D1560054

The Myth of Constitutionalism
in Pakistan

The Myth of Constitutionalism in Pakistan

Zulfikar Khalid Maluka

Karachi

Oxford University Press

Oxford   New York   Delhi

1995

Oxford University Press, Walton Street, Oxford OX2 6DP
Oxford   New York
Athens   Auckland   Bangkok   Bombay
Calcutta   Cape Town   Dar es Salaam   Delhi
Florence   Hong Kong   Istanbul   Karachi
Kuala Lumpur   Madras   Madrid   Melbourne
Mexico City   Nairobi   Paris   Singapore
Taipei   Tokyo   Toronto
and associated companies in
Berlin   Ibadan

Oxford is a trade mark of Oxford University Press

© Oxford University Press 1995

ISBN 0 19 577572 4

Printed in Pakistan at
PanGraphics (Pvt) Ltd., Islamabad
Published by
Oxford University Press
5-Bangalore Town, Sharae Faisal
P.O. Box 13033, Karachi-75350, Pakistan.

Dedicated to all those citizens of Pakistan who believe in constitutional democracy and have fought for its restoration in the country.

CONTENTS

ABBREVIATIONS

ANP	Awami National Party
CMLA	Chief Martial Law Administrator
COAS	Chief of the Army Staff
CPC	Civil Procedure Code
COP	Combined Opposition Parties
DAC	Democratic Action Committee
Cr.P.C.	Criminal Procedure Code
EBDO	Elective Bodies (Disqualification) Order
FC	Federal Court
FSF	Federal Security Force
FSC	Federal Shariat Court
GIK	Ghulam Ishaq Khan
IJI	Islami Jamhoori Ittehad
MNA	Member National Assembly
MPA	Member Provincial Assembly
MRD	Movement for the Restoration of Democracy
NAP	National Awami Party
NPT	National Press Trust
NWFP	North-West Frontier Province
PNA	Pakistan National Alliance
PPC	Pakistan Penal Code
PPP	Pakistan People's Party
PDA	Peoples Democratic Alliance
PLD	All Pakistan Legal Decisions
PPA	Political Parties Act
PODO	Public Offices (Disqualification) Order
PRODA	Public Representative Offices (Disqualification) Act
RTC	Round Table Conference
SC	Supreme Court

PREFACE

This book is the quintessence of a decade of research and academic labour. I have tried honestly to put forward an undiluted expression of the whole truth about constitutionalism in Pakistan. The treatise has the specific aim of exposing the penchant of the ruling elite for throwing the norms of constitutionalism to the winds. To that end, I have been guided by the paramount consideration of the survival of Pakistan as a nation: if we are to survive as a nation, a great creative effort is required to evolve an innovative consensus on the perennial political contentions in the domain of Pakistan's constitutional jurisprudence. Whether I have been successful in my endeavours in identifying remedies for our constitutional maladies, I leave it to my readers to judge.

The Pakistan of today is precariously balanced between her quest for orderly procedures of constitutional democracy and the lingering arbitrariness of authoritarianism. The more I ponder on the crises of constitutionalism in which Pakistan has got entangled, the more I am convinced of the imperativeness of constitutional democracy. As I have uncovered the successive ruling elite's lust for absolutism, disdain for constitutionalism, indulgence in deceit and huckstering, unbridled ambitions, and reckless pillaging of the national exchequer, I am driven to ask the citizens of Pakistan one question: Are we so hardened of heart, so deadened of conscience, so pusillanimous politically, so corrupt morally, and so degraded socially that we prefer to groan under the dictator's heel rather than uphold constitutionalism? Let us put an end to such organized hypocrisy.

At a time when Pakistan is passing through the vortex of great crises, in which a false move might well mean disaster for the nation, I ask my readers to believe, that I have tried to restrict myself to merely reflecting the truth, though it is very difficult to eliminate one's own political predilections.

The last three chapters of the book were written under the impact of unfolding political and constitutional events in Pakistan. The *terminus ad quem* of the book is February 1995. Research work for the book began in the mid 1980s. The collection of research material and my mode of working on this study can be compared to an ant's futuristic sense, which compels it to work persistently and patiently on collecting its tiny particles of food. This it does as an inalienable part of its natural instinct and futuristic stratagem for survival in a harsh milieu. I can say with pride that I have learnt the same strategy from this tiny creature. However, in my quest for survival, the one person who has suffered and made innumerable sacrifices, and who has always stood by me is my wife, Farhat, a companion par excellence and my most valued critic, she has neglected her own interests to sustain me intellectually. This work is my personal tribute to Farhat.

Islamabad
23 March 1995   Zulfikar Khalid Maluka

1

INTRODUCTION

CONSTITUTIONALISM, FEDERALISM, AND POLITICAL LEGITIMACY

Full of unanswered challenges, overburdened by ideological cliches, wrecked by ambitious power-seekers, and subjected to forcible dismissal of governments by the men on horseback, Pakistan has been literally transformed into a laboratory for various constitutional experiments. The country's ruling elite (well-versed in the Machiavellian art of statecraft), while grafting rough and ready constitutional formulae on the state structure, have always projected Almighty Allah's pleasure as the reason for every abortive constitutional system in Pakistan.

Writing in the late 1950s, Keith B. Callard, an American political scientist opined: 'No one is willing to die for the preservation of the Constitution in Pakistan.'[1] The truth of such a painful prophecy has been vividly demonstrated throughout the chequered constitutional history of the country. The civil and military bureaucratic despots, from Ghulam Muhammad to Ghulam Ishaq Khan, have indulged in the most malevolent acts of abrogating, holding in abeyance, and violating various Constitutions of the land. For the Pakistani nation, a constitutionally-limited government seems to be a 'luxury' that could only be afforded under a certain fortunate political milieu.[2] Because its autocracy is ever willing and ready to subvert those conditions and to reassert unashamedly its ignominious rule in the country, the people's demands for constitutionalism, political propriety, and democracy have been painted as being close to treason, and thus intolerable.

The constitutional malaise and systematic marring of the representative system in Pakistan could rightly be compared to a classic French joke. Prior to the advent of the Fifth French Republic (1958), a political scientist visited a bookstall in Paris and asked for a copy of the French Constitution. 'Sorry' was the prompt and plain reply of the proprietor of the bookstall, who added with a sarcastic smile: 'We do not sell periodicals here.' Such an oft-quoted gibe in the parlance of constitutional law is extremely apt in the context of crises of constitutionalism in Pakistan.

Nonalignment in foreign affairs, and a federal, parliamentary, and democratic Constitution—based on social justice, equality, and fairplay, not any theocracy—were the two most cherished ideals of the Father of the Nation, Quaid-i-Azam Mohammad Ali Jinnah. While shady political characters and the British-trained bureaucratic clique compromised Pakistan's non-aligned status, as envisaged by Jinnah, forging military pacts with a superpower, the *de facto* rulers treated the constitution-making (or even unmaking/abrogating) process as a casual assignment. That is why Pakistan's crises of constitutionalism have not yet ended, though the country has painfully experimented with almost eight 'late Constitutions' so far.[3] Besides 'the late Constitutions', Pakistan has to its democratic discredit various constitutional drafts—demonstrating interesting, provocative, contradictory, and conflicting outlooks, obsolete religious extrapolations, and, above all, demanding theocratic-administrative set-ups, i.e. the *Imamate*, the *Caliphate*, and even the Presidential form of government; the latter being depicted as 'close' to Islam.

A country's Constitution is fundamentally a regulatory interface between the people and their government, ensuring stability, social justice, and welfare of the State. However, in Pakistan the search for a Constitution has become 'an end in itself'. The constitution-makers, 'far from looking to the needs of the future', says an analyst, 'have sought to constitutionalise the position and immediate requirements of those in power.'[4] Pakistan's constitutional tragedy is that not a single Constitution has been allowed to outlive the stipulated tenure of the government of its founding father. This is understandable, because not even the founding fathers of various 'late' Constitutions in Pakistan had any respect for their own products. They found excessive faults with their own brainchild and finally mutilated the creation of their own constitutional engineering.

Undeniably, the overwhelming majority of those entrusted with the prestigious task of constitution-making were neither competent craftsmen nor visionary and futuristic leaders. They tended to indulge in abject compromises with their personal, parochial, and group interests. Their products never represented the spirit and growth of the nation, nor could they be called symbols of national integration of diverse ethnolinguistic and regional aspirations. Even if some of them endeavoured sincerely to bestow a Constitution upon their nation, at most they were, in the candid observation of Professor Carl J. Newman, bad tailors who purchased expensive pieces of cloth from distant lands and produced a garment that did not fit the customers.[5]

A constitutional instrument requires the citizens, the judiciary, and the government functionaries to conform to its mandate voluntarily. An emotional attachment to a Constitution is most essential, for it ensures its functioning on a permanent basis. If the constitutional instrument is not looked upon with respect, nay reverence, the net result would be an invitation to social strife, political tension, and civil war in a State. Intense patriotism, a sociopolitical virtue, and tolerance, a philosophical virtue, are the two main pillars of constitutional democracy in any civilized society. The former teaches sacrifice for the sake of national interest, and the latter leads to national integration and social harmony.

Unfortunately, for want of the two essential ingredients mentioned above for the successful running of constitutional democracy, the history of constitution-making in Pakistan has been long and chequered. Above all, it was a history of constitution-breaking and of disfiguring democracy. Though achieved strictly on the basis of the constitutional and democratic process of the transfer of power, Pakistan, within a few years of its emergence, was placed completely in the hands of a 'be-all and end-all' bureaucratic clique which readily dispensed with constitutional democracy altogether. The democratic norms and imperatives of constitutionalism restrained a man of the stature of Jinnah from dictating a Constitution to his personal liking. But it could not hold back ambitious strongmen from being the sole lawgivers and from arbitrarily amending or mutilating the whole Constitution to serve their own ends.

Being a concord among the federating units of the State, a Constitution is a fundamental framework of immense importance for political interaction, co-operation, crisis management, and conflict resolution among them. A Constitution contains those primary rules of law and those binding conventions which regulate the structure of the main governmental organs, their operating principles, their relationship with one another and with the citizens of the State. In the contemporary norms of constitutional democracies, civilized people consider the Constitution as the supreme law of the land and, therefore, an inviolable and enduring agreement amongst themselves or the federating units, laying down the political methodology and a quasi-permanent set of principles for governing the national affairs of a State. In a federal state like Pakistan, it becomes almost a sacrosanct national and moral obligation of the citizens and the State functionaries—who swear allegiance and fidelity to the Constitution— to preserve it with all its commas, semi-colons, and full stops.

In Pakistan, the adoption of extra-constitutional methods for ulterior motives, suspension and abrogation of Constitutions as mere pieces of paper to be easily scrapped, have had an extremely negative impact on democratic trends, national integration, and, indeed, on the future of the country itself. While the ruling elite in Pakistan has wrecked constitutional democracy by resorting to unconstitutional manipulations, the ever-assertive and uncompromising religious pressure groups have tended to complicate and thwart the constitution-making process by their biased and narrow interpretations of the 'Two-Nation Theory'. The abject conspiracy of power-hungry men to usurp high public offices, the ugly phenomenon of autocratic and arbitrary power-wielding for self-aggrandizement, and, above all, the frequent intervention by martial law dispensations 'to save the nation from within', have given birth to constitutional *ad hocism* and temporization of the various forms of government in Pakistan.

Pakistan's national polity was founded, sustained, and has remained as a federal system—at least in the constitutional documents. Nothing has been more damaging to national integration than the inability of almost all federal governments to ensure an undiluted democratic order and to observe, in letter and spirit, the principle of federalism in relations between the Federation and its components. Far from appreciating the pluralistic nature of Pakistan's geopolitical, ethnolinguistic, and sociocultural structure, the ruling elite took steps to vest overarching coercive powers in the hands of the federal government *vis-à-vis* the ever-subservient provincial governments. While institutionalizing the colonial legacy of political discrimination against the federating units, they took persistent steps to marginalize the spirit of provincial autonomy, so that it now has a farcical status.

So far, the issue of provincial autonomy has remained the most important yet unanswered question, i.e., the regional parties, having electoral strongholds other than the Punjab, demanding maximum provincial autonomy along with foolproof constitutional guarantees.[6] Retrospectively, the adoption and modification of the Government of India Act of 1935, alongwith the Indian Independence Act, 1947, as the Provisional Constitution of Pakistan had all the potential of fulfilling aspirations for provincial autonomy. The grave political differences between the federation and its components on the allocation of seats in the Parliament, division of powers between the Centre and the provinces, the status of regional languages and culture, and the equitable distribution of national and regional resources, etc. inordinately delayed the constitution-making process in the country.

The ruling political party, the Pakistan Muslim League, which consistently pursued the issue of provincial autonomy *vis-à-vis* a strong Centre, as provided in the Government of India Act, 1935, resorted to precisely the opposite practice after Independence. The abominable legacy of a federal constitutional structure, intelligently crafted to suit the political exigencies of the British colonialists, was kept intact, as if the ruling elite intended to whip a subject people in the new state of Pakistan. The constitutionally weak provincial executives were required to carry out all the instructions of the federal government. The provincial governments were dismissed on minor pretexts of maladministration or their failure to carry out the instructions of the federal government. Notwithstanding the distinct regional and cultural status of the provinces in West Pakistan, their amalgamation into One Unit in 1955 for so-called administrative convenience, was a complete negation of the principle of federalism.

Throughout the first decade of Pakistan's independence, the Bengali penchant for seeking political and constitutional domination on the basis of their numerical strength continued to be pitted against the Punjabi-dominated federal structure of the country. When the 1956 Constitution was formulated, the general pattern of centre-province relations remained almost the same as in the Government of India Act, 1935.[7] The 1956 Constitution was not a purely federal Constitution, and the executive and legislative powers conferred on the federating units were much less than those exercised by the federal government.

The martial law regimes of Ayub Khan and Yahya Khan arrogated to themselves sweeping powers, unhesitatingly centralizing the already semi-federal structure of the state. Ironically, when the political parties with strong roots elsewhere than in the Punjab were demanding provincial autonomy from the Ayub Government, the then Law Minister, Mr S. M. Zafar warned the people on his President's behalf that the statements calling for 'greater provincial autonomy' would henceforth be considered as 'a treasonous act' and that its protagonists 'would be identified, hunted, crushed and destroyed.'[8]

Far from visualizing the disastrous consequences of centralized rule at the expense of paralysing the provinces, many, particularly in the province of Punjab, were taken in by the official anti-autonomy propaganda. They began to dub the adherents of the autonomy issue as 'traitors'. However, when the people of Pakistan awakened from the long spell of Ayub's dictatorial centralization, they found themselves in the damaging grip of Yahya Khan's Legal Framework Order (LFO). The patient then was, to use the late Zulfikar Ali Bhutto's political analogy, 'in the last stages of tuberculosis'.[9] Thus, it was too late to seek its survival.

The demands of provincial autonomy from the insensitive centre had assumed the vital character of separatism. The December 1970 elections were held against the backdrop of perennially ignored regional aspirations and attempts at over-centralization on the model of the Government of India Act of 1935. That occasion provided the political parties, contesting elections on the plank of greater provincial autonomy, with a recipe for the final breakup of the state.

After the falling apart of the Federation in 1971, the framers of the 1973 Constitution faced up to the question of provincial autonomy with greater consciousness. The prevalent forms of federalism were discreetly maintained in the 1973 Constitution, to the political satisfaction of all the federating units, and Article One of the Constitution provided, *inter alia,* that Pakistan shall be a Federal Republic.

Though it deserves credit for giving the nation a unanimously evolved Constitution, the popularly elected government of Premier Zulfikar Ali Bhutto could not 'resist the temptation to make serious inroads into the rights of provinces'.[10] When it came to the mechanics of managing centre-province relations, the Bhutto Government demonstrated visible inability 'to comprehend the need for a stable federal system and democracy', preferring to rule by edicts.[11] The complete extirpation of the non-PPP Governments in the NWFP and Balochistan in the 1970s vindicates such an assertion.

While holding the 1973 Constitution in abeyance, Zia's prolonged martial law 'lost no time in smothering the expectations for elections and parliamentary rule and appointed pro-consuls to rule the Provinces in a manner that wholly negated the spirit of provincial autonomy.'[12] The continuation of the central *diktat* in right royal fashion and vice-regal traditions accentuated provincial feelings and obliged the autonomists to vociferously demand their rights. Zia's holding of local bodies elections as well as the 1985 general elections on a non-party basis hampered the sense of brotherhood among the federating units. The polls were largely contested on the bases of region, language, caste, and creed. The military dictator's ruthless tactics of playing on inter-provincial tensions for the prolongation of his personal rule did not augur well for the working of the federal principle in the country.

The contemporary centre-province row over the sharing of national resources and distribution of power today presents a formidable challenge to the Federation of Pakistan. In today's federal polity, the question of provincial autonomy has become too serious to be subjected to political polemics. It seems likely to acquire momentum in the foreseeable future, and, if unresolved, it might pose a serious threat to the integrity of the Federation.

The penchant of Pakistan's ruling elites for authoritarianism and strident centralism is a basic hurdle in the smooth running of constitutional democracy in the country. Constitutionalism and federalism, the bases and imperatives of Pakistan's national edifice, are antidotes to the aforementioned inclinations of the ruling elite. Constitutionalism and federalism reinforce each other, ultimately stabilizing the democratic process. Evidently, in the contemporary constitutional history of many developing nations, the absence of one erodes the roots of the other. If one is progressing, that will have a healthy effect on the other, and vice versa. Both principles need a written Constitution, and an effective and independent judiciary for their smooth operation in any national polity.

The preceding thesis may be summarized thus: that absolutism is the arch-enemy of constitutionalism and federalism. If the former advances, the latter recedes, and vice versa. If one were to pinpoint the main malcontent disfiguring democracy, constitutionalism, and federalism, it would be the civil and military bureaucratization of politics. The first military dictator, Field Marshal Ayub Khan, thwarted the first general elections and kept the people away from the democratic order. He considered the people of Pakistan a 'wild horse that had been captured but not yet tamed.'[13] Such a shortsighted and parochial goal of taming the people's aspirations for constitutional democracy, constitutionalism, and federalism, and above all, equating such ideals to a 'wild horse' have been the prime motivation of the civil and military bureaucracy in Pakistan. Besides, they have directed the bureaucratization of politics in order to weaken the will of the people and erode the basis of an all-Pakistan leadership. They have made systematic attempts to create intellectual confusion and generate controversies over settled national and constitutional issues.

Now it is sufficiently clear from Pakistan's own experience and the glaring examples of the militarily-ruled overwhelming majority of developing countries, that the supremacy of the military over national affairs is anathema to the institution-building process. After the Second World War, whenever and wherever in the developing countries the armed forces have intervened to wield civil authority, that country has never won a war.[14] Indeed, the dubious interplay of the civil and military bureaucracy erodes the very basis of the democratic state and its social system. In the opinion of Dr Mubashir Hasan, a former federal minister, 'if Pakistan is to survive, the army must be subordinate to civil authority.'[15]

The three martial laws of Ayub Khan, Yahya Khan, and Ziaul Haq apart, the short civil interregnums have failed so far to subordinate the military to the nation's political will. Having tasted the dismissals of Muhammad Khan Junejo's government on 29 May 1988, by the COAS/President Zia, Ms Benazir Bhutto's government on 6 August 1990, and that of Nawaz Sharif on 18 April 1993, by Ghulam Ishaq Khan, fully backed by the military, political thinkers and politicized laymen alike increasingly question the future of not only the democratic process but that of the State itself. Given the track record of the military's interest and intervention in national politics, public opinion seems to be that it is very difficult to bridle the intractable horse in the foreseeable future.

Neither Zia's lifting of martial law in 1985 nor the crash of 17 August 1988 ensured the total withdrawal of the army from civil affairs. Ayub Khan, Yahya Khan, and particularly Zia deliberately allowed the army to diversify its hydra-headed interests in civil affairs. Zia actively encouraged and never 'interfered with the money grabbing operations of his colleagues and subordinates.'[16] Barrister Makhdoom Ali Khan opines that:

> ... the army has such a large monetary stake in the country that it will never allow a populist civilian government to interfere with the *status quo*. A civilian government may be permitted to continue only so far as it does not interfere with the financial interests of the army. Only a revolution may bring about a change in this state of affairs. Any civilian government brought into office by normal sedate democratic channels will neither have the

strength nor will it be permitted to pursue a political or economic policy which the military does not regard as conducive to its interests[17]

Unless effective political and national institutions are strengthened via the democratic process, the military may well continue to remote control the civil governments. Having failed to establish their supremacy and democratic representation in their own house, the Bengali politicians in the 1960s came to the conclusion that it was impossible either to share power or rule the country under the dominating shadow of the military hailing from the Punjab. Rao Rashid, a former Inspector General of Police, relates an eye-opening turning-point in the thinking of Sheikh Mujibur Rehman, which led to the separation of East Pakistan in December 1971.[18] He says in his book, *Jo Mein Ney Dekha (What I Saw)*, that prior to the holding of the 1970 general elections, Mujib visited London and met Bengali intellectuals and politicians. They reminded Mujib that he could easily secure a majority in the National Assembly, and on that strength he could also become the Prime Minister of united Pakistan. But they questioned: what would you do with the military which belonged to West Pakistan? Would it allow your political supremacy over the national institutions? Mujib had no answer to these questions. But the military had! Because it could easily dispense with him at any time after his assumption of office as the premier of united Pakistan. Mujib's London visit, in the considered opinion of Rao Rashid, proved to be decisive in moulding his decision to abandon all pretensions of being an all-Pakistan leader.

Jinnah, the Father of the Nation, had given to his nation the supreme democratic motto of self-reliance, 'Unity, Faith, and Discipline', to follow for its survival in any harsh milieu. Yet the manner in which the three martial law governments of Ayub Khan, Yahya Khan, and Zia manipulated the motto was vividly explained by the late Allama Ahsan Illahi Zahir. While addressing a public rally at Liaquat Bagh, Rawalpindi, Allama Zahir opined that the first martial law of Ayub Khan took away the 'Discipline' of the nation; the second martial law imposed by Yahya Khan did away with the 'Unity' of the country; and that Zia's martial law snatched away the 'Faith' of the nation— because of Zia's questionable 'Islamization'.

The judiciary is considered the guardian and the ultimate interpreter of the Constitution—the highest law of the land. For such an avowed task, constitutional safeguards discourage any alignment or political proximity between the judiciary and the executive. That is why, in all civilized societies, judicial decisions independently arrived at have acquired historic importance and are widely quoted elsewhere. However, the manner in which the higher judiciary in Pakistan conducted itself at critical political turning points, has raised doubts about its independence and autonomy in dispensing justice. Yet, through the anachronistic colonial concept of 'Contempt of Court', it continued to be self-protected as a sacred cow. By making themselves readily available to various authoritarian regimes as a convenient and pliable mechanism to be used for the abrogation of Constitutions, for validating seditious, illegal, and unconstitutional acts, for liquidating political forces, and for allowing individuals to amend the Constitution, the concerned Courts seem to have indulged in 'judicial misconduct' and 'corruption of justice'.[19] By legalizing clear instances of high treason under the 'Doctrine of Necessity', the Courts deprived themselves of the credit for some of their popularly acclaimed landmark decisions. The way the highest Court of the land allowed culprits to dismantle legally formed governments, dissolve parliaments, and subvert the Constitution, is evident from the following observation of an analyst:

> Each successive martial law came under review before the Supreme Court and this Court had to pronounce its verdict on the *vires* of such action. The martial law of General Ayub was challenged in the case of Dosso, that of General Yahya in that of Asma Jilani and General Zia in Begum Bhutto's. A detailed analysis of the judgements reveals that the track record of the Supreme Court in these cases is uninspiring, to say the least. While deciding these cases, this Court has followed a consistent pattern of condoning the act of usurpation, validating the action and justifying Martial Law. This was done on one pretext or other. In the process, of course, the Court discovered some queer notions of law and principles. If support was found for Ayub in Kelsen's theory of 'revolutionary legality', justification was sought for Zia on 'the doctrine of necessity.' Each time the Court's judgement lent support to the incumbent military regime and offered justification for its rule.[20]

The higher Courts in Pakistan thus robbed themselves of the judicial distinction of being the custodians of the fundamental law of the land. They have seldom enjoyed a reputation for applying judicial checks and balances to the arbitrary use of state authority. Ignoring the imperatives of constitutionalism, sustained and administered by the judicial system, they readily acquiesced in the imposition of authoritarian laws by the strong. The deliberately-contrived situations for ousting constitutional governments and abrogating Constitutions were provided with the blanket cover of legality. The courts would term a military *coup d'etat* as a phase of constitutional deviation, and thus curtail their own jurisdiction by adjudging martial law to be superior to the constitutional government. For instance, in the Begum Nusrat Bhutto case, Zia became the sole law-giver as later he always claimed power, *vide* his Court-approved Martial Law, to amend the Constitution. The wholesale legal endorsement of commissarial dictatorships forced the people to live under the dark shadows of arbitrariness.

The most humiliating yet somewhat factual comments on the Supreme Court's decision in the Haji Saifullah case, i.e., terming Zia's dissolution of the National Assembly on 29 May 1988 illegal and unconstitutional, came from the two sons of Zia. In a press conference in Rawalpindi on 8 October 1988, Zia's sons asserted that, had their father been alive, the Supreme Court's verdict would have certainly been different, implying thereby the pressure and executive influence of the rulers on the judiciary in Pakistan. By a curious coincidence, in 1993, Mirza Aslam Beg, the ex-COAS, blew the whistle on the independence of the judiciary, confessing that he had sent a candid message to the Supreme Court asking it not to restore the government of Muhammad Khan Junejo, which had been dismissed by Zia on 29 May 1988. Beg's remarks were like the proverbial cat let loose among the pigeons.

Given the four-decade long record of the higher judiciary in the country, popular perceptions and criticism, particularly of its judgments on constitutional petitions, have crystallized on the following:

1. Whenever martial law has been imposed, the Courts seemed to have been waiting in the wings to provide it legal cover of validation.

2. The Courts in Pakistan have hardly ever pronounced any judgment against any ruler while he was in office. The

overall pattern: the law of necessity was applied to all the incumbent rulers; but when they fell, their acts were depicted as usurpation, illegal, and unconstitutional (as in the Asma Jilani case).

3. The general appraisal of the higher judiciary seems to be: 'senior members of the judiciary, particularly those holding the august office of Chief Justice in Supreme Court or High Courts, have, by playing political roles in affiliation with the Government, undermined the credibility of their high office. Apart from the question of conflict of interest in such situations, holding patently political offices tends to put judges on the same level as any other job seeker like a retired bureaucrat or a general or an opportunistic politician.'[21]

4. The factors of political instability and socio-economic insecurity imbued the intelligentsia's character with 'opportunism' and scant respect for principles. Such traits are also reflected in the judiciary, stultifying its image, prestige, and credibility as an impartial and independent custodian of justice and as the guardian of the law of the land.

5. In 1993, all honour to the Supreme Court of Pakistan which did not follow in the footsteps of its predecessors, but discarded the abhorrent vestiges of the 'Doctrine of Necessity'. The fatal blow struck by the Supreme Court, in defence of constitutionalism and against authoritarianism, is a triumph for the rule of law in Pakistan. Amidst passionate pleas, a campaign of vilification and even intimidation, the Supreme Court held its own, unaffected by the frowns or approving nods of those in power.

Untrammelled by historical considerations, the orthodox *ulema, muftis*, and grand *muftis* have been demanding the immediate imposition of *Nizam-i-Islam* on the model of the *Khilafat-i-Rashidah* in Pakistan. Ever since the independence of Pakistan, they have been trying to persuade the people to turn to orthodoxy. They call it 'returning to the roots', the wellsprings of a vanished golden age. While arguing in favour of the complete and conventional imposition of *Shariah* as understood by them, they reject democracy, modern state structure, and its constitutionalism, as ideas unsuitable for assimilation in an Islamic State.

However, this class of traditional interpreters of Islam has often aligned itself with the despots while opposing the adherents of constitutional democracy to the teeth. Without any remorse, some self-styled protagonists of the 'Law of Islam' and *de facto* custodians of the 'ideological frontiers' of the state, have more than often contributed to pulling down the fragile constitutional structures of Pakistan. They seem to realize little that the founding of a state and the conception of its Constitution are inalienable in Islam.

Constitution-making and its adoption on a priority basis are the *Sunnah* of the Holy Prophet Muhammad (pbuh). The stiff opposition of Mecca's pagans to Muhammad's (pbuh) preaching of monotheism had compelled the latter to migrate in AD 622 to Yathrib—a city 280 miles to the north of Mecca. At the time of the arrival of Muhammad (pbuh) at Yathrib (renamed Medina), the city was in utter political chaos. To protect his followers and his nascent religious doctrines from the wrathful vengeance of the Qureshite of Mecca, the Prophet (pbuh) employed his political and diplomatic skills to knit together his actual and potential adversaries at Medina into a meticulously worked out sociopolitical contract. Commonly known as the *Charter of Medina,* the document is of indubitable authenticity—'the embryo constitution' in the annals of political constitutionalism.[22]

Consisting of fifty-three clauses, the *Charter of Medina*, evolved and adopted on contemporary political contours, offered to its adherents the supreme principles of civic equality, religious tolerance, and freedom of worship, rejecting a politico-administrative coercive apparatus. For its formulation, the founder of the Islamic state travelled from tribe to tribe, from one entity to another, and indeed far and wide, in search of political consensus, ascertaining the fundamental aspirations of the would-be federating units of the state. Since he had the highest regard for the imperatives of peaceful co-existence among various religious and tribal entities, the Holy Prophet Muhammad (pbuh) was successful in bringing together the representatives of the would-be federation at an assembly in Medina. The assembly of heterogeneous entities so gathered agreed upon and sanctioned in writing the supreme law of the state. Keeping all other considerations pending, the Holy Prophet (pbuh) accorded top-most priority to constitution-making as the best device for saving the Islamic State from the scourges of internal and external disruptions. Such an act of the Holy Prophet (pbuh) has left the following indelible footprints and guiding principles pertaining to the State and Constitution for the whole of humanity:

1. Constitution-making and its adoption on a priority basis is the *Sunnah* of the Holy Prophet (pbuh).

2. The free will and willingness of the signatories could be construed as the modern democratic process of arriving at agreements. Neither an individual, nor any particular group is vested with the sacred task of bestowing a Constitution upon the whole nation.

3. Only a government based on a Constitution and run in accordance with the imperatives of the law of the land is entitled to be called Islamic.

4. A balanced and unanimously adopted written Constitution can guarantee the solid foundations of a federation.

5. Constitution-making is a collective, co-operative, and political act of free will of the participants.

6. Liberally interpreted in the light of modern constitutionalism, the rudimentary form of a written Constitution (i.e., the *Charter of Medina*) envisaged a complete absence of theocracy and accorded full autonomy of peaceful co-existence to all faiths and communities, regardless of their caste, creed, and tribal affiliations.

7. Based on innovative integrating political principles of 'unity in diversity', the *Charter of Medina* aimed at creating an embryonic form of federalism (communities with diverse socio-religious traits as its federating units), untainted by ideological encumbrances.

8. The adoption of a democratically formulated Constitution is the first step towards humanity's breaking away from the bondage, ills, and evils of kingship and abject state coercion.

9. Aversion to the Constitution invariably leads to authoritarianism.

10. The penultimate clause of the *Charter of Medina* provides that the breach of agreement (i.e., Constitution) shall be treated as *zulm-o-fasad* i.e., high treason.

Fourteen centuries after the adoption of the *Charter of Medina*, Quaid-i-Azam Mohammad Ali Jinnah, the founding father of Pakistan, reiterated the letter and spirit of the *Sunnah* of the Holy Prophet (pbuh) pertaining to constitution-making, in his speech before the Constituent Assembly on 11 August 1947. Leaving the sacred task of constitution-making to the representatives of the people in the Constituent Assembly, Jinnah pledged equal national rights to all the citizens of Pakistan. Having successfully led his nation to the 'promised land', Jinnah, a first-rate constitutionalist, was in a position to thrust his own version of the Constitution on the new entity. Yet he preferred that the Constitution be formulated through the free will of the people's representatives. Jinnah believed in and upheld the inalienable right of civil liberties. This is evident from his stiff opposition to the Rowlatt Act of 1919—a black law, passed against the spirit of the British Constitution. Indeed, he categorically termed the law as even beyond the rudimentary conception of a civilized government and resigned from the legislature in protest.

In the light of the aforementioned historical legacies, it is sufficiently clear that to abrogate, put in abeyance, suspend, or fundamentally alter the law of the land is not only an uncivilized act but a negation of the *Sunnah* of the Prophet (pbuh) as well. The sanctity and priority to be accorded to constitution-making was demonstrated by the Holy Prophet (pbuh) himself when he prioritized the *Charter of Medina* even over the construction of the *Masjid-i-Nabvi*. The establishment of the first Islamic state was followed by the formulation of the *Charter of Medina* and construction of the *Masjid-i-Nabvi*, in that order. Moreover, clause 43 of the *Charter* termed the place where the assembly of the tribes and religious entities passed the prestigious document inviolable, sacred, and secure.

As against the sanctity accorded by the Holy Prophet (pbuh) to his Constitution, many authoritarian caliphs, absolute kings, and ruthless rulers in Muslim history accorded scant respect to the Constitution. They and their coteries indulged in ghastly acts of suppression of human free will, denial of human rights, and indeed, to sullying the sacred name of Islam. Such unsavoury practices have continued in modern Pakistan as well. Here, the spectres of martial law and authoritarianism have never allowed the Constitution and associated democratic institutions to take root. The civil and military bureaucracy, feudal lords, the *nouveaux riches*, and the industrialists seem to be in constant search of authoritarianism and dictatorship. They have prospered at the cost of the annihilation of democratic institutions and Constitutions.

Dr Muhammad Yusuf Goraya, a prominent scholar and intellectual, opines that the concepts of Pharaoh, dictator, and Chief Martial Law Administrator (CMLA) are one and the same in practical dispensation.[23] The Pharaoh said to the people: 'I am your Chief Lord.' The same sentiments were expressed by the military dictators of Pakistan (i.e. Ayub Khan in October 1958, Yahya Khan in March 1969, and Ziaul Haq in July 1977): 'I am your Chief Martial Law Administrator.' To Dr Goraya, the words 'Chief Lord' and 'Chief Martial Law Administrator' are the same in their theoretical meanings and practical conceptions. Both the Pharaoh and the CMLA became sole masters of the country's resources, the fountainhead of law and administration, and applied the coercive levers of the state for the satisfaction of their whims and vendettas.

Using the foregoing reflections on the constitutional history of Pakistan encapsulated in the preceding pages as a starting point, this study offers a critical evaluation of the constitutional flux in an Islamic state. An attempt is made to identify various factors leading to constitution-making, constitution-breaking, and the continuous constitutional malaise in the forty-seven year history of Pakistan. What went wrong with almost eight 'late' Constitutions of Pakistan that the search for, or restoration of an appropriate Constitution is still on? Why were the ambitious strongmen with their ulterior motives (couched in messianic appeals) and simplistic solutions to the problems of a plural society and federal state allowed to indulge excessively in constitutional engineering of the worst kind in the country? Why has the high mortality rate of Pakistani constitutions become a puzzle to political scientists and constitutional experts, both within and outside the country?

These and other similar subtle yet vital questions will be dealt with within this study. The aim is to make sufficiently clear what the sources of the present-day constitutional confusion in our political system are and their possible effects on the future of constitutional democracy in the country.

In the attempt to discover the truth by uncovering blatant lies, the main thrust of the study is on the following focal points:

- Pakistan's constitutional crises, with continuous references to the presence, abeyance, or absence of constitutional democracy in the country;

- The politico-historical circumstances leading to the promulgation or abrogation of any particular Constitution in the state;

- The tendency of the ruling elite to disregard the norms of constitutionalism and federalism, preferring power to flow from the top downwards, without legitimately sharing it horizontally, i.e. with the federating units;

- Popular remedies and recipes in the context of political and constitutional, rather than that of bureaucratic-authoritarian-elitist solutions to the existing and seemingly endless problems facing Pakistan's democratic order shall be examined; and

- Finally, throughout the book, I have been guided by a single consideration: that if Pakistan is to survive as a nation, great creative efforts are required to hammer out an innovative consensus on the country's perennial political conflicts in the parlance of its constitutional jurisprudence.

2

MAINSPRINGS OF POLITICAL CONSTITUTIONALISM: A CONCEPTUAL ANALYSIS

For analysing the Constitution and the state system in general and the crises of constitutionalism in Pakistan in particular, it is imperative to carry out a brief conceptual analysis of some basic constitutional issues. These issues taken together would be 'all-embracing', and would help students of constitutional law, political scientists, and lay readers to understand the constitutional problems of a developing state. An attempt has been made to define, interpret, and elaborate such concepts as they are understood in modern writings on political constitutionalism and liberal democratic orders. It may be mentioned that the constitutional concepts defined and explained here in an encapsulated form are philosophically, historically, and analytically very vast. The purpose is to understand them as they influence the potentials and limitations of Pakistan's fragile constitutional and democratic order.

CONSTITUTION

To protect their fundamental rights and to promote common interests, the people usually prefer an organized political society to anarchy—for the latter is the antithesis of the former and the only conceivable alternative to constitutional rule. For the successful evolution and operation of higher institutions, every political society has a body of fundamental rules which facilitates interaction and interdependence among its various governmental organs and its citizens. The collection of principles forming the frame for any political society is called its Constitution.

In the modern era, a Constitution is required to set limits on the arbitrary powers of levers of the state, to ensure the fundamental rights of the governed, and to ensure a smooth relationship between the two. Thus, a Constitution is generally thought to be a national manifesto, a statement of national ideals and aspirations, a fundamental law of the land, an abiding charter of the land, a social contract, and, above all, a written confession of the political faith of a state.[1]

In its broadest sense, a Constitution is defined as 'a body of rules governing the affairs of an organized group'.[2] However, most of the definitions, in their formal and legal sense, have been drawn from that put forward by James Bryce in his Oxford lectures of 1884.[3] Bryce defined a Constitution as 'a frame of political society, organized through and by law; that is to say, one in which law has established permanent institutions with recognized functions and definite rights'.[4] Except in the case of the United Kingdom and Northern Ireland, whose governments function mostly in the absence of a single written constitutional document, the general practice is to define a Constitution on the presumption of a written national document. This, to some, is a narrow perspective, and a wider definition is usually based on that offered by Bolingbroke in the following:

> By constitution, we mean, whenever we speak with propriety and exactness, that assemblage of laws, institutions and customs, derived from certain fixed principles of reason ... that compose the general system, according to which the community hath agreed to be governed.[5]

Whatever the scope and limitations of definitions offered by various constitutional historians and legal experts, the overwhelming thrust of all is to depict a Constitution as the full and free political expression of an organized society. Such an inherent and inalienable right of the people was elaborated by Thomas Paine in his definition of a Constitution:

> A constitution is a thing *antecedent* to a government, and government is only the creature of a constitution ... A constitution is not the act of a government, but of a people constituting a government; and government without a constitution, is power without right.[6]

What a wonderful liberal democratic order shall emerge if the developing societies, reeling under abhorrent military dictatorships, absolutism, and kingship were to follow Thomas Paine's definition of a Constitution! However, from the foregoing conceptions, the two-fold essence of a Constitution is inferred:

1. It establishes the fundamental structure and functions of the different organs of a government;

2. It regulates the relations of those governmental organs to one another and to the people. Applied to the organizational principles of a political society, a true functional Constitution embraces the following three essential dimensions:

- organization of various governmental organs;
- the distribution/demarcation of power between those organs; and
- the manner and mode in which such power is to be exercised in relation to one another and to the people of that political society.

An instrument of national interaction, prestige, and survival, a Constitution symbolizes a country's credentials of nationhood for the world at large. In addition to performing the functions of constitutionalism, the Constitution of a country legitimizes the power base of its rulers. In the exclusive domain of political stability, a Constitution is an instrument of immense significance, for it facilitates the legitimate transfer of power or change of government in a prescribed manner. Excluding the prospective functions as expected from any good constitutional instrument, various constitutions in the modern world are aimed, says an American political scientist, Professor William G. Andrews, at the following:

> Constitutions are baptismal certificates to newly independent nations, so are they marriage contracts for federations. They are convenient and necessary instruments for spelling out the rights and obligations of separate political units that are merging into one State structure. The pie of public authority is sliced up between national and regional governments and their relationships are prescribed. Constitutions assign some powers to the component units and some to the national government; others are shared or denied to both. The federation may bring together previously independent States or it may simply recognise substantial cultural or historical differences among several geographic areas of an existing State.[7]

From the advent of written constitutions and constitutional governments, it seems that there is no uniform pattern in the evolution, adoption, and promulgation of various constitutions in the modern world. Even a single country which has practised more than one constitutions may present different modes of adopting it. For instance, Pakistan's Provisional Constitution (1947–56) was promulgated (via the Indian Independence Act of 1947) by Governor-General Jinnah. The 1956 Constitution (though a result of behind-the-scene compromises) was adopted by the Second Constituent Assembly of the country. The 1962 Constitution was bestowed on the nation by an individual, i.e., Field Marshal Ayub Khan. Yahya Khan promulgated his Legal Framework Order, and Zia bestowed the PCO on his captive nation. Only the 1973 Constitution was a unanimously adopted document (by the National Assembly).

Contrary to popular assertions and general presumptions, 'a constitution is never made directly by the people and no constitution has ever been adopted by them unanimously'.[8] Some may cite the institution of referendum, yet that too remotely resembles free choice, the availability of all possible options, and unanimity of the whole people. The presentation of an already drafted constitution for 'yes'/ 'no' to the people cannot be construed as their direct and free involvement in the constitution-making process. A former Chief Justice of the Supreme Court of Pakistan, Muhammad Munir, holds the following possible authorities behind a Constitution:[9]

1. an alien paramount authority giving a Constitution to the people under its sovereignty, i.e., the Government of India Act of 1935;

2. a popularly-elected Assembly formulating a Constitution, i.e., the 1956 and the 1973 Constitutions of Pakistan;

3. the people themselves consenting to a Constitution in a referendum;

4. a *de facto* sovereign authority terminating (voluntarily or under the force of circumstances) its authority, and transferring power to other hands by a constitutional document, ultimately becoming a Constitution of that political entity; and

5. a hitherto sovereign authority imposing governing limits on its power, i.e., the British Constitution.

The making and adoption of a Constitution usually follows some fundamental political/historical event(s)[10], such as the conferment or achievement of independence, on or by a satellite/colonial territory; the setting up of a new constitutional government after a successful revolution or political upheaval; for example, the Constitution of the Islamic Republic of Iran in 1979; the emergence of a new state after the existing political entities have agreed to federate under a common government, e.g., the Constitution of the United States of America; and a major reconstruction of a country's institutions, following a huge natural calamity or a catastrophic war.

Besides the functions of a Constitution briefly mentioned in the preceding pages, a Constitution may contain some prospective functions. The prospective functions may be summarized in the following:[11]

- A Constitution may articulate the ideas, aspirations, and ambitions of the political society it serves. Such functions are usually mentioned in the preamble of a Constitution. Though never going beyond the stage of rhetoric, almost all the late Constitutions of Pakistan contained such ideals, mostly relating to democracy, an Islamic welfare state, etc.

- Most of the Constitutions in the world contain a comprehensive list of the fundamental rights of the citizens.

- A Constitution may describe details of territory under a country's sovereign jurisdiction or may also refer to territories lost to an alien actor.

- It may contain the economic and social policies of the state.

Professor Andrews maintains that though 'constitutions rarely perform according to expectations', yet to realize the prospective functions seems to be the most difficult task. In his opinion:

> It is much easier to forbid a government to trespass in a given area than to instruct it in the substance of policy formulation or execution. In the area of human rights, for instance, it is much easier for a constitution to deny the government the power to restrict freedom of speech than to succeed in requiring it to set up printing plants in order that all political groups might have the means to disseminate their opinions. On government, as on fractious horses, reins are easier than spurs to use effectively.[12]

CONSTITUTIONALISM

Constitutionalism is a very complex concept and seems attractive to the people, yet very distasteful to the ruling elite, ever prone to an arbitrary manner of government. From antiquity down to the modern era, philosophers and political scientists, in their constitutional and democratic conceptions, have placed emphasis on the urgent need and imperatives of constitutionalism and the rule of law. For instance, Aristotle, in contrast to Plato's search for and training of philosopher-kings to rule the state, eulogized constitutionalism as the best guarantee of state stability, progress, and the rights of the people. To Aristotle, constitutionalism meant that 'Government must be responsible to the governed, that citizens should be involved in the process of making laws, that they are obliged to obey, and that, however else men may be unequal, they are equal under the law'.[13]

Literally, constitutionalism means a government according to a Constitution or adherence to constitutional principles. The evolution of political constitutionalism in the modern democratic era has come to mean succinctly a 'limited government', in which 'power is proscribed and procedure prescribed'.[14] Professor Andrews calls it the 'libertarian and procedural sense of constitutionalism'. By the 'libertarian' sense of constitutionalism, he means that 'authority to take certain actions regarding the members of the community is withheld. The State is forbidden to trespass in areas reserved for private activity'. By the 'procedural' sense of constitutionalism, he means a state of affairs in which 'directions are set forth determining the manner in which policy shall be formulated and implemented within the areas of jurisdiction of the State. Government institutions are established and their functions, powers, and interrelationships are defined'.[15] More or less in the same sense, yet very cogently, Justice Munir dilated on these concepts of constitutionalism when he wrote, that 'it is customary for a constitution to limit the powers of the government and thus to operate as a bulwark for protection of private rights'.[16]

The basic rationale of almost every written Constitution is to control and regulate the functions of various organs of government. The concept of Constitution itself originated in the belief that it might achieve the long-cherished human ideal of 'limited government'. Such an assertion is borne out by Professor Vile when he says that:

[I]nternational theorists have concerned themselves with
the problem of ensuring that the exercise of governmental power, which is essential to the realisation of the
values of their societies, should be controlled in order
that it should not itself be destructive of the values it was
intended to promote.[17]

Written Constitutions in modern political systems seem to be the
'documentary embodiment of constitutionalism', for the latter proudly stands 'in a position of co-legitimacy with democracy'.[18] However,
many countries in the world in general and the developing countries
in particular do have Constitutions, yet without constitutionalism. In
such cases, the prospective trends for democratization have been
gravely undermined because 'tyrants, whether individual or collective, find that constitutions are convenient screens behind which they
can dissimulate their despotism.'[19]

Over two centuries ago, when the American Constitution was
written and adopted, Thomas Paine claimed that written Constitutions are 'to liberty, what grammar is to language'.[20] Detested for his
pro-people views (by none other than the then President of the United
States of America) as 'a dirty little atheist', Paine laid down a
constitutional maxim of immense importance, that a government
acting contrary to the constitution was an unconstitutional act of
'power without right'. From his definition of Constitution, as mentioned in the foregoing pages, the following principles of constitutionalism can be inferred:[21]

- There is a fundamental difference between a people's
  government and a people's Constitution, whether the
  government happens to be entrusted to a king or to a
  representative assembly.

- The Constitution is antecedent to the government.

- The Constitution defines the authority which a nation
  commits to its government and, in so doing, limits it.

- Any exercise of authority beyond the prescribed limits by
  any government is 'power without right'.

- Finally, in a state which is ignorant of the subtle distinction
  between the government and the Constitution, there is no

Constitution at all. There, the will of the people has no checks and limits upon the government and that state demonstrates despotism.

When developing countries like Pakistan are hanging in the balance between orderly procedures of constitutional democracy and the arbitrariness of growing authoritarianism, the most cherished dream and unswerving faith in the sanctity of the individual and the nation can be realized by observing the letter and spirit of constitutionalism. The people of Pakistan must be allowed to apply limits within which self-rule would become possible. Only then could constitutionalism mean constitutional democracy, the system of laws, customs, and conventions 'in which the individual can play a creative role, where his individuality will not be dwarfed and where his capacity for personal growth and expansion will not be surrendered at the altar of collectivistic and unrestrained, untrammelled regimentation'.[22]

THE DOCTRINE OF RULE OF LAW

Rule of law is the fundamental and legitimate concern of every citizen in the modern state system. Throughout the annals of known civilization, human instincts have striven for the Rule of Law—the principal and the most sacred pillar of justice. The concept of the Rule of Law is rooted in the spirit of man—being a victim of the arbitrary exercise of governmental power and attempting to seek justice and control of the genie of political and economic power. The sovereignty of constitutional rule over the absolute and arbitrary wielding of power is the quintessence of the doctrine of the Rule of Law.

Rule of Law is said to prevail where men are ruled by law and not subjected to caprice. 'Inalienable rights', 'natural rights', and 'human rights' are all sociopolitical and philosophical expressions which fall within the doctrine of the Rule of Law. That law must be triumphant over all other considerations was the essence and gift of Greek political theory. Aristotle was perhaps the earliest thinker who laid down the principle of the supremacy of law in his *Politics*: the Rule of Law must prevail and should be preferable to the will of an individual. The supremacy of law was, to the Greek philosophers, the mark of a good state. The Rule of Law, or constitutional rule, as understood from Aristotle's political philosophy, is summarized by George H. Sabine in the following:[23]

- it is rule in the public interest and distinguished from a factional or tyrannous rule in the interests of a ruling elite;

- the government is run by regulations, not by arbitrary decrees, and it does not flout customs and the conventions of the Constitution; and

- a constitutional government is distinguished from despotic rule supported merely by force.

The constitutional law of the present-day world has been greatly transformed from what it was in the late nineteenth century, yet A.V. Dicey's intellectual influence on the conception of the Constitution and the Rule of Law still remains a guiding star. The lectures which Dicey delivered as Vineriam Professor of English Law at Oxford, first published in 1885 under the title *Introduction to the Study of the Law of the Constitution*, a most influential treatise, not only catapulted him to fame as a first-rate constitutional authority but also rigorously moulded the constitutional thinking of successive writers. While expounding the supremacy of law, Dicey accorded the following three meanings to the doctrine of the Rule of Law:[24]

- the absolute supremacy or predominance of regular law as opposed to the influence of arbitrary power ... or even the wide discretionary authority on the part of government ... a man may be punished for a breach of law, but he can't be punished for anything else;

- 'equality before the law or the equal subjection of all classes to the ordinary law of the land administered by the ordinary law courts'. By the second principle of the Rule of Law, Dicey in fact contrasted the superiority of the British system of ordinary courts to that of the *Droit Administratif* in France; and

- the third principle of Dicey reflected the political environment in which he intellectually grew up and lived. For him, the Constitution is the result of the ordinary law of the land, i.e., forming part of the ordinary law as administered by the law courts.

More than a century after Dicey evolved his concepts of the Rule of Law, the doctrine has been immensely enlarged and made universally applicable by various international organizations, consisting mainly of jurists and political thinkers. Among others, the International Commission of Jurists has attained prominence. Thus, the doctrine of the Rule of Law could not be better comprehended than by reference to a maxim, 'Respect for the supreme value of human personality', propounded by the International Commission of Jurists, an affiliate of UNESCO. In its historic moot in New Delhi, the Commission gave material content to the Rule of Law, an expression used in the Universal Declaration of Human Rights. Based on a questionnaire distributed to 75,000 lawyers the world over, and on the deliberations of jurists from more than fifty countries, the Rule of Law, in the perspective of 'the Declaration of Delhi, 1959' includes the following:[25]

1. *The legislature:* there is a right to representative and responsible government, and there are certain minimum standards or principles for the law, including those contained in the Universal Declaration and the European Convention and in particular, freedom of religious belief, assembly, and association, and the absence of retroactive penal laws;

2. *The executive:* especially that delegated legislation should be subjected to independent judicial control, and that a citizen who is wronged should have a remedy against the state or government;

3. *The criminal process:* a 'fair trial' involves such elements as certainty of criminal law; the presumption of innocence, reasonable rules relating to arrest, accusation, and detention pending trial, the giving of notice and provision for legal advice; public trial; the right of appeal; and the absence of cruel or unusual punishment; and

4. *The judiciary and the legal profession:* this requires the independence of the judiciary and proper grounds and procedures for the removal of judges; and it imposes a responsibility on an organized and autonomous legal profession.

A constant struggle is going on between those who intend to balance, diffuse, or devolve political power, and those who seek to monopolize, concentrate, or consolidate it for a particular ruling elite in developing countries like Pakistan. Here, power has been misused by tyrants. However, the modern era can no longer endure tyranny, and democracy has taught people to resist the wrongful exercise of power. A. K. Brohi maintains that the combination of power with 'pride' is 'disease', and the contemptuous attitude of the wielders of power towards the people is perhaps its symptom. Therefore, 'the Rule of Law is the only effective antidote' against it.[26] For humbling the ruling elite and making them realize that the power they wield is conditional and that the poisonous shafts of their pride are temporary, Robert Briffault maintains the following:

> Every form of pride and ostentation is a display of power; despotic pride, aristocratic pride, material pride, pride of birth, pride of wealth—the glorification of abused power. Is not pride the last and most persistent attribute of the wielder of power, his infirmity? When all is lost, when he has been dispossessed, brought to justice, a grand heroic aureole will yet surround him to the last, wherein he will with magnificent gesture cloak himself, and contemptuously turning to the canaille proudly proclaim: I have treated you all as dogs.[27]

FEDERALISM

Federalism is a dynamic democratic process based on 'interdependence', 'co-operation', and 'sharing of powers' between the centre and its units, as provided for in the written Constitution of a state. The concept of federalism is derived from various theories of 'social contract' and, both theoretically and practically, it is strongly animated by characteristics of co-ordination, co-operation, and partnership, rather than a subordinative relationship, and it stresses specifically the devolution of powers to the federating units.[28] Federalism aims at voluntary unification of multilingual, multi-ethnic, and diverse cultural entities with substantial latitude in self-political operation. It is a linkage of the people and their institutions by mutual consent and homogeneity of fundamental interests, enabling all 'to share in the system's decision-making and decision-executing processes'.[29]

Federalism is a concept theoretically attractive yet practically distasteful to the ruling elite of almost every federation in the world.

Political constitutionalism and federalism, two closely related concepts, have been rated high in the constitutional debates and propaganda of many governments. But practically, most of them have swung towards authoritarian centralization. Seemingly, those political systems which are imbued with the letter and spirit of federalism have been by far the most stable entities in the modern era.

Federalism, in the perspective of a Pakistani jurist, A. K. Brohi, can be defined as 'a constitutional device by which a system of double government is made to operate in one and the same state'.[30] Robert Garran, an eminent Australian scholar, defined federalism as: 'A form of government in which sovereignty or political power is divided between the central and local governments, so that each of them within its own sphere is independent of the other'.[31] K. C. Wheare in his prestigious constitutional work, *Federal Government*, defines the federal principle as: 'The method of dividing powers so that the general (i.e., the Central) and regional (i.e., the Provincial) governments are each, within a sphere, coordinate and independent'.[32] Besides the division of specific powers between the Centre and the Provinces, the federal principle requires, in the perspective of some, that 'the residue' be left with the latter.[33] However, Wheare opines that whoever is the 'residuary legatee', the specific demarcation of powers should be made in such a way that neither the Central nor the Provincial government is 'subordinate' to the other. And if the federal principle is predominant in a Constitution, that Constitution may be called 'a federal constitution'.[34]

Externally, a federal state might seem a unitary style of government, yet it is the internal division of powers that gives to it the distinguishing character of federalism. The autonomous existence and functioning of the provincial governments within the organic whole (i.e., the federation), take place through constitutionally prescribed limits. The federation and the units independently supplement each other, are masters in the spheres of their allotted constitutional jurisdiction, never encroach upon the other's exclusive sphere of influence, and finally, they have the constitutional option to refer their conflicts and grievances for adjudication to the higher courts of the land. For explication of the foregoing federal imperatives, one may refer to a scholarly observation of Lord Bryce, who described the two levels of governments in the same state as 'distinct and separate in their action'. Explaining the philosophy of the federal system, he said it was 'like a great factory wherein two sets of machinery are at work, their revolving wheels apparently intermixed, their bands crossing one another, yet each set doing its own work without touching or hampering the other'.[35]

The New Federalism

After defining federalism, it seems pertinent to ask: why is there a renewed interest in the systematic study of federalism in the modern era when the trends indicate a global village phenomenon? In view of the ascendancy of authoritarianism in the post-First World War political systems, critics like Harold J. Laski were obliged to sound the death-knell for it, when he observed in 1939 that 'the epoch of federalism is over'.[36] Even Professor Wheare, a leading exponent of federalism, had to concede in 1945 that the prevalent trends in the socio-economic and political milieu of the world were discouraging for the federal form of government. However, in the early 1950s, another noted political scientist, Max Beloff, noticed that federalism was attaining 'a widespread popularity such as it had never known before'.[37] Evidently, it is the pragmatic political philosophy of federalism and the federal principle which seem to have dominated the modern state structure. When old empires were falling, to give way to the modern nation-states, the philosophy of federalism was invariably employed in aid of ethno-linguistic and territorially-centred nationalism. However, in the modern era, the emphasis has been reversed, i.e., application of the federal principle to unify the multi-faceted societies and units into a federal state structure.

Contrary to the predominant imperialistic tendencies in most of the political systems, a German political scientist, Althusius, in the sixteenth and seventeenth centuries methodically visualized the procedural framework of federalism. While recognizing cities, districts, and provinces as microcosms, (i.e., units) inside the macrocosm (i.e., the federal state), he assigned sovereignty to the federation and statutory rights to the units, which could not be violated.[38] Just as the American practice of the federal system has become the prototype of modern federations in the world, the two German connotations, i.e., *Staatenbund* (confederation) and *Bundestaat* (federation), have contributed to the political theory of prevalent federalism.

Having little regard for the universalization of federalism, the inimical tendencies towards centralization have become a dominant feature in many developing states. The national systems and their

Constitutions founded upon the pragmatic federal principle have turned out to be, in many cases, highly centralized and unitary in practice. From such practices stems the conclusion that a government may have a federal Constitution yet in actual operation it may well be a non-federal or quasi-federal structure.[39] Thus, it is predominantly the practice of the letter and spirit of the federal Constitution which determines the character of a federal government. Such an assertion could be substantiated from Pakistan's constitutional history in which the system, constitutionally visualized as federal, was deliberately allowed to degenerate into a highly centralized and non-federal one in practice. All the constitutional restraints and reverence for federalism in the three Constitutions of 1956, 1962, and 1973, were sacrificed by every regime, to the patent slogan, 'The centre should be strong', thus making a farce of provincial autonomy.

Confederation

A confederation is essentially an association of sovereign states in which the confederal components retain their political supremacy and governmental autonomy, except as they voluntarily delegate certain powers to the confederation. The fundamental difference between the federal principle and confederal government is that 'the authority of the confederation does not directly reach over to and operate upon the people. It operates through the intermediary governments which stand, as it were, midway between the people and itself'.[40] The second major difference between the two is that in the case of a confederation, sovereignty rests with the component states, while in the case of a federation, the federating units give up sovereign claims in favour of their federal union. The third difference between the two is that confederations, as compared to federations, have proved to be loose, fragile, and temporary structures.

Representing a transitional stage in the political association of sovereign entities, confederations have often been terminated and rarely transformed into federations. The outstanding examples of confederations are the Hanseatic League, the Holy Roman Empire, and, more recently, the old German Confederation (1815-66), the Swiss Confederacy (1815-40), the Union of American States (1781-89), and the UAR (United Arab Republic), consisting of Egypt and Syria (1958-61). Among the avowed objectives of such confederations were external security, cultural unity, and uniformity of socio-economic intercourse, etc.

Essentials of Federalism

In order to enable the federal principle to succeed in its actual operation, various theorists have stipulated the following conditions:[41]

1. The existence of units/provinces/states, closely connected by locality, by history, race, or the like, being capable of fostering in their citizens an impress of common nationality. Federalism does flourish among units which have already been loosely connected. The desire for union and pro-federation sentiments among the inhabitants of units are most essential. Geographic contiguity is certainly a very favourable factor in a cohesive federation, and, if the federating units are wide apart (as in the case of pre-1971 Pakistan), a persistent pretext obliges the regional leadership to opt for insurrection and secession.

2. The formation of a Constitution, under which powers between the federal and provincial governments are specifically stated and demarcated, enables both governments to draw their authority and legitimacy from the supreme national law. In federalism, the federal Constitution constitutes the highest law of the land, and it should be written and rigid.

3. If statesmen are interested in making their states, in the words of an American Chief Justice, Salmon P. Chase, 'an indestructible Union, composed of indestructible States' (Texas v. White, 7 Wallace, 1869), they must apply the principle of non-centralization in their federal systems. The rationale of Justice Chase's argument is the splitting of the powers of the federation among the co-ordinative units.

4. Inbuilt or even acquired ability in the federal system to build consensus rather than operating through coercive levers *vis-à-vis* the units.

5. The essence of injecting the federal principle in any political system visualizes the following:[42]

i) The strength of the federation does not stem from the federal government but from the devolution of power upon the nation as a whole;

ii) Both the federal government and the governments of the units exercise only delegated powers; and

iii) Resort to constitutionalism and self-restraint, (i.e., minimizing blackmail and the abject use of coercion), on the basis of the national written Constitution, is the hallmark of federalism.

Pakistan: Centralists versus Federalists and Confederalists

The aforementioned elaboration of federalism and the federal principle notwithstanding, we will be confronted with three other related concepts (though purely in the Pakistani context) in the succeeding chapters of this work. They are: the centralists, the federalists, and the confederalists. Ever since its inception, Pakistan's much trumpeted federal polity and its constitution-making as well as constitution-breaking history, have involved dealing with the unpalatable consequences of denying autonomy to the federating units. With various efforts to suppress the whole issue, political sentiments and social aspirations associated with provincial autonomy have been neglected so far. The heart-rending tale of deliberately preventing the federal principle from taking root has sharply divided popular politics and the political parties (particularly those based in the smaller provinces) on this vital issue.

To begin with, the centralists treat the provinces as mere administrative units and increasingly paint the 'autonomists' as 'traitors', working against the solidarity of the state itself. Ignoring regional political aspirations, sentiments, cultural ethos, linguistic, and social traits, the centralists advance the 'Islamic brotherhood' argument as the basis and source of the country's unity and its national integration process. Though they have never so far openly advocated, the ingredients of the Government of India Act of 1935, strong Presidential rule and One Unit are the ideal contours of a Constitution for the political aspirations of this group. The ideal working model for the Federation of Pakistan aspired to by this group is the CMLA dictating to the DMLAs (the proconsuls of the Byzantine empire) at the provincial levels, and so on, down to the district level. The federal bureaucracy, the military generals during the martial law eras, and invariably the ruling elite in power at the centre, are the chief adherents to this model.

Inspired by the federal principle and all the political idealism associated with it, the federalists opine that the legitimate rights of all distinct and larger regional, linguistic, cultural, or racial entities should be safeguarded. Shunning the domination of one group or region by another, the federalists demand power devolution and power-sharing in the Federation of Pakistan. Often described as the 'autonomists', they favour the substantive devolution of legislative, financial, and executive powers to the federating units of the country. An almost overwhelming majority of political parties (mostly when they are out of power at the Centre) call for the immediate introduction of the federal principle in Pakistan. The political forces based in East Pakistan prior to its separation in 1971 and the regional parties hailing from the smaller provinces in the 'new' Pakistan have been in the forefront in demanding provincial autonomy.

As against the federalists and the centralists, the confederalists maintain that Pakistan's polity is a structure of heterogeneous entities. They stress confederation, not federation, as the best constitutional device for its survival. They consider the text of the March 1940 Resolution (i.e., the Pakistan Resolution) as the rationale for their arguments in favour of a confederal Constitution for Pakistan. They not only demand greater provincial autonomy but want to vest a very limited number of subjects (i.e., foreign affairs, defence, communications, and currency) in the Centre. They opine that because of the machinations and exploitation of the civil-military bureaucracy (hailing from the Punjab), the federal experience in Pakistan has failed so far. That is why only a confederal Constitution could guarantee the rights of the smaller units of Pakistan. Punjabi domination, they maintain, has forced them to adopt confederal demands in the Constitution.

The professions and conceptual bases of the centralists, federalists, and confederalists notwithstanding, I will endeavour to analyse in the succeeding chapters why the adherents of such constitutional principles are inconsistent, unprincipled, and mostly opportunistic in what they demand, and why they practise the opposite of what they preach. Why do the political personalities and parties demanding provincial autonomy when they are out of power, suddenly become the champions of a strong centre after attaining power? For instance, the ruling party in the 1950s, the Pakistan Muslim League, was the major exponent (both in theory and in practice) of a strong centre. But the same party had based its demand for Pakistan, besides other factors, on the plank of maximum provincial autonomy in the 1940s. The examples could be multiplied but the discrepancy in profession and practice of the aforementioned groups shall be exposed at a later stage of this work.

THE DOCTRINE OF SEPARATION OF POWERS

Locke viewed government as a federative entity in the nature of a Board of Trustees and the effective way to limit the possible abuse of powers by the trustees was to separate the legislative and executive organs of the state. The executive, in Locke's conception, was supposed to be visibly subordinate to the supreme organ of the legislature; the former had to be given the powers of issuing ordinances in case the latter was not in session. Upon Locke's visualization of parliamentary priorities, Montesquieu built his proposition that the political functions be classified as legislative, executive, and judicial. He professed to have discovered the doctrine of separation of powers from Locke's conceptions of democratic measures against despotism and by studying the English Constitution itself.[43] However, almost all the English constitutionalists and political scientists are of the unanimous view that Montesquieu's understanding of the eighteenth century Constitution was patently 'imperfect'. Montesquieu was primarily concerned with the preservation of individual liberty, and he felt that this could be realized through the doctrine of separation of powers as echoed in his work, *Esprit des Lois* (1748):

> Political liberty is to be found only when there is no abuse of power. But constant experience shows us that every man invested with power is liable to abuse it, and to carry his authority as far as it will go ... To prevent this abuse, it is necessary from the nature of things that one power should be a check on another ... when the legislative and executive powers are united in the same person or body ... there can be no liberty ... Again, there is no liberty if the judicial power is not separated from the legislative and the executive ... There would be an end of everything if the same person or body, whether of the nobles or of the people, were to exercise all three powers.[44]

What the doctrine of separation of powers was meant to realize, as elaborated by Montesquieu and his contemporaries, was the prevention of 'tyranny'. Tyranny to them was the obvious result of concentration of powers in a few hands which usually enact tyrannical laws and execute them in a tyrannical manner. Following in the footprints of Montesquieu, the English jurist Blackstone, in his *Commentaries on the Laws of England,* echoed the imperatives of separation of powers in almost identical terms:

> In all tyrannical governments, the supreme magistracy, or the right both of making and enforcing the laws, is vested in one and the same man, or one and the same body of men; and whenever these two powers are united, there can be no public liberty. The magistrate may enact tyrannical laws, and execute them in a tyrannical manner, since he is possessed in quality of dispenser of justice with all the powers which he as legislator thinks proper to give himself . . . Were it (the judicial power) joined with legislative, the life, liberty, and property of the subject would be in the hands of arbitrary judges, whose decisions would be then regulated only by their own opinions and not by any fundamental principles of law; which, though legislators may depart from, yet judges are bound to observe. Were it joined with the executive, this union might soon be an overbalance for the legislative.[45]

The doctrine of separation of powers has received the most positive response in the Western democracies, securing in the process the independence of the judiciary from the executive. Contrary to such practice, the doctrine has been reduced to a farcical concept in the totalitarian states of the developing world. The extent to which separation of powers, both in theory and practice, exists in any given society, depicts the extent of democratic freedom and the rule of law in that state. The Constitution of the United States has applied this doctrine more than any other in the world. It is based on the actual doctrine of separation of powers, i.e., one branch of the state must not have the whole of another branch vested in it, nor can it obtain control over another branch. The three branches, i.e., executive, legislative, and judicial, should be interrelated and yet act as 'checks and balances' on one another.

Article XXX of the Massachusetts State Constitution of 1780 explained the doctrine as follows:

> In the government of this commonwealth, the legislative department shall never exercise the executive and judicial powers or either of them; the executive shall never exercise the legislative and judicial or either of them; and the judicial shall never exercise the legislative and executive powers or either of them to the end and it may be government of laws and not of men.

For a further exposition of the aforementioned observation, one may cite *The Federalist* (an American classic in the annals of constitutionalism), Essay 47:

> The accumulation of all powers, legislative, executive, and judiciary, in the same hands, whether of one, a few, or many, whether hereditary, self-appointed, or elective, may justly be pronounced the very definition of tyranny.

THEORY OF DIVINE RIGHT OF RULERS

For their vested interests and for maintaining themselves in power till Doomsday, the rulers, in their active connivance with the contemporary religious institutions, propagated among the masses the belief that authority to rule was granted by God, that the subjects were duty-bound to obey their rulers. The theory of the divine right of rulers is based upon the following assumptions:

1. A state is a consequence of direct divine intervention/creation.

2. The rulers possess the divine sanction to control the affairs of the state.

3. The rulers are accountable to none but God alone.

The theory of the divine right of rulers significantly supports the claims of many rulers to govern absolutely, without any semblance of accountability to their people. For instance, James I of England once told his Parliament:

> A king can never be monstrously vicious. Even if a king is wicked, it means God has sent him as a punishment for

people's sins and it is unlawful to shake off the burden which God had laid down upon them. Patience, earnest prayer and amendment of their lives are the only lawful means to move God to relieve them of that heavy curse.[46]

The exploitative and coercive levers of this notorious theory were imitated and adopted with immense benefits by the Muslim rulers as well. While styling themselves as *Zil-e-Subhani* or *Zil-e-Ilahi* ('the shadow of God'), they would loudly assert that their personal rule and commands were 'the will of God', 'a manifestation of God', and 'the decree of God'. High-sounding titles, the king being the shadow of God, were invariably arrogated to themselves by the Muslim kings of Persia, the Mughals of the subcontinent, and the Ottoman Turk sultans.

The institution of kingship and its 'divine attributes' were exalted by the Muslim rulers to the extent that the Mughal king, Akbar the Great, bestowed upon himself the title of 'Incarnation of Supreme Light' on earth. While the Muslim rulers had a readily available and equally pliable class of *ulema* and *muftis* to support the sanctimonious basis of their monarchies, the kings in the West were no less fortunate in having a similar class of bishops and archbishops to perform the same task.

Both the Muslim and the Christian rulers, following in the footprints of the Pharaohs of Egypt, the Kings of Persia, and the Byzantine emperors glorified and rationalized the parameters of the theory of divine right of kings by playing upon the sheer ignorance of the masses. However, political philosophers like Hobbes, Locke, Montesquieu, Rousseau, and others began to demolish the theory by expounding the theories of the social contract of the masses, and of sovereignty belonging to the people and not to the rulers. By championing the rights of the people and the individuals, these philosophers dealt a severe blow to the outmoded theory.

Notwithstanding such setbacks at the hands of political philosophers of yore and of modern times, the advent of the age of science and industrialization, the theory of the divine right of rulers still seems attractive to some in developing countries like Pakistan. For instance, the former military dictator, General Ziaul Haq, and his theocratic supporters seemed bent upon availing it for their dubious ends. Zia openly proclaimed in a speech at Quetta that 'he was sent by God to Islamize the Pakistani society'.[47] He often talked about 'a mission' (perhaps a divine one) to complete in the society of Pakistan. More than often, he claimed that, for fulfilling his mission, he used to do *istikhara* (seeking divine instruction), thus seeking direct guidance from Almighty Allah. Having dismissed the government of Prime Minister Muhammad Khan Junejo on 29 May 1988, Zia publicly claimed that he did so after performance of *istikhara*. Although the benefits of *istikhara* could not save him from the ill-fated crash of 17 August 1988, he definitely joined those despots of yore who claimed direct communication with God to befool the masses.

THEOCRACY

The concept of theocracy or *Hukumat-e-Illahiya* (literally meaning 'kingdom of God') has evolved from time immemorial. Theocracy is a word derived from the Greek 'theos' meaning 'god'. The dictionary defines theocracy as 'a system of government in which laws of the state are believed to be the laws of God'—implying a government by priests or a priestly class. It is a system of government in which the priestly class reigns supreme on the presupposition of being an intermediary between men and their Creator. Thus the title is attached to those states governed by God directly or through a sacerdotal class. Because God could not look after states or empires personally, the cumbersome duty thus devolved on the high priests as the spiritual and temporal representatives of the Lord!

The socio-political life of the ancient states, theocratic in substance, revolved around the main temple, the abode of gods.[48] The process of the evolution of state allowed the rulers to wield immense power and to amass immense wealth. With the passage of time, the priests became jealous of the kings who monopolized the institution of 'representing' God on a piece of territory, (empire, kingdom, or state) on earth. The theocrats put forward, though off and on, the divine theory. They began to articulate views that, as the pious and chosen people, they were best suited to perform the administrative functions of a state. Both Christianity and Judaism perceived the state as a divine institution and, hence, divine rule over it of utmost importance.

Sibte Hasan, a Pakistani intellectual, draws a graphic sketch of the ancient theocratic monarchies in his work, *The Battle of Ideas in Pakistan* :

> Rulers in the days of theocracy used to perform their
> religious duties punctually. They would regularly visit the

temple to pay homage to their god, participate in religious ceremonies and festivals, oblige the priests with precious gifts and allocate large endowments of land to their establishments. Yet they never allowed the priestly class to interfere in affairs of the State. . . . Priests were duty-bound to interpret the laws of god to suit the personal idiosyncrasies of monarchs and expediencies of the State. And woe to the swollen-headed priest who dared to defy the king's command. This pattern of relationship between the State and the custodian of religion remained an accepted norm all over the world till the end of feudalism. The pagan Roman emperors and their Christian counterparts at Byzantium, the Umayyads and the Abbasids, the Pathans and the Moghals all kept the priestly class subservient to them.[49]

While the rulers used the priestly class for the prolongation of their autocratic rule, the latter, becoming somewhat indispensable to the former, subjected the masses to the mercy of *taqdeer* (fate) and *karma*. Whenever the people began to attain any awareness of their exploitation, the priests would divert their attention by preaching sermons to the poor that they better prepare for the beautiful world of the Hereafter. Sibte Hasan dilates on the ghastly role of priestly orthodoxy against the masses in the following words:

People suffered under the . . . priestly orthodoxy. Bound to the chariot of superstitions, beliefs and costly rituals and ceremonies, they had no escape. From birth to death, every step in their life was controlled by priests. Even their agricultural activities like ploughing, sowing and harvesting required the blessings of the priest who was paid for it by them. The priests stuck to their life like leeches and would never have them think freely for themselves or act as they willed . . . .[50]

The emergence of the modern state and the obsolescence of the old order of empires, kingdoms, and emirates made it imperative that the people adjust and adapt by utilizing their rationalistic faculties in contemporary situations and settings. However, the idea of people managing their own affairs seemed unacceptable to the religious elite, particularly in developing countries such as Pakistan. Openly challenging the people's sovereignty over state affairs, they began twisting the purely religious conceptions of divine revelations which speak of God as 'sovereign in heaven and earth' into modern political literature.[51] The *ulema's* insistence that the Constitution of the state must recognize the sovereignty of God seems loaded with ulterior intent, i.e., ultimately seeking their own supremacy as the custodian and sole interpreters of *Shariah* in the Kingdom of God. The *ulema's* exhortations that sovereignty belongs to God in an Islamic state allowed the critics to ridicule the nation as if 'in officially atheistic countries God had set up governments-in-exile'.[52] The *ulema*, while making themselves readily available anti-people levers in the hands of the ruling elite, have been using religion as a revivalist weapon to convert Pakistan into a theocracy on medieval lines.

THE STATE

The state as an organized political community, aiming at a cohesive social order and manifesting its united power, has existed in human history from very early times. Not involving oneself with the intricacies associated with the definitions offered by renowned political scientists and jurists of yore, one may follow a very brief yet comprehensive definition of the modern state put forward by an American President, Woodrow Wilson: 'A State is a people organised for law within a definite territory'. Such an organized though artificial legal entity has been depicted by various names, at various places, and at various stages of known human history.

The ancient Greeks used to call it *polis* (city-state), and the Romans *respublica* (commonwealth), *civitas* (community of citizens), and *regnum* (realm or kingdom).[53] The widely accepted word, *status*, from the Latin, was adopted as *stato* by the Italians. The French pronounce it *état* and the English *state*. While Plato dilated on its characteristics in his *Republic*, Thomas Hobbes labelled it *Leviathan*. The Christian theologians aspiring for high office in the Mediaval Ages would call it *respublica christiana* (the commonwealth of Christendom). Among the three early expressions of state i.e., *polis, civitas,* and *respublica*, the former two became outdated as narrow terms because the latter was sufficient to express the large territorial entities as they grew in the form of empires.

Sultanate, mulk, and *mamlikat* are the oriental expressions. The first model of an Islamic state was set up by the Prophet Muhammad (pbuh) in the city of Yathrib, later named *Medina-tul-Nabi*, which ultimately evolved into its present form of Medina. After the death of the Holy Prophet, when the Muslim head of state was given the title of *Khalifa* (i.e., Caliph), such an entity increasingly came to be known as the Caliphate. *Imamate* has a somewhat similar connotation, and is loaded with purely theological overtones. *Dawlah* is the modern version of *state* in the Arabic language.

3

THE MODERN STATE AND CONSTITUTIONALISM: ISLAMIC THEORY AND PRACTICE

This chapter deals with some vital questions as to the contents, characteristics, and forms of an Islamic state and its Constitution. Does the Holy Quran or the *Sunnah* of the Holy Prophet Muhammad(pbuh) prescribe any particular form of government or constitutionalism for an Islamic state ? What is the actual period and mode of functioning of the true Islamic state? Contrary to traditional writings, it is argued that the contents, approach, and the spirit of the Islamic state and its Constitution are not based on theological deductions. An attempt will be made to draw conclusions from the crucible of the actual historical experience of the Islamic state. Buffeted by a perennial barrage of problematic, complex, and sweeping theological generalizations, mainly raised by the so-called doctors and professors of Islam in Muslim countries like Pakistan, one is compelled to invoke the purely historical practice of the Islamic state and the salient political ideas that support it.

Unlike the evolution and growth of other legal and constitutional systems of the modern world, traditional Muslim jurists have often asserted that, with the death of the Prophet, the revelation of divine commands ceased, thereby making the Law of Islam perfect. Such notions obliged latter-day generations to treat the principles of Islamic Law and Jurisprudence as something static and immutable— indeed, as the irrevocable Will of God. More than that, they rested the basis and parameters of Islamic Law and Constitution upon divinely sanctioned Ordinances which should be universally accepted, respected, and upheld by all people. They propounded the theory that the validity and applicability of Islamic Law and the state, and its actual letter and spirit could never be destroyed in any time or space. Such cliches helped to fossilize the spirit of the Prophetic State and Constitution, i.e., the *Charter of Medina*.

This chapter concentrates on the thesis that 'Islam is a society, not a political system', and that the traditional theory aimed at establishing a universal Islamic state, (i.e., the Caliphate), transcending all geographical, racial, linguistic, and sectarian barriers has become redundant in the modern era; that Islam is a system of societal integration and socio-religious thought of its followers; that the modern day Muslim states are national, geographic, ethnic, and linguistic in their substance and practice.

The self-styled protagonists of the 'Universal Islamic State' may eulogize the institution of the Caliphate till the end of the Ottoman Caliphate in 1923. They may even cite rare and scattered precedents of piety and benevolence usually enveloping obsolete institutions. Yet, in its ideal practice, it crumbled after the *Khilafat-i-Rashidah*. Later, the unending saga of Muslim dynastic and despotic rules seems to have penetrated the nascent doctrine of an Islamic state and its institutions. It may be mentioned here that this chapter begins and ends in the context of latter-day controversies relating to the origin and practice of the Islamic state and Constitution in Pakistan.

I

AN OVERVIEW

Untrammelled by historical considerations, socio-economic realities, and political evolution of the modern state and constitutionalism, the orthodox *ulema*, *muftis*, and grand *muftis*, have been making demands for the immediate imposition of *Nizam-i-Islam* on the model of *Khilafat-i-Rashidah* in Pakistan. The traditional jurists, theologians, and protagonists of the political theory and practice of an Islamic state invariably refer to the model institutions and precedents of a state as practised by the first four caliphs only. For reasons well-known to themselves, they 'seldom refer to the Prophet's era, as if no state existed in that period, or the practice of the Prophet carried no legal value in this matter'.[1] They indeed isolate a period of twenty-three years (i.e., the time between the death of the Prophet and the assassination of Ali), and hold it aloft—characterizing it as the complete theory and practice of an Islamic state, thereby fit for complete adoption in modern territorial entities.

The *ulema* and the *muftis* have been pressing governments and trying to persuade the people to quickly return to orthodoxy. They call it 'returning to the roots'—the wellspring of a vanished golden age of the *Khilafat-i-Rashidah*. While arguing in favour of complete imposition of *Shariah*, they reject democracy, modern state structure, and constitutionalism as ideas unsuitable for assimilation in an Islamic state.

In the perspective of A. K. Brohi and Professor Qamaruddin Khan, the word *dawlah*, conveying the idea underlying the term 'state' as implied by modern political scientists, is neither found in classical Arabic literature nor is there even a passing reference to it in the Holy Quran.[2] When, in the early 1950s, a fierce controversy as to the configuration of the future Constitution of Pakistan was going on, Brohi (then Advocate-General of the Sindh Chief Court) deplored the continuous 'wrong insistence' of the traditionalists in vociferously demanding a Constitution based on the injunctions of the Quran and the *Sunnah*.[3] He characterized the position of the *ulema* for the inclusion of the *Shariah* in the state structure and its Constitution as 'paradoxical' and asked them to give the nation 'the contents of that constitution'. He stunned the clergy by pledging to pay a sum of five thousand rupees if any religious scholar could point out the Quranic text considered pertinent to becoming the foundation of a Pakistani Constitution.

Except branding Brohi as a narrow-minded constitutionalist, who was trying to conceal the truth and was ignoring the ideals of the Pakistan movement, the ensuing debate could not properly answer such a formidable challenge. On 21 September 1952, Brohi asserted that none of his critics had provided any pattern of the executive, the legislative, or the judicial organs of the state, based on the Quran, thereby concluding that the Holy Book offered no explicit guidance on the specific issues of the state and its Constitution.

The fundamental source of the Law of Islam, the Quran, opines Professor Khan, refers to some ancient Kings—David, Solomon, Saul(Salut), Goliath(Jalut), the Pharaoh, and a prince of Egypt, purely in a moral and religious context, and no political theory can be construed from these stories. He further states that 'the Quran does not aim to create a state but to create a society' and hence, 'whatever the form and shape of the state—if the Quranic society is realised in it, it may bear the designation of the Islamic state. The omission of the details is therefore the great blessing to the Muslim community, because it makes it possible for Islam to march with the progress of time and adjust itself with new conditions and new environments'.[4]

Indeed, the Holy Book provides a broader framework of the limits, the crossing of which is detrimental to its own upholders, and allows the community to liberally interpret its tenets in the changing conditions of the world. The moment any self-styled professor of religion attempts to reduce the spirit of Islam to specific regional and parochial objectives, he strips Islam of its universality. That is why Brohi maintains that 'the conception of an Islamic state as it is propounded by those who claim that they understand it, is not a clear one and there appear to be as many varieties on the theme of an Islamic state as there are the expounders of it'.[5]

The form, content, and political character of an Islamic state are neither fixed nor stereotyped, as is fallaciously assumed by many *ulema* in Pakistan and elsewhere. Such an assertion is borne out by the following observations of Muhammad Asad, a widely respected scholar on Islamic thought and jurisprudence:

> The *Shariah* does not provide any definite pattern to which a state should conform, nor does it elaborate in detail a constitutional theory, but on the contrary, allows for greater latitude in governmental methods and administrative procedures . . . . Being a Divine Ordinance, the *Shariah* duly anticipates all possibilities and necessities of historical evolution and confronts man with no more than a very limited number of fundamental political laws to which any constitution must conform if the state is to be Islamic; beyond that, it leaves a vast field of constitution-making activity (of legislation generally) to the *Ijtehad* of the time concerned . . . There is not only one form of Islamic state but many; and it is for the people of every period to discover the form most suitable to their needs.[6]

In the background of efforts to equate religion with the state and its constitutionalism, one could pose a pertinent question as to why the traditionalists are taking pains to propound a form of government whose parameters are unclear, controversial, and contradictory in themselves. Both the modernists and traditionalists are unanimous in their analyses that there has never existed a truly Islamic state after the assassination of Ali, the fourth Caliph. Even in that period, neither the Quran nor the *Sunnah* had prescribed any particular form of government or the procedure for selecting its head. The whole state structure and its constitutional scheme seem to have been left to the free will, willingness, and sense of proportion of the Muslims themselves.

II

THE STATE UNDER THE PROPHET

It seems befitting to cast a cursory glance at the governmental and constitutional milieu in which the Prophet was born. The whole of Arabia, save some territories, was independent; it was, however, divided into tribal principalities. With a rudimentary political organization, Bedouin tribalism was the salient feature of Arabia. Each tribe was headed by some Shaikh or Syed, the first among equals, to whom the tribal members owed their allegiance. Advised and assisted by a council of elders(*majlis*), the tiny 'government' of every Shaikh acted in a manner of arbitration rather than command.[7] Plagued with inter- and intra-tribal hostilities and conspicuously devoid of any central authority, the anarchical Arab society could succumb to conflicts at the slightest pretext. However, because of the tremendous regard for the precedents and practices of their ancestors, the tribal chief and his *majlis* were a symbol of tribal prestige and honour.

Law, in its strict sense, was not prevalent among the Arabs, though the tribes and their individuals interacted through customary law and the precedents of their ancestors. But 'it was protected by no sanction, and enforced by no authority. If both parties chose to invoke it, well; if not, neither had anything to fear but the anger of his opponents'.[8] Blood feuds were another distinct feature of the general anarchy in Arabia. Polytheism, polygamy, slavery, and superstitions were the social heritage of that society. The status of women was generally worse than chattels. Though not very different from the rest of Arabia, then at the fringes of Byzantine and Persia's sociocultural milieu, the social organization at Mecca was slightly distinct. The organizational principles of the Meccan polity could roughly be compared to a 'merchant Republic governed by a syndicate of wealthy businessmen'.[9] Freedom of trade, action, and limited public authority—purely moral and persuasive—were the chief traits of that city-state. In this city stood the holy shrine, Kaaba, a centre of pilgrimage.

It was from Mecca that the magnetic voice of Muhammad(pbuh), after being vested at the age of forty with the sacred office of prophethood, drove his followers to vast territorial limits, thereby laying the foundations of an Islamic state. The stiff opposition of

Mecca's pagans to Muhammad's preaching of monotheism compelled the latter to migrate (AD 622) to Yathrib—a city 280 miles to the north. At the time when Muhammad(pbuh) arrived at Medina, the city, inhabited by various antagonistic parties, was in utter political chaos. The Muslims who migrated with the Prophet to Medina were named *Mohajireen* (refugees). Prior to undertaking the journey to Medina, the Prophet had reached an understanding with the leaders of Banu Aws and Banu Khazarij at Aqaba, tribes who had embraced Islam, and came to be known as *Ansar*(helpers). Living in an unending saga of tribal strife, both the Banu Aws and Banu Khazarij were split into twelve clans. Consisting of ten clans, the Jews alongwith other citizens of the city welcomed the Prophet. In return for Jewish goodwill, the Prophet not only extended recognition to their divine religion and Scriptures, but even adopted some of their salient customs and traditions.

For establishing his paramountcy in the city-state of Medina, the Prophet, cognizant of the heterogeneous character of the local population, preferred a sociopolitical policy of 'live and let live'. To protect his followers and his nascent religious doctrines from the vengeance and wrath of the Qureshite of Mecca, the Prophet employed his political and diplomatic skills to knit together the actual and potential adversaries at Medina into a meticulously worked out contract. Commonly known as the *Charter of Medina*, the document is of indubitable authenticity, 'the embryo constitution'[10] in the annals of political constitutionalism. Written and issued at the initiative of the Prophet, the Charter offered to its voluntary adherents the supreme political principles of civic equality, religious tolerance, and freedom of worship, thus rejecting a politico-administrative coercive apparatus. (The salient features of the *Charter of Medina* are mentioned in Chapter One of this study).

The adoption of the *Charter* by all the significant parties in Medina established the paramount political status of the Prophet as an arbitrator in all disputes in the city-state. The *Charter* depicted the fathomless political ingenuity of the Prophet because it successfully excluded any possibility of collusion between any local group and the Qureshite of Mecca. Ensuring safety at home, he could now confidently confront the pagans of Mecca.

Interpreted liberally in the light of modern constitutionalism, the rudimentary form of this written Constitution envisaged a complete absence of theocracy and accorded autonomy and peaceful co-existence to all faiths and communities, regardless of their caste, creed, and tribal affiliations. The will and willingness of the signatories could be construed as the democratic process of arriving at agreements. The rights and obligations of the parties concerning the city-state were set down in black and white. Based on the innovative and integrative political principles of 'unity in diversity', the *Charter* aimed at creating an embryonic form of federalism (communities with diverse socio-religious traits as its federating units), untainted by ideological encumbrances. Though short-lived and completely ignored by the later generations of Muslims, the *Charter of Medina* was a 'social contract' of immense importance. Such political constitutionalism, which became the fundamental written document of the nebulous city-state, was essentially devoid of preconceived theological generalizations.

The second landmark after the *Charter of Medina*, relating to modern-day constitutionalism and the prospective functions of a democratic Constitution, is the last address of the Holy Prophet, which deserves the supreme title of the *Charter of Human Rights*. The address envisaged welding of the high and the low, the rich and the poor, white and black, Arab and non-Arab, men and women, master and slave, into a coherent fraternity by emphasizing noble, humane, and eternal principles. The Farewell Address of the Holy Prophet unequivocally affirmed the equality of man and the inviolability of his person, property, and reputation. The Holy Prophet proclaimed:

> O people, Allah says: O people We created you from one male and one female and made you into tribes and nations so that you could be identified. Verily in the sight of Allah, the most honoured amongst you is the one who is the most God-fearing. There is no superiority for an Arab over a non-Arab, and for a non-Arab over an Arab, nor for the white over the black, nor for the black over the white, except in piety. All mankind is the progeny of Adam and Adam was fashioned out of clay. Behold, every claim of privilege, whether that of blood or property, is under my heels . . . Behold, all practices of the days of ignorance are now under my feet . . . O people, verily your blood, your property, and your honour are sacred and inviolable until you appear before your Lord, as the sacred inviolability of this day of yours, this month of yours and this very town of yours.

Founded on an unswerving faith in monotheism, the Muslim community, with a universal outlook and common religious ties, did transcend tribal, racial, and geographic barriers under the dynamic leadership of Muhammad(pbuh). The Holy Prophet engendered the supranational synthesis of the masses by emphasizing the common origins of mankind and its faith in monotheism. The territorial state, as understood in the modern political sense, was not the ultimate end of the Prophet's mission. Through the eternal message of the Quran, he impressed upon his followers the imperative of a cohesive social fabric which would be a 'mere reflex of the way in which an individual lives in peace with himself and in peace with the world of external relations'.[11]

III

ADVENT OF THE CALIPHATE

Except for his own mode of heading the Muslim community and the nascent state, the Prophet never expressed anything on either succession or a particular form of the future state and its constitutionalism. The Prophet had no surviving son, nor did he appoint a successor to head the expanding Muslim community after his departure. By his deliberate silence on his possible successor, the Prophet left certain things to the people themselves so that they could make a free political choice in keeping with their interests in the changing circumstances.

However, the demise of the Prophet created a dilemma for the Muslim community regarding the selection of his successor. The contending claims of various parties, i.e., the *Mohajireen*, the *Ansar*, and the aristocrats of the house of Umayyad for the high office of the caliph, generated an unfortunate controversy—culminating in perpetual schism among the ranks of Muslims. While the Prophet's dead body awaited burial, the political haggling to nominate a caliph from amongst the various contending claimants continued for several hours. Ultimately, the claims of the Medinites on the sheer strength of their majority and services to the cause of Islam were silenced through a politico-racial argument: firstly, that Arabia would acknowledge no master but from amongst the Qureshite; and, secondly, by quoting a controversial *Hadith* of the Prophet that 'the caliphate would always belong to the Qureshite'.

To the utter chagrin of local Medinites, Abu Bakr was nominated as the first caliph. Although the prompt nomination of Abu Bakr as the caliph averted temporary confusion and potential disunity among the Muslims, the politico-racial superiority argument and the controversial *Hadith* cited in favour of his nomination constituted a clear contravention of the Prophet's last historic address only two months earlier at Mecca. Indeed, it was the beginning of all confusions, arch rivalries, and political uncertainties that were to limit, thwart, and, later, wreck the unity of the Muslim polity. A handful of people and influential members of the early Muslim community hailing from Mecca elected the first caliph, and the rest of the community was asked to give the hand-grasp of fealty. Even Ali, the son-in-law of the Prophet, did not take the oath of allegiance for six months, and it was only after the death of his wife (the daughter of the Holy Prophet) that he paid homage to Abu Bakr as the caliph.

The accession of Umar to the caliphate was a quiet act because he was nominated by the first caliph, Abu Bakr, during the latter's life-time, overruling the apprehensions of some as to the harsh temperament of the former. Some call it an act of *quid pro quo* between the first two caliphs, yet the arguments advanced by Abu Bakr in favour of nominating Umar cannot be disregarded. He said: 'I have done my best to choose the fittest . . . I have appointed over you none of my kin, but Umar, son of Khittab'.[12]

Abu Bakr's sincerity in nominating Umar to succeed him was above-board, as he had nominated a person of stature, who was not his son or brother but who had foresight and the potential to be a good ruler and organizer, and was a devout Muslim.[13] Though the nomination had no legal or constitutional precedent, Abu Bakr's nominee was subsequently endorsed by the general Muslim community after his death.

The victim of an assassin's dagger, Umar was on his deathbed when he constituted an electoral college comprising six chief Companions, i.e., Abdur Rehman, Zubeir, Saad, Ali, Usman, and Talha. In addition to the six electors/candidates for the office of Caliphate, Umar placed the name of his son, Abdullah bin Umar, on this list to arbitrate in case of a tie, explicitly excluding him from standing as a candidate for the succession. Amidst unprofitable wranglings that continued for two days, Abdur Rehman voluntarily offered to forego his own claim to the Caliphate on condition that he would be accepted as the final arbitrator. On the third day of Umar's death, when the people were getting restive, Abdur Rehman, after questioning both Usman and Ali as to their future conduct of the Caliphate, arbitrarily decided in favour of Usman.

Lacking the administrative skills of the Caliph Umar, Usman fell easy prey to the exploitive and crafty skills of his dynasty, the Umayyads. However, contrary to allegations of nepotism by his critics, Usman considered it an act of piety to have special solicitude for his kith and kin and to exercise his authority for their benefit.[14] Usman's leniency in dealing with his corrupt Umayyad officials, and the traditional jealousies between the house of Hashim and that of the Umayyads, constituted two of the major causes of sedition against him, ultimately resulting in his assassination. The effects of Usman's accession to the Caliphate, his turbulent reign, and his consequent assassination, 'led to dissensions which for years bathed the Muslim world in blood, threatened the existence of faith, and to this day divide believers in hopeless and embittered schism'.[15]

After the assassination of Usman, anarchy and chaos were rampant in the horror-stricken city of Medina. The regicides had blatantly refused to leave the capital until the election of the new Caliph, and the restoration of the state to its normal functioning. Meanwhile, the people gathered in front of the house of Ali and frenziedly requested him to be their Caliph. Pressed by the threats of the regicides and entreaties of all in the city, Ali hesitatingly decided to accept the august office of the Caliphate, provided the Muslim community openly took oath of allegiance to him in the Mosque of the Prophet. Ali's resort to the free will and willingness of the people, to accord him the hand-grasp of fealty openly in the mosque, was a radical departure from the traditional pattern of selecting a caliph through a limited council of elders. Ali's choice of going for an open and direct backing of the populace had all the potential of modern-day republicanism.

From its beginning to its end, the cries for avenging Usman's death plagued and haunted Ali's Caliphate. The lenient administrative apparatus of Usman had allowed seditionists to become demanding and to create huge dissensions among the Muslims. Usman's assassination had provided them with an opportunity to rise in rebellion. The hysterical demands made on Ali's Caliphate to quickly and adequately punish the assassins led to civil war; firstly, between Ali and Ai'shah (one of the Prophet's wives), which resulted in the killing of many Muslims including such notables as Talha and Zubeir;

secondly, there was war between Ali and Muawiyah, the latter employing clever political tactics and abject intrigue to wrest the Caliphate from the former. Ultimately, with Ali's murder, the true Islamic Republic, though somewhat limited in scope, thanks to the Arab tribal milieu, gave way to an unending autocratic dynastic rule in Islamic history. From the foregoing analysis, the following broad conclusions can be drawn:

1. The successors of the Holy Prophet adopted different modes of accession; hence, no uniform pattern of election or selection of the head of the modern state can be tangibly construed.

2. Except for Ali, who was extended open allegiance by the community in the Mosque of the Prophet, the first three Caliphs were first selected by a very limited council of elders and then presented themselves for acceptance to the general public.

3. Hereditary rule was conspicuously absent in the case of the accession of the first four Caliphs.

4. Women were never publicly excluded from expressing their opinion in the selection or election of the Caliph.

5. Consequent upon the murderous assaults of assassins, three Caliphs met unnatural ends. Invariably, each succession to the high office created a legacy of intense controversies.

Ali's murder practically meant the end of the pious Caliphate. The unique constitutional principle left by the pious Caliphate was the system of both direct and indirect election to that high office. In the lingering tribal structures of Arabia, the presentation of the nominated Caliph to the general community and seeking the handgrasp of fealty were cardinal republican principles. However, devoid of a definite and uniform pattern of election, the system's inbuilt contradictions led to chaotic political disputes and bitter legacies in the Islamic polity, gave way to civil wars, and weakened the republican edifice.

The consultative council(*Shura*) of the pious Caliphate had all the constitutional potential to assume the contemporary status of a legislature. Except for *Shariah*, there were no constitutional and political limitations on the authority of the Caliph; yet, by virtue of a convention left by the Holy Prophet, the pious Caliphs discharged the affairs of state in consultation with the *Shura*. But, like the system of election, it lacked definite composition, function, and procedure. The *Shura's* sessions were not a regular feature and it depended on emergent situations.

IV

THE UMAYYADS

With the advent of Amir Muawiyah's rule in AD 661, the characteristics of absolute kingship were injected into the veins of the nascent Muslim state. The administrative structure and succession by the first four pious Caliphs were reduced to mere fiction and formalities, hence ushering in an era of the imperial Caliphate, ultimately turning it into an empire. By nominating his son, Yazid, as his successor, Amir Muawiyah radically changed the concept of Caliphate, thus making it into dynastic rule. Trampling upon the republican principle, Muawiyah's setting of the hereditary rule of succession was followed throughout later Muslim history. The Umayyad's preference for hereditary kingship over the rudimentary democratic mode of the Caliphate has been defended by some on the bankrupt plea of averting the impending disintegration of the Muslim polity.[16] Muawiyah proudly asserted that he was the first king of Islam.

Under the Umayyads' dynastic rule, the moral and religious traits associated with the Chief Executive began to acquire secular trends, based on the predominant Arab caste. With their imperial bent of mind, the Umayyads patterned their hereditary rule on Hellenistic-Roman traits and court practices. Amidst luxury and splendour, they introduced absolute kingly prerogatives, with utter disregard for the cardinal principle of public accountability. After the first centennial of the Prophet Muhammad's(pbuh) death, the extent to which the conceptual parameters and practical mode of the Islamic state had transformed itself under the Umayyads could be ascertained from the following sketch of the court life of the Umayyads:

> In the heart of the city [Damascus] stood the glittering palace of the Umayyads, commanding a view of flourishing plains which extended south-westward to

> mount Hermon with its turban of perpetual snow. Its builder was none other than Muawiyah, founder of the dynasty, and it stood beside the Umayyad Mosque .... In the audience chamber a square seat covered with richly embroidered cushions formed the caliphal throne, on which during formal audiences the Caliph, in flowing robes, sat cross-legged. On the right stood his paternal relatives in a row according to seniority, on the left his maternal relatives. Courtiers, poets and petitioners stood behind ...[17]

While nominally retaining some of the essential forms of their predecessors, the Umayyads dyed their imperial Caliphate with the hues of Arab supremacy by placing a premium upon the Arab social traditions. Such pretensions relegated the non-Arab Muslims to the status of mere clients—*mawali*. Contrary to the spirit of human rights in Islam, as propounded by the Prophet in his last address, the Umayyads held non-Arabs in scant respect and unabashedly imposed *jizya* and *kharaj* on them. Such humiliating treatment meted out to *mawalis* compelled them to expedite the process of the Umayyads' downfall. Because of the Umayyads' misdeeds, Muslim jurists had to plunge into an ever-widening gulf between the ideals of Islam and the dictates of the changing times, in order to provide a rationale for the heretic state practices and conduct of the rulers.

With the passing of the age of the first four pious Caliphs, the vested interests and dynastic rule began to create a great corpus of traditions with legal implications—that too by falsely ascribing them to the Holy Prophet. Later on, the collection, authentication, and indeed conflicting interpretations of those traditions introduced immense controversies, flouting the actual social spirit of Islam. While the original message and spirit of Islam began to wane, personal pronouncements and commands in the name of Islam began to gain ground.

The Umayyads retained the divine law, though only as a facade, as they did not dare to scrap it; yet they did not allow it to grow. Mainly for the perpetuation of dynastic rule, the utility and full significance of the traditions of the Holy Prophet were evident to the Umayyads. One of the sources of divine law, the traditions proved 'to be an enormous power in the hands of the authorities to shift the responsibility for any decision and to give it stability by referring to the alleged reports of the practices of the Prophet which could be so easily manufactured'.[18]

V

THE ABBASIDS

The Abbasids overthrew the Umayyad dynasty in AD 749. Founded on the wholesale butchery of the Umayyads, their rule spanned the next five centuries, with thirty-seven Caliphs succeeding one another. The Abbasid empire met its end at the hands of the savage Mongols, led by Halaku Khan, who ransacked Baghdad, and indiscriminately put the populace to the sword in AD 1258.

The Abbasids shifted the capital of the Muslim empire from Damascus to Baghdad on the Tigris, the meeting point of Persia, Syria, and Arabia, with the implicit objective of integrating these territorial and sociocultural entities, 'for the only hope of permanence to the empire lay in welding these into a unity'.[19] The Abbasids had seized power by organizing an armed insurrection of discontented elements against the Umayyads. To justify their rebellion against the authority of the Umayyads, the Abbasids had sought veneering *fatwas* from the pliable *ulema*, maligning the Umayyads, and accusing, them of indulging in unIslamic practices and observances. Once they succeeded in uprooting their rivals, apprehensive of the backlash of the earlier *fatwas* impeaching the Umayyads, the Abbasids employed the same class of *ulema* to reinterpret their *fatwas*, prohibiting rebellion against the ongoing Caliphate. Throughout their dynastic rule, the Abbasids persistently courted the ever-available coterie of *ulema* to lend legitimacy to their hereditary kingship, by playing upon the theocratic inclinations of the masses. Contravening the precedent of the pious Caliphs of preference for the titles of 'Deputy of the Prophet of Allah' or 'Commander of the Faithful', the Abbasids took to high-sounding connotations i.e., 'Deputy of God' or 'the Shadow of God', with the ulterior intent of claiming from Allah the Almighty the authority of ruling the people.

Though they retained Arabic as the official language and Islam as the state religion, the location of the capital at Baghdad initiated the permeation of the sociopolitical influence of Persia through the Abbasid Caliphate.The Caliphate evidenced 'a revival of Iranian despotism and less an Arabian Shaikhdom. Gradually, Persian titles, Persian wine and wives, Persian mistresses, Persian songs, as well as Persian ideas and thoughts, won the day. Their influence softened the rough edges of the primitive Arabian life and paved the way for a new era distinguished by the cultivation of science and scholarly pursuits'.[20]

Unrestrained by limitations on their monarchical absolutism, the Abbasids followed the precedent set by the Umayyads in nominating their successors, i.e., sons, brothers, or any other close member of the dynasty, to the office of the Caliph. They introduced the novel practice of 'double nominations' for succession, which often plunged the Caliphate into palace intrigues and internecine wars.

Basing their source of authority on divine origins, the Abbasids increasingly depended on the hierarchical bureaucratic structure. Theoretically subjecting themselves to the Law of Islam, they exercised authority through various *dewans*, headed by a *wazir* at the centre and the governors in the provinces. They established *qazi* courts to administer justice, though a new precedent of withdrawing criminal cases from *qazis* was set by the later Abbasid Caliphs and princes.

Save for the employment of repressive measures for the perpetuation of their dynastic rule, no significant theory of state and constitutionalism can be construed from the Abbasid Caliphate. The salient act distinguishing the Abbasids from the Umayyads was the elevation and induction of *mawalis* in the hierarchical administrative structure. However, it was a personal favour of the sovereign to help individuals with pro-empire talents to scale the pinnacles of high offices in the empire. This policy of the Abbasids arrested, though temporarily, the racial tendencies of separatism in the Muslim empire.

The reign of Harun ar-Rashid (AD 786-809) and his son, Mamun (AD 813-833) marked the apogee of grandeur of the Abbasid Caliphate; and then it began to decline. By that time, Baghdad, the capital of the Muslim empire, had grown to 'a city with no peer throughout the whole world'.[21] The legend of the 'Arabian Nights' era began and ended with Harun, and his victorious campaigns spread his name far and wide in the world. Apart from its well-filled harems, eunuchs, concubines, and slaves, and all the extravaganza of its court, the Abbasid era undeniably has to its credit innumerable and invaluable advances made by Muslim scientists in all disciplines, especially the natural sciences.

The Fatimids

Alongwith the Abbasid Caliphate, there emerged two other Caliphates in the Muslim world, one in Cairo, ruled by the Fatimids, and the other in Cordova, led by the Umayyads. The addition of two Caliphates to the one in Baghdad shattered the theological myth of a universal Caliphate in the Muslim world. Moreover, when the Caliph in Baghdad was killed by the invading Mongols, the Muslim world remained, for about three years (AD 1258-61) without a Caliph.

The Fatimid dynasty was an offshoot of the Ismaili sect of the Shi'ite Muslim community that struck roots in Sanaa, Yemen. Thereafter, a descendant of the Ismaili sect, Muhammad al-Habib, sent an envoy to North Africa to propagate their transcendental doctrine. By organizing the Berber army, that envoy overthrew the local ruling Aghlab dynasty. After gaining a foothold in North Africa, he invited Obeidallah, son of Muhammad al-Habib, who claimed to be the much-awaited *Mahdi* and who established the Fatimid dynastic rule. After conquering Egypt and Syria, the Fatimid Caliphate shifted to Cairo where it was ultimately uprooted by Sultan Saladin. Working cohesively and in full conformity with the Ismaili theorists and their theological doctrines, the Fatimid Caliphate was fully sovereign. With the passage of time, like their Sunnite counterparts in Baghdad, they were overwhelmed by the inexorable expanding military machine of the Berbers and ultimately reduced to puppets in their own realm.

The Umayyads In Spain

Having escaped the massacre of his house in Palestine at the cruel hands of the Abbasids, Abdur Rahman, a member of the Umayyad family, managed to reach Spain. With the active help of the Yemenites, the Syrians, and the Kharijites, all of them weary of discord, he succeeded in establishing unquestioned sway over Spain. Under his dynamic leadership, the Umayyad dynasty implanted its Caliphate in Spain, even though it was ruthlessly exterminated in Damascus.

VI

POLITICAL AND CONSTITUTIONAL HERITAGE

The Abbasid Caliphs acted more autocratically than their predecessors, the Umayyads, yet they were fortunate in that they had a galaxy of jurists who painted their dynastic political system in theological colours. With the advent of the Abbasids, attempts at formulating a political theory to justify a theocratic Caliphate were made by relying on unauthentic traditions of the Holy Prophet. Stray verses from the Quran were separated from their original context, twisted, over-stretched, and interpreted to suit the ambitions of the *status quo*-oriented dynastic rulers.

The political and constitutional theory during the Abbasid era mainly centred on the institution of the Caliphate. The propounders of such a bankrupt political theory were not concerned about the imperatives of the state. They only highlighted the Caliphate as a unique institution, and concocted and employed a swelling mass of *Hadith* to suit its exigencies. The Caliphate, a law unto itself, was an unrivalled overlordship of the Muslim community and *Darul Islam*. Whenever any Muslim philosopher or political scientist reminded those demigods and self-styled 'shadows of God on earth' of their sheer abuse of power, they were bribed, corrupted, cajoled, and often co-opted into the system; or, if they resisted, they were imprisoned and often poisoned.

Al-Mawardi (AD 940-1058)

Among the jurists who articulated Islamic political theory, Al-Mawardi was at the forefront and spearheaded the political venture of constructing an idealistic theory of the Caliphate, which was an apologetic compromise with historical facts.[22] Basing his interpretation on mere pragmatic considerations and dogmatic theology, he advocated the supremacy and dominance of religion in Muslim statecraft in such a manner that no Muslim thinker or writer could ever dare to question his political constructions regarding temporal authority. Those who sincerely endeavoured to propound even a single new concept readily earned the general reprobation and censure of the *ulema*.[23] Al-Mawardi's widely quoted work, *Al Ahkam al Sultania*, with the reputation of an authoritative reference work on Muslim political theory, favoured the Catholic taste of the Caliphs, their dynastic and elitist process of selection, much to the disadvantage of democratic norms.

Almost all the Muslim political writers working under the shadow of the Caliph's court, including Al-Mawardi, have paid 'scant attention to the rights and claims of the people. The lack of the idea of the fundamental rights of man has been one of the principle sores in Muslim polity for ages, and has been mainly responsible for the almost complete absence of the growth of democratic life in Muslim lands'.[24]

In view of the modern-day emphasis of Mufti Abduh, Rashid Rida, and Allama Iqbal on democratic political thought and consultative and legislative assemblies in the twentieth century, Al-Mawardi's favouring of the selection of the Caliph by the elite renders the full significance and relevance of his conceptions in contemporary political constitutionalism irrelevant. Professor Qamaruddin Khan, author of *Al-Mawardi's Theory of State,* pronounces the following judgement on this medieval jurist:

> He was not a political thinker, and hence could not evolve a philosophic conception of the state. He could not develop the full idea of the state. He does not discuss the meaning, scope, jurisprudence, responsibilities and obligations of the state, gives no conception of sovereignty, and seems to be completely ignorant of the idea of constitution. The lack of constitutional theory has not only very much reduced the value of al-Mawardi's work, but has its deadening effect on the later development of Islamic political thought.[25]

The most remarkable political and constitutional merit, and the relieving articulation in Al-Mawardi's theory of state lies in his suggestion to the people to refuse obedience to the unjust, illegal, and illegitimate rule of tyrants. But as a civil servant (judge), working under the impotent Abbasid Caliphs *vis-à-vis* the omnipotent Shi'ite Buwahid Amirs, Al-Mawardi for obvious reasons could not elaborate the mode and methods of his theory of rebellion, nor, perhaps, had he any example in Muslim history to draw on. He advanced his theory of rebellion on the basis of a ruler going against the creed of Islam, yet he himself diluted the significance of his theory, opining that the rule of the usurping Amir was legitimate if he obtained a letter of investiture from the central Caliphate, did not openly defy the Caliph, and ruled in accordance with the injunctions of *Shariah*. In propounding this theory, Al-Mawardi was adjusting the foundational parameters of the theory of rebellion with the prevalent objective conditions, i.e., legitimizing the Buwahid control of the state structure. The limitations of Al-Mawardi's theory of rebellion against unjust and tyrant rulers have been summed up by Professor Qamaruddin Khan in the following:

> No machinery has been proposed by means of which the will of the people may be ascertained or the Imam may be voted out of power. There is no precedent in Islamic history when an Imam may have been removed from office by legal or peaceful means. And since the Imam is the supreme authority, not responsible to any tribunal, it is obvious that he cannot sit to impeach himself or allow others to interdict him. On the contrary, there are numerous examples in history when tyrant Imams persecuted pious and innocent people and even sent them to the gallows.[26]

Supposedly on the imperatives of the notorious contemporary doctrine of necessity, Al-Mawardi, contrary to apologetic conceptions of his theory of rebellion, indulged in deliberate omission in case a licentious person succeeded in scaling the pyramids of power. Indeed, this was to provide justification for the selfish ends of the Buwahids, who wanted the Caliph to plunge himself into pleasure-seeking, thereby allowing them free exercise of actual political authority. Moreover, the prescription of a long list of pious qualifications for candidacy for the Caliphate was meant to give somebody a bad name and then exclude him from being chosen Caliph. Al-Mawardi's prescriptions and the rationale behind his philosophy were fully utilized for the 'Islamization' process of Zia's regime in Pakistan. The insertion of 'pious qualifications' as a part of the Eighth Amendment to the 1973 Constitution was to achieve the same end—the exclusion of all actual and potential rivals from participation in the elections.

Ibn Taymiyah

The complete erosion of the Abbasid Caliphate at the hands of the savage Mongols, in AD 1258, not only obliterated the myth of a universal Caliphate but also marked the practical disappearance of the institution itself. With the advent of the powerful Mongol and Turk Sultans, the mythical insistence of the Sunnite theology that the Caliphate could only be presided over by a 'Qureshite' was laid to rest permanently. Recognizing the stark reality that the fiction of a so-called obligatory universal Caliphate could no longer be sustained, Ibn Taymiyah opined that men required authority (temporal rule), whether its holder was just or unjust, elected or imposed.[27]

Standing in marked contrast to other Muslim jurists of the medieval ages, and far from falling prey to apologetic compromises on the precedents of the Caliphate, Ibn Taymiyah, in the estimation of Rosenthal:

> is very critical of its theoretical foundation. He does not insist on the ideal qualifications of the *Imam*; in fact he never discusses them. He dispenses with the election and even the designation of the Caliph: God designates the sovereign through the infallible voice of the community, the *ijma*. It is clear from this attitude that the centre of gravity has shifted from the *khilafa* and the *khalifa* to the community . . . he pleads for close cooperation between the *Imam*—the necessary authority—and the community.[28]

Convinced of the human need for co-operation, association, and mutual aid for survival and welfare, Ibn Taymiyah recognized the imperatives of autonomous territorial and political entities. The existence of the state to him was 'neither a divine commission nor a power-state based on sheer military might; it is a cooperation between all members of the community to realize certain ideals', i.e., the *Shariah* law, the organic unity of the civilization, and its collective life.[29] Laying great emphasis on justice, Ibn Taymiyah held the head of the orderly state to be at once the proxy (*vakil*), the guardian (*wali*), and the partner *(sharik)* of those over whom he ruled. Moreover, he categorically rejected the myth that the head of the community should belong to the Qureshite lineage, possessing special qualifications. He believed that the unity of Islamic people could be realized through their co-operation and free choice. Recognizing the historical fact that the Muslim community could no longer be carried back to the ideal Caliphate of the pious Caliphs, he opined that an ideal society could be built by seeking guidance from the Quran and *Sunnah* in the light of new realities.[30.]

Ibn Taymiyah essentially visualized Islam as a social order—the law of Allah reigning supreme in the universe. He did not find any basis of the theory of the Caliphate and its so-called divine origins in either the *Sunnah* or the Quran.[31] The state was to Ibn Taymiyah simply a religious necessity where the authority of *Shariah* reigned supreme, appealing essentially to the Quran and *Sunnah*, and not to historical precedents. Instead of propping up shadowy Caliphs by propounding new juridical and theoretical foundations as Al-Mawardi did, he attempted at reform and restatement of the relationship between the community and the law of Allah.[32] The views of Ibn Taymiyah, a distinguished political scientist, are a stark reminder to those who are confusing the people in the state of Pakistan by their emotional appeals to historical dogma.

Ibn Khaldun (AD 1332-1406)

The officious Muslim jurists, overwhelmingly accustomed to propounding and rationalizing the theories of Caliphate by blending theology and politics, were plunged into oblivion after the demise of the institution itself. The emerging pattern of sultanates and kingdoms with secular ordinances had rendered the old political system of the Muslim world ineffective. The inauguration of the sultanate era, based on power, paved the way for the emergence of several dynasties with parochial sentiments, confronting the *Shariah* with new challenges. Meanwhile, 'the destruction wreaked by external foes and senseless conquerors, and the loss of political unity were paralleled by the loss of intellectual and cultural unity, when the monopoly of the Arabic language was broken by the revival of Persian and later by Turkish'.[33]

In the given milieu of huge structural changes, while other Muslim jurists, ignoring the systematic sociological approach, simply offered politico-theological apologia, Ibn Khaldun, with his high sense of history, rationalized the sociopolitical realities of his age, becoming a rare exception in his intellectual pursuits. Having served different rulers, Ibn Khaldun was familiar with the systematic operation of a number of states, distinct in culture, dialect, history, environment, and administration. He prefaced his clear vision of the factors responsible for the rise and fall of Islamic principalities to a long dissertation on history. In his famous *Muqaddamah* or *Prolegomena,* which forms a salient contribution to his political philosophy, Ibn Khaldun drew bold and scholarly conclusions about a variety of socio-political entities, terming them essential for the higher aspirations of rational man and human civilization.

Far from expounding the divine right of the rulers (an obsession with his predecessors and successor Muslim jurists), Ibn Khaldun's down-to-earth approach led to clarification of his political conceptions about the state thus:[34]

1. Avoiding drawing wild conclusions from the customary blend of theology and politics, he distinguished between them, thus propounding the basis of political authority.

2. Without labouring with juridical devices to fill the widening gaps in the theory and practice of the Caliphate, he accepted and appreciated the new political realities.

3. Substituting the already exploded myths of *shura, ijma,* and *baiah,* he based the power theory of *mulk* on the *asabiyah* (i.e., mutual affection and willingness to fight and die for one another), 'a driving force in the formation of state and dynasties'.

On the basis of his criterion of *asabiyah,* Ibn Khaldun analysed the rise and fall of the Arab Muslim Caliphate. The institution of the Caliphate was essentially a product of the Arab age of Islam, and he attributed its decay to the fall of *asabiyah* of the Arabs, leading to ascending *asabiyah* of other socio-racial groups, i.e., the Turks in the eastern Islamic world, and the Berbers in the west.[35] He considered the combination of religious conviction and *asabiyah* the ideal form of political power, though subject to change in the changing circumstances, which primarily led to the asendancy of the Umayyad and the Abbasid dynasties. For Ibn Khaldun, 'only a strong attack, backed by the *asabiyah* of tribes and clans, can remove rulers and destroy the edifice of their states which are firmly established'.[36]

Ibn Khaldun considered the Caliphate a social and institutional organization, not an immutable article of faith, which pretended to protect religion and exercise political power in the state. Based on historical facts, he divided the history of Muslim rule as follows:

•   the era of the classical/orthodox Caliphate;

- an era of transition, in which the institution of the Caliphate cohabited with the emerging features of kingship/sultanate in the Muslim world; and

- the final transformation of the Caliphate into kingships/sultanates.

The emergence of kingship meant power-state based on *asabiyah* and coercion of the rulers, not on the predominance of *Shariah* as a restraining force. Initially, the institution of the Caliphate combined in itself the theological and secular bases, the former being dominant over the latter. In the second stage of transformation in Muslim history, religion and politics were disentangled; and in the third phase, there emerged secular monarchies, nominally professing subjection to *Shariah*. To Ibn Khaldun, the ideal political organization was the state of the first four Caliphs, yet he impressed upon the Muslims, confronting difficulties in restoring the earliest Caliphate, that they should prefer secular monarchy, based on *asabiyah* of the politically dominant group or dynasty exercising rational laws.[37]

VII

NEW ENTITIES

The savage devastation of the Abbasid Caliphate by the Mongols had exploded the myth of the universal Caliphate. There emerged four distinct Muslim empires, i.e., Mamluk Egypt, the Turkish Ottoman empire (which styled itself on the model of the defunct Caliphate), Safavid Persia, and Mughal India. If the Mongols had obliterated the Abbasids, Western and Russian imperialism eliminated the remaining Muslim entities at the end of the eighteenth and beginning of the nineteenth centuries.

While the Muslim rulers ran their empires, kingdoms, sultanates, and emirates with secular ordinances, laws, and decrees, the *ulema* always impressed upon the masses that they should readily submit even to illegitimate and coercive rules, thus saving such entities from pro-people revolutions. Thus, throughout Muslim history, barring the state under the Holy Prophet and the *Khilafat-i-Rashidah*, 'passive obedience to any *de facto* authority governing by consent remains an unknown concept; autocracy has been the real and, in the main, the only experience'.[38] The doctors of Islam, associated with the courts of the rulers, labelled the community as 'a trust from God to the ruler'. Whether their rule was benevolent or tyrannical, it was incumbent upon the subjects to extend unqualified obedience to the rulers, so the *ulema* exhorted them.

Far from evolving any coherent political theory to guide and educate the masses, official apologists like Ibn Jamaa (AD 1241- 1333) put forward strange and defeatist concepts to the people, i.e., the ruler was a necessity; that if 'one is deposed by another, the other must equally be obeyed—we are with whoever conquers'.[39] If any reform movement or liberal sentiment emerged anywhere in the Muslim entities, it was crushed, coerced, and eliminated, via the *fatwas* of the jurists, on the abhorrent rock of absolutism.

VIII

THE FUNDAMENTALISTS CONTENTIONS

The death of the Mughal king Aurangzeb, in 1707, gave birth to an unending saga of weak and rapid successions to the throne in Delhi. While such a state of affairs produced the myth of the 'later Mughals' ruling India, in reality, British colonization of the subcontinent had reduced Muslim rule to bondage. The colonial domination began to dye the social, cultural, political, and religious heritage of the Muslims in the region in entirely new and unknown hues. Excessively nostalgic about their past as they always were, the Muslims failed to come to terms with the advent of British rule.

Despite the disastrous consequences of the 1857 uprising, Muslim fundamentalists in India failed to appreciate the future role of the technologically superior, politically cohesive, educationally advanced, and culturally pervasive British in the subcontinent. Unable to come to grips with the political genius and traditions of the mighty intruders, the Muslims miscalculated the winds of fortune. Instead of saving the Muslim community from the scourge of Hindu majority rule in any eventual introduction of a Westminster-style of government in the subcontinent, the *ulema* advocated joining hands with the Hindus in their futile bid to oust the British.

On the other hand, while deliberately avoiding any possible head-on collision course with the then omnipresent British, Sir Syed

Ahmed Khan concentrated on his enlightened educational, social, and religious reforms, which he considered vital for bringing his nation out of the doldrums. Misconstruing his policies, the *ulema* immediately boycotted his educational programme, poured scorn on his social reforms, and labelled him a 'heretic' on account of his radical, scientific religious interpretations. Confronted with the new political order set in motion by the British, the *ulema*, instead of extending a helping hand to Sir Syed Ahmed Khan, rejected his efforts to establish a modern educational institution. Nay, in their Friday prayers, they beseeched Almighty Allah 'to destroy the institution and its founder'.

Being the ostensible adherents of the Islamic identity, the *ulema*, in their blind bid to oppose the British, increasingly identified themselves with the All India National Congress. Such a miscalculated action turned them against their own ideals and history. In order to save his nation from falling prey to any eventual identity crisis, Sir Syed Ahmed Khan was vehemently opposed to its entry into the Congress-dominated political permutations of the subcontinent, whereas the *ulema* stressed Muslim co-operation with the Hindu Congress.

In their orthodox enthusiasm, the *ulema* established their own *madrasahs* which eventually led to their 'splendid isolation' from Muslim political aspirations. Having denounced modern political ideas and educational systems, the *ulema* failed to appreciate the imperatives of elections, local self-government, and constitutionalism introduced by the British. In their considered opinion, the whole exercise of electioneering and constitutionalities was against the spirit of *jihad*. While resisting the inevitability of such institutions, they considered them obstructions in the way of re-establishing Muslim dominance in the subcontinent.

The Muslim community paid little heed to the *ulema*'s perspectives. That is why the latter had to confine themselves to the four walls of their *madrasahs*. However, the 'balkanization' of the Ottoman empire provided them an opportunity to stir again by launching the *Khilafat* movement for the restoration of the obsolete order in Turkey. Through processions, rallies, *fatwas*, and similar ways and means of exerting pressure on the British Government, the *ulema* made their presence felt on the political stage for several years. However, Mohandas Gandhi, in pursuance of his ambitious bid to monopolize Indian politics, seized upon the *ulema* lever. While steering the 'Gandhi-Khilafat express'[40] to scale the heights of political popularity and promote his personal charisma, Gandhi betrayed the *raison d'etre* of the Khilafat movement.

In order to restore the defunct institution of the *Khilafat,* and that too in co-operation with the Hindus, the fundamentalists threw the Muslim League and its leadership into oblivion. Having failed in their pan-Islamic objective and finding themselves on the point of crumbling, the *ulema* in their desperation hurriedly declared the sub-continent as *Darul Harb.* In compliance with this *fatwa,* the gullible Muslims started migrating to neighbouring countries, facing untold hardships and miseries in the process.

Far from extending their co-operation to the Muslim League and its cause, the innumerable religious pressure groups, namely, Majlis-i-Ahrar-i-Islam, the Khaksars, Jamiat-i-Ulema-i-Hind, Jamiat-i-Ulema-i-Islam, Jamaat-i-Islami, etc. drifted away from Muslim separatism, and often threw themselves into the Congress camp. Besides this, the Khudai Khidmatgars, based in the NWFP, always remained a source of irritation to the Muslim League leadership. Their pettiness, prejudice, lack of a sense of direction, and wholesale greed, more often than not, led them to commit political somersaults.

After the 23 March 1940 Lahore Resolution, the overwhelming majority of the religious pressure groups considered the Muslim League's demand for 'Pakistan' at variance with their pursuits of *Hukumat-e-Illahiya.* As the concept of Pakistan was perceived to be short of all the requisite ingredients of *Hukumat-e-Illahiya,* the Muslim League and its leadership too did not come up to the rigid standards of 'Islamic leadership and organization' as propounded by the *ulema.* They labelled Quaid-i-Azam Mohammad Ali Jinnah as *Kafir-i-Azam.* Through a *fatwa* in 1945, Maulana Husain Ahmed Madni, President of Jamiat-i-Ulema-i-Hind asked the Indian Muslims not to join the Muslim League on the grounds that its demands and actions were contrary to the dictates of Islam.[41]

Among the *ulema* opposing the Muslim League's leadership and its cause, Maulana Abul Ala Maudoodi, founder and Amir of the Jamaat-i-Islami, was the most critical, when he wrote:

> From the League's Quaid-i-Azam down to the humblest leader, there was no one who could be credited with an Islamic outlook and who looked at the various problems

from an Islamic point of view ... one cannot discover even
a hint of Islam in the ideas, ideals and political style [of
the Quaid-i-Azam].[42]

However, the emergence of Pakistan left the *ulema* high and dry.
While leaving their followers in the lurch in post-Independence India,
the self-styled protagonists of the 'Law of Islam' fled to 'Islamize'
Pakistan. And ironically, without any remorse, they posed as the *de
facto* custodians of the 'ideological frontiers' of the new state.

Soon after independence, when the administration of the new state
was coping with huge problems arising out of the partition of the
subcontinent, the *ulema* began arousing the religious passions of the
people to get an 'Islamic Constitution' passed by the Constituent
Assembly. They invoked the 'Law and Islam of Mecca' to be the only
raison d'etre of Pakistan. The conflict between the approach of the
adherents of the Pakistan movement and the fundamentalists' version
as to modern versus theocratic state led critics to ridicule the basis of
Pakistan. The rationale of the criticism of the ruling Congress and
numerous other Hindu organizations in India was obviously clear, yet
the presentation of Pakistan as a theocratic state, demands for 'a
hundred per cent Islamic Constitution', and an excessive display of
pan-Islamic inclinations, invited some Muslim countries to pass their
sacrilegiously-worded verdicts on the new state. For instance, King
Faruk of Egypt used to gibe at Pakistan's overzealous devotion to
Islam by saying 'Don't you know that Islam was born on 14 August
1947?'[43] To many critics:

> Pakistan appeared as a country where fanaticism was
> swallowed as food, where orthodoxy was preached as a
> code, where bigotry was practised as an art and religion
> was administered as dope. They had hardly any hesitation
> in referring to us as a nation of religious fanatics and
> sentimental fools who were so inseparably allied to the
> Islamic way of life that they did not even want to profit
> from Western advances in the economic and political
> fields.[44]

IX

CONSTITUTION: JINNAH'S VISION AND VISUALIZATION

The preceding brief overview of the *ulema's* rigid perspectives on the future parameters of Pakistan's Constitution, can be contrasted with the vision of Jinnah, the Father of the Nation. Imbued with nationalistic sentiments, Jinnah had no love for the white man's rule. For his avowed national objectives and political strategy, Jinnah believed in and adopted political means. Politics and religion were two different domains in Jinnah's perspective and, contrary to the tendencies and inclinations of his contemporaries, he never thought of fusing the two. Straightforward in his religious outlook, neither a bigot nor a fanatic, progressive not retrogressive, free from theological orthodoxies, and keeping the theologians, high priests, and orthodox missionaries at bay, Jinnah aspired to complete independence of the subcontinent, where all nationalities and communities, irrespective of size, caste, and creed could co-exist in harmony.

Since Jinnah accepted the undeniable fact of the existence of different and antagonistic nationalities in the subcontinent, he endeavoured to hammer out and reconcile their outstanding conflicts within an acceptable constitutional framework. However, parochialism and the pro-majority politics of the Congress forced him to pursue the 'Two-Nation' thesis as the final solution to the subcontinental political question.

Having successfully led the Muslim nation to the 'Promised Land', Jinnah endeavoured to solve the constitutional problems connected with the sovereignty and independence of the new state. Being a democrat, a great constitutionalist, and a firm believer in the rule of law, Jinnah never forced his personal version of constitutionalism on his people. However, his ideas and idealism about the future Constitution of Pakistan can be ascertained from his speeches and statements

Sovereignty

Jinnah had unswerving faith in the wisdom and invincible power of the people. On many occasions, he had categorically rejected the orthodox theocratic concept of sovereignty. For instance, in an interview he gave in 1946 to Don Campbell, the Reuter correspondent in New Delhi, he asserted: 'The new state would be a modern democratic state with sovereignty resting in the people and the members of the new nation having equal rights of citizenship regardless of their religion, caste, or creed'.[45]

Form of Government

Jinnah had explicitly declared that the system of government in Pakistan would be federal and parliamentary, envisaging Islamic social justice, equity, and fair play for everybody. However, Jinnah's pursuance of the Two-Nation Theory and oft-cited references to Islam and Quranic injunctions have deliberately been misconstrued by the ruling elite throughout the chequered history of Pakistan. Contrary to the *ulema*'s concept of Islam and their concept of government, aimed at prolongation of repression, and permitting social stagnation, economic exploitation, the persistence of religious dogma, and superstitious thinking, Islam to Jinnah, was the anchorsheet and bedrock of social egalitarianism and economic brotherhood.

To differentiate Jinnah's concept of government from the *ulema*'s exaltation of a theocratic structure to suppress the masses, one could contrast their diametrically opposed perceptions, attitudes, and outlook on the *Khilafat* Movement in the subcontinent. Kemal Ataturk of Turkey had frustrated the attempts of the *ulema* from within and without the country to restore the obsolete institution of the Caliphate. While the *ulema* were groping to revive their umbilical relationship with the Turkish style of Caliphate in some new form, Jinnah, being well aware of the retrogressive nature of the defunct Caliphate, never provided them an opportunity nor ever succumbed to their demand that the concept of people's sovereignty be tied to the apronstrings of theocratic superstructures.[46]

Theocracy

Jinnah's attitude towards the *Khilafat* Movement manifestly contradicted concepts like *Caliphate, Imamate, Darul Islam, Darul Harb*, etc. Jinnah's interpretation of the 'Law of Islam' was liberal, enlightened, and broad, contrary to the conflicting, confusing, sectarian expositions of the *ulema*, which were completely devoid of *ijtehad*. Though Jinnah would never have visualized formulating constitutional principles repugnant to the injunctions of the Holy Quran and the *Sunnah*, his aversion to sectarian interpretations of *Shariah* by the *ulema* is evident from the following statement:

> · Whose *Shariah*? *Hanafis*? *Hambalis*? *Sha'afis*? *Ma'alikis*? *Ja'afris*? I don't want to get involved. The moment I enter this field, the *ulema* will take over for they claim to be the experts and I certainly don't propose to hand over the field to the *ulema* ... I don't propose to fall into their trap.[47]

In his broadcast to the people of Australia on 19 February 1948, Jinnah had said that Pakistan was not going to be a theocracy, and he repeated this view in his broadcast to the people of the United States. He said, 'In any case Pakistan is not going to be a theocratic state to be ruled by priests with a divine mission'.[48]

From similar other bits and pieces of Jinnah's pronouncements, one can safely conclude that Jinnah never visualized religion to be the state system. Moreover, he never 'aimed at converting the state of Pakistan into a laboratory of religious experiments in which Muslim divines and *ulema* would be acid-testing the faith of the Muslims'.[49]

Status of Minorities

Iqbal, the poet-philosopher who envisioned the future territorial entity of Pakistan, and Jinnah, who gave practical shape to Iqbal's vision, considered minorities at par with the citizens of the majority community. A pointer to such an assertion is Iqbal's liberal and flexible declaration to this effect: 'Nor should the Hindus fear that the creation of autonomous Muslim states will mean the introduction of a kind of religious rule in such a state'.[50]

Minorities, in Jinnah's constitutional parameters, had a very special place in any civilized society. This can be ascertained from Jinnah's criticism of the Nehru Report, which had disregarded the constitutional safeguards and political rights of the minorities. He believed that:

> Every country struggling for freedom and desirous of establishing a democratic system of Government has had

to face the problem of minorities wherever they existed, and no constitution, however idealistic it may be, and however perfect from the theoretical point of view it may seem, will ever receive the support of the minorities unless they can feel that they, as an entity, are secured under the proposed constitution and government, and whether a constitution will succeed or not must necessarily depend as a matter of acid test on whether the minorities are in fact secure.[51]

Jinnah, being conscious of such a fundamental fact, stressed time and again the necessity for safeguarding the inalienable rights of the minorities. It is in the fitness of things to state the concept and vision of Jinnah about minorities. Speaking for himself on the Communal Award in the Central Assembly on 7 February 1935, Jinnah defined minorities:

What are the minorities? Minorities mean a combination of things. It may be that a minority has a different religion from the other citizens of the country. Their language may be different, their culture may be different, their race may be different, and a combination of all these elements—religion, culture, race, language, art, music and so forth—makes a minority a separate entity in the state, and that separate entity wants safeguards. Surely, therefore, we must face this question as a political problem, we must solve it and not evade it.[52]

To Jinnah, the rationale of Pakistan was the protection of the fundamental rights of the Muslims (the largest minority in undivided India) from brute majority rule in the Westminster-style of democracy, before and after Partition. He was well aware of the inalienable rights of the minorities as equal citizens of the new state. Being the Father of the Nation, the undisputed President of the Muslim League, and the Governor-General to be of Pakistan, Jinnah addressed the first Constituent Assembly of the newly created state on 11 August 1947; in this speech, he outlined the role and status of the minorities as following:

If you change your past and work together in a spirit that everyone of you, no matter to what community he belonged, no matter what relations he had with you in the past, no matter what his colour, caste, or creed, is first, second, and last a citizen of this state with equal rights, privileges and obligations, there will be no end to the progress you will make . . . We are starting with this fundamental principle that we are all citizens and equal citizens of one state . . . Now I think you should keep that in front of us as our ideal, and you will find that, in course of time, Hindus would cease to be Hindus, Muslims would cease to be Muslims, not in the religious sense, because that is the personal faith of each individual but in the political sense as citizens of the state . . . You are free to go to your temples, you are free to go to your mosques, or to any other place of worship in this state of Pakistan. You may belong to any religion or caste or creed . . . that has nothing to do with the business of the state.

Constitution Through Democratic Means

Being a first-rate barrister, a member of the Central Legislature, and having actively participated in various conferences aimed at evolving the future constitutional set-up of British India, Jinnah understood all the intricacies of constitutionalism and its interpretation. Moreover, as he had a prestigious status in the new state, Jinnah was in a position to impose his own version of the supreme law of the land. But as a true democrat, he believed that such an authority resided in the elective representatives of the people of Pakistan. The following remarks made by Jinnah are ample evidence of this:

> The Constitution of Pakistan has yet to be framed by the Pakistan Constituent Assembly. I do not know what the ultimate shape of this constitution is going to be, but I am sure that it will be of a democratic type . . .[53]

Women

Jinnah firmly believed that women should participate in the social and political affairs of the state. In Jinnah's perspective, no nation could progress if half of its population were to remain passive and away from national affairs. Addressing the students of the Aligarh

Muslim University in 1936, he stressed upon the youth to awaken Muslim women:

> Having freed ourselves from the clutches of the British, the Congress, the reactionaries and the *moulvis*, may I appeal to the youth to emancipate our women. This is essential. I do not mean that we are to ape the evils of the West. What I mean is that they must share our life, not only social but also political.[54]

From Jinnah's speeches, statements, interviews, and, above all, from his political career, the following broad principles relating to the Constitution can be ascertained:

1. Jinnah never visualized a theocratic state and did not believe in the theory of divine rights, where the high priests with a divine mission were not accountable to the people. He never wanted to confer a veto power on theocrats who could flout the aspirations of the people of Pakistan.

2. In emphasizing Islamic principles, Jinnah understood a society based on social justice, equality, brotherhood, religious tolerance, equity, justice, and fair play for everybody, regardless of colour, caste, or creed.

3. In Jinnah's constitutional parameters, there was only one nation in the country, and that was the Pakistani nation, because he believed in Pakistani nationalism, not in Muslim nationalism or pan-Islamism.

4. Religion was the personal domain of an individual and had nothing to do with the administration of the state.

5. He visualized a democratic and parliamentary form of government for Pakistan.

6. A Constitution was to be evolved and adopted by the Constituent Assembly of Pakistan.

7. He abhorred extra-constitutional methods and agitational politics.

X

THE OBJECTIVES RESOLUTION

The Quaid's death on 11 September 1948 exhilarated the *ulema* who were waiting in the wings to seize upon such 'an opportune moment' to vociferously demand the immediate imposition of *Shariah* in the state. The early accomplishment of the task of constitution-making by the Indian Constituent Assembly in 1948 put an obligation on the people of Pakistan to exert pressures on their government and the Constituent Assembly to evolve their own Constitution as well. Amidst such a favourable political milieu, the *ulema* felt no compunction in playing upon public passions and sentiments. On the other hand, the level-headed politicians were reminding the nation that the blueprint of the 'Islamic way of governing', to which the fundamentalists ceaselessly referred as part of their slogan-mongering campaign, existed nowhere. Thus, the question of its immediate imposition in Pakistan was beyond comprehension. Moreover, they were advised that 'instead of endlessly repeating the call for an Islamic state, the enlightened *ulema*, in concert with experts in law and other fields, should try to study the teachings of the *Quran* and the *Sunnah* from the standpoint of present-day conditions and evolve a suitable body of *Shariah* law for enforcement in Pakistan'.[55]

Undaunted by such limitations, and temporarily riding on the tide of the people's emotions, which seemed to be running high on the issue of Constitution and an Islamic state, the *ulema* did not want to miss the opportunity. It was in these circumstances, notwithstanding Jinnah's ideas and aspirations for the future Constitution of the state, that Liaquat Ali Khan had to acquiesce in the *ulema's* demand by introducing the Objectives Resolution in the Constituent Assembly, a resolution having theological overtones.

The Objectives Resolution, entitled 'Aims and Objectives of the Constitution', passed in March 1949, affirmed that sovereignty over the entire universe belonged to Almighty Allah alone, and declared that Islam would be the foundation of the new state. It envisaged that the power of the state would be exercised 'through the chosen representatives of the people'. It also talked of the people's resolve 'to frame a Constitution for the sovereign, independent state of Pakistan'.

Devoid of any legal validity, the vaguely-worded Objectives Resolution was contradictory in itself and at variance with modern democratic norms and mores. It was primarily adopted to appease the agitating theologians. Far from serving any national purpose, the Resolution generated many fundamental queries such as how the injunctions of *Shariah* should be incorporated in the country's political framework. The *ulema's* pronouncement of sovereignty belonging to Allah, in the context of the ambiguous and imprecise Resolution, had ridiculed the word 'sovereign' itself. However, 'the recital of such a simultaneous sovereignty' belonging to both Allah and the state, seemed misleading.[56] In the perspective of an analyst, the Resolution had made 'God sovereign, the people sovereign, parliament sovereign, and the state sovereign in Pakistan'.[57] Such inbuilt contradictions in the Resolution were also taken cognizance of by the Court of Enquiry (constituted under the Punjab Act II of 1954), i.e., the Munir Report which stated *inter alia*:

> The authors of that Resolution misused the words 'sovereign' and 'democracy' when they recited that the constitution to be framed was for a sovereign state in which principles of democracy as enunciated by Islam shall be fully observed . . . When it is said that a country is sovereign, the implication is that its people or any other group of persons in it are entitled to conduct the affairs of that country in any way they like . . . An Islamic state, however, cannot in this sense be sovereign, because it will not be competent to abrogate, repeal or do away with any law in the Quran and the *Sunnah*. Absolute restriction on the legislative power of a state is a restriction on the sovereignty of the people of that state.[58]

The passage of the Objectives Resolution came as a bolt from the blue for the minorities who had been assured of their equal status in the future constitutional set-up of the state by the Quaid in his address to the Constituent Assembly on 11 August 1947. In addition to the theocratic colour of the Resolution, the acrimonious remarks made by the *ulema* against the future role of the minorities, substantially contributed to the arousal of certain well-grounded apprehensions:[59]

- it would make them 'drawers of water and hewers of wood' as they would have to play the part of 'second fiddle' and be confined to the status of plebians i.e., *dhimmis*;

- the Resolution potentially excluded them from the decision-making process on matters vital to the state's safety and security; and

- the fusion of politics and religion would be detrimental to their fundamental rights.[60]

Far from appeasing the *ulema*, the Objectives Resolution fomented intense religious controversies that delayed the constitution-making process. It proved to be an effective weapon in the hands of the ruling elite to create rifts in the national polity with the effect of prolonging their ignominious rule.

XI

DATELINE: A SEMINAR

Burdened by the theological accretions and speculations of the so-called doctors of Islam, the erstwhile simplicity and clarity of the spirit of the state and the Constitution under the Holy Prophet have been deliberately deformed by despotic interests. The *fatwas* of self-seeking *ulema* always discouraged the initiation of a movement for democratic rights, polity, and institutions in the Muslim world. Now they pronounce democracy to be foreign and against the genius of Muslims and the principles of an Islamic state and Constitution. The democratic stirrings, though always weak among the Muslim people, seem anathema to those with vested interests. However, with full-throated assertions that the modern parliamentary system is unIslamic, the fundamentalists also 'aver that the Islamic system once fully introduced will, in a miraculous way, combine all the advantages of autocratic rule with the benefits of Western democracy.'[61]

Both in the Quran and the *Sunnah*, the two moral and spiritual bases of the Muslim society, 'forbidden things are very few and permitted things are innumerable'.[62] With such a cardinal principle, based on unshakeable foundations it seems that:

> In some Muslim countries highly respected intellectuals including high court judges, speak most irresponsibly and say that there is no democracy in Islam, no parliament,

> no party system, and no election, because these things are
> not mentioned in the Holy Quran. One may ask, are these
> things prohibited by the Quran? If not, then have these
> people taken over the Divine agency to legislate on behalf
> of God?[63]

Besides the proponents of above-mentioned thesis, who readily
discard the modern state system and constitutionalism as unIslamic,
there is another equally strong, vocal, and ambitious group of Islamic
jurisconsults and retired high court judges in Pakistan which, off and
on, yearns for complete revival and imposition of the earliest model
of the Islamic state in contemporary Pakistan. While working on the
bankrupt cliche of the late CMLA/COAS/President General Muhammad
Ziaul Haq, that 'the Islamic system is the end—democracy is the
means',[64] they have created self-contradictory analogies between the
modern conceptions of state, Constitution, and democracy, and those
of the earliest controversial (i.e., in terms of Shia-Sunni perspectives
about its legitimacy and duration) Islamic state. The majority of the
adherents of Zia's thesis were at the forefront at an international
seminar, *Application of Shariah in Pakistan,* sponsored by the Organization of the Islamic Conference in Islamabad on 9-11 October 1979.
Among the partcipants was Justice (retired) Hamoodur Rehman,
whose paper entitled 'Islamic Concept of State' helped in fulfilling
the preconceived notions of the participants as well as the wishes of
Zia, the self-styled 'Commander of the Faithful', whose bankrupt
thesis was fully supported by the one-time Chief Justice of the
Supreme Court of Pakistan.

While inferring concepts of democracy, fraternity, accountability,
justice, liberty, sovereignty, and the Caliphate from the Holy Quran
and the *Sunnah*, the Justice concluded that the following were the
main characteristics of the *Nizam-i-Islam* and the Islamic state of the
earliest Islamic era:[65]

1. That it was an institution established through a democratic
    process, viz., the free will and accord of the people desiring
    to form the same and to accept the Holy Prophet as the
    paramount authority.

2. That it was a constitutional organization functioning under
    a written charter *(Charter of Medina).*

3. That it was a federal structure that comprised of two communities, the Muslims and the non-Muslims, and not two territories.

4. That it was an ideological state based on the concepts and fundamental principles embodied in the Holy Quran.

Barring the last conclusion, which seems a factual distortion, one may agree with the conclusions of Justice Rehman. The city-state established under the *Charter of Medina* (as discussed in the *Introduction*) was not based on any express Quranic revelation, and was thus free of all ideological encumbrances. However, after dilating on the aforementioned four vital elements of the Islamic state, Justice Rehman built the theory of the Caliphate mainly on the generalizations of Al-Mawardi's political apologia and on compromise with historical facts. The most intriguing aspect of the author's whole exercise and the scheme of the paper was that his analogical deductions favoured General Zia's self-sustaining and self-perpetuating exercise of *Nizam-i-Islam*. While jumping on the band-wagon with the other ideologues present in that seminar, he opined:

> There is no scope for the British type of democracy or parliamentary or party government under the Islamic system. The Presidential system appears to be more akin to it, provided the cabinet of ministers or council of advisors is selected purely on the basis of merit from among the members of the *Shura*. The President [implying 'life-long'] will only be removable by impeachment, and that too by a special majority of votes in favour of such impeachment.[66]

Finally, expressing his full satisfaction over the revolutionary 'advancement' of *Nizam-i-Islam*, from the stage of mere talk to its 'practice' in the Zia era, Justice Rehman pinpointed the 'Islamic' qualifications which he advised for incorporation in the Constitution of the Islamic Republic. He recommended, in line with 'Islamic concepts', that the President be elected 'by an electoral college consisting of very highly qualified persons . . . both elected and *ex officio* members representing all shades of public opinion'. The members of such an electoral college, termed *Majlis-i-Shura*, should 'not be tied to any political party'.[67] While considering the novel recommendations for the Islamic state and its Constitution by the participants of the seminar, one must bear in mind the background of the worthy Justice's candid observations.

The seminar was organized by General Ziaul Haq and was sponsored by the Organization of Islamic Conference (OIC), dominated by Saudi interests and thinking, favouring absolute kingship and dynastic rule. Zia, with his cherished designs to be the lifelong COAS/CMLA/President of the Islamic Republic, had instituted his *Majlis-e-Shura*, a hand-picked motley collection of sycophants, self-seekers, and discredited *ulema*, *muftis*, *mushaikhs*, feudal lords, etc. The year was 1979, the tyrant's military rule at its height. Amidst a 'galaxy' of scholars and jurisconsults, who had gathered to shower praise on Zia for the latter's pious and endless efforts to 'practically' introduce *Nizam-i-Islam* among the 'infidels' of Pakistan, the inferences of a person of the stature of Justice Rehman (the author of the Hamoodur Rehman Commision's Report and the famous Miss Asma Jilani judgment) seemed self-contradictory.

At the beginning of his paper, like many other participants of the seminar, he had concluded that the nascent Islamic state under the Holy Prophet (pbuh) and the first four Caliphs was constitutional, democratic, and the embodiment of welfare and social justice, fraternity, liberty, and accountability. Yet, at the end of his paper, like the rest of those present at the seminar, Justice Rehman was at pains to equate the presidential system, the *Shura*, the non-party electoral college, and lifelong office of the head of the state, with that of the early Islamic system. With all respect and reverence for the worthy former Chief Justice of the Supreme Court, one may ask him and other proponents of this theory, if any of them could cite any one quality or attribute of the Islamic state under the Holy Prophet (pbuh) and the pious Caliphs which was present in the *Nizam-i-Islam* of Zia. One may equally question the other conclusions that if party-based polls, parliamentary democracy, and so on, were unIslamic, was martial law, and all the ills associated with this abhorrent system, Islamic? Was it the *Sunnah* of the Prophet and the tradition of the Caliphs to scrap the Constitution? If not, then Justice Rehman and the like were simply sugar-coating repressive military rule in theological pronouncements on the model of medieval Muslim jurists.

4

CONSTITUTIONAL IMPERATIVES OF
THE PAKISTAN MOVEMENT

Socially coercive, culturally repressive, economically exploitative, and politically and institutionally alien, yet the English colonial policy of representative and constitutional 'democracy by instalments' radically transformed the mental make-up and political outlook of the people of the subcontinent. Notwithstanding all the ills and curses intrinsically associated with imperialistic rule, the penetration of British thought and education helped shake off the local people's apathy and complacent acquiescence in the obsolete order, aroused nationalistic aspirations, stirred the urge for fundamental rights, remodelled medieval institutions on modern lines, and prepared minds for self-rule.

Besides offering an appraisal of these developments, this chapter concentrates on the constitutional developments and the emergence of political schism between the Hindus and the Muslims which led to the creation of India and Pakistan. It focusses on vital questions such as why the Hindus and the Muslims could not be brought together through an acceptable constitutional set-up (via the British colonial system) in a region where they had been living side by side for centuries. This chapter begins with the advent of constitutional developments in the subcontinent, and ends with the emergence of India and Pakistan inheriting the colonial legacies of British constitutionalism and federalism in the region.

Part I of the chapter deals with the advent of British colonial rule and its constitutional and administrative impacts, particularly on the Muslims, the Two-Nation perspective, and other associated issues bearing on the constitutional developments of that era. Part II deals with the injection of the federal principle (via the Government of India Act, 1919) in the colonial political set-up in India. Part III of the chapter critically analyses that how and why the Hindu chauvinism, and the niggard response of the Congress towards the Muslims' constitutional demands, cemented the latter's separatism? Why the Congress continued to insist on a Contitution with strong centre, and the League stood with the federating units and for their distinct autonomous status?

I

MUSLIM RULE

In the seventh century AD, the Muslims came to the subcontinent as conquerers of the local faith and lands, and, in the process, they dominated the Hindus socially, politically, economically, and militarily for about a thousand years. The Muslim conquerers were, firstly, the Arabs, and, later on, the Turkish soldiers of fortune who laid the foundations of Muslim rule in the subcontinent. With the decline of the Abbasid Caliphate at Baghdad, the Muslim rulers and dynasties holding sway over India, or a substantial part of it, were virtually independent from the Caliph's directives. The overwhelming majority of the Muslim conquerers from the north were neither missionaries of Islam nor state-builders in the modern sense. Their invasions and conquests were actuated by several factors, such as wealth, glory, annexation, conquest, and so on. However, their military assaults created great cracks in the age-old Hindu order, and facilitated the spread of Islam in the region.

The Ghaznavids, the Ghauris, the so-called Slave dynasty, the Balbans, the Khiljis, the Tughlaqs, and finally the Syeds and Lodhis all ran their sultanates on a feudal basis. Adopting a policy of religious tolerance, they never interfered in the religious beliefs of any group, unless it affected the basis of their dynastic rule. Their rule was always central in nature and practice, and its effectiveness depended on the strengths and weaknesses of the ruler's personality. The potential and actual rivals were always waiting in the wings to take advantage of the weaknesses of the ruler. Every ruler was free from any checks to enjoy, in any way he wished, the fruits of his hard-won military victories.

The sultanates under various dynasties were neither consolidated entities nor did they present uniformity in the dispensation of justice and administration. The unrestrained power of the sultan, and his whims and wishes were the law of the land. Each sultan used to divide his territorial fortune into provinces (*subas*), run by provincial governors (*subedars*). Magnificent and luxurious courts, reward for obedience, suppression of dissension, pious disposition, and instilling of fear and awe in the hearts of the ruled, rather than seeking the consent of the people, were the chief traits of such rule. The Sultanates were neither inspired by any political theory, nor were they based on divine law. They were won and sustained by the sheer strength of the ruler's sword and his military machine; the sultans were always confronted with the formidable task of suppressing revolts and breaking the backbone of the centrifugal tendencies of their own governors. Contrary to what the court historians of various Muslim dynasties would have us believe, Muslim power and rule in India were Muslim in name only and resembled any secular and repressive kingship anywhere in the world. More often than not, the ruler, for his personal pleasure, used to exploit Muslim religious sentiments to validate his regal pursuits.

Lack of an enduring relationship with the people over whom they ruled as demi-gods, failure to evolve an effective and uniform pattern of government, and pernicious immoral pursuits of the sultans led to the disintegration of the Muslim sultanate at Delhi. Following in the footprints of other invaders of yore, Babar, a descendant of Genghis Khan, laid the foundations of the Mughal empire by defeating the local sultan, Ibrahim Lodhi (a nominal ruler of the Afghan dynasty) at Panipat in AD 1526. Babar's victory at Panipat was the first step in the assiduous task of Mughal empire-building. Barring the Sher Shah Suri interlude, the Mughal empire thenceforth began to expand and to incorporate vast territories from Kabul to Bengal in its imperial realm. It was with the death of Aurangzeb on 3 March 1707 that the mighty empire began to disintegrate, giving birth to the fiction of later Mughal rule in India.

Permeated with corruption and inefficiency, and lacking a firm basis of succession and government, the declining Mughal rule invited the menace of foreign invasion. The opportunity was availed by the Persian invader, Nadir Shah, who ransacked Delhi in 1739. He was followed by an Afghan ruler, Ahmed Shah Abdali, who led several military expeditions into India from AD 1748–67. All such attacks and the internal weaknesses of the dwindling empire inevitably broke the central authority at Delhi, and led to the establishment of the writ of independent principalities, i.e., the Deccan, Oudh, Bengal, etc.

The Mughal imperial government was centralized in nature and operation. Possessing unlimited powers, the emperor was a law unto himself; none could dispute his imperial will. Pleased to be called 'the fountain of justice', *Zil-e-Illahi,* and *Zil-e-Subhani,* the Mughal emperor was the supreme authority in his autocratic state. For transacting the affairs of state, the Mughal emperors appointed heads of various Departments: the Imperial Household under the *Khan-e-Saman,* the Imperial Exchequer under the *Diwan,* the Military Pay Department under the *Mir Bakhshi*, the Judiciary under the *Chief Qazi*, Religious Endowments and Charities under the *Sadrus Sudur*, and the *Mohtasib*, who used to censor public morals. Barring the *Fatwa-e-Alamgiri* and the twelve ordinances of Shahinshah Jahangir, no codified law existed in the Mughal era. The Qazi courts usually followed the medieval interpretation of the divine law by eminent Muslim jurists.

The Mughal empire was initially divided into twelve provinces and finally rose to fifteen during the reign of Aurangzeb. Following in exact miniature the central administration at Delhi, the provinces were further divided into districts and subdivisions. *Mansabdari* was the chief trait of the Mughal army, never national in composition and outlook, but an amalgamation of adverse elements, groups and interests. The redeeming feature of the Mughal state and its administration was the free process of the Hindu-Muslim rapprochement, never allowing it to degenerate into intense antagonism. Though Muslims in outlook and practice, the Mughals never adopted discriminatory policies against the Hindus.

The Mughal imperial order, till the death of Aurangzeb, was very efficient and effective by contemporary standards. The Mughal government freely borrowed and adopted Perso-Arabic rules of governance and mixed them with elements and institutions of Hindu empires of yore. Even with their despotic dispositions, most of the Mughal emperors never allowed their imperial rule to degenerate into unbearable tyranny for the masses. By patronizing art and architecture, education, and literature, the Mughal imperial order left behind lasting footprints. However, like any other imperial order, the Mughals were prone to centralization and discouragement of political awakening of the masses. That is why the impact of Mughal patronage of education remained confined to the outskirts of Delhi and the provincial capitals of the empire.

II

ENTER THE BRITISH

AD 1857 marks the practical end of the later Mughals' impotent rule over India. Until the death of Aurangzeb in 1707, the Mughal imperial writ reigned supreme from the Bay of Bengal to the inhospitable mountains of Afghanistan. Whether we call it sheer irony of fate or blissful ignorance of the universal maxim of survival of the fittest, the last Mughal emperor, Bahadur Shah Zafar, stood helplessly before the so-called English court to listen to the following scornful and savage pronouncement against him of 'high treason' on 21 September 1857:

> For that he, being a subject of the British Government in India and not regarding the duty of his allegiance, did at Delhi on the 11th May, 1857, or thereabouts, as a traitor against the state, proclaim and declare himself the reigning king and sovereign of India and did then and there traitorously seize and take unlawful possession of the City of Delhi . . .[1]

What else could he expect from the mighty intruders except that he was presented with the chopped-off heads of his two sons at breakfast! With wresting away of all powers from the Muslims, the British indulged in massive repression and wholesale massacre. Why was an alien actor from a distance of 7,000 miles able to encroach upon the local riches and hold sway over the people of the subcontinent? Behind such a distasteful development, there lay the systematic planning, modern technology, and intense patriotism of the intruders, factors which were conspicuously absent in the fragmented polity of the region. Moreover, the British adopted rigorous principles of organization and government which seemed new in practice in the subcontinent. The British ascendancy snatched away the vigour and vitality of the Muslims, and the latter began to sink to a secondary position in every sphere of life. They were lowered rapidly from a proud all-India overlordship to a persecuted minority, and fully exposed to face the unpalatable socio-economic and political consequences of territorial conquest by a technologically superior, socially cohesive, politically ambitious, and well-organized alien actor.

Crown Replaces Company

The reign of terror let loose by the East India Company, wholesale economic exploitation of local resources, and, above all, the storm of hatred and suspicion between the victors and the vanquished, led to the 1857 catastrophe. The East India Company's abject discrimination, territorial annexations through the notorious 'doctrine of lapse', and other innumerable administrative measures to ruin the old system, obliged the British Crown to directly assume the responsibility of the Government of India through a Secretary of State in 1858.

In the considered opinion of London, it was dangerous to continue 'to legislate for millions of people with few means of knowing, except by a rebellion, whether the laws suit them or not'.[2] Thenceforth, the British began to introduce the representative principle, though in a very restricted sense, into various constitutions enacted from time to time for their Indian colony. This, indeed, was the beginning of the political education of the Indian people, about which Lord Macaulay had warned: 'having become instructed in European knowledge, they (i.e., Indians) may in some future demand European institutions'.[3]

After transfer of Indian sovereignty to the British Crown, various Acts, i.e., the Government of India Act of 1858, the Council Acts, 1861 and 1892, etc. were passed, aimed at assuaging the local bitterness and discontentment against the Company's oppressive rule. Throughout the second half of the nineteenth century, the Crown introduced administrative, educational, judicial, and local self-government reforms of far-reaching implications. The reforms introduced by various Acts were not adequate to fulfil local aspirations, yet they definitely helped in awakening political consciousness among the masses, particularly the Hindus.

While the Muslims under the aegis of the new system were deprived of their lucrative and prestigious economic and political posts, i.e., in the military service, collection of revenue, and judiciary, the Hindus benefitted both politically and economically at the expense of the former. For the Hindus, it was a mere question of changing masters, i.e., from the Muslims to the English. For several decades, the panoply of a *fait accompli*, forced upon the Muslims by the imperatives of the new order, essentially remained vindictive and parochial in nature.

Having reconciled themselves *ab initio* to the new order in the subcontinent, the Hindus would often describe the Muslim rule in the region as oppressive and aggressive and thus 'welcomed the British rule as a more acceptable substitute for the Muslim domination'.[4] Since, in the wake of the 1857 uprising, the British accused the Muslims of deep-seated hostility in attempting to uproot the former's newly established sway, the consequent discriminatory policies against the Muslims seemed golden opportunities for the Hindus.

The hostile and non-cooperative response of the Muslims to British domination seemed natural; yet, in the given circumstances, they had penalized themselves by creating a wide gulf of hatred and suspicion *vis-à-vis* the omnipresent British in the subcontinent. In the face of British-Muslim confrontation, 'the Hindus readily learnt the English language, acquired the Western culture, and made themselves as indispensable to the new rulers of India as they had become to earlier conquerers'.[5] Given the Muslims' attitude, and the fact that they demonstrated no immediate signs of revival, the Hindus, through their flexible responses, succeeded in replacing the Muslims in the fields of administration, warfare, business, education, etc.

Ahmed Khan's Remedies

In reaction to such a difficult situation, the Muslim responses assumed two parallel (though antithetical) approaches. The first was a fundamentalist religious revival called *Wahabism*, which sought to strip modern innovations and western influences, both educational and social, from the Islamic faith. Recalling the triumphs of their ancestors, the Wahabi movement asked the Muslims to go 'back to the Quran'. The second was a policy of reconciliation with the British rulers, attempts at modernization of religious attitudes, and endeavours at modern and scientific education modelled on the Western style.[6]

The second approach, essentially secular in nature, was a reaction to *Wahabism* and Muslim militancy. It was advanced and advocated by Sir Syed Ahmed Khan, the founder of the Aligarh Muslim University, who has proudly been called by many 'the first Pakistani'.[7] While accepting the *fait accompli* of the advent of British rule, Ahmed Khan, a visionary, progressive, a pragmatist, and above all a well-wisher of the Muslim nation, advised the latter to acquire modern and scientific education. In his intellectual discourses, writings, and speeches, Ahmed Khan (often dubbed as a 'heretic' by the orthodox *ulema*) concluded that the following factors were mainly responsible for the decadence and fast deteriorating social, economic, and political position of the Muslims of the subcontinent:

1. The superstitious beliefs and practices that had entered the character of Indian Muslims and their religion;

2. Lack of emphasis on the assimilative and universal character of Islam; and

3. The aversion of the Muslims (mainly as a result of the *fatwas* of the *ulema*) to Western education.

The fundamental thrust of Khan's argument in favour of modern education was that Islam, contrary to the propaganda of many, erected no barriers whatsoever to scientific thinking, planning, action, and social progress. While deploring the prevalent hostility and ill-conceived reaction of the Muslim religious scholars preaching a life-and-death struggle against the British in India, Sir Syed Ahmed Khan urged them to conform to the new sociocultural and politico-economic realities and to fit into the contemporary system 'by conscientious service to the state, to play their full part in the new regime, as they had done under the Mughal rule'.[8]

Ahmed Khan's educational reform policy and his efforts to bring about reconciliation between the Muslims and the British coincided with the sudden emergence of the aggressive, dogmatic, and militant Hindu religious organizations, such as the Hindu Mahasaba which preached violence against both the British and the Muslims. The British-sponsored All India National Congress, which was formed in 1885 at the official behest and patronage, was often led by fanatical Hindus, such as Tilak, who alienated the Muslims through their non-stop preaching of violence and hatred. Such a state of affairs convinced Ahmed Khan of the unfolding course of Hindu-Muslim relations:

> Hindus and Muslims will never be able to unite. The unpleasantness created between the two peoples by educated Hindus is nothing compared to what is coming in the future. With the progressive spread of education among the Hindus, there will develop more bitterness between the two peoples.[9]

The revival of Hinduism began to acquire the aggressive and militant form of Hindu nationalism 'which first made its appearance in Bengal and then spread to other parts. Thus, there developed a community of interests between the Muslims and the British, just as there had been a community of interests between the Hindus and the British when the British first appeared in India. The British began to fear for their empire at the hands of the Hindu majority and the Muslims for their future as a backward minority, should the British be forced to depart from the scene'.[10]

Besides the British colonial compulsions to avoid the pitfalls of one-sided leanings and to consolidate their rule through a balanced relationship with the two major nations of the subcontinent, the Muslims were also forced, through the bitter taste of increasing Hindu chauvinism, to reassess their future political course if they were to survive as a distinct nation in the Hindu-dominated region. Through the Urdu-Hindi language controversy (Hindu agitations against the imposition of Urdu as an official language in some parts of India), the Hindu organizations had clearly demonstrated that they would no longer tolerate the social norms and nomenclature associated with the Muslims in the subcontinent. Because of increasing Hindu extremism, the socio-economic and political conflict between the Muslims and the Hindus had intensified. However, the emerging British-Muslim reconciliation, though short-lived, was a great morale boost for the latter.

Realizing the futility of any co-operation with the Hindu-dominated Congress, and also wishing to avoid any chance of political confrontation with the British, Sir Syed Ahmed Khan, his colleagues, and successors passionately advised the Indian Muslims to keep themselves aloof from politics, devote time to Western education, and serve the British wholeheartedly. While laying emphasis on the non-political activities of the Muslims and the restoration of British confidence in the loyalties of the Muslims towards the Raj, Khan and his followers scorned the All India National Congress's idea of composite nationalism in India—anathema in every respect to the rights of the Muslims. Against the Congress demands that elections be held on a composite basis, Ahmed Khan pleaded for an election system which could ensure that the Muslims were given separate nominations in the municipal bodies which had been created by Lord Ripon. In Khan's perspective:

> In a country like India, where caste and religious distinctions still flourish, where there is no fusion of various races, where education in its modern sense has not made equal progress among all the sections of the population, I am convinced that the introduction of the principle of election, pure and simple, for representation of various interests on the local boards and district councils would be attended with evils of greater significance than purely economic considerations.[11]

Being well aware of the centuries-old conflict between the Muslims and the Hindus, Ahmed Khan asked the former to deliberately avoid joining the enthusiasm of the latter for the British introduction of self-government in the prevailing political conditions of the sub-continent. A great visionary and futurist, championing the cause of his nation, Khan visualized the emergence of the Hindu-Muslim schism in the following:

> Is it possible that under these circumstances two na-tions—the Mohammedan and the Hindus—could sit together on the same throne? Certainly not. It is neces-sary that one of them should conquer the other, and thrust it down. To hope that both could remain equal is to desire the impossible and the inconceivable.[12]

The All India Muslim League

In 1885, the Indian National Congress was conceived in an English mind, Allan Octavian Hume who, at the behest of his fellow English rulers, wanted the gathering together of the colony's intelligentsia—hand-picked men and highly educated Indians—to deliberate and possibly be a thinking-link between the masses and their masters. Visualizing the future course of events, Ahmed Khan had dissuaded the Muslims from joining the Congress, because their participation in political activities might arouse the British grudge, which would deal a fatal blow to his strategy of Muslim-British conciliation. But at the turn of the nineteenth century, the fast-changing events in the form of the emergence of Hindu organizations, the peculiar parochial orientations of the Congress, and sympathetic British understanding of the socio-economic malaise of the Muslims, resulted in the cementing of Muslim separatism in the subcontinent.

The aforementioned trends and events forced the Muslims to safeguard and protect their rights by forming their own political platform. The division of Bengal had given the Muslims a majority area, yet the Congress, heavily dominated by Hindu interests and Hindu symbolism and mythology, began a campaign, both anti-British and anti-Muslim, to annul the partition of Bengal which the Muslims had welcomed as a sign of relief and a huge concession by the Crown. While the partition presented new opportunities for the Muslims of East Bengal, they lacked the organization and guidance to consolidate such a useful gain.

For such an avowed objective and to present the Muslim case for future constitutional legislation, a deputation of leading Muslims met Lord Minto at Simla on 1 October 1906. The British Viceroy responded positively, appreciated the representative character of the delegation, and agreed to its basic constitutional demands: i.e., effective representation in the Imperial Council and a system of separate electorate for the Muslims.[13] In pursuance of their negotiations with the Viceroy and in response to the political imperatives of the time, on 30 December 1906 the All India Muslim League was founded at Dhaka, with the following objectives:

- to promote among the Muslims a sense of loyalty to the British royalty;

- to look after their political rights and interests; and

- to cultivate better understanding between the Muslims and other communities of the subcontinent.

The Indian Councils Act, 1909 (Minto-Morley Reforms)

The Indian Councils Act, 1892, had recognized the principle of election, representation, and association of Indians in the administration of the country. However, in view of the growing dissatisfaction and discontent among the masses, the British authorities felt that something had to be done to win over a sizeable segment of the people.

Besides enacting repressive laws, i.e., the Seditious Meetings Act and the Explosives Act, the Government of India recommended to the Home Secretary in London acceptance of the principle of giving separate representation to the Muslims. In 1908, Lord Morley (Secretary of State for India) introduced his famous Bill (i.e., the Indian Councils Act, 1909) in the House of Lords.

The Minto-Morley reforms enlarged the size of the legislative councils and the Act provided for separate or special electorate for the due representation of different communities, classes, and interests. The functions of the Legislative Councils increased, and rules were made to discuss various matters, i.e., budget, taxation, etc. Although the Act did not fulfil all the aspirations of the Indians, the Muslims were pleased because, in addition to the partition of Bengal in 1905, the Minto-Morley reforms bestowed upon them the rare political privilege of separate electorate, the two main and visible concessions of the Muslim-British rapprochement.[14]

Meanwhile, the British government repeatedly assured the Muslim League that the partition of Bengal was 'a settled fact' and it would not be revoked under pressure. Contrary to such assurances, the British Government hurriedly united the two parts of Bengal in 1911, and that too, to avoid Hindu demonstrations which could possibly mar the celebrations at the forthcoming visit of the English King and Queen to India to hold a royal *darbar* in Delhi.

In the wake of the annulment of the partition of Bengal, the Muslims faced a dilemma: they could not trust the British who had defied their own solemn assurances, and were also unable to reconcile themselves with the Congress, whose utilizing of the Hindu anthems and gods in its campaign against the partition of Bengal were still fresh in the memory of the Muslims and the Muslim League. Besides in the prevalent bitter situation, the annulment of the partition of Bengal had fully convinced the Muslims that agitations led by popular will would be successful in the unfolding political course and that they themselves urgently required means and ways of fortifying their political position in any such eventuality.

III

GENESIS OF PROVINCIAL AUTONOMY

Pre-independence Federalism

The Congress-Muslim League demands to be represented in the governmental affairs of the subcontinent and the lengthy process of constitutional evolution under the British colonial authority proved instrumental in generating the demands for provincial autonomy. Though the Indian Councils' Act, 1909 (better known as the Minto-Morley Reforms), had established non-official majorities in the then Provincial Councils, it fell short of the expectations of the local people. The famous constitutional document, 'Report on Indian Constitutional Reforms' (known as the Montague-Chelmsford Report), was published in July 1918. The report contained a critical analysis of the prevailing constitutional system in the subcontinent and made new proposals for the reconstruction of the whole constitutional structure, because the Minto-Morley Reforms of 1909 had failed to satisfy the political aspirations of the people.

The constitutional recommendations of the Montague-Chelmsford Report were incorporated in a Bill, which was passed by the Commons and the Lords into law in 1919. Sir Reginald Coupland, in his constitutional work, *The Indian Problem:1833-1935*, summed up the main provisions of the Act of 1919 as follows:[15]

1. It established a measure of provincial autonomy by devolving authority in provincial matters on to the provincial governments and freeing them to a large extent from central control.

2. It began the process of materializing responsible government in the provinces by dividing the field of government (dyarchy). While such vital subjects as law and order were 'reserved' for the control of the Governor and his Executive Councillors, responsible as before to the Secretary of State and Parliament, the rest of the field was 'transferred' to Indian Ministers, responsible to their Provincial Legislatures.

3. It converted the existing Central Legislative Council into a bicameral legislature for British India, directly elected for the most part on a national or unitary basis. Dyarchy was not introduced at the Centre, the whole Executive remaining responsible to the Secretary of State and Parliament.

4. It established a Chamber of Princes, representing the rulers of Indian states, for deliberative purposes.

5. It provided, lastly, for the appointment of a Statutory Commission in ten years time to consider the possibility of the further extension of responsible government.

The system of government introduced by the Government of India Act 1919, was dyarchy—meaning dual government. The subjects reserved for the provincial governments were divided into two parts: 'transferred' and 'reserved'. The reserved subjects were administered by the Governor with the help of an Executive Council and the transferred subjects were dealt with by the Governor with the help of provincial ministers. Such a dyarchical system proved to be unworkable and less than satisfactory for the ever-growing Indian constitutional demands.

The Act of 1919 had an adverse effect on Muslims' interests, particularly in Bengal and the Punjab, where their slight margin of majority was readily transformed into a minority. Amidst denunciations both by the Congress and the Muslim League that the constitutional reforms were disappointing, the introduction of the dyarchical system had provincialized political activities. In the 1920s, the sharp rise in communal tensions began to frustrate the constitutional understanding between the League and the Congress, eventually obliging both the political parties to adopt divergent perspectives. The 1921 session of the All India Muslim League was addressed by an eminent Muslim intellectual and leader, Hasrat Mohani (1878-1951), who demanded 'a loose federation of fully autonomous provinces'.[16] In pursuance of such a perspective, the Muslim League in its special session at Lahore in 1924 passed a resolution demanding revision of the 1919 Constitutional Reforms and future constitutional enactments favourable to the Muslim interests.[17] The following are the highlights of the resolution. It visualized:

- a Federation of India with fully autonomous provinces.

- preservation of Muslim majorities in the Punjab, Bengal, and the NWFP, in all circumstances.

- weightage in legislature to small minorities, without prejudicing the interests of the majorities in the provinces.

- maintenance of the system of separate electorate, provided any community could rescind the decision in favour of joint electorate.

- withholding of any legislation affecting any community to which three-fourths of its representatives were opposed.

The constitutional proposals contained in the League's 1924 Lahore Resolution continued to be the basis of the League-Congress dialogue, aimed at settling the communal problem once and for all. However, in March 1927, thirty Muslim leaders advanced some new proposals (i.e., the Delhi Muslim Proposals). The Delhi Manifesto agreed to forego the system of separate electorate for the Muslims provided that:[18]

- Sindh was constituted into a separate province.

- Constitutional reforms were ensured in the form of provincial self-government for the NWFP and Balochistàn on an equal footing with other provinces.

- Muslim representation in the Punjab and Bengal should be proportionate to the Muslim population in these provinces.

- Finally, reservation of not less than one third of the seats for the Muslims in the central legislature in the future federal polity of United India was guaranteed.

While the whole Muslim League political cadre was unanimous in demanding greater provincial autonomy, the issue of giving up the separate electorate system created a split within the party. Moreover, Congress favoured a strong unitary Centre, and the Muslim majority provinces advocated a weak Centre and demanded delegation of overwhelming constitutional powers to the provinces. While Jinnah was busy reconciling the divergent Congress-League constitutional perspectives on centre-province powers and the issue of provincial autonomy, Motilal Nehru presented his report to the Congress in August 1928, rejecting unilaterally all constitutional concessions to the Muslims in the future political set-up of India. Indeed, the Nehru Report, instead of seeking the voluntary and intelligent co-operation of the various communities of the subcontinent, aimed at deliberately conceding to 'an ungenerous majority' unprecedented political sway, both at the central and provincial levels, over 'the dynamic minority' in the future constitutional set-up of undivided India.[19] The publication of the Report sent chilling reminders to various Muslim factions, who termed it 'a pious fraud' in the name of nationalism, and above all, 'a death warrant' for the minority.

Sensing the callous attitude of the Congress towards Muslims' constitutional demands, Jinnah drafted his famous fourteen points in 1929, demonstrating his political and constitutional acumen. Jinnah's political and constitutional proposals provided a basis for negotiations with the Congress and the British. The first and second points in Jinnah's political demands urged a federal Constitution, provincial autonomy to all provinces, and the residuary powers in the Constitution to be vested in the provinces.[20] While advancing the Muslim aspirations for greater provincial autonomy and the separation of Sindh from Bombay to form an independent province, Jinnah and his League emerged as the champions of Muslim rights.

The Government of India Act 1919, had provided for the setting up of a Statutory Commission within ten years of the passing of the Act, to report as to whether and to what extent it was desirable to establish the principle of responsible government or to extend, modify, or restrict the degree of responsible government then existing in India.[21] The Commission was also required to report on whether the establishment of the second chamber of the provincial legislature was desirable or not. Although, as per the constitutional requirement, the Statutory Commission was to be appointed around 1930, in view of the gravity of the political situation and the demands of the political parties for substantial constitutional reforms, the British colonial authorities announced its formation under the presidency of Sir John Simon in 1927. Despite its boycott by all shades of political and constitutional opinion in British India, the Simon Commission published its survey of the Indian system of government with the following major recommendations:[22]

- By extension of the principle of responsible government and devolution of power from the centre, the provinces should be accorded greater autonomy.

- For the ultimate objective of establishing an all-India federation, the Central Legislature should be reconstituted on a federal rather than a unitary basis.

- The Legislature should be based on a wide franchise, and 'the official bloc' should disappear.

- Sindh and Orissa should be separate provinces.

In view of the wholesale condemnation of the Simon Commission Report by Indian political parties, the British Government decided to convene a Round Table Conference in November 1930. Three sessions were held in London, in 1930, 1931, and 1932. The most outstanding and substantial outcome of the London Round Table Conference was the agreement between Indian representatives on the formation of 'a federal constitution' with responsible government, operating fully (though subject to specific safeguards) in the provinces and partially at the centre. After the deliberations of the Round Table Conference, the British Government published its recommendations in a White Paper. After scrutiny by a Joint Select Committee of the British Parliament, the White Paper formed the basis of a Draft Bill, which subsequently became law as the Government of India Act, 1935.

The Government of India Act, 1935

Being the outcome of a seven-year (1927-34) investigation of the Indian system of government, constitutional discussions, and political compromises, the Government of India Act, 1935, provided for a 'Federation' of India, comprising both provinces and states. Though the term 'provincial autonomy' had not occurred in the Act of 1919, the partial extension of the federal principle and introduction of responsibility to the provinces in the Government of India Act, 1935, was a continuation of the earlier process initiated in the form of 'dyarchy' in 1919. The Joint Select Committee of the British Parliament, on the basis of the White Paper, had explained the term 'provincial autonomy' as follows:

> The scheme of Provincial Autonomy, as we understand it, is one whereby each of the Governor's Provinces will possess an Executive and a Legislature having exclusive authority within the Province in a precisely defined sphere, and in that exclusively provincial sphere broadly free from control by the Central Government and Legislature. This we conceive to be the essence of Provincial Autonomy.[23]

In theory, the system of dyarchy was abolished in the Act of 1935, yet it continued to function in accordance with the provisions of the Act of 1919. A large measure of provincial autonomy and self-government was conceded to the provinces and the provincial governors were entrusted with the responsibility of protecting the rights of minorities, the civil service, and the 'law and order' situation.

There was no mention of the 'Dominion' status of India in the Act; and it was primarily enacted to perpetuate colonial rule, not to relinquish it. While firmly holding on to the vital attributes of sovereign power at the centre, only the provincial part of the Act of 1935 was allowed to function. Equipped with immense 'discretionary powers', the Governor-General could stamp his authority, at both the federal and provincial levels. The Act was immediately termed 'a steel frame' for checking the divisive tendencies, inimical to lasting colonial Raj in the subcontinent.[24]

The Federal Legislature was to be bicameral, consisting of the Assembly and the Council of States—both Houses were modelled half-way between Westminster and Washington-style Constitutions. There was a large number of subjects of vital importance, where the prior sanction of the Governor-General in respect of the Federal Legislature, and of the Governor in the case of the Provincial Legislature, was required to initiate them for legislation. The chapter titled 'The Provincial Legislature' was mostly a reproduction of the chapter titled 'The Federal Legislature'. Invariably, all the powers which the Governor-General possessed in relation to the federal legislature, i.e, powers of promulgating ordinances and enactment of acts, were provided to the Governors in their provincial domains. Pakistan's Federal Court in the *Federation of Pakistan v. Maulvi Tameez-ud-Din Khan*, explained the foregoing position of the Governor (as provided in the Government of India Act, 1935) in the following words:

> The position in the Provinces was similar to that at the Centre. The Governor was appointed, like the Governor-General, by his Majesty by a Commission under the Royal Sign Manual. He was also to have a Council of Ministers, and in certain specified matters, was required to act in his discretion, or in exercise of his individual judgement, and, when so acting, he was subject to the general control of the Governor-General. He had the power to summon, prorogue or dissolve the Assembly. He could withhold assent to bills of the Provincial Legislature, or reserve them for the consideration of the Governor-General, who could either assent to the bill, or withhold his assent therefrom, or reserve it for the significance of His Majesty's pleasure thereon. Apart from this, His Majesty had the power to disallow Acts passed by the Provincial Legislature. The Governor could either in his discretion, or in exercise of his individual judgement, promulgate ordinances during the recess of the Legislature, and with respect to certain subjects, at any time. He could also enact Acts concerning matters which were within his discretion, or his individual judgement. If at any time he was satsified that a situation had arisen in which the Government of the Province could

not be carried on in accordance with the provisions of the Act, he could, by Proclamation, assume to himself all or any of the powers vested in, or exercised by, any Provincial body or authority.[25]

Though the Act of 1935 had definitely widened the functions of the popular provincial ministries and had made them responsible to the legislatures, the aforementioned position of the Governor reduced their responsibility substantially. The poet-philosopher, Allama Sir Muhammad Iqbal, expressed his views (even prior to the formal announcement of the Act of 1935) that the British appeared to create in the persons of the Provincial Governors 'White Rajas in addition to the Brown Rajas in the states'.[26]

By according distributed functions to the federation and the provinces, the latter appeared as separate personalities in the 1935 Constitution, yet they could not assume distinct personalities because of the following reasons:

- The Governor-General and almost all the Governors being non-Indians, the former were to exercise full control over the latter, with their huge executive and legislative powers in the provinces.

- Sections 122 and 126 provided executive and legislative supremacy to the federation, 'to secure respect' for the laws of the Federal Legislature and Executive authority. Besides 'giving instructions', the Federal Legislature was also empowered 'at any time', with the prior approval of the Governor-General, to increase 'duties' and 'taxes' by 'surcharge for Federal purposes and the whole proceeds of any such surcharge' were to 'form part of the revenues of the Federation' (Section 137). These and other similar powers of the federal government, and that too without the actual functioning of the federal part of the Government of India Act, 1935, made the existing status of the provinces subordinate to the British Government of India.

- While wide discretion was provided in the 1935 Constitution to the Indian princes to determine their position in the Federation, including the right to approach the Federal Court for adjudication, no such discretion or redress was available to the provinces (Sections: 6,127).

- By envisaging numerous safeguards and reservations, and conferring discretionary powers and functions on the Governor-General and the provincial Governors, the Act of 1935, being of an illiberal character, impeded, though temporarily, constitutional and political advance in the subcontinent.

The Government of India Act, 1935, partly came into force on 3 July 1936, when the electoral provisions began to operate, and completely on 1 April 1937, when the provincial governments assumed their responsibility after the elections. The unwillingness of the princely states to accede to 'the Federation' of India, as contemplated in the Act of 1935, and opposition of both the Muslim League and the Congress to what they maintained was an 'undemocratic' and 'irresponsible' centre in the Constitution, obliged the British Government to postpone indefinitely the implementation of the federal part of the Act.

Far from resolving the Hindu-Muslim conflict, the Act of 1935 deviated from the federal principle, mainly to back the Congress penchant for a strong centre, and to fulfil the colonial urge of the British to retain full control over the provinces. The executive was not completely responsible to the legislature, and the centre's 'discretion' in appointing and dismissing provincial governors, and dislodging deviant provincial governments via the readily available constitutional weapon of 'emergency proclamations', gave birth to an all-pervasive super-centre. Above all, the system of semi-responsible governments at the provincial level was essentially aimed at provincializing all-India politics, thus keeping the major political parties at bay. In the analysis of Ayesha Jalal:

> By granting provincial autonomy and beating a retreat to the Centre, the British planned to give autonomy to their friends and collaborators, and to retain control at the top. Encouraging provincial ambitions and keeping the Centre firmly in British hands was not a strategy for getting out of India, but a way of staying on . . . . the most disturbing feature of the Act, from the point of view of those familiar with the constitutional law, was the clear disjunction between provincial autonomy and the creation of an all-India federation.[27]

The Muslim League and Jinnah had opposed the federal part of the Act of 1935 in order to avoid the authoritarian and expansionist 'Hitlerism' of the Hindu-majority rule in the future political set-up of united India, as well as the persistence of the Byzantine-type British bureaucracy. The All-India Muslim League, in its 1936 session at Bombay, accepted provincial autonomy and the Communal Award, but rejected the federal provisions of the Government of India Act, 1935, describing it as 'fundamentally bad . . . most reactionary, retrograde, injurious and calculated to thwart and delay indefinitely the realisation of complete responsible government, and is totally unacceptable'.[28] Ironically, the part of the Act relating to provincial autonomy, for which the Muslim League had made concerted efforts, operated after the formation of the 1937 Congress Ministries in nine out of eleven provinces, to the detriment of Muslim interests.

The 1937 provincial elections and the introduction of the parliamentary form of provincial governments under the Act of 1935 resulted in the permanent parting of the ways between the Hindus and the Muslims. The two and a half year rule of the Congress proved to be a blessing in disguise for the Muslims and the Muslim League:

- The Congress leadership refused to allow any representation from the Muslim League in the provincial governments. The Congress 'in its wild jubilation at the election victory, forgot the agreement made at the [London] Round Table Conference (1930-32) to give adequate representation in the provincial governments to the Muslims as forming the largest minority'.[29]

- The Muslims living in provinces then under Congress rule began to complain of Hindu atrocities. Congress workers initiated systematic attacks on the lives, property, and culture of the Muslims. Leaders like Jinnah, who still had vague hopes of Hindu-Muslim co-operation to work together for the independence of India, were completely disappointed at the anti-Muslim attitude of the Congress Ministries. In Jinnah's words, the Congress had 'killed every hope of Hindu-Muslim settlement in the right royal fashion of Fascism'.[30]

Having tasted the bitter implications of Congress rule, and that too only in nine provinces and under the dominating shadows of British Governors, the Muslim leadership began to think of securing the 'legitimate interests' of the Muslim nation, ultimately leading to 'full independence'.[31] Even prior to the partial working of the Act of 1935, Allama Sir Muhammad Iqbal had in the 1930 Allahabad session of the Muslim League, called for the amalgamation of (at least) the Punjab, the North-West Frontier Province, Sindh, and Balochistan into a single Muslim entity. On similar lines, Chaudhary Rahmat Ali (1897-1951) visualized in his famous 1932 pamphlet, *Now or Never— Are We to Live or Perish?*, a federation of the Muslim majority provinces in the north-west of the subcontinent.[32]

Notwithstanding the Muslim League's demands for complete provincial autonomy, some Muslim intellectuals put forward various schemes for the confederation of India. For instance, Syed Abdul Latif (1893-1972), a professor at the Osmania University, Hyderabad Deccan, spoke of the division of India into fifteen cultural zones, i.e., four for the Muslims and eleven for the Hindus, all linked through a loose confederal structure.[33] Writing under the pseudonym of 'A Punjabi', Mian Kifayat Ali published his confederacy scheme under the title of *Confederacy of India*, in the late 1930s.[34] The author of *Confederacy of India* proposed the making of five independent countries (the Muslim majority areas in the north-west and north-east of the subcontinent forming two countries), linked at the centre through a confederal Constitution. More or less the same pattern was followed by numerous other schemes aimed at solving the Muslim dilemma in the future polity of the subcontinent. Although the idea of Muslim separatism was an old one, the schemes and suggestions for the redistribution and rearrangement of powers in the existing constitutional structure, a loose union, or alliances with Hindu-dominated provincial entities, were the gist of various new intellectual constitutional exercises. It was evident to the Muslim League's leadership that the federal part of the Government of India Act, 1935, would never be operative, and was already obsolete. Therefore, new constitutional imperatives had become essential. An eminent Pakistani historian, K. K. Aziz, opines that, around 1940, amidst the continuing search for remedies for the Muslim problem, everyone was aware that:

> If a solution had to be found, this had to be done without
> further loss of time. It was common knowledge that the
> Muslim League was in the process of reaching a decision.
> Those who wanted to avert a partition, hastened to air

their views in order to influence the League. Those who believed that division alone could lead to freedom were also quick to put their opinions on record, and this with a double purpose. They wanted to throw their weight on the side of partitioners, lest the League might choose anything less than division; they also wanted to prescribe a solution in the hope that ultimately the League would select their particular scheme for adoption.[35]

Throughout the 1920s and 1930s, the Two-Nation theory and the vehement constitutional demands for greater provincial autonomy for the Muslim majority provinces remained the corner-stone of the League's manifesto. After suffering a debacle in the 1937 elections to the provincial legislatures, and having experienced the Congress ministries maltreatment of the Muslim minorities in the Hindu-dominated provinces, the Muslim League was anxious to seek out new avenues, instead of conventional remedies, to preserve the autonomy of the Muslim nation. Prior to the outbreak of the Second World War, Jinnah in his parleys with the Viceroy had asked for the indefinite postponement of the application of the 1935 Constitution, and impressed upon him the imperatives of including the Muslim League in the making of any constitutional plans for the future of the subcontinent.

The Muslim League projected the federal scheme embodied in the Act of 1935 as unacceptable to Indian Muslims, because this and other similar schemes would definitely allow a permanently hostile community to trample upon the interests of the Muslims. Meanwhile, an article written by Jinnah was published in the London-based *Time and Tide* (19 January 1940), in which he categorically echoed the Indian Muslim thinking that was irrevocably opposed to any federal objective because it meant Hindu-majority rule. Therefore, in pursuance of its apprehensions, experience, and political thinking on the future constitutional set-up of the subcontinent, the Muslim League in its historic session at Lahore on 23 March 1940 demanded an independent territorial entity for the Muslims:

> It is the considered view of this session of the All India Muslim League that no constitutional plan would be workable in this country or acceptable to the Muslims, unless it is designed on the following basic principle, viz., that geographically contiguous units are demarcated into

regions which should be so constituted, with such territorial adjustments as may be necessary, that the areas in which the Muslims are numerically in a majority, as in the North-West and Eastern zones of India, should be grouped to constitute 'Independent states' in which the constituent units shall be autonomous and sovereign.[36]

The words 'Independent states' with 'autonomous and sovereign units' in the 'geographically contiguous' Muslim regions, led various critics of the Pakistan movement to narrow interpretations, as if the Resolution envisaged plural independent states. Jinnah had ascribed the words 'states' appearing in the original Resolution to 'a misprint' and had directed that it be substituted with the singular 'state'.[37] Some political scientists opine that, like other matters of detail concerning 'Pakistan', the Muslim League deliberately refrained from clarifying the ambiguity arising out of the word 'states'.[38] And such vague terminology was advanced to appease provincial feelings that differed in character and experience.[39] However, in view of the various meanings and interpretations of the Lahore Resolution, and to avert confusion over the future parameters of a Muslim territorial entity, the 1946 Delhi convention of the Muslim League legislators to the central and provincial legislatures rectified the plural sense of the wording of the Resolution to the singular one:

> That the zones comprising Bengal and Assam in the North-East, and the Punjab, North-West Frontier Province, Sind and Baluchistan in the North-West of India; namely Pakistan zones, where the Muslims are in dominant majority, be constituted into a sovereign independent state and that an unequivocal undertaking be given to implement the establishment of Pakistan; that two separate constitution-making bodies be set up by the people of Pakistan and Hindustan for the purpose of framing the respective constitutions.[40]

Even after the passing of the Lahore Resolution in March 1940, the Congress repeatedly asked the British that the destiny of ninety million Muslims be entrusted to it in the future Indian federation. Jinnah, who had emerged as the sole spokesman of the Indian Muslims, disputed Congress claims. He was of the view that 'notwithstanding the thousand years of close contacts, the nationalities (i.e. Hindus,

Muslims, Sikhs, etc.) which are as divergent today as ever, cannot any time be expected to transform themselves into one nation merely by means of subjecting them to a democratic constitution and holding them together by the unnatural and artificial methods of British Parliamentary statutes'.[41]

The British declaration of India as a belligerent in the allied cause of the Second World War placed the Congress in a more difficult position than it did the Muslim League and Jinnah.[42] Many in the Congress thought that Britain's difficulties in the long war were godsent opportunities for the Congress and India. Therefore, they demanded immediate independence for India and the formation of a constituent assembly to arrange for the transfer of power. The League's resolution, while repudiating the claims of the Congress to represent the whole of India, asked for guarantees from the British that no scheme of constitutional reform would be enforced without its approval.[43] The British authorities, who wanted to avoid a League-Congress united front against them, at least during the war period, assured the Muslim League that they would avoid one-sided constitutional dealings with Congress alone. The British Viceroy in India, Lord Linlithgow, went to the extent of saying that 'So long as the Congress failed to meet Muslim demands, it was a mistake to try swapping horses or doing anything which might lose us Muslim support'.[44]

In the early 1940s, the British Indian authorities were determined to block Congress demands 'for a national government during the war, stand pat at the centre and run the provinces wherever necessary through section 93' of the Act of 1935.[45] Moreover, 'if the Congress did not bend, it would be broken', was the ultimate resolve of the government. For the time being, 'if Congress resorted to its ultimate agitational weapon, civil disobedience', the government seemed fully prepared 'to crush the organisation as a whole'.[46] So as to save face and press ahead for something new, Congress launched its civil disobedience movement. The subsequent arrest of Congress leaders allowed Jinnah, who in his political strategy was waiting upon events, to work in a complete void and exploit the situation to the advantage of his community.

Given the British hesitation to settle the Indian problem in a manner exclusively favourable to Congress inclinations and demands, the latter announced a political struggle in 1942, asking the British to

'Quit India'. While remaining aloof from the agitational politics of Congress, the Muslim League gave its own slogan, i.e., 'Divide and quit India', which corresponded to its demand for a separate Muslim entity. With the Congress leadership imprisoned, the Muslim League, which remained free to function, regarded the former's demands as 'directed not only to coerce the British Government into handing over power to a Hindu oligarchy but also to force the Mussalmans to submit and surrender to the Congress terms and dictatorship'.[47]

Cripps Mission

The British, who were completely bogged down in the Second World War in Europe and the Far East, intended to keep India free from any internal disruption and chaos. Relying on India's vast resources for their war-making, war-sustaining, and war-winning strategy, the British made efforts to reconcile the antagonistic constitutional views of actors who mattered in the subcontinental problem. Besides the Congress opposition to 'Pakistan', the British authorities themselves were in search of a formula that could simply guarantee Muslim rights within a single united polity.

Amidst the deadlock on hammering out a constitutional consensus, Sir Stafford Cripps, a British Cabinet Minister, came to India in April 1942 with some specific proposals regarding the Interim Government at the end of the Second World War. Cripps' negotiations with the League and Congress leaders ended in failure, yet 'the cause of Pakistan was advanced because the British Government for the first time had recognised the right of an individual province to stay out of the proposed Indian Union and to form a separate federation'.[48] However, the League opposed the creation of a single Union and also proposed a system of a single electoral college and proportional representation.

Congress-League Dialogue

In September 1944, C. Rajgopalacharia made efforts to resolve the League-Congress deadlock over the Interim Government and the future constitutional set-up of the subcontinent. Consequently, Jinnah-Gandhi negotiations took place. Jinnah insisted that Congress should first concede that 'the two zones of Pakistan would comprise the six provinces of Sindh, Balochistan, the North-West

Frontier Province, the Punjab, Bengal and Assam'. Gandhi's position was that Muslims could claim only those parts of the Punjab, Bengal, and Assam where they were in an absolute majority.[49] Besides their differences over the question of future confederal and federal schemes in the subcontinent, Gandhi was also hesitant to recognize the Muslims as a separate nation. Ultimately, the Gandhi-Jinnah parleys failed.

After the failure of the Gandhi-Jinnah negotiations, Bhulabhai Desai successfully endeavoured to reconcile the League-Congress political cleavages. Desai's efforts bore fruit and the Desai-Liaquat formula of January 1945 was agreed upon as to the future Interim Government at the Centre. However, the futile attempts to solve the overall Indian political problem, and that too without dividing it territorially, continued amidst plebiscitary elections in 1946.

The 1946 Elections

The 1946 elections in the subcontinent gave a new turn to the League's demand of Pakistan. The elections convincingly proved the truth of the League's claim that it alone represented the Muslims of the subcontinent. While the Muslim League bagged the majority of the Muslim seats, the Congress was equally successful in the Hindu-majority provinces. The League's electoral success virtually eliminated its erstwhile Muslim splinter groups, thereby allowing it and Jinnah to speak politically on behalf of the 100 million Muslims against the 250 million Hindus in the subcontinent.

With its proven electoral strength, contrary to the Congress perspective on future independence, the League made the demand for Pakistan its non-negotiable and ultimate goal. Amidst increasing communal polarization and a bloody civil war, the Congress-League antagonistic 'lines were clearly drawn for the claims and counter-claims of the end game':[50]

> Congress still wanted independence to come before settling the communal problem. This meant having an essentially unitary form of government—one constitution and one nation—strong enough to fulfil the purposes for which independence was being sought, while appeasing the fears of provinces and minority groups. In contrast, Jinnah and the League reiterated their demand that the first

step must be to accept Pakistan in principle, now that the Muslim electorate had given its verdict in favour of it.[51]

The Cabinet Mission Plan

For seeking the co-operation of the parties who mattered in the Indian problem and to hammer out a consensus on the future Constitution of independent India, three members of Premier Attlee's Cabinet, Lord Pethick-Lawrence, Sir Stafford Cripps, and Lord Albert Alexander, began their visit to India from 24 March 1946. Having ascertained the views of Indian representatives and political parties on the future political and constitutional set-up of the subcontinent, the Cabinet Mission announced its three-tier Federation scheme on 16 May 1946. A kind of loose confederation envisaged in the Cabinet Plan was to create 'three groups' of provinces and states, i.e., two eastern and western groups claimed by the Muslim League, and a third group, comprising the rest of British India. The centre visualized in the three-tier Federation was to be responsible for foreign affairs, defence, and communications. All other subjects were to be assigned to the provinces with the residuary powers. The princely states were to be admitted in the Federation on negotiated terms and conditions. The second part of the Cabinet Mission Plan was related to the future constitution-making machinery and the third concerned with proposals on the Interim Government. As the Cabinet Mission, which seemed averse to the partition of the subcontinent, could not initially reconcile the divergent League and Congress constitutional and political perspectives, it recommended that the new Constitution of India be drawn up on the following pattern:

- A Union of India, embracing both British India and the states, should deal with specific subject, i.e., foreign affairs, defence, and communications, and should have the necessary powers to raise the finances required for the Union's subjects.

- The Union's Legislature and Executive be based on provincial and the states' representatives.

- All subjects other than the Union subjects, and all residuary powers, should vest in the provinces.

- The states should retain all subjects and powers other than those ceded to the Union.

- Provinces should be free to form 'groups' with executives and legislatures, and each group could determine the provincial subjects to be taken in common.

- The Constitution of the Union and of the group should contain a provision whereby any province could, by a majority vote of its Legislative Assembly, call for a reconsideration of the terms of the Constitution after an initial period of ten years and at ten yearly intervals thereafter.

Despite the rejection of its 'Pakistan scheme' in the Cabinet Mission Plan, the Muslim League saw a great 'tactical' advantage in the grouping of the provinces on communal lines.[52] With greater provincial autonomy, the Muslim majority regions grouped in Sections B and C offered an optional separation in the form of Pakistan after ten years of initial stay in the Union. Keeping in mind the latter fact, the Muslim League agreed, on 6 June 1946, to accept the Plan. Though obviously unhappy with the grouping scheme of the Plan, Congress initially accepted it on 26 June in the hope that it would never work in future united India.

After acceptance of the Cabinet Plan, the next important step was to form an Interim Government consisting of five nominees each of the Congress and the Muslim League and four representatives of other parties and interests. Interestingly, the British had stipulated on 16 June 1946 that, in the event of the two main parties or either of them refusing to join the Executive Council, the Viceroy would proceed to form a government from among those who were willing to accept the Cabinet Mission Plan. Consequent upon the Congress demand that it be allowed to nominate a Muslim representative as well, the Muslim League pleaded with the Viceroy that it alone had the right to nominate all the Muslim representatives. Amidst controversy, the Congress refused to participate in the Interim Government. Such a development created an unpalatable situation for the Viceroy who, according to his own pledges, was supposed to invite the Muslim League to form the Interm Government. This deviation infuriated the Muslim League and its leadership, who withdrew their acceptance of the Cabinet Mission Plan, and declared 16 August 1946 as 'direct action day', if the Muslim demands concerning Pakistan were not fulfilled.

While claiming to play the role of an 'honest broker' between the two communities, the British had exhausted their options for settling the Indian problem in a manner acceptable to both the Hindus and the Muslims. Amidst proposals and counter-proposals concerning an acceptable constitutional edifice, the antagonistic communities seemed to be waiting in the wings to get at each other's throats, if they were let loose by their leaders. In the given tense circumstances, 'If that were to happen, the leaders would cease to lead, the followers would not follow and that thin crust of order which the British and their collaborators had maintained for a century and a half of rule, would break down, with disorders on a scale never before seen in India, and certainly in Britain's experience overseas'.[53]

The Muslim League seemed determined to seek Pakistan; the Congress leadership was equally vehement in opposing it tooth and nail. On 5 April 1946, Jawaharlal Nehru said that 'Congress is not going to agree to the Muslim League's demand for Pakistan under any circumstances whatsoever, even if the British Government agrees to it. Nothing on earth, not even the UNO is going to bring about Pakistan which Jinnah wants'.[54] In the same tone, Gandhi declared on 31 March 1947: 'If the Congress wishes to accept partition, it will be over my dead body. So long as I am alive, I will never agree to the partition of India. Nor will I, if I can help it, allow Congress to accept it'.[55]

In his disregard of all the solemn pledges and promises made to the Muslim League in seeking the latter's co-operation during the difficult war years, the decision of the British viceroy, Lord Wavell, to invite Mr Nehru to constitute an Interim Government, proved to be disastrous.[56] Such an unprincipled step led to a bloody communal civil war between the Hindus and the Muslims on an unprecedented scale. A civil war, in the form of wholesale butchery, huge and horrible, set the principal towns of the subcontinent ablaze. In a debate in the House of Commons in December 1946, Winston Churchill, while condemning the British government's decision on the interim regime in India as 'a cardinal error', observed: 'It is certain that more people have lost their lives or been wounded in India by violence since the Nehru government was installed in office four months ago than in the previous ninety years'.[57]

Realizing the gravity of the deteriorating communal situation in the subcontinent, the British government convened a conference of the Congress, the Muslim League, and the Sikh representatives in London in December 1946. The significant outcome of the London Conference was the abandonment of the Cabinet Plan; it also raised the hope for the Muslim League that Pakistan in some form might be conceded.[58] When the Cabinet Mission's suggestions and recommendations seemed dead, the partition of the subcontinent became inevitable. Stripped of their global sway and military reach, the British were in a hurry to leave India at the earliest. They were no longer in a position to 'divide and rule'; instead, they immediately set about a 'divide and run' policy.[59]

On 20 February 1947, British Prime Minister Attlee's Labour Government announced that the final transfer of power to the Indians would take place no later than June 1948. Meanwhile, Lord Wavell was replaced by Lord Louis Mountbatten as the Viceroy of India, with the clear mandate to transfer power and withdraw as quickly as possible. On his arrival, Mountbatten found that the all-India unitary talks between various actors in the Indian problem had failed, and there seemed no alternative except to partition the subcontinent. Acting on the advice of V. P. Menon, his Indian constitutional adviser, Lord Mountbatten proposed the partition of the subcontinent, including the provinces of the Punjab, Assam, and Bengal, and the establishment of two separate constituent assemblies and two governments as the only possible solution to the Indian problem. Such a plan was accepted by all the concerned parties, i.e., the Sikh, the Hindu, and the Muslim leaders. Thus, on 3 June 1947, Lord Mountbatten, with Nehru on his right and Jinnah on his left, announced in Delhi that the subcontinent would be partitioned to form India and Pakistan.

The procedural plan for the ultimate territorial shape of the two countries was ready in the debilitating summer of 1947. The Radcliffe Award performed major and painful surgery on Punjab and Bengal, and handed over arbitrarily determined shares to India and Pakistan. Having performed 'the greatest administrative operation in history', the British authorities felt 'miraculously lucky' at the success of their 'divide and run' strategy in the political and communal quagmire of the subcontinent.[60]

IV

THE COLONIAL CONSTITUTIONAL HERITAGE

The Hindu-Muslim conflict had existed even prior to the advent of British colonial rule in the subcontinent. Sir Syed Ahmed Khan's perspectives on the deep-rooted Hindu-Muslim cleavage and the various remedies put forward by him for the cultural, social, economic, and political ailments of the Muslims, and his incessant efforts for the realization of a distinct Muslim political entity, had ultimately prevailed in the form of Pakistan. Jinnah, who had initially set his mind on reconciling and blunting the sharp edges of Hindu-Muslim antagonism through constitutional guarantees on an all-India basis, had to give in to the 'Two-Nation Theory' propounded by Ahmed Khan.

Sir Syed Ahmed Khan had perceived and prophesied the ultimate shape of the Hindu-Muslim conflict through his visualization of unfolding trends and events. Jinnah, on the other hand, through most of his political life, pursued the principle that the rights of the Muslims, as the major and dynamic minority, be adequately and constitutionally safeguarded on an all-India basis. He, however, was forced to retreat to Khan's line of thinking (i.e., the Two-Nation Theory), after experiencing the authoritative, uncompromising, discriminatory, relentless, and high-handed repression against the Muslims by the Congress Ministries in the late 1930s. However, Jinnah and his party, like Ahmed Khan, were pitted not only against the British and the Hindus, but they also had to face and counter the retrogressive and short-sighted Muslim fundamentalists both within and without the Muslim League.

The All India National Congress persistently maintained that the Muslims of the subcontinent had everything in common with the Hindus save religion, and that Pakistan would be the culmination of British intrigues and a manifestation of a classic case of the 'divide and rule' strategy. In conceding Pakistan, the British were all out to partition the subcontinent; the Congress did little (at least as regards accommodating the Muslims' minimum constitutional demands) to dissuade them from falling back upon such an extreme move. Influenced by emergent Hindu chauvinism, the Congress leadership's niggardly attitude towards the Muslim League's demands for political autonomy and constitutional guarantees within an all India federal or confederal structure, singularly contributed to the evolution of the latter's separatism.

The advent and continuous expansion of British colonial sway in the subcontinent led to the formation of administratively convenient territorial units, called provinces. Numbering fourteen about the year 1919, all the provinces were not uniform nor were they territorially drawn on any natural, ethno-cultural or linguistic lines. The unitary style of government, operating through British Parliamentary supremacy, was vested in the Governor-General, who received and obeyed the orders of the Secretary of State for India. The provincial governments were under the direct superintendence, direction, and control of the Governor-General. Being merely administrative units, the provinces were not vested with their own powers, and hence one finds no trace of the federal principle prior to the introduction of the Act of 1919. The provincial governments, working under the Byzantine-type British bureaucracy, were merely the agents of the centre.

In view of the Indian demands for constitutional reforms and responsible government, the British had begun, in 1909, the gradual process of bestowing on India 'a large measure of self-government'. However, it was the Act of 1919 which injected the federal principle, though on a limited scale, by introducing the devolution of authority from the centre to the provinces. Under the Constitution of 1919, with the dyarchical principle operative in the provinces, the local representatives had executive authority and in its exercise were responsible to elected politicians in the provincial councils.

Unlike the Congress, which stood for a strong centre, the Muslim League had recognized (besides its advocacy of the separate electorate system) the supreme value of federal principles as an effective deal for religious, linguistic, and cultural minorities. A pointer to such an assertion could be the 1924 Resolution of the Muslim League, demanding constitutional reforms 'on a federal basis so that each Province shall have full and complete provincial autonomy'. The federal principle and full provinical autonomy suited the dynamic Muslim minority to mitigate the weight of the Hindu majority at the centre, and strengthen the political position of the Muslim majority provinces.

If the Muslims detested British colonial rule, they were equally apprehensive of brute Hindu majority rule in the possible federation of united India. Federal versus unitary, full provincial autonomy versus a powerful centre, and finally a separate versus a joint electorate system, remained the main constitutional contentions of the League and the Congress throughout the 1920s and the 1930s. Whether it was the 1930 Simon Commission Report dealing with the subcontinental constitutional malaise, and its recommendations on improving the Act of 1919; or the 1933 White Paper (based on the British decisions and recommendations arrived at in the light of the London Round Table Conference), the afore-mentioned League-Congress constitutional contentions did surface to add new dimensions to the already aggravated communal conflict.

From the British colonial point of view, the Government of India Act, 1935, was a Constitution that suited 'the genius' of the subject people. However, in the language used by Mr Jinnah, the 1935 Constitution being 'thoroughly rotten, fundamentally bad and totally unacceptable', was a colonial scheme thrust upon the local people. Passed by the British Parliament, the Act of 1935 never gave the local people full control over the government of their country. They could neither amend nor change the Constitution: they were simply supposed to obey it.

Though the undemocratic and irresponsible centre and the absolute powers conferred on the provincial governors (as agents of the Governor-General at the centre) were great impediments to the realization of full-fledged reponsible government, at least in the provinces, the new scheme was an improvement on the limited federal system visualized in the Act of 1919. Departing from the old unitary form of government, the Act of 1935 subjected India, at least in constitutional theory, to a federal form of government. The provinces for the first time in the whole history of the subcontinent were recognized in the Constitution as distinct legal entities. They were to exercise executive and legislative powers in their own spheres and were to a great extent free from the overlordship of the centre. Though the centre was empowered to infringe upon the whole field of provincial autonomy during war or emergency, and governors were vested with huge discretionary power, yet what else could be expected from the colonialists who were still anxious to stamp their authority even in that period of transition?

The question of 'residuary powers', which Professor Kenneth Wheare considers a test of the federal principle, was deferred to avoid any unpleasant encroachment on British colonial sway. Despite conceding provincial autonomy, the Act of 1935 envisaged a unique federation. The profession of the federal principle in the Constitution of 1935 notwithstanding, the federal part of the Act was substituted for a unitary type of government functioning at the centre in actual practice. Unlike the federal practice evolved elsewhere (i.e., the USA, Canada, the Commonwealth of Australia, etc.), with the autonomous units surrendering their powers voluntarily through a pact to the federation, here it was the centre which devolved authority on provinces with arbitrarily drawn boundaries. The provinces which got provincial autonomy from the centre were devoid of any legal authority to surrender power to the latter.

Unlike the provinces, the princely states possessed a unique legal status in the 1935 Constitution. Envisaged as part of the federation, the states were given the option of either joining the federation on negotiated terms or staying out. While the members from British India were to be elected by the people, the states were allowed to nominate their quota in the Council of States and the Federal Assembly. The British could thus use the pliable and handpicked nominees of the states to serve their colonial interests. It was on account of this and similar other undemocratic provisions that Dr Keith was obliged to denounce the federation in the Act of 1935, as 'bastard Federalism'.

In spite of the British desire to retain full control over the centre, owing to the opposition of both the Congress and the League to what they considered as an irresponsible and undemocratic centre, the federal part of the Act of 1935 never came into actual operation. Only that part of the Constitution which related to the provinces was enforced. The administrative evils practised in the form of dyarchy in the provinces under the Act of 1919 were repeated at the centre in the Constitution of 1935.

The working of the provincial governments, though detrimental to the Muslim interests in the late 1930s, nurtured a strong sense of the value of provincial autonomy among the provinces. Moreover, the confederal and zonal schemes advanced by some Muslim thinkers and political scientists, as part of solving the problem of Hindu-Muslim communalism, pampered the distinct character and status of the provinces. Having persuaded the Viceroy to defer indefinitely the operation of the federal part of the 1935 Constitution, Jinnah and his League presented their case for a separate Muslim entity on the strength of Muslim majority provinces in the north-west and north-east of the subcontinent. They urged the British to reconsider the constitutional and political problem *de novo*. The timing of the 1940 Pakistan Resolution and the League's demand for 'Independent

States', based on 'autonomous and sovereign units' was meant to deliberately arouse the much-cherished ambitions of the provinces for greater provincial autonomy and thus keep alive its strategy of separatism.

Throughout the 1940s, while the Congress continued to harp on a Constitution with a strong centre, Jinnah and his League firmly stood with the provinces and their distinct autonomous status. The 1946 Cabinet Mission Plan and its constitutional strategy of a three-tier federation was more akin to the Muslim League's political demands than to the Congress's quest for a strong centre to overwhelm the provinces. Possessing such a pivotal position in the League's strategy of achieving Pakistan, both the states and provinces were imbued with a strong sense of provincial autonomy, and looked forward to ensuring their distinct and autonomous status in the new set-up.

5

PAKISTAN: 1947-1958

MOCKERY OF CONSTITUTIONALISM AND FEDERALISM

This chapter is divided into three parts. Part I deals with the chequered constitutional developments which eventually led to the adoption of the 1956 Constitution. The overwhelming thrust of this part will be on the political impediments to the injection of the federal principle in the constitutional formulations put forward by the Constituent Assembly of Pakistan. The most vital question of provincial autonomy, finally degenerating into the Bengali-Punjabi controversy, will form part of this section.

Part II is devoted to constitutional politics relating to the practice of provincial autonomy between the years 1947-58. It will be shown that, notwithstanding the Muslim League and its leadership's stand and promises on federalism and constitutionalism (as evident from the preceding chapter), the ruling elite at the centre preferred to dole out mere palliatives to the federating units on these vital issues. Did the ruling elite lack political means that they opted for utilizing the notorious clauses of the Government of India Act, 1935, in order to dismiss and wreck the provincial governments in the country? Part III contains a general assessment of the leaders who defied constitutionalism in Pakistan.

I

THE PROVISIONAL CONSTITUTION

In accordance with the legal provisions of the 3 June 1947 Plan to partition the subcontinent into two independent states, the British Parliament enacted the Independence Act, which came into force on 18 July 1947. With the enactment of the Independence Act of 1947, the process of constitutional developments climaxed in the middle of August 1947, when India and Pakistan were inaugurated as two independent dominions with the British Crown as the nominal head.[1] Until the formulation of a new Constitution for each dominion, the Act of 1947 divided the 450 member Constituent Assembly into two legislative bodies, exercising all the powers hitherto applied by the central legislature. Each dominion and its provinces were to be governed in accordance with the Government of India Act, 1935. The Governor-General of each dominion was empowered to modify or adopt the Constitution of 1935, and to bring the provisions of the Independence Act of 1947 into effective operation and for other legal purposes.

The Act of 1947 provided for the termination of the suzerainty of the Crown over the Indian states, and continuation of the existing arrangements between the princely states and the new dominions till negotiations on a new constitutional relationship were completed. The system of dyarchy at the centre and the issuing of 'the Instrument of Instructions' to the Governors were done away with. The dominion of Pakistan was to include the provinces of Sindh, the NWFP, British Balochistan, East Bengal, West Punjab, and the states which acceded to it. Pending the framing of a new Constitution, Pakistan adopted the Government of India Act, 1935, with some adjustments and amendments, as its Provisional Constitution.

The Provisional Constitution seemed repugnant to the aspirations of the people of Pakistan and was demonstrably unable to respond to the emerging character of the nation. For framing a befitting Constitution for the new state, the previous indirectly elected members from the provincial legislatures and the princely states (elected on a 14% franchise based on property and education) in the 1945-6 elections were co-opted in accordance with the provisions of the Independence Act, 1947, to the first Constituent Assembly of Pakistan. The first session of the Constituent Assembly of Pakistan (CAP) was held on 10 August 1947 and the next day it unanimously elected Jinnah as its first President.

On the eve of independence, eight members (including Abul Kalam Azad) of the CAP renounced their membership, left Pakistan, or remained in India.[2] Thus, additions had to be made to accommodate representatives from the states which had acceded to Pakistan, the Tribal Areas, Balochistan, and the refugees from India.[3] After adjustments and readjustments of the members of the CAP, its final strength rose from 69 to 79. The territorial distribution of the CAP was: East Pakistan 44; Punjab 22; Sindh 5; NWFP 3; Balochistan 1; and one member each to represent the Balochistan States Union,

Bahawalpur, Khairpur, and the NWFP princely states.[4] The Muslim League, with 59 members, represented the Government. The opposition was mainly represented by the Pakistan National Congress (12 million Pakistani Hindus), initially consisting of 16 members, but its membership had dwindled to eleven by 1953.[5]

Many of the CAP members were also members of the provincial legislatures, and ministers in the federal and provincial governments. Some even held ambassadorial posts abroad. Besides two women members, the CAP included: Jinnah, the first Governor-General of Pakistan; Liaquat Ali Khan, the first Prime Minister of Pakistan; Khawaja Nazimuddin, who succeeded Jinnah; Abdul Ghaffar Khan (who remained under detention for about six years); Maulana Shabbir Ahmed Osmani, representing the theocracy; Mian Iftikharuddin, representing the view-point of the left; and intellectuals like Professor I. H. Qureshi and Omar Hayat Malik.[6] Considering the limited basis of the franchise of the CAP, the membership allocation in the Assembly never fully represented the actual federating units. For instance, as many as six members of the CAP from East Pakistan, including Premier Liaquat Ali Khan, Maulana Shabbir Ahmed Osmani, Khan Abdul Qayyum Khan, and Ghulam Muhammad, were non-Bengalis.[7]

STATUS OF THE FEDERATING UNITS

The legal and political (though disputed) stand of Pakistan on Jammu and Kashmir, Hyderabad, and Junagadh apart, its federation consisted of fifteen separate entities: four Governors' Provinces, i.e., East Bengal, West Punjab, Sindh, and the NWFP; ten princely States, i.e., Bahawalpur, Khairpur, the four Balochistan States of Kalat, Kharan, Mekran, and Lasbela; the four Frontier States of Swat, Chitral, Dir, and Amb; and the centrally administered Chief Commissioner's Province of Balochistan. Barring this last mentioned province, all other federating units had equal status under the Government of India Act, 1935. East Bengal possessed a 'dual status' in the federation: firstly, it was one of the four Governors' Provinces, and secondly, being about one thousand miles away from the western wing, it contained the majority of the population, though in area it was one-sixth of Pakistan.

In comparison to the heterogeneous nature of the western wing, East Bengal demonstrated ethnic and linguistic unity. The Sylhet district and East Bengal (forming a province of Pakistan) were one of those regions where the British colonialists had applied their initial administrative and constitutional experiments. Thus, the people of Bengal were politically more conscious compared to the rest of the federating units of Pakistan.[8] Such an earlier political awakening in Bengal obliged it to provide initial leadership for the nationalist movement against imperialism. In the 1920s and the 1930s, Bengal 'eagerly took to the politics of violence'.[9] After its partition into two Bengals (i.e., East Pakistan and the Indian state of West Bengal) in 1947, the volatile and turbulent politics of the region left three conspicuous legacies for the new sovereign entities of India and Pakistan. They were: a vigorous demand for Bengali autonomy, tactics of violence, and leftist leanings.[10]

After its annexation in 1849, the British had introduced constitutional reforms in Punjab under the Act of 1909. Like Bengal, the Punjab was partitioned into two parts in 1947, west Punjab forming a province of Pakistan. NWFP, which was carved out of the Punjab in 1901 as a distinct administrative unit, was deprived of constitutional reforms under the Acts of 1909 and 1919. After violent protests and rallies, constitutional reforms were introduced in the NWFP in the early 1930s. Through a referendum, whether to join Pakistan or India, the NWFP decided in 1947 to join the former.

As a result of great struggle by the people and repeated demands of the Muslim League, Sindh was detached from the Bombay Presidency and declared a province under the Government of India Act, 1935. Consisting of a Chief Commissioner's Province and four princely states, Balochistan was directly governed by the British through a political agent of the Governor-General. Despite consistent demands of the Muslim League, the British never introduced constitutional reforms in Balochistan. The tribal elders of British Balochistan, by a unanimous vote, decided to join Pakistan on 29 June 1947. The exception was Kalat (the Khan of Kalat was not represented at the Jirga of Chiefs which voted to join Pakistan) and its annexation was negotiated between the Khan of Kalat and Governor-General Jinnah in April 1948. In 1954, all the princely states and the Chief Commissioner's provinces were merged, and, later on, consolidated into the One Unit System.

With the foregoing disproportionate entities (both provinces and princely states) in its federation, Pakistan began its independent life.

Karachi was made its capital, and a new Federal Court was created on the pattern of its predecessor in British India. Prior to the emergence of Pakistan as a sovereign federal entity, the issues relating to federalism and provincial autonomy had eventually culminated in the Government of India Act, 1935. Notwithstanding its limitations (mainly because of sustaining colonial rule), the 1935 Constitution with its fundamental constitutional foundations had left the following three indelible legacies of federalism for the new state of Pakistan:

- Being a model Constitution and written on federal lines, it conceded provincial autonomy in principle and established a full regime of responsible government, with division of powers between the centre and the provinces;

- It created a Federal Court, a promise and anchorsheet of federalism, and the ultimate judicial device to settle centre-province disputes;

- Finally, being the penultimate chapter of British constitutional reforms since the Act of 1858, the 1935 Constitution remained the Provisional Constitution (1947-56) of the Federation of Pakistan. Moreover, it demonstrated all the potential of an adaptable model for various 'future Constitutions' in the country.

The Government of India Act, 1935, with necessary omissions, additions, adaptations, and modifications, had established a federation, though highly centralized, in Pakistan. Contrary to their stand on greater provincial autonomy in pre-partitioned India, the rulers of newly-independent Pakistan changed the distribution of powers between the centre and provinces further in favour of the former. While constitutionally reducing the status of provinces to mere agents of the central government, the provinces were handicapped by the superior powers of the centre in legislative, financial, and political spheres. The Act of 1935, being the Provisional Constitution, empowered the federal government to control provincial politics via the Governor who, in his relations with his ministers, was to act as the agent of the Governor-General. The lack of adequate financial resources and the federal government's powers with regard to taxation as a major source of revenue made the provinces highly dependent on the centre.

Considering the consensus in the ruling party on the federal principle and greater provincial autonomy in the pre-independence era, it was unfair and indeed detrimental on its part to work against the spirit of federalism. Justification for a strong centre in order to avert the sufferings of the country's birth pangs seemed a bankrupt argument. Provincial autonomy having been advocated earlier, the imperatives of federalism had assumed sensitive dimensions, which required careful handling in the ensuing centre-province relations. Far from advancing an adequate response to the challenge, the ruling elite allowed the provincial autonomy issue to degenerate into an intractable problem. For instance, the Governor-General's power to proclaim an emergency was further augmented by successive amendments by the CAP in Section 102 of the original Act of 1935 in 1947, 1948, and 1950, which enlarged its scope. The amended Section thus read as follows:

> The federal legislature shall, if the Governor-General has declared by proclamation that a grave emergency exists, whereby the security or economic life of Pakistan or any part thereof is threatened by war or internal disturbance or circumstances arising out of any mass movement of population from or into Pakistan, have power to make laws for a province or any part thereof with respect to any matter enumerated in the provincial legislature list or to make laws, whether or not for a province or any part thereof with respect to any matter not enumerated in any of the lists in the seventh schedule to this Act or to make laws, notwithstanding anything in any other provision of this Act, relating to the custody, management and disposal of the property of any person concerned in any mass movement as aforesaid.

The existence of such powers in the hands of the federal legislature to make laws on matters exclusively mentioned in the provincial list was to erode *ab initio* the letter and spirit of the federal principle. While Section 122 ensured respect for federal laws in the provinces and the federal government could also function directly through its own officers posted in the provinces, Section 92-A was inserted in the Provisional Constitution to make the provinces almost subservient administrative units. This section, which reads as under, subsequently resulted in the suspension of constitutional machinery in the Punjab, East Bengal, and Sindh:

> If at any time the Governor-General is satisfied that a grave emergency exists whereby the peace or security of

Pakistan or any part thereof is threatened or that a situation has arisen in which the government of a province cannot be carried on in accordance with the provisions of this Act, he may by proclamation direct the Governor of a province to assume on behalf of the Governor-General all or any of the powers vested in or exercisable by the provincial body or authority. Any such proclamation may contain such identical and consequential provisions as may appear to the Governor-General to be necessary or desirable for giving effect to the objects of the proclamation including provisions for suspending in whole or in part the operation of any provision of this Act relating to any provincial body or authority.

In view of the aforementioned deadly constitutional device to control and guide the provinces on desired lines, little scope was left for provincial autonomy to exist in relation to a dominant centre. Notwithstanding the distinct legal entity of the provinces, whatever autonomy existed in the provinces was at the mercy of the centre. Ignoring the cardinal principle that provincial autonomy was an inevitable corollary of the federal system, the Federation amassed powers to the extent where the federal principle began to be diluted through the centre's excessive interferences. Trampling upon the strong spirit of provincial autonomy (based on the Muslim League's promises in pre-partition India), the centre's successive assaults on the federal principle scuttled provincial rights, leading to the unending saga of centre-province conflict.

FEDERAL ISSUES

Pakistan, being a secular, federal, and parliamentary state under the existing constitutional arrangements of the Act of 1935, confronted the following major issues in the formulation of its Constitution:

- The East Bengal-West Pakistan power balance.
- The Islamic state issue.
- The language controversy.
- The joint or separate electoral system.

Barring the Islamic state issue, the other matters could safely be treated in the context of Pakistan's search for a federal constitutional order. The national imperatives, the dynamics of independence, and the Muslim League's constitutional remedies promised to the masses and the federating units, necessitated that the constitution-making process be accomplished at the earliest. The geopolitical contours, linguistic contrasts, divergent cultural ethos, and the plethora of the problems associated with the emergence of a new sovereign entity, demanded a national Constitution for the steady growth of Pakistan's federal body politic.

For nineteen months after its first meeting under the one-day chairmanship of Jogendra Nath Mandal on 10 August 1947, the CAP transacted no constitutional work of any significance.[11] Having a prestigious status in the new state, and being familiar with all the skills and intricacies of constitution-making and constitutionalism, Jinnah was in a position to impose a Constitution of his personal choice[12]. Yet, as a true democrat, he believed that such an authority was vested in the elected representatives. Having left the Constitution to be evolved and formulated by the CAP, Jinnah never saw its outcome. After Jinnah's death on 11 September 1948, the CAP's enthusiasm began to effervesce and it took its job as a 'casual assignment'.

The nation, despite glaring ethno-cultural, geographic, and linguistic contrasts, was knit together, via the still reverberating common national struggle and unswerving faith in its unique achievement. Thus, initially it was easy to hammer out a consensus on constitutional complexities relating to federalism, which, as time rolled by, began to multiply and deadlocked the constitution-making process itself.

While the administration of the new state was trying to cope with huge problems arising out of the partition of the subcontinent, the religious elite began to arouse the passions of the people, to get 'a hundred per cent Islamic Constitution' from the CAP. Jinnah's death led to an acceleration in the ulema's demands for the immediate imposition of *Shariah* in the state. Despite constant reminders to the *ulema* by the level-headed national leaders that the blueprint of the Islamic way of governing, to which they were ceaselessly referring, existed nowhere in the modern world, the former felt no compunction in playing upon public emotions and religious sentiments.

It was in these circumstances that Prime Minister Liaquat Ali Khan introduced the Objectives Resolution, loaded with theological undertones, in the CAP on 7 March 1949. Beginning with the name of Allah, the Beneficient and the Merciful, the Objectives Resolution was hailed as the landmark in constitution formulations of the new state. Far from appeasing the agitating *ulema*, the Objectives Resolution created intense religious controversies that delayed the constitution-making process. It proved to be an effective weapon in the hands of the ruling elite to create rifts in the national polity to the effect of prolongation of their ignominious rule. Its theological undertones apart, the Objectives Resolution stated that Pakistan 'should form a Federation, wherein the provinces would be autonomous, with such limitations on their powers and authority as might be prescribed'.[13] The salient provisions of the Resolution were:

- Sovereignty belongs to Allah, and it will be exercised by the people in accordance with tenets of the Holy Quran and the *Sunnah*.

- The principles of democracy, freedom, equality, tolerance, and social justice shall be observed.

- The state shall exercise its powers and authority through the elected representatives of the people of Pakistan.

- Equal fundamental rights for all the citizens of Pakistan.

- Pakistan should be a federation.

Besides the contentions between moderates and fundamentalists as to the inclusion of Islamic clauses in the future Constitution of the country, public opinion in both the wings of Pakistan was sharply divided on the federal principle. The majority of political leaders from West Pakistan (particularly the Punjab) 'argued that each of the units should have an equal degree of autonomy and equal representation in a federal upper house. East Pakistanis insisted that their isolated province was *sui generis* and entitled to a greater degree of autonomy than was practicable for the units of West Pakistan and, because of its population, was entitled to a majority voice in national affairs'.[14]

The clamouring of the *ulema* (overwhelmingly based in the western wing) for imposition of *Shariah* apart, the constitution-making process was confronted with two major issues:

1. The representation of each zone in the national federal institutions; and

2. The distribution of powers between the centre and the
    provinces.

The vital question of translating the federal principle into the form
of adequate constitutional representation for the federating units of
Pakistan 'proved to be no less baffling to the constitution-makers
than the issue of the place of Islam in politics'.[15] While the demands
for an Islamic Constitution were exclusively confined to the western
wing, the sharp differences between East Pakistan and West Pakistan
over their mutual constitutional relationship began to complicate the
future federal set-up of the state, finally degenerating into an ugly
Bengali-Punjabi controversy.

BASIC PRINCIPLES COMMITTEE'S REPORT

On the same day that the Objectives Resolution was passed (i.e., 7
March 1949), the CAP appointed the Basic Principles Committee
(BPC) to evolve the fundamental principles of the country's future
Constitution. With Maulvi Tamizuddin Khan as its President, and
Liaquat Ali Khan as its Vice President, the BPC consisted of
twenty-five members (with the legal right to co-opt more members
if required). To prepare a comprehensive document to be presented
before the CAP, the BPC constituted three sub-committees to deal
with:

- The federal and provincial constitutions, and distribution
  of powers between the centre and provinces;

- Matters relating to franchise;

- The judiciary's status.

The popular urge for a Constitution and the political dictates of
the time notwithstanding, the BPC published its first report more
than a year after its formation. The report overwhelmingly based itself
on the Government of India Act, 1935. The following were the main
recommendations of the first interim report of the BPC, presented to
the Constituent Assembly on 28 September 1950:[16]

- Executive power would be vested in the Head of State,
  acting on the advice of the Ministry.

- The Head of State would appoint a Prime Minister, the Cabinet being then appointed on the advice of the Prime Minister.

- The Federal Legislature would consist of the House of Units (elected by Provincial Legislatures), and the House of the People (directly elected).

- The two Houses would have equal powers and would, under certain extraordinary circumstances, meet in joint sessions.

- Each province would have a unicameral legislature, elected for five years, with executive power to be exercised by the head of the province.

- The subjects for legislation would be divided into those reserved for the Federal Legislature, and those reserved for the Provincial Legislatures. In the case of any conflict between Federal and Provincial Legislation, the former's legislation from the concurrent list would prevail.

- The Head of State could proclaim an emergency and suspend the Constitution in whole or in part.

- Bills passed by the Federal Legislature would be presented to the Head of State, who would either stamp his assent or return it.

- The official language of the state would be Urdu.

- Teaching of the Holy Quran would be compulsory and *waqfs* (trusts) and mosques would be run on modern lines.

The report invited a barrage of scathing criticism from the fundamentalists (who were insisting on an Islamic Constitution) and the protagonists of provincial autonomy. The moderate political elements condemned it as anti-democratic and wholly against the spirit of the Pakistan movement. The fundamentalists dubbed the report as secular and an abject insult to Islam, smacking of a fascist approach, and subversive of the ideology of Pakistan.[17] The absence of adequate and substantial provincial autonomy sparked off a very violent reaction in East Pakistan, where public opinion characterized it as 'a fatal stab', 'a shameless conspiracy against their province', 'a murderous scheme' cleverly devised by the 'power-drunk oligarchical ruling clique in Karachi' for its nefarious aims of imposing 'a dictatorship under the camouflage of Islam and the Objectives Resolution'.[18]

Besides the aforementioned highly critical comments of the Dhaka-based *The Pakistan Observer*, the Lahore-based *Nawa-i-Waqt* described the report as a 'negation of provincial autonomy and a mockery of federalism'.[19] Amidst wholesale condemnation of the report, the consensus was that over-centralization and conferring of dictatorial powers on the Head of State, working at the apex of the constitutional pyramid, would definitely expose the centre to the temptations of interfering in the affairs of the provinces.[20]

The choice of Urdu as the official language and the proposal to grant the House of Units (in which all provinces would have equal representation) equal powers with the House of the People (elected on population basis) were severely criticized in East Pakistan as 'designedly framed' to cripple that wing.[21] Agitational rallies were brought out in East Pakistan, dubbing the report as 'anti-Bengali'. Faced with charges and counter-charges against the report, the government of the day felt guilty and apologetic, and vainly tried to defend it with assertions that there was nothing contrary to the fundamentals of Islam and precepts of democracy and federalism. However, in view of growing opposition, the report was finally withdrawn for 'further consideration'.

With the sudden withdrawal of the BPC's first report, the persistent controversy over constitution-making and its final outcome now centred on two thorny issues, i.e., the Islamization of the state structure and the adequate quantum of provincial autonomy. While Liaquat Ali Khan was busy in reconciling the divergent perspectives, he was assassinated in Rawalpindi on 16 October 1951. His assassination put Khawaja Nazimuddin in the saddle; he endeavoured to work out a viable and acceptable formula to the constitutional crisis. On 23 November 1952, the Government presented the second revised report of the BPC to the CAP, containing the following salient features:[22]

- The Head of State would be a Muslim.

- There would be parity of representation between East Pakistan and West Pakistan in both the House of Units (120 members) and the House of the People (400 members). The units composing West Pakistan would be represented in each House in proportion to their respective population.

- Separate representation was recommended for minorities in the Federal and Provincial Legislatures.

- Elections were to be held through secret ballot.

- The Cabinet would be responsible only to the House of the People.

- No law would be made in violation of the tenets of the Quran and the *Sunnah*.

- Provisions would be made for a religious advisory board.

- The official language issue would be referred to the Constituent Assembly.

Besides the above-mentioned broad principles, the BPC's report had an appendage on Directive Principles of State Policy. They were as under:

- The state should be guided by the Objectives Resolution.

- Activities subversive of the Objectives Resolution should be forbidden.

- Steps should be taken to enable Muslims to order their lives in accordance with the dictates of the Quran and *Sunnah*.

- Existing laws should be amended/repealed in accordance with the tenets of the Quran and *Sunnah*.

- Efforts should be made for the abolition of illiteracy.

- National integration should be encouraged and parochialism discouraged.

- A pious and upright person should be elected as the Head of State.

- Separation of judiciary from executive within three years was recommended.

- Protection of minorities and their legitimate rights was stressed.

THE PARITY FORMULA

Political weightage and due representation to both wings of the country in the federal legislature proved to be a hydra-headed, intractable problem. In the early 1950s, provincial feelings had manifested themselves. The tedious constitution-making process reflected political fear, hysteria, mutual distrust, and suspicions of ultimately being overwhelmed by the other, between East Bengal and West Pakistan (particularly the province of Punjab). To avert any possible head-on-collision between East Bengal and the centre, the government of Khawaja Nazimuddin came out with what is known as the principle of parity as the basis for resolving the inbuilt potential for conflict between the two zones of Pakistan.

The parity formula—equal representation to both wings of the country in the federal legislature being the cardinal principle of second BPC report—came to be viewed overwhelmingly as a flagrant violation of the principle of universal franchise. The politicians and political parties in East Bengal criticized it for its anti-democratic bias, and 'a death blow' to East Bengal whose four per cent majority in the total population of the country was being utilized 'to arouse provincial animosities and rivalries'.[23] Opposing the parity formula, H. S. Suhrawardy termed it 'sheer sentimentalism that East Pakistan would dominate the legislature'.[24] He opined that it was 'the same dread of one section for another section of the people, which assumed the shape of communalism between the Muslims and the Hindus and led to the division of India on communal lines, is being imported in Pakistan in another shape, and is being applied to the provinces'.[25]

If East Pakistan was opposing Nazimuddin's parity formula because the representation in the federal legislature was not based on population, Punjab also showed its opposition to it. Those representing it saw no logic in treating a single unit, i.e., East Bengal, at par with all other units put together. Behind the Punjabi opposition to the parity formula (i.e., one unit with its 54 per cent population being equal to the rest of the units and sub-units) was the apprehension that East Bengal, by forging political alliances with one or more units of West Pakistan, could easily render the influence and weightage of the Punjab ineffective in the Federation.[26] Except Punjab, all other units of West Pakistan seemed favourably disposed towards the BPC's report, but the effective Punjabi opposition, creating a deadlock in the CAP, proved counterproductive in East Bengal.

Amidst charges and counter-charges between the Bengali and Punjabi leadership on the intriguing political aspects of the parity formula, the confederal principle as an absolute necessity began to be revived, particularly in the Punjab. Interpreting the 23 March 1940 Resolution as having visualized two autonomous regional governments, the leaders of the Azad Pakistan Party, including Mian Iftikharuddin and Sardar Shaukat Hayat Khan, and other notables like Maulana Zafar Ali Khan, Begum Shahnawaz, and Choudhry Nazir Ahmed, supported the confederal principle as a viable alternative.[27] The discussion in the Punjab on the confederal option as an effort at aggregating the interests of both zones was readily adopted in East Bengal where public opinion termed it the best solution: leaving West Pakistan to run its separate federation, and allowing both wings to be associated in a loose confederation.[28] In view of the peculiar geographic conditions of Pakistan, the confederal idea was appreciated by saner political elements but it was unacceptable to the central government, and Khawaja Nazimuddin bulldozed it by saying that it would 'be the end of Pakistan.'[29]

The evasiveness of the Punjab Chief Minister, Mian Mumtaz Muhammad Khan Daultana, in facing up to the religious storm, and his ulterior intent in politicizing the purely law and order situation throughout the whole bitter episode of the 1953 Ahmadiya riots, cost him his Chief Ministership.[30] The lingering religious controversies, deteriorating economic situation, and inability of the CAP to hammer out a consensus on the future Constitution of the country, obliged the Governor-General, Ghulam Muhammad, to unceremoniously dismiss the Prime Minister.

Needless to say, the whole incident dealt a severe blow to the cause of democracy. While overruling the case of the State v. Dosso (PLD 1958 SC 533) in the Miss Asma Jilani v. the Government of Punjab and others case, the Supreme Court of Pakistan described the illegal, unconstitutional and arbitrary act of the Governor-General as the 'first constitutional mishap' of Pakistan's crises-ridden history. In the words of the Supreme Court's verdict:

> In April 1953, Mr Ghulam Muhammad dismissed Khawaja Nazimuddin and his Cabinet although he commanded a clear majority in the Constituent Assembly and made another civil servant, Mr Muhammad Ali Bogra, then Pakistan's ambassador to the United States of

America, the Prime Minister . . . This was the first constitutional mishap of Pakistan as Governor-General Mr.
Ghulam Muhammad was only a Constitutional Head. He
had to act on the advice given to him by the Prime
Minister and under the Constitutional Instruments (Indian Independence Act, 1947, and the Government of
India Act, 1935), he had no legal authority to dismiss the
Prime Minister and assume to himself the role of
sovereign.[31]

BOGRA FORMULA

Neither a member of the Constituent Assembly nor of any political
party, Muhammad Ali Bogra, ambassador to the United States, was
summoned by the Governor-General to assume the premiership of
Pakistan. Working on a version of the parity formula proposed by
the government of his predecessor, Khawaja Nazimuddin, Bogra
successfully evolved a new constitutional formula, guaranteeing
equality for the two zones in the overall composition of the federal
parliament. Announced on 3 October 1953, the Bogra formula
envisaged the following for Pakistan:

- A bicameral legislature, i.e., the Upper House and the
  Lower House.

- The number of units in West Pakistan were reduced to four.
  It limited the strength of the Upper House to fifty, and
  provided for election of the Lower House on the basis of
  population.

- In the federal legislature, the total members from East
  Pakistan and West Pakistan would be equal, i.e., East
  Pakistan having 10 members in the Upper House and 165
  in the Lower House (out of a total of 300), West Pakistan
  40 in the Upper House and 135 in the Lower House.

- If the Head of State were to be elected from one wing, the
  Prime Minister would belong to the other wing.

- On disputed bills and ousting of the Head of State, it was
  stipulated that such matters could only be passed provided
  the majority of the two Houses sitting together included
  thirty per cent of the members from each wing.

Those favouring the formula endorsed it as 'singularly appropriate to the genius of our people and the geography of Pakistan.'[32] However, the critics in both wings of the country denounced it as 'uncouth and cumbersome', dangerous, and anti-democratic, aimed at giving a 'fillip to provincialism'.[33] Amidst apprehensions voiced about the domination of one zone over another, Prime Minister Bogra presented his formula, alongwith the report of the BPC to the CAP on 7 October 1953.

While the process of constitution-making in the Assembly was in progress, elections to the provincial legislature were held in East Pakistan. The United Front, commonly known as the 'Jugto' Front, a motley collection of four political parties, contested the elections on its unanimously drawn-up manifesto of 21 points. Besides other demands with a regional bias, one demand of the Jugto Front's manifesto was 'full and complete autonomy' for East Pakistan, leaving defence, foreign policy, and currency with the Centre.[34] Contesting elections on the attractive demands of complete provincial autonomy and representation in the federal legislature on population basis, the Front routed the Muslim League completely, and hence deprived it of its representative character in the CAP. The Muslim League could secure only 10 out of 310 seats.

The March 1954 elections in East Pakistan had changed the whole political milieu in which the Bogra formula was presented in the CAP. One constitutional alternative after another on the question of East-West representation in the federal legislature having been tried, the emergence of East Pakistan's monolithic electoral verdict reinforced the Punjab's apprehension that the eastern wing's political ascendancy might overwhelm it in the future. Such underlying feelings of fear and distrust led to a fresh constitutional deadlock in the CAP.

LANGUAGE FORMULA

Besides the problems of representation on 'parity' basis and the distribution of powers between the Centre and the provinces, the language controversy was the third most important federal issue. Along with geographic contrasts, Pakistan had inherited a multilingual polity. The overwhelming majority of people in East Pakistan spoke Bengali, while in the western wing a number of distinct languages, i.e., Pushtu, Sindhi, Punjabi, Seraiki, Brahvi etc. were spoken. The question of an official language presented Pakistan *ab initio* with an intense problem. In February 1948, the Congress members in the CAP hailing from East Bengal had demanded equal representation of Urdu and Bengali as the state languages. Amidst the row over this issue, Jinnah defended Urdu as the only state language in his famous Dhaka speech on 21 March 1948:

> Let me tell you in the clearest language that there is no truth that your normal life is going to be touched or disturbed so far as your Bengali language is concerned. But ultimately it is for you, the people of this province, to decide what shall be the language of your province. But let me make it very clear to you that the state language of Pakistan is going to be Urdu and no other language. Any one who tries to mislead you is really the enemy of Pakistan. Without one state language, no nation can remain tied up solidly together and function.[35]

The Bengali reaction to Jinnah's assertion was very violent; the students of Dhaka University went on strike and organized processions in favour of Bengali as one of the state languages. In the wake of the East Pakistan reaction on the language issue, many in West Pakistan readily pronounced their verdict that 'the demands for making Bengali a state language were unIslamic and expressed fears that if the demand was accepted, it would strengthen Bengali nationalism'.[36] Levelling such irresponsible insinuations that Bengali owed its origins to Hindu civilization, the protagonists of Urdu as the only state language advanced the following arguments:[37]

- With its close association with the Muslims and the Pakistan movement, Urdu was the *lingua franca* of the Muslim nation;

- Urdu alone could provide linguistic unity, a vital precondition for national integration.

The aforementioned bankrupt arguments could not assuage the injured sentiments of the Bengalis, who attributed it to the discriminative and contemptuous attitude of the West Pakistanis from whom it was futile to expect fairplay and justice to their cultural ethos. In 1952, a second language movement was launched and its violent manifestation changed the political complexion of East Pakistan. It contributed in fostering a kind of linguistic nationalism, and emerged as a symbol of the Bengalis' struggle for political, economic, and cultural equality. Impressed by the pro-Bengali agitations, the party in power in the East Bengal Legislative Assembly was obliged to pass a unanimous resolution, urging the CAP to recognize Bengali as one of the state languages. Moreover, the United Front made language and representation in the federal legislature on the basis of population the two major issues of its electioneering in the 1954 elections in East Pakistan, thus inflicting a crushing defeat on the ruling party, the Muslim League.

On 7 May 1954, Bengali wrath on the issue of language was forcefully brought home to the CAP which, by modifications in the BPC's report, adopted the following eight point formula as a viable and satisfactory solution of the language controversy[38]:

1.   Bengali and Urdu should be the official languages of Pakistan. The Head of State, on recommendation by the provincial legislature, might accord official status to any other regional language.

2.   In addition to English, the members of the Assembly/Parliament would have the right to speak in Urdu and Bengali.

3.   Notwithstanding the two abovementioned resolutions, for a period of twenty years from the coming into force of Pakistan's Constitution, the English language would continue to be used for all official purposes.

4.   For the Central Services Examination, all provincial languages would be placed on an equal footing.

5.   Provisions should be made for teaching of Arabic, Urdu, and Bengali in secondary schools, in addition to the language used as the medium of instruction.

6.   The state should take measures for the development of a common national language.

7.   A commission should be appointed ten years after the promulgation of the Constitution to make recommendations regarding the replacement of English.

8.   Notwithstanding anything in the aforegoing resolution, the Federal Legislature may provide for the use, after the

expiry of twenty years from coming into force of the
Constitution, of the English language for such purpose
as may be specified by the law.

DISSOLUTION OF THE CONSTITUENT ASSEMBLY

The ugly Punjabi-Bengali tussle for constitutional and political
ascendancy, particularly after the 1954 provincial elections in East
Pakistan, had deadlocked the constitution-making process. Public
opinion had begun to deplore the intriguing delay in constitution-
making and voiced concern over the futility of the CAP. Amidst a
rising crescendo of disappointment on its competency to deliver a
Constitution, the CAP began to move fast on the constitution-
making process, perhaps to silence its many critics. Meanwhile, the
emergence of East Pakistan as a monolithic voice on constitutional
issues in general and provincial autonomy in particular had placed
the Punjabi leadership on the defensive. The unity of East Pakistan
led the Punjabi politicians to advance the idea of merging all the
units of West Pakistan into One Unit, a solid block counter-
balancing East Pakistan on all national forums.

Besides the One Unit system, a new scheme of zonal sub-federation
was presented by Malik Firoz Khan Noon, the then Chief Minister of
the Punjab. This scheme visualized that the Punjab, with forty per
cent, and the rest of the units in West Pakistan with sixty per cent
representation should form a zonal government, and the Punjab and
East Bengal combined would have eighty per cent representation in
the Federal Government and the rest of the twenty per cent representation would be vested with the rest of West Pakistan. Foreseeing
a fast erosion of their distinct entity in the new schemes, the smaller
provinces joined hands with the Bengali members in the CAP to
oppose the idea *ab initio*. Noon's insistence on getting his zonal
sub-federation passed by the CAP was criticized by other units as
'unrepresentative' and a part of the Punjabi 'power politics' game.
When placed before the CAP, both schemes, i.e., One Unit and zonal
sub-federation were outrightly rejected.

The two aforementioned schemes had the blessings of Ghulam
Muhammad, the Governor-General, who pressurized the members
of the CAP to support the move, failing which he threatened to

initiate disqualification proceedings via PRODA (Public and Representative Offices Disqualification Act) against them.[39] Increasingly aware of the Governor-General's veiled threats against its members and his reckless precedent of dismissing Nazimuddin's ministry, the CAP thought it appropriate to amend Sections 9, 10, 10-A, 10-B, and 17 of the Government of India Act, 1935, to reduce him to the position of merely a constitutional head. On 21 September 1954, a Bill to this effect was introduced and passed in the CAP within ten minutes to curtail the discretionary powers of the Governor-General, while the latter was convalescing in the Northern Areas of Pakistan. That Bill had the following four main provisions:

- The Governor-General would appoint as Prime Minister a member of the Federal Legislature who enjoyed the confidence of the majority of the members.

- Ministers would be appointed from amongst the Legislative members.

- The Cabinet would be collectively responsible to the Assembly.

- The Governor-General would be bound by the advice of the Ministers.

Such a constitutional development was wholly unpalatable for the Governor-General who could not tolerate having his discretionary powers curtailed, making him dependent on the Federation and the Constituent Assembly. He issued a Proclamation of Emergency on the pretext that the Constituent Assembly could no longer function because it had lost its representative character over the years and that the constitution-making machinery had failed in the realization of its original objective, necessitating new elections to the Assembly. Thus, on 24 October 1954, the first Constituent Assembly was dissolved by the Governor-General, who knew full well that the draft of a Constitution based on the Objectives Resolution was ready. This was the second great constitutional mishap in Pakistan.[40]

The dissolution of the Constituent Assembly as a sovereign body had wide ranging adverse implications for the future of Pakistan. Such an act of the Governor-General plunged the country into political chaos and constitutional and legal crises of a serious nature. Had the validity of the unconstitutional action of the Governor-General in arbitrarily dismissing Prime Minister Khawaja Nazimuddin in 1953 been challenged in the higher Courts, the Governor-General would have refrained from taking this far more drastic step of dissolving the first Constituent Assembly.[41]

Consequent upon the dissolution of the Constituent Assembly by the Governor-General, its President, Maulvi Tamizuddin Khan, filed a writ petition under Section 223-A of the Government of India Act, 1935, in the Chief Court of Sindh praying that a writ in the nature of mandamus be issued against the Federation of Pakistan and the members of the reconstituted Council of Ministers, restraining them from implementing the aforesaid proclamation and prohibiting them from interfering in the exercise of Maulvi Tamizuddin Khan's function as President of the Constituent Assembly.[42] Another writ of *quo warranto* prayed that the appointment of the newly reconstituted Council of Ministers be declared invalid.

The constitutional petition was contested by all the respondents who raised various pleas, the main plea being that the Chief Court of Sindh had no jurisdiction in the writs prayed for. According to this plea, the Government of India (Amendment) Act, 1954, by which Section 223-A was inserted in the Government of India Act, 1935, and under which such writs could be issued, had not received the assent of the Governor-General. It was, therefore, not a valid law. While setting aside the plea of the Government, the Chief Court of Sindh held that the Acts of the Constituent Assembly, when it was not functioning as the Federal Legislature, did not require the assent of the Governor-General; that Section 223-A of the Government of India Act, 1935, was a valid law; and that the dissolution of the Constituent Assembly was *ultra vires* and void.

On appeal by the Federal Government, the matter was referred to the Federal Court. The Federal Court did not go into the question of whether the Governor-General's act of dissolving the Assembly was valid; it set the Chief Court's verdict aside on a technical ground, that the Act, by virtue of which the Court issued the verdict 'was not yet law', because it had not received the assent of the Governor-General. The Federal Court held that the Governor-General was part and parcel of the Constituent Assembly and all such laws passed by it as had not yet been assented to by the Head of State stood null and void. Contrary to the learned Court's verdict, it may be mentioned:

> Many constitutional Bills passed by the Constituent Assembly under this rule since 1948 were authenticated

without the assent of the Governor-General and neither the first nor the second nor the third Governor General, Ghulam Muhammad himself, raised the question that the Acts of the Constituent Assembly were invalid for want of assent. The Sind Court referred to an order of the Governor-General only four days before the dissolution of the Constituent Assembly under an Act passed without his assent. It was stated before the Court that even the superior courts in Pakistan in a number of cases had accepted the proposition that enactments of the Constituent Assembly required no assent.[43]

Running parallel to the abovementioned legal point, seventeen years after the announcement of the Federal Court's verdict, one of the learned judges of the Supreme Court of Pakistan, while dealing with this subject in the Asma Jilani case, expressed the following dissenting opinion:

> The assent of the Governor-General was, therefore, not necessary to give validity to the laws passed by the Constituent Assembly. With great respect to the learned Chief Justice, the interpretation placed by him on Section 6 and 8 of the Indian Independence Act, 1947, as a result of which the appeal was allowed, is *ex facie* erroneous though we do not propose to examine in detail the reason given in the judgement.[44]

The obvious consequence of the Federal Court's verdict was that forty-four Acts on the statute book, which were not assented to by the Governor-General prior to the dissolution of the Assembly, stood invalid. Prominent among them was an Act which had given the Governor-General discretion to pass constitutional enactments by Ordinance; this also became invalid. However, the developing constitutional crisis took a new turn when, on 27 March 1955, the Governor-General promulgated the Emergency Powers Ordinance IX of 1955 and assumed powers to:

1. Make provisions for framing the Constitution of Pakistan.

2. Make provisions to constitute the province of West Pakistan.

3. Validate laws which had been passed by the Constituent Assembly but had not received the assent of the Governor-General.

4. Authenticate the Centre's budget.

5. Name East Bengal as East Pakistan.

While hearing the appeals in Usif Patel v. the Crown case and two other cases, the fact of validating and enacting the abovementioned laws through the Emergency Powers Ordinance IX of 1955 was brought to the notice of the Federal Court. The Court held that the said Ordinance was invalid, as the Governor-General alone could not enact constitutional laws but could only give his assent to such laws as passed by the Constituent Assembly.[45] Addressing the Advocate General, the learned Chief Justice reportedly remarked that 'if you ride rough-shod, you will bring disaster to this country. You do not have validating machinery nor do you intend to create one.'[46]

The Court's verdict created a constitutional crisis of supreme magnitude. Amidst such grave constitutional complexity, the Governor-General filed a reference in the Federal Court and sought to validate certain Constitutional Acts of the Constituent Assembly, by giving his assent with retrospective effect. The Federal Court with dissenting opinion (2:3) applied the principle of state necessity and validated the Governor-General's Act in those extraordinary circumstances. Chief Justice Muhammad Munir, in dealing with the principle of state necessity, observed that:

> Subject to the condition of absoluteness, extremeness, and imminence, an act which would otherwise be illegal becomes legal if it is done *bona fide* under stress of necessity, the necessity being referable to an intention to preserve the Constitution, the state, or the society, and to prevent it from dissolution, and affirms . . . that necessity knows no law . . . necessity makes lawful which otherwise is not lawful . . . refers to the right of a private person to act in necessity, in case of the Head of State's justification to act must *a fortiori* be clearer and more imperative.[47]

In view of the Federal Court's verdict on 10 May 1955, that the Governor-General had legal authority to dissolve the Assembly, to summon a new Assembly, and validate laws retrospectively during the interim period, but that he could not nominate the members of the

Constituent Assembly which must be a representative body, the following four propositions about the late CAP were established:[48]

- The CAP had been unable to formulate a Constitution in more than seven years of existence.

- It had become an unrepresentative body.

- The CAP had practically assumed the form of a perpetual legislature.

- Contrary to the law, the CAP had asserted that the constitutional provisions made by it did not need the assent of the Governor-General.

Following the Federal Court's verdict in Usif Patel v. the Crown, the Governor-General had to abandon his cherished pretensions of formulating a Constitution through 'a Constituent Convention', and thus ordered the election of a new Constituent Assembly on 28 May 1955. The second CAP elected on 21 June 1955 consisted of eighty members, each wing being represented by forty members. The new Assembly, which had its first meeting in Murree on 7 July 1955, was elected indirectly by the members of the Provincial Legislatures. The Muslim League, which had had a majority in the first CAP, had suffered a set-back and it had only twenty-five members in the second Assembly. Most of the members of the first CAP were defeated and only fourteen of them managed to return to the second CAP.

In the absence of even a marginal majority for any party, a coalition of the Muslim League and the United Front was sought under Chaudhry Muhammad Ali, the former Finance Minister, as the Prime Minister of Pakistan. While addressing immediately itself to the constitution-making process, the second CAP revalidated all laws and statutes which had become null and void by the verdict of the Federal Court. The next highly controversial legislation of the Assembly was to evolve a plan for integration of all units in the western wing of the country into One Unit.

ONE UNIT

'A good many eggs were broken in the making of the "One Unit" omelette', said the London-based *Economist*, 'but they were mostly addled ones.'[49] The One Unit system, as later events indicated, proved to be an administrative encumbrance and wholly against the spirit of federalism. To borrow its characterization from Professor Wheeler, it was 'a painful process of grudging concession' by the smaller units in the western wing, who were coerced into making such an unpalatable omelette.[50] This was the disastrous engineering of the West Pakistan leadership in general and of the Punjab in particular, aimed at fulfilling their desire for an equal degree of autonomy and an equal say in all national affairs.

In pursuance of his 'parity formula' between the two wings of the country, Muhammad Ali Bogra had announced the merging of the existing three provinces and the princely states in the western wing into a single electoral unit and making Pakistan a federation of two units, i.e., East Pakistan and West Pakistan. Bogra's announcement was followed by the Governor-General's order establishing the single province of West Pakistan under an Emergency Ordinance, which was subsequently declared null and void by the Federal Court's ruling in the Usif Patel v. the Crown case.

After the second Constituent Assembly was elected, the advocates of One Unit within the administration, after having failed to introduce their much-cherished scheme, decided to get it through the legislative process. With little regard for the political aspirations of the people of the merging provinces and princely states and without even seeking their free consent, the Provincial Legislatures were coerced into agreeing to the establishment of One Unit. Thus, on 30 September 1955, the Assembly passed a bill merging the former provinces of Sindh, Punjab, and the NWFP, the federally administered territory of Karachi, the former states of Balochistan, Bahawalpur, and Khairpur, the former Frontier states, and the Chief Commissioner's province of Balochistan into a single province, West Pakistan.

The question of establishing West Pakistan as One Unit and treating both wings of the country at par was hotly debated in the Constituent Assembly between the antagonists and the protagonists of the One Unit system in the following manner:

Advantages

The advocates of One Unit argued that the merger of the provinces would bring in a host of benefits and advantages, e.g:[51]

- It would simplify the federal structure of the proposed new Constitution; constitution-making would be made easier by getting rid of the complexities and intricacies of bicameral legislation;

- West Pakistan being a single 'hydraulic unit', the One Unit administration would facilitate the pace of progress by solving problems of irrigation, rooted in inter-provincial conflicts;

- It would save millions of rupees, minimize corruption, and promote efficiency by bringing merit to the top;

- It would destroy the monster of provincialism, kill the moves for 'Pakhtunistan', and bring democratic rights to the people of the princely states;

- It would provide scope for administrative reforms, economic readjustments, and political reorientation, to the benefit of the whole population; and

- It would promote the much sought after goal of national unity and integrity.

Disadvantages

The antagonists saw things differently:

- They maintained that the arbitrary demolition of established provincial boundaries was not a sufficient guarantee to suppress the hydra-headed provincial rivalries and jealousies. On the contrary, it might exacerbate the centrifugal tendencies among the federating units.

- It was widely apprehended that the formation of One Unit would establish 'Punjabi sway' in the economic and administrative spheres of West Pakistan.[52]

- Bengali opposition to One Unit, as propounded by Suhrawardy, was that the origins of the One Unit idea lay in 'the fear of domination by East Pakistan over the western wing and to capture power at the centre'.[53]

- The former Chief Minister of the NWFP maintained that it was 'the outcome of an intrigue to split the country.'[54]

- Sindh described it as 'ill-conceived and short-sighted', 'unhistorical, unfair and anti-Pakistan', 'an attempt to destroy the very foundation upon which Pakistan was conceived', 'an unpatriotic move to liquidate the three smaller provinces' and a 'hostile act against Sindh'.[55]

- The apprehensions of the antagonists were further strengthened due to the way in which the Bill was passed by the Second Constituent Assembly: (i) 'support for the plan had been obtained through coercion and intimidation; ministries were dismissed, people were threatened, interned or externed for opposing the merger plan';[56] (ii) 'officers were transferred, fake charges were framed against inconvenient persons, elections were interfered with and solemn pledges were broken'.[57]

Far from achieving any national objective, the One Unit scheme disappointed the electorate throughout the country. While East Pakistan was deprived of the benefits of its numerical electoral strength, the intrinsic values of quasi-racial and linguistic identities of the distinct units in the western wing were artificially liquidated for the ruling elite's electoral and administrative convenience. Federal and regional loyalties are the prerequisites of any stable federation. The regional loyalties, upon which rested the very foundation of Pakistan, were sought to be destroyed, intensifying provincialism in the process.

FEDERALISM IN THE 1956 CONSTITUTION

Almost nine years after Independence, the Second Constituent Assembly was able to prepare a constitutional draft which was adopted by it on 29 February 1956. Governor-General Iskandar Mirza enacted it formally on 23 March 1956, substituting it for the Provisional Constitution based on the Government of India Act, 1935. The nation felt miraculously lucky to have its own 'first' Constitution.

The Constitution contained a Preamble, 234 Articles, and was divided into 13 parts and 6 Schedules. It was one of the lengthiest written Constitutions in the world. Based on 'parity' between the two wings of the country, the 1956 Constitution envisaged in Article 1 that

Pakistan shall be Federal Islamic Republic. By its centripetal bias and emphasis on the One Unit system, the Constitution empowered the Centre to politically strangulate the provinces. By clubbing the three minority provinces in the western wing into forming the artificial nexus of One Unit and then making a Federation of two provinces, the Constitution thwarted the politico-cultural aspirations of these units and reduced the due share of East Pakistan in federal power.[58]

The President, the Cabinet, and the unicameral National Assembly were the three organs of the Federal Government. The Federal Executive consisted of the President and the Cabinet. The President 'in his discretion' would appoint from amongst the members of the Assembly, a Prime Minister 'who in his opinion' was 'most likely to command' the confidence of the majority of the members (Article 37). Ministers and ministers of state would be appointed and removed by the President. The Prime Minister was to hold office during the pleasure of the President. The President could dismiss him if he was satisfied that the Prime Minister did not command the confidence of the majority of the National Assembly members.

The head of the executive authority in each province would be a Governor, to be appointed and dismissed by the President. Each province was to have a cabinet headed by the chief minister whose functions and responsibilities corresponded to those of the federal cabinet. The fifth Schedule of the Constitution spelled out the powers to be distributed between the centre and the provinces. The distribution of responsibility between the centre and the provinces theoretically corresponded to the policy of provincial autonomy. However, the 1956 Constitution invested in the federal government certain arbitrary powers of 'direction' to the provincial governments, by virtue of which the Centre could convert to a unitary style of government. Such provisions did curtail the quantum of provincial autonomy. The provincial governor, as a representative of the President, was vested with discretionary power over the chief minister and his Cabinet.

Article 193 in the 1956 Constitution (like 92-A in the amended Act of 1935) empowered the Centre to dismiss the provincial government and impose direct rule in the province. The 1956 Constitution had followed the contours of the Act of 1935 on the provincial autonomy issue. By retaining full powers of direction and emergency control, the Centre empowered itself to completely suspend provincial autonomy on the pretext of unforeseen contingencies.

Thirty subjects were alloted to the Federation, including defence, foreign affairs, citizenship, trade and commerce between the provinces, currency and coinage, public debt, copyright, navigation and shipping, posts and census. Nineteen subjects were enumerated on the concurrent list, and ninety-four items were included in the provincial list. Parliament had power to legislate for the provinces on matters enumerated in the provincial list if the Provincial Assemblies passed a resolution to that effect. Parliament was also invested with powers to make laws for the whole or any part of Pakistan for implementing any treaty with the outside world.

THE ELECTORATE BILL ISSUE

During the 1956 Constitution-making process, the Second Constituent Assembly, having failed to achieve a consensus on the separate versus joint electorate issue, preferred to defer it for future legislation. Most of the parties in the United Front, including the Nizam-i-Islam Party, the East Pakistan Awami League, and the Hindu community (then about twenty-five per cent of the total population of East Pakistan) vehemently favoured the system of joint electorate.[59] On the other hand, the Muslim League was all for a system of separate electorate. Thus, a debate arose over the electorate issue in the National Assembly which delayed forthcoming elections and struck at the very roots of the Two-Nation thesis and, above all, favoured the ruling elite's attempt to perpetuate its despotic rule. Being the leading exponent of the separate electorate system, the Muslim League leadership advanced the following main arguments:[60]

- The ideology of Pakistan was based on the 'Two-Nation' theory which established the cardinal principle of separate electorate.

- Such a system ensured the protection and adequate representation of minorities in national affairs in accordance with their numerical strength.

- Islam being the only link between the two wings, if non-Muslims were to participate in joint elections (as was envisaged in the joint electoral system), they might infiltrate the higher ranks of the Muslim political parties, thus subverting the ideology of Pakistan.

The defenders of the joint electorate system came up with equally compelling arguments in support of their stance.[61] They maintained that:

- In the system of separate electorate, with the exclusion of 25 per cent non-Muslims (mainly the Hindus in East Pakistan), and with parity representation between the two wings of the country, the Bengali Muslims would be reduced to a permanent minority *vis-à-vis* West Pakistan.

- Apprehending its eventual failure to win over the Hindu voters in any future electoral process, the Muslim League was designedly trying to exclude them from the mainstream of Pakistani national politics.

- The system of separate electorate was in complete contravention of the solemn pledges given by Jinnah to the minorities on various occasions.

- If the Two-Nation theory held good (even after the achievement of Pakistan), the minorities would be obliged to demand a separate state 'to preserve their respective identities', following in the footsteps of the Muslims in British India.

- If both the Muslims and the non-Muslims could jointly elect the President of the Islamic Republic of Pakistan, how could they be debarred from jointly electing the members of the National Assembly?

- The joint electoral system might help national integration.

As if the crisis generated by separate versus joint electorate system was not sufficient to rock the boat, another Bill, envisaging joint electorate in East Pakistan, to allay fears of the Hindus and Bengalis, and separate electorate in West Pakistan, to acquiesce in the fundamentalists' motives of splitting the national polity beyond repair, was passed by the National Assembly in October 1956. However, the ensuing resentment in the public impelled the government of the day to introduce an amended version of the above-mentioned Bill, the Electorate Amendment Bill, in the National Assembly in April 1957, providing for joint electorate system in both wings of the country. The Bill was subsequently passed, ultimately paving the way for the Election Commission to make preparations for the general elections to be held on the basis of universal franchise in 1958. Like the rest of the constitutional controversies, the separate versus joint electorate issue suited the ruling elite's strategy for prolonging their rule, and that too, without facing the people of Pakistan at the hustings. Instead of picking up the pieces to integrate the nation, the electorate bill issue created undesirable cleavages between the two wings of the country. Ironically, unlike the politics of the Pakistan movement, this time it was the majority which entertained fears of being overwhelmed by the minority: the old persecution complex had again taken hold of the Muslim multitude.

II

FEDERALISM AND CONSTITUTIONALISM: THE UNANSWERED CHALLENGE

The unanswered challenge can never be disposed of, and is bound to present itself again and again until it either receives some tardy and imperfect response or else brings about the destruction of society which has shown itself inveterately incapable of responding to it effectively.

Arnold J. Toynbee

Having dealt with the painful drama of Constitution formulations (1947-56) and the step-motherly treatment to the federal principle, it seems appropriate to evaluate the practice of provincial autonomy between the years 1947-58. Such a survey may cause extreme embarrassment to the souls of some of the Federation's founding fathers. Yet their political bickering and abject intrigues in the dismissing of federal ministries and routing of the provincial governments (via the notorious clauses of the Act of 1935) with swift strokes wrecked the very object of the democratic federal state, born through constitutional means.

Apart from the dabbling of the fanatical *ulema* in constitutional politics for ulterior ends, the decade-long unconstitutional and anarchical politics in the theoretically federal set-up of Pakistan centred on denial of provincial autonomy to the federating units, keeping East Pakistan at bay, lest it dominate the centre, and on highly undemocratic personalized politics.

The paranoid majority-minority syndrome, reminiscent of the Congress-League politics in the pre-independence era, and the irresponsible pronouncements to the effect that the autonomists were 'traitors', hardly demonstrated the ruling elite's faith in democracy and federalism.[62] Having openly professed to the Muslim masses and the federating units the vital principles of democracy and federalism, the axiomatically contrary practice charted a disastrous course for the country. The rationale of the analysis in the succeeding pages is to demonstrate the glaring discrepancy between the profession and practice of the ruling elite on two vital constitutional principles, namely, constitutionalism and federalism.

The first part of this chapter demonstrated that the superficial, evasive, and meaningless efforts of the ruling elite in the sphere of constitution-making had culminated in the compromise Constitution of 1956. This was essentially a centrist document which provided the ruling elite at the Centre with a wide range of discretionary powers to damage the federal system itself. We have also seen that, in the presence of representative assemblies, the governments of the day used to promulgate anti-democracy and anti-federal ordinances, aimed at crushing political dissidents and the provinces. Indeed, the whole history of constitution-making in Pakistan was a severe blow to the letter and spirit of constitutionalism and federalism, the two essentials for maintaining a viable federation.

For substantiation of the foregoing assertion, suffice it to say that for nineteen months from its first session, the CAP transacted no constitutional work of significance, except fixing of salaries and allowances for its members, ministers, and the Governor-General.[63] To its own discredit, the CAP passed the notorious Bill known as the Public and Representative Offices Disqualification Act, 1949, excessively utilized by the Centre for sheer victimization of political dissidents and autonomists. Ironically, for the first eleven years of the country's history, the Assembly was in session for 338 days only (or for an annual 30 days), every session lasting only a few hours.[64] While the legislature in these years enacted not more than 160 laws, the Head of State promulgated (or manufactured) 376 laws and ordinances.[65]

The will of the Federal Government was readily transmitted to the CAP because most of its members were ministers, chief ministers, and governors of the provinces. For filling vacant seats, the CAP adopted the undemocratic method of co-option rather than popular will. Put succinctly, the track record of the CAP amply demonstrates how the federal principle could not acquire strong roots in a sordid, squabbling political milieu where to grab power, centralize it, and then allow the anarchical situation to drift for years had become the usual practice. To expect a national Constitution to be drawn up on federal lines from such an Assembly was unrealistic.

THE NORTH-WEST FRONTIER PROVINCE

For seven years after the emergence of Pakistan, the Muslim League ruled both at the Centre and in the provinces. Barring the NWFP, where a Congress Ministry was in power, the Muslim League was successful in forming governments in all the provinces. Despite the referendum of 1947, overwhelmingly resulting in favour of Pakistan, the Congress Ministry headed by Dr Khan Sahib continued to retain a parliamentary majority in the NWFP provincial legislature. After the 1946 elections, the League had reportedly made pleas to the British Government to dismiss it. But the latter refrained from taking such a distasteful action on the pretext of 'constitutional impropriety'.[66]

Having failed to tilt the referendum in favour of India, the Congress Ministry in the NWFP 'facilitated' its own demise by refusing to take oath of allegiance to the new state and deliberately declining to attend the hoisting ceremony of the Pakistani flag.[67] Notwithstanding its umbilical links with the Indian National Congress, it must have dawned on the Khan's ministry that the people of the NWFP, whom it represented, had expressed their popular free will (via the recently held referendum) to join Pakistan. Thus, it was incumbent on it to swear the oath of allegiance to the new state and to respect its flag. Such recalcitrancy infuriated public opinion, obliging the Governor-General to order the ministry's dismissal under sub-section 5 of Section 51 of the Government of India Act, 1935, within a few days of the emergence of the new state.

Having dismissed Khan Sahib's ministry, the following constitutional and democratic options were available to the Centre:

- Impose Governor's rule in the province.

- Order fresh elections to elect new members to the Provincial Legislature.

- Form a new ministry which enjoyed the confidence of the House.

Knowing full well the democratic and constitutional limitations, the Centre imposed Khan Abdul Qayyum Khan, who did not enjoy a majority in the Legislature, as the new Chief Minister. Though leading a minority, Qayyum managed to retain power (with the connivance of Liaquat Ali Khan) by the novel and undemocratic device of restraining the Assembly from meeting till March 1948.[68] After that, by persuasion and cajolement, he was able to win over seven members of the Congress and thus constitutionally consolidated his precarious position.

However, had the Muslim League ministry been formed through obtaining a new mandate from the electorate in the province or even on the strength of the majority *ab initio*, it would have established a better democratic precedent. It was not on account of dismissing Khan Sahib's ministry that the Centre could be censured for acting in an anti-democratic and anti-federalist way, but rather for installing Qayyum's ministry, which initially represented a minority in the House. Secondly, in the whole unpleasant episode, it was the people of the province who were betrayed; they had categorically rejected Khan Sahib's ministry's campaign in the referendum to join India, thereby renouncing its anti-Pakistan programme. Indeed, this was the people's 'no confidence' vote in the Congress ministry. The natural outcome of such an historic decision was fresh elections. Yet, far from ascertaining their new electoral mandate, the people of the NWFP were made to live with a ministry which did not enjoy the confidence of the redundant House, albeit for a short time. The onus of perpetrating such an unconstitutional, undemocratic, and unjust precedent lay with the Centre.

Qayyum Khan, known for his highhandedness in dealing with provincial opponents, was allowed to employ the full weight of government and party machinery to rig the 1951 provincial elections and continued to preserve himself in power with the blessings of the Centre.[69] The unpalatable and undemocratic practice of the Centre's interference in the provincial domain assumed new heights in April 1953. On the Governor-General's directive, Qayyum Khan was elevated to the post of minister in the federal government, and the vacant post of chief ministership was filled by Sardar Abdul Rashid, the Provincial Inspector General of Police. Rashid, the nominee of Qayyum Khan, was ordered by the Centre to resign on telephone and assume the highest political office in the province.[70]

SINDH

The arrival of refugees in Sindh and the induction of non-Sindhi officials in the provincial administration gave birth to the unending saga of Sindhi-non-Sindhi conflict in the province. Besides the Sindhi landed aristocracy's resentment over the refugee phenomenon, the declaring of Karachi as the Federal Capital was also taken as an encroachment on provincial rights. The provincial ministry led by Muhammad Ayub Khuhro unanimously passed a resolution against the federal government's order making Karachi a federally-administered territory. Amidst brewing ethnic politics and the Khuhro-led ministry's staunch opposition to the Centre's decision on Karachi's federal status, the Governor-General ordered the Governor to dismiss the Khuhro ministry on 26 April 1948, on charges of corruption, maladministration, and misconduct. On 3 May 1948, a new ministry was installed under Pir Ilahi Bukhsh who, after a year in office, was found guilty of corrupt practices. Thus, he was disqualified from even being a voter in the Sindh Assembly for the next six years.[71]

The successive dismissals of provincial governments in Sindh mainly centred on the protests the local politicians would mount against the Centre's capricious attitude on the issues of the federal capital, refugees from India, or integration of provinces and princely states into One Unit. However, the Centre continued to advance lame excuses of maladaminstration or corruption charges against the ministries. For instance, the Centre dismissed the ministry of Abdus Sattar Pirzada in Sindh on the ground of maladministration, but Pirzada would always assert that the action was taken against him because of his opposition to One Unit.[72] His place was taken by M.A. Khuhro who had earlier been dismissed by no less a person than Governor-General Jinnah himself. While One Unit was a popular phrase among the Punjabi politicians, it always annoyed the leaders in Sindh, who saw it as a conspiracy against their provincial rights. The background to the dismissal of a majority of provincial administrations in the 1950s, whether in Sindh or elsewhere, was the opposition to the scheme of One Unit.[73]

PUNJAB

The feudalistic factional strife in the Punjab had begun during Governor-General Jinnah's life, and it assumed acrimonious dimensions in the Nazimuddin-Liaquat era. The Daultana-Mamdot tussle for political ascendancy in the provincial Legislative Assembly had obliged Premier Liaquat Ali Khan to openly favour the former. On Daultana's persuasion, the Centre utilized the full force of Section 92-A of the Provisional Constitution in dissolving the Mamdot Ministry and the Legislative Assembly on 25 January 1949. The unpleasant mode of dismissing the Mamdot ministry had detrimental undemocratic dimensions, i.e., the central government had dissolved a provincial government which enjoyed a clear majority and the confidence of the House.[74] Secondly, this precedent underlined the role of personalities, not principles, for the ruling party, (both at the Centre and in the provinces). Party and democratic principles began to be sacrificed, giving birth to an unending phenomenon of personality cult in the national polity.[75] Not only was the dismissal of the Punjab ministry arbitrary, the newly appointed Governor of the province, Sardar Abdur Rab Nishtar, overstepped 'his constitutional position by presiding over the Muslim League party meetings and identifying himself with the party in numerous ways'.[76]

In the 1950s, the destiny of the provinces and the popular ministries throughout the country was mortgaged to the mighty figure of the Governor-General and, later on, the President. The Centre and its administration would erect all kinds of safeguards merely for perpetuation of its dictatorial writ throughout the country. The Punjab, like other federating units, witnessed ministerial reshuffles and that too at the whim of the Centre. Mian Daultana and later Firoz Khan Noon and their ministries fell victim to the personalized politics of the politicians ruling the Centre.[77]

EAST BENGAL

The declaration of Urdu as the only state language by Governor-General Jinnah was taken as denying to East Bengal (a monolithic linguistic unit where the majority of the federation's population lived) a sense of linguistic and cultural identification. The frustration was heightened when the policy-makers in Karachi constantly rejected the pleas for induction of Bengali as a state language on the flimsy pretext of being it 'permeated with Hindu imagery'.[78] Such irresponsible, unpatriotic, and anti-federal behaviour injured the majority's cultural feelings.

By 1950, the vehement demands for the provincial autonomy of East Pakistan had assumed concrete dimensions. Because of the federal government's excessive and blatant interference in provincial administration, the idea of provincial autonomy (which the federating units had hoped for) had been negated so far. Besides the making of Bengali a state language, the East Pakistan-based political parties demanded equal shares in the revenues and budget of the Centre. The economic and financial policies of the Centre were depicted as deliberately causing disparity in the eastern wing. As is evident from the preceding part of this chapter, throughout the 1950s the Bengali politicians continued to press ahead for accommodation of their political voice on the basis of their population as well as according to their distinct province for its special status in the federal set-up.

By the time the 1954 elections took place in East Pakistan, the Bengali masses had hardened their perceptions about the Centre's discriminatory attitude and dominating tendencies on the following issues:

- The central government had neglected the socio-economic needs of the province.

- Bengali, though the *lingua franca* of the majority, was not made the state language.

- Punjab-based bureaucrats, with their jaundiced views, were completely ignorant of and unsympathetic to the aspirations of the people, and above all, were foisted from above on the province. When the Bengalis saw that their civil-military representation at the Centre was lower than that of West Pakistan, they propounded maximum autonomy as the only realistic alternative to such an offending scenario.

- The unpopular governments led by the Muslim League were constantly forced upon the people by arbitrary extensions at the Centre.

The Muslim League and its leadership had portrayed the United Front as traitors, secessionists, communists, pro-India, and anti-Islam.

Despite such abusive propaganda, the resounding electoral victory of the Front (as it secured 309 seats as compared to the League's 10) was a stark indicator of the Bengali public opinion. It was a no-confidence vote against the unpopular government, undemocratic and anti-federalist policies pursued by the Muslim League both at the Centre and in the provinces. The overwhelming electoral triumph of the United Front demanded a radical restructuring of the constitutional arrangement, in which all the federating units in general and the eastern wing in particular would enjoy maximum provincial autonomy.

After the complete electoral rout of the League in the 1954 elections, A. K. Fazlul Haq (the Lion of Bengal) took over the Chief Ministership of East Pakistan. For the first seven years of the country's independence, the United Front had formed a non-League Ministry. When Haq assumed his responsibilities, the excessive labour unrest and riots had given birth to a law and order situation in his province. Within a few weeks of assuming power, Haq visited Calcutta, where he reportedly made pleas for co-operation with West Bengal and ridiculed the partition of the subcontinent.[79] On his return to Dhaka, Haq contradicted such statements, yet his political opponents continued to paint him as an anti-state politician. While Premier Bogra openly called him a 'self-professed traitor' to his country and province, Haq's political opponents and the media urged the Centre 'to do its duty no matter who or what seeks to thwart it'.[80]

On 30 May 1954, after two months in office, Haq's ministry was dismissed by the Centre by invoking Section 92-A of the Act of 1935. Iskandar Mirza (then Federal Defence Secretary) was appointed the Governor of East Pakistan, and every trick was used to dismember the United Front. Having been directly ruled by the Centre since A. K. Fazlul Haq's Ministry was dismissed in May 1954, Governor's rule over East Pakistan was lifted by Prime Minister Bogra on 2 June 1955, in a grotesque manner.

Bogra, who had openly charged Haq with treachery to his country, found himself in a very precarious political situtation. The Muslim League, of which he had been foisted as chief by the intrigues of Governor-General Ghulam Muhammad, had lost the election to the United Front. Constitutionally, he could remain in office if he was elected to the new CAP; for this it was necessary for Bogra to be indirectly elected by the Legislative Assembly of his home province, i.e., East Pakistan. For such an objective, he had no option except to look to the goodwill and support of the non-League members in the

East Pakistan Assembly. Ignoring all political niceties, democratic norms, and personal integrity, Bogra unhesitatingly 'put power back into the hands of the "traitor" for whose overthrow he had fervently solicited the nation's support about a year back'.[81] A popular ministry headed by Abu Husain Sarkar (a nominee of Haq) was installed, with the active connivance of Haq and Bogra—the worst kind of horse-trading for political expediencies.

If, for election to the second CAP, Bogra had installed Haq's nominee as the Chief Minister, Chaudhry Muhammad Ali (the successor to Bogra) transgressed political and federal norms a step further. He allowed Sarkar's ministry to remain in office without facing the Provincial Assembly for a whole year. Moreover, Prime Minister Chaudhry appointed Haq the Governor of East Pakistan (a step which even Bogra had not dared to take), for the purely political objective of prolonging Sarkar's ministry. Thus, the pursuit of power, besides running the government in a unitary style, seemed the ultimate objective of the executive and 'no means were too mean to achieve it'.[82]

By the mid-1950s, the Bengali politicians were openly complaining about the neglect of their province and of wholesale political exploitation by the ruling elite based in West Pakistan. By that time, Bengali public perceptions that the Centre 'was fundamentally hostile to all things Bengali' had assumed concrete shape.[83] In the prevailing circumstances, 'for many Bengalis the real issue was not to secure provincial autonomy, important though that might be, but to obtain fair recognition, in theory and practice, of the claim of the east wing to equality with the west'.[84] In the perspective of Keith Callard, the following factors added to their 'despairing of Bengali equality on a national' basis, so that 'they turned increasingly to proposals for home rule' for East Bengal.[85]

> Whether through Bengali ineffectiveness or the Machiavellian wiles of their opponents, Bengali influence had never been decisive. Nazimuddin had been Governor-General, but the real power lay with Liaquat Ali, Nazimuddin became Prime Minister, but lacked force of will, and was ultimately dismissed by the [Punjabi] Governor-General. Muhammad Ali [Bogra] was brought in as Prime Minister but, though a Bengali, he remained the captive of the West Pakistan group that provided the main strength of his government. The Bengali

members attempted to use their majority to diminish the powers of the Governor-General, but as a result they found themselves out of their own jobs. The electorate of East Bengal had repudiated the Muslim League, but the outcome was rule for more than a year by West Pakistan bureaucrats. The armed forces were West Pakistani, the national civil service was predominantly West Pakistani, and trade and industry were largely in the hands of non-Bengalis ...

In the image of the foregoing summary of Bengali grievances and feelings of neglect, the bitterness of the Bengali perspective was crystallized in a speech by Ataur Rahman Khan, an opposition Bengali member in the second CAP:

Sir, I actually started yesterday and said that the attitude of the Muslim League coterie here was of contempt towards East Bengal, towards its culture, its language, its literature and everything concerning East Bengal.... In fact Sir, I tell you that far from considering East Bengal as an equal partner, the leaders of the Muslim League thought that we were a subject race and they belonged to the race of conquerers.[86]

III

DEFIANCE OF CONSTITUTIONALISM AND FEDERALISM

Unwilling to accept constraints on their authority, the ruling elite indulged in excessive political manipulations to make the Centre all-powerful, reducing the federating units to mere extensions rather than autonomous and co-ordinative partners. The intriguing policy of strident centralism never allowed democracy and federalism to take root in the country. Increasingly aware of their complete rout at the hustings, the ruling elite, rather than facing the electorate, opted for prolongation of constitution-making via the CAP, the latter perpetuating itself to maintain unrepresentative anarchy.

The death of Jinnah in September 1948 'removed from the scene the one man who would have stiffened the resolve and discipline of the Assembly; it is hard to believe that he would have tolerated a situation in which years went by without the provision of a Constitution'.[87] Khawaja Nazimuddin, as successor to Jinnah, acted merely as Head of State. The full weight of political and constitutional power was monopolized by Liaquat Ali Khan, the Prime Minister. Effective in decision-making and policy-execution, Liaquat had to work in an uncomfortable milieu of regional, religious, and parochial rivalries. In the sphere of constitution-making, his 'outstanding' achievement was the Objectives Resolution.

Premier Liaquat Ali Khan's track record on the vital issue of provincial autonomy and federalism was very grim. He embraced M. A. Khuhro, whose Ministry was dismissed by no less a person than Jinnah, and quashed corruption charges levelled against him under PRODA on technical grounds. Much to the chagrin of the provincial Legislature, Premier Khan dismissed the Mamdot ministry in Punjab, though the latter commanded the confidence of the Assembly. Besides his open campaigning for Daultana in the Punjab provincial elections in 1951, he sustained the minority ministry of Qayyum Khan in the NWFP. While tolerating the ineffective provincial ministries like that of Nurul Amin in the East Bengal, the rationale of Premier Khan's whole exercise was to prop himself up and enlarge his powers at the Centre.

After his gruesome assasination on 16 October 1951, Premier Khan (the *Quaid-i-Millat*) was succeeded by Khawaja Nazimuddin, who stepped down from the office of Governor-General to become the second Prime Minister of the country. The putatively pious Nazimuddin could not effectively maintain his supremacy over the executive. His insistence on Urdu as the only state language of Pakistan generated the 1952 language riots in East Pakistan. His politico-constitutional overtures to the agitating *ulema* encouraged them to indulge in the 1953 Ahmadiya riots in the Punjab. Amidst a mess of political problems of Nazimuddin's own making, the personal 'virtues which had eminently qualified him for the office of the Governor-General, could not sustain him in the office of Prime Minister against more assertive and capricious claimants to power'.[88] In April 1953, the Nazimuddin ministry, which had just passed the national budget, was dismissed by the Governor-General, who neither believed in democracy nor in fair and equitable treatment for East Bengal, and who, above all, considered himself the sole interpreter of popular will.

The illegal and unconstitutional dismissal of the Nazimuddin ministry was 'neither publicly debated nor judicially determined.'[89] Besides these two aspects, the remedy for such an irresponsible act actually lay in political means. The Constituent Assembly, as the sovereign body (being the constituent and the legislative forum), was the right place to determine an issue of such awesome national significance. But to the utter chagrin of the people of Pakistan, on whose behalf it was functioning, the CAP never expressed its disapproval of the illegal act, either by passing a vote or resolution of censure of the Governor-General or reaffirming its confidence in Premier Khawaja Nazimuddin.

Far from registering its protest in any form or on any forum, it accepted the new Prime Minister, ambassador Muhammad Ali, who was neither a member of the CAP nor head of the ruling party, the Muslim League. This demonstrated its unashamed acquiescence in the Governor-General's illegal and discretionary act. This also set the undemocratic precedent of accepting a person as the Prime Minister of the country who was not even a member of the Assembly. The CAP's treacherous silence in conceding its afore-mentioned prerogatives was indeed an act of placing its own fate in the hands of an irresponsible and reckless Governor-General who, firstly, had demolished (by dismissing Nazimuddin's ministry) the tradition of the Governor-General's impartiality, and secondly, was soon to set his heavy hands on the CAP itself.

If the CAP remained silent on an unconstitutional change, loaded with distasteful r epercussions, Khawaja Nazimuddin equally committed a political blunder by opting for tranquillity instead of challenging his dismissal in the higher courts, because Ghulam Muhammad's drastic and unconstitutional action was directed as much against the CAP as against the Nazimuddin ministry. In the analysis of Keith Callard, in those extraordinary circumstances:

> The price of the Governor-General's *coup* was high. Three major conventions of the cabinet government had been destroyed or gravely weakened. First, the tradition of the impartiality of the Governor-General had been demolished. Second, the convention of cabinet and party solidarity had been disregarded. Third, the role of the Legislature as the maker and sustainer of governments had been impugned.[90]

THE MOHAFIZ-I-MILLAT

After the *Quaid-i-Azam* and the *Quaid-i-Millat*, Governor-General
Ghulam Muhammad had arrogated to himself the high-sounding
title of *Mohafiz-i-Millat* (guardian of nation), though he always acted
contrary to what his self-acquired title suggested. In the words of
Air Chief Marshal (Retired) Asghar Khan, 'half-dumb, half-
paralysed', and at least partially insane, Ghulam Muhammad was
successful in exploiting the assassination of Liaquat Ali Khan on
16 October 1951. What an intriguing political transformation the
assassin's bullet had wrought! It can best be understood in the words
of an Indian political scientist, M. S. Venkataramani, in the following:

> Within hours after Liaquat Ali's assassination, Pakistan
> had a new Prime Minister, Khawaja Nazimuddin! The
> Governor-General stepped down—was made to step
> down—to the office of Prime Minister. To the position
> vacated by the pliable Nazimuddin ascended the Minister
> of Finance, Ghulam Muhammad. In a remarkably short
> time it became common knowledge in Pakistan that the
> real centre of power and authority in the new Govern-
> ment was Governor-General Ghulam Muhammad. It was
> a fantastic rise for a man who, but a few years earlier, had
> been a mere officer in the Indian Audit and Accounts
> Service, serving his British masters with diligence and
> skill. A bureaucratic dark horse had outwitted the feuding
> and confused political war horses of Pakistan. The *munim*
> who rose to be a *vazir* had turned himself into a sultan![91]

Having consolidated his supreme position (along with his coadjutor, Iskandar Mirza) in the otherwise parliamentary system of
Pakistan, the Governor-General often acted against constitutional
propriety. The inexplicable suddenness with which he dismissed the
Nazimuddin ministry and the politicians' and the CAP's treacherous
silence in readily acquiescing in such a dangerous precedent, were the
beginning of a continuing attack on democracy and federalism.

Summoning of a serving ambassador, Muhammad Ali Bogra (not
even a member of the CAP) to be the Prime Minister was the height
of interference in the democratic process. Ironically, all the cabinet
ministers and their portfolios were selected by the Governor-General

himself.[92] The dissolution of the CAP was the culmination of the undemocratic and unconstitutional arbitrary actions taken by Governor-General Ghulam Muhammad. The legality of dissolving the Assembly was open to question and such an irresponsible action plunged the state into a terrible constitutional crisis. From the very outset, 'the entire foundation of the legal order in Pakistan was called into question and the situation was only resolved by the use, for the first time, but not the last time, of the doctrine of "state necessity" by the Federal Court'.[93]

Having been barred by the Federal Court from bestowing a Constitution on his nation through a Constitution Convention, Ghulam Muhammad asked Bogra to form a new ministry which was responsible to and removable by the Governor-General—or the Governor-General's Council.[94] Being the titular head of government, Bogra resigned (or was made to resign) from the premiership, returned to Washington (the place from where he was 'made' the Prime Minister of Pakistan) to assume his ambassadorial duties. Having suffered a series of severe heart attacks, Ghulam Muhammad had to vacate his high office for Iskandar Mirza on 6 October 1955 (Mirza had already assumed office as acting Governor-General on August 7). The fallen *Mohafiz-i-Millat* gave the following 'farewell message to the nation':

> As I bid you a sincere and heart-felt good-bye, I feel fortified by the belief that when, on the day of final reckoning, I appear before the Throne of Divine Providence, I shall be able to say with humility that I tried to serve my country honestly and to the last limit of human energy.[95]

ISKANDAR MIRZA

With the end of Ghulam Muhammad's unpalatable 'services' to the nation began the sordid era of his former adjutant, Major-General Iskandar Mirza. To the discredit of the whole nation, the dismissal of Nazimuddin's ministry, the foisting of Bogra, the maltreatment meted out to the autonomists in general and Haq's ministry in particular, the dissolution of the CAP, and strident centralization were the outstanding 'services' of Ghulam Muhammad. Mirza surpassed him in every respect.

Mirza had brought to his job of Pakistan's third Governor-General 'the full bag of tricks he had learnt as a British Political Agent on the North-West Frontier.'[96] After assuming the presidentship under the 1956 Constitution, 'his style of political agentry and viceroyalty' meant manipulation, coercion, and boudoir intrigues to rout and create ministries. By changing the federal and provincial ministries in quick succession, and that too in the right royal fashion of Machiavellianism, the sole aim was to try every politician of some public siginificance, get them labelled as ineffective, and then kick them out as 'incorrigible rogues'. The single objective was to make the people believe that the God-gifted President was a 'good guy'.[97]

Iskandar Mirza had, via the 1956 Constitution, coined for himself an official designation, viz., President of the Islamic Republic of Pakistan, a title that had not been accorded to the *Quaid-i-Azam*, the *Quaid-i-Millat*, or even to the so-called *Mohafiz-e-Millat*. Expert as he was in the 'intrigue-ridden game of formation and dismissal of ministries', Mirza, alongwith General Ayub Khan, 'manipulated party positions, tried every permutation and combination to create situations under which as many as four Ministries fell like pins, the last short-lived one being the one headed by I. I. Chundrigar.'[98] It lasted for only 59 days. General Ayub Khan, as a vital pillar of the unholy trinity (i.e., Ghulam Muhammad, Mirza, and Ayub) had shared power. Yet, later on, while absolving himself completely from the abject part he played in the sordid political drama of palace intrigues, Ayub characterized the era of Iskandar Mirza thus:

> Shrewd as he was, he could see how the Constitution could be used to promote political intrigues and bargaining. No one knew any longer who belonged to which political party; it was all a question of swapping labels: a Muslim Leaguer today, a Republican tomorrow; and yesterday's 'traitors' were tomorrow's Chief Ministers, indistinguishable as Tweedledum and Tweedledee.[99]

On Bogra's exit (11 August 1955), Chaudhry Muhammad Ali was raised to the premiership by Iskandar Mirza. Heading the Muslim League-United Front coalition ministry, he was successful in getting the scheme of One Unit passed by the CAP. Attaching overriding significance to the framing of a Constitution, he succeeded in hammering out (though via compromise) the 1956 Constitution. For such an avowed objective, the Prime Minister had to embrace the publicly declared 'traitors' i.e., Fazlul Haq as Governor of East Pakistan and Dr Khan Sahib (Mirza's personal friend and nominee) to head the League Ministry in the newly created province of West Pakistan.

While foisting Dr Khan Sahib (a non-Leaguer) as the Chief Minister on West Pakistan, Mirza openly eulogized his invaluable leadership qualities and services for the solidarity of West Pakistan.[100] However, knowing the anti-Pakistan track record of Dr Khan Sahib and his Congress party, his nomination as the Chief Minister was widely resented within the ranks of the public and the Muslim League. When opposition to Mirza's nominee grew stronger, he was quick to denounce such 'elements' as anti-state and advised them 'to quit Pakistan'.[101]

The continuation of Dr Khan Sahib in power could rightly be attributed to active connivance between the Prime Minister and the Governor-General. Out of the 310 Provincial Assembly members, 245 belonged to the League, which had not only passed a resolution against Dr Khan Sahib's nomination but had selected Sardar Bahadur Khan as its parliamentary leader. Obviously displeased over such an unpleasant reaction, Dr Khan asserted his 'constitutional prerogative' to remain in office till ousted by a no-confidence motion.[102] Besides such a grotesque assertion, he began to hurl threats by branding the said Assembly as being of an 'unrepresentative character' and declared his 'right to seek its dissolution and order its general election in case it did not repose confidence in him.'[103] Having adopted such an unprincipled and unconstitutional stand, the Provincial Governor continued to delay the summoning of the Assembly, almost certainly to allow time to the Centre and Dr Khan Sahib to translate their parliamentary minority into a majority.

After Chaudhry Muhammad Ali's 13 months stint (i.e., August 1955-September 1956) as Prime Minister, came the government of Huseyn Shaheed Suhrawardy. Gifted with exceptional parliamentary talent, a brilliant legal mind, oratorical skills, and political dynamism, H. S. Suhrawardy belonged to the category of those politicians who had the requisite courage and will to face the masses directly. However, his nomination by the President, and his changing parties in the past definitely placed him in the class of power-seekers who were ready to sacrifice their 'commitments' (i.e., those of the party and the national political system).

Having initiated a vigorous political campaign to incite popular sentiments, Suhrawardy (as a member of the CAP) had refused to sign the 1956 Constitution.[104] Yet six months later, he was sworn in by President Mirza, to preserve and defend the same document, as the Prime Minister of Pakistan. Working under the overlordship of Iskandar Mirza, Suhrawardy had to defend policies and perspectives which he had detested in the past. Like his predecessor, Suhrawardy, after remaining in office for about thirteen months (September 1956-October 1957), was made to resign. He was replaced by I. I. Chundrigar, a leader of the opposition in the National Assembly. Remaining in office for 59 days, Chundrigar was replaced by Malik Firoz Khan Noon, the last pawn on Mirza's chess board.

THE NETWORK

Under the practice and tradition of the parliamentary system of government, the Governor was supposed to be a mere figurehead. However, during the period under review in this chapter, the Governor, being the nominee and representative of the Centre, was vested with substantial discretionary powers which allowed him to indulge in political activities.

The Governors were instrumental in the making and unmaking of ministries and would often influence the Chief Ministers to induct or drop particular individuals to and from their cabinets. Such an abominable practice was prevalent in all the federating units. For instance, in the analysis of Rounaq Jahan, the five Governors of East Pakistan who succeeded the first English Governor there, remained continuously active in provincial and national politics.[105] They are: Firoz Khan Noon, who after his East Pakistan governorship (1950-3) was elevated to the position of Chief Minister of the Punjab (1953-5) and Prime Minister (1958); Chaudhry Khaliquzzaman, who was Governor of East Pakistan (1953-4), later became President of the Muslim League; Major-General Iskandar Mirza, (who remained Governor after the suspension of the Haq ministry, till 1955), first became defence and interior secretary in the Federal Government, and later the Govenor-General and the President of the country; A. K. Fazlul Haq, whose ministry was dismissed on anti-state charges, remained unofficial head of his party even during his governorship of East Pakistan.

By the time the One Unit system was imposed on the reluctant units in West Pakistan, the abrupt manner of installing and disposing of governments (both central and provincial) had become a notorious feature in Pakistani politics. Using the analogy of Khan Abdul Qayyum Khan, the provincial ministries were 'dismissed with even less formality than in dismissing "chaprasies" (i.e., peons)'. The new ministries were 'nominated in the same manner Mughal emperors used to appoint their "subedars" (i.e., governors) in the provinces'.[106] As the prelude to the formation of One Unit, the foregoing saga manifested itself in an abrupt fashion. In November 1954, the Bahawalpur Assembly was dissolved and Hasan Mahmud's ministry dismissed, and the state's neighbouring province, Sindh, met the same fate, where Pirzada Abdus Sattar's ministry was routed. Both ministries were reluctant to integrate their units into One Unit. The same treatment was meted out to the Noon ministry in the Punjab in May 1955, and two months later to the Rashid ministry in the NWFP.

The ruling elite, who dominated the new state structure, mostly hailed from regions that were no longer part of Pakistan, and had lost their political and electoral constituencies in the new set-up.[107] Despite the oligarchic nature and function of this elite in the new state:

> They were reluctant either to broaden their ranks by including the regional leaders from within Pakistan or to risk an election, for fear of losing power. As the 'national' political elite continued to avoid elections, their mandate grew stale and the ranks of the opposition (mainly regional leaders) swelled. In their bid to stay in power, the 'national' political elite found an ally in the civil-military bureaucracy, whom they often used (or were used by) for political purposes'.[108]

In every way, Pakistan *ab initio* operated as an 'administrative state' because the all-pervasive and 'be-all and end-all' type of bureaucracy became an active instrument in halting the pragmatic advance towards a federal polity. Trained in the colonial pattern of controlling and ruling the subject people, the bureaucracy did not for a moment give up its inclination for dominating the government of the new state.[109] Habitually prone to the unitary rather than the federal style of government, the bureaucracy never allowed the weak political leadership to promote and sustain provincial autonomy or to decentralize local administration. Being the most effective instrument of centralization, the Civil Service of Pakistan 'manned most of the key decision-making posts in both the centre and the provinces'.[110] Working under the dominating shadows of a constitutionally strong governor (a nominee and representative of the Centre), the provincial political leadership felt handicapped in the presence of the CSP network intricately connected with the Centre.

Having engaged themselves in the art of arbitrarily dismissing majorities and installing minorities (both at the Centre and the provinces), the men who ruled the federation had relegated the essential norms of constitutionalism and federalism to secondary considerations. Besides the *ulema*'s religious squabblings, Pakistan's constitutional flux mainly centred on the quantum of provincial autonomy, east-west representation in the federal structure, and, finally, the ruling elite's cherished pretensions to remain perpetually in power.

The Bengali politicians continued to complain about the conspiratory bids of the Centre and the civil-military system (based in the Punjab) to keep their distant majority province politically impotent and socio-economically backward. Given the fissiparous tendencies in East Pakistan, the foisting of unrepresentative figures, and the 'steamroller' of One Unit in West Pakistan had hastened the inimical trends towards provincialization of politics in the professed federal set-up of the country.

With the ascent to the high office of Head of State of Ghulam Muhammad and then Major-General Iskandar Mirza, the excessive bureaucratization of the constitutional and political milieu of the country began. With the politicians fighting like Kilkenny cats, both Ghulam Muhammad and Mirza set aside constitutional conventions and ruled by ordinances. Excessive centralization in the otherwise federal polity of Pakistan was their ambition, and outfoxing the feuding politicians became their cherished creed. The prospect of general elections was like a death-knell to their ignominious position. Both were masters in guillotining popular ministries and patronizing the ever-tightening grip of the bureaucracy, a notorious residue of colonial rule. Besides institutionalizing the growing ascendancy of the civil-military role in national affairs, both Ghulam Muhammad and Mirza marred the parliamentary and federal form of the political system in the country. While weakening federalism, the trinity (i.e., Ghulam Muhammad, Mirza, and Ayub) systematically shaped centre-province relations on a monolithic pattern, like the CMLA dictating to the DMLAs during martial law rule.

Amidst such an abominable logrolling and wire-pulling political milieu, the gathering storm in the shape of constitutional flux, chronic political violence, frenzied rioting, assaults on the Assembly Speakers, the ruling elite's undemocratic tactics to avoid general elections, and their utter disregard for constitutional and federal norms took its toll in the form of the imposition of authoritarian military rule. However, prior to moving on to the next chapter, it seems worthwhile to recount the glaring abberations concerning constitutionalism and federalism, as discussed in the preceding pages.

Vital Signposts

- Except for Liaquat Ali Khan, no Prime Minister sought (or was asked to seek) a vote of confidence from the Federal Legislature.

- Some of the Prime Ministers/Chief Ministers who were imposed on the centre/provinces (via palace intrigues) were initially not even members of the Assemblies. Sardar Abdur Rashid (serving Inspector-General of Police) and Muhammad Ali Bogra (serving ambassador) were made chief minister of the NWFP and Prime Minister of Pakistan respectively, vivid examples of such arbitrariness.

- During the first eleven years of the country's independence, no government (either at the federal or provincial level) was changed through a no-confidence motion in the legislature. Barring Liaquat Ali Khan's assassination, the governments were either dismissed or had to resign under pressure.

- The singular case of Nazimuddin apart, no Governor-General/President in the first eleven years of Pakistan's parliamentary history acted merely as the Head of State.

- Men publicly condemned and officially declared as 'traitors' to the state were inducted into responsible posts in the government. Dr Khan Sahib from the NWFP and A. K. Fazlul Haq from East Pakistan are examples.

- During the same period, the federal governments persuaded the provincial governments not to bolster federalism or uphold any democratic norm but to have provincial heads amenable to their pressures.

- During the years 1948-58, the working of the federal principle in the Pakistani polity could be generalized on a singular pattern: the CMLA (Chief Martial Law Administrator) dictating orders to the DMLAs (Deputy Martial Law Administrators) in the provincial capitals, and so on.

- During the whole period under review in the preceding pages, neither the CAP nor the National Assembly had a second chamber, thus depriving the federating units of equal representation in the upper house of the Parliament.

- Between the years 1948 and 1954, the CAP passed 44 acts, mostly by making amendments in the Act of 1935, with the sole aim of increasing the powers of the Centre.

- The first CAP was primarily a constitution-making body but it acted as a federal legislature too.

- Following the dissolution of the CAP by Governor-General Ghulam Muhammad, Pakistan was governed for about ten months without a federal legislature.

- During the first eleven years of its history, Pakistani cabinets and assemblies were installed and dismissed surreptitiously; the country had seven prime ministers in that interregnum, and that too without a single general election in the country.

- From the time that Ghulam Muhammad became Governor-General, serving and retired bureaucrats tended to dominate the federal polity. It was the height of undemocratic practices when Ayub Khan, serving as the C-in-C, was made the defence minister in the Cabinet.

- The vicious process of deliberately wrecking an all-Pakistan leadership, though perfected in the Ayub era, was initiated by the elevation of Ghulam Muhammad to the office of Governor-General in 1951.

6

AYUB KHAN'S AUTHORITARIANISM: 1958-1969

This chapter is divided into four parts. Part I deals with constitutional developments under the military regime (1958-62). Having contrived a coercive arbitrary governmental apparatus to keep the politicians and their demands for a federal parliamentary system at bay, Ayub Khan continued to remain as the sole source of executive, judicial, and legislative authority in a pyramidic system.

While referring to the principle of federalism in its Preamble, rather than in Article One (like that of the late 1956 Constitution), the 1962 Constitution completely distorted the federal structure of Pakistan. Being exclusively Ayub Khan's brainchild, the 1962 Constitution provided for a vertical power structure, in which state power flowed from the mighty President down to the Basic Democrats, without being shared with horizontal structures.

Part II concentrates on the how and why of the decidedly centripetal scheme in the 1962 Constitution, for the ulterior motives of an individual in authority at the Centre.

Part III analyses the frustrations of the autonomists, particularly the political forces in East Pakistan, which were almost convinced in the Ayub era that they could never get just and fair treatment from the Centre. The major emphasis in this section will be on evaluating the demands for provincial autonomy by the various political parties which found themselves pitted against the ruling elite who clung to the unitary centre and centripetal system of Ayub Khan.

Part IV centres on the Two Economy thesis versus the centralized economic development planning during the Ayub era.

I

ENTER MARTIAL LAW

The general elections under the 1956 Constitution were drawing near. The bright prospects of politicians getting back into power by directly facing the masses at the hustings was nightmarish for both

Iskandar Mirza and General Ayub Khan. Having no respect for the intelligence of the masses, both eulogized 'tight rule' under the 'genius' of planners like themselves and their bureaucratic clique.[1] Although both viewed the politicians as corruptible rogues and disruptive evil forces, Ayub Khan also perceived 'Mirza as a crooked politician incapable of giving Pakistan the kind of leadership that the time called for'.[2]

Besides the politicians, including Iskandar Mirza, Ayub Khan admits 'hating' *(Friends Not Masters)* the Constitution and constitutionalism. Having schemed to betray the people of Pakistan and grab power since 1954, Ayub Khan thought the following would be his best political strategy:

> He would wreck the Constitution by using the Constitution. He would use the legally-elected President, the man who had taken oath on the Koran to protect and defend the Constitution, Iskandar Mirza, to destroy the Constitution—and then he would destroy Iskandar Mirza . . . .[3]

While 'blaming everybody except himself', President Iskander Mirza, on the evening of 7 October 1958, issued a proclamation to the following effect:

- the Constitution of 23 March 1956 was abrogated;

- the National Parliament and Provincial Assemblies were dissolved;

- all the political parties were abolished;

- federal and provincial governments were dismissed forthwith;

- until alternative arrangements were made, Pakistan would come under Martial Law, General Ayub Khan being the Chief Martial Law Administrator, with all the armed forces placed under him.

- The Constitution(abrogated) was seriously threatened, claimed Mirza, 'by the ruthlessness of traitors and political adventurers. The Constitution is so full of dangerous compromises that Pakistan will disintegrate internally if the inherent malaise is not removed . . . my intention [is] to devise a Constitution more suitable to the genius of the

172 The Myth of Constitutionalism

> Muslim people. When it is ready, and at the appropriate
> time, it will be submitted to a referendum';

- finally, in Mirza's 'appraisal', the vast majority of Pakistani
  people 'no longer has any confidence in the present system
  of government'.[4]

Projecting himself as 'Mr Clean', Iskandar Mirza, in his fourteen
hundred word proclamation, pronounced the following harsh judgement on his country's politicians:

> For the last two years, I have been watching with deepest
> anxiety the ruthless struggle for power, the corruption,
> the shameful exploitation of our simple, honest, patriotic
> and industrious masses, the lack of decorum, and the
> prostitution of Islam for political ends . . . These
> despicable political activities have led to a dictatorship of
> the lowest order; adventurers and exploiters have
> flourished to the detriment of the masses . . . . some of our
> politicians have lately been talking of bloody revolution.
> Another type of adventurer among them thinks it fit to
> go to foreign countries and attempt direct alignment with
> them which can only be described as high treason.
> . . . the political adventurers, the smugglers, the black
> marketeers, the hoarders, will be unhappy, and their
> activities will be severely restricted. As for the traitors,
> they better flee the country if they can, while the going is
> good.[5]

Vaguely specifying 'the ultimate aim' of the martial law regime to
'restore democracy', Ayub Khan said in his broadcast on 8 October
1958, 'but when that time will be, events alone will tell'. Allying
himself with President Mirza and his charges against politicians, Ayub
had the following to say about martial law, the 'drastic and extreme
step taken with great reluctance':

> Politicians have started a free-for-all type of fighting in
> which no holds were barred. They have waged a ceaseless
> and bitter war against each other regardless of the ill
> effects on the country, just to whet their appetites and
> satisfy their base motives. There has been no limit to the
> depth of their baseness, chicanery, deceit and degradation.

Having nothing constructive to offer, they use provincial feelings and sectarian, religious, and racial differences to set Pakistani against Pakistani. The country and people could go to the dogs as far as they were concerned.[6]

Dispelling 'doubts' about his motives and personal ambitions for clamping martial law and abrogating the Constitution, Ayub said:

You may not know, but I refused, on several occasions, the late Ghulam Muhammad's offer to take over the country. I did so in the belief that I could serve the cause of Pakistan better from the place where I was, and I also had a faint hope that some politicians would rise to the occasion and lead the country to a better future. Events have failed those hopes . . . .[7]

The 'two-man regime' had not specified any law to govern the country in place of the abrogated Constitution. The first legal dilemma arose just three days after the imposition of martial law, when the Dhaka High Court, claiming lack of jurisdiction, refused to administer the oath of office to the Governor-designate of East Pakistan.[8] To fill this and other innumerable constitutional lacunae that might have confronted 'the revolutionary' regime, the Laws (Continuance in Force) Order, 1958, was promulgated. Consisting of seven short Articles, dubbed 'the shortest Constitution in the world',[9] it provided for running the country as nearly as possible in accordance with the abrogated Constitution and that all courts would continue to function. The Supreme Court and the High Courts would have jurisdiction to issue writs of *habeas corpus*, *mandamus*, prohibition, *quo warranto*, and *certiorari*. No writ could be issued against the Chief Martial Law Administrator or any other person under his authority, and the courts could not question the validity of Martial Law Regulations and the orders of the President.

Legalizing an Illegality

Prior to the imposition of martial law and abrogation of the 1956 Constitution, certain cases were pending in two benches of the High Courts at Peshawar and Lahore. Arising out of the proceedings taken under the Frontier Crimes Regulations (No.III/1901), striking down of this notorious law was prayed for on the plea that it was in contravention of the fundamental rights granted under Article 5 of the 1956 Constitution. In one of these cases, the petition was referred to the Council of Elders (*Jirga*) and was therefore dismissed in 1957, while the rest of the petitioners, including Dosso, were granted the writs prayed for. The government filed an appeal before the Supreme Court of Pakistan against the decision of the High Court. Meanwhile, martial law was proclaimed, the 1956 Constitution abrogated, and the Laws (Continuance in Force) Order, 1958, promulgated.

On 13 October 1958, the Supreme Court of Pakistan, while hearing the above-mentioned appeal, was confronted with three main constitutional intricacies:[10] whether the President's proclamation of 7 October 1958 was rightly promulgated; whether in pursuance of that proclamation, the President had the power and authority to issue the Laws (Continuance in Force) Order, 1958; and whether the writs issued by the High Court in the above-mentioned cases had abated under Clause (7) of Article 2 of the Laws (Continuance in Force) Order, 1958.

As to the first constitutional question, the learned Chief Justice held that 'a victorious revolution and a successful *coup d' etat* is an internationally recognized legal method of changing a Constitution(via Hans Kelsen, *General Theory of Law and State:* 1945) and that, after a change of that character has taken place, the national legal order must for its validity depend upon the new law-creating organ'. It was also held that 'if the territory and the people remain substantially the same, there is, under the modern juristic doctrine, no change in the corpus of international entity of the state, and the Revolutionary Government and the new Constitution are, according to international law, the legitimate Government and the valid Constitution of the state.'

With regard to the second point, it was held that 'where revolution is successful, it satisfies the efficacy and becomes a basic law-creating fact. On that assumption the Laws (Continuance in Force)Order, however transitory or imperfect, was a new legal order and it was in accordance with that order that the validity of the laws and the correctness of the judicial decisions had to be determined.'

On the third question, the learned Chief Justice held that since Article 5 of the late Constitution itself had now disappeared from the new legal order, the Frontier Crimes Regulation(No.III/1901) by reason of Act IV of the Laws (Continuance in Force) Order,1958, was still in force and all proceedings in cases in which the validity of that regulation had been called in question having abated, the conviction recorded and the references made to the Council of Elders were good.

The Court's judgment in the Dosso case had far-reaching implications on the constitutional developments of the country. Unlike the Federal Court's firmness in Usif Patel v. the Crown (binding the Governor General, who had endeavoured to arrogate to himself the role of constitutional dictator, to summon the new Constituent Assembly through elections), the Supreme Court in Dosso's case legalized an avowed illegality by conferring upon the President the role of a constitutional arbitrator. This verdict retroactively deprived the petitioners, including Dosso, of their fundamental rights.

The learned Chief Justice Muhammad Munir's excessive reliance and copious lecturing on Hans Kelsen's scholastic expositions(in which he 'was trying to lay down a pure theory of law as a rule of normative science') invited Chief Justice Hamoodur Rehman's criticism as recorded in the Asma Jilani case:

> The learned Chief Justice [Muhammad Munir] not only misapplied the doctrine of Hans Kelsen, but also fell into error that it was a generally accepted doctrine of modern jurisprudence. Even the disciples of Kelsen have hesitated to go as far as Kelsen had gone ... I am unable to resist the conclusion that [Muhammad Munir C J] erred both in interpreting Kelsen's theory and applying the same to the facts and circumstances of the case before him. The principle enunciated by him is . . . wholly unsustainable, and I am duty-bound to say that it cannot be treated as good law either on the principle of *stare decisis* or even otherwise.[11]

It is also said that by his wholesale reference to the Kelsen's theory, the Chief Justice 'deliberately tried to evade legalistic discussion on the political situation prevalent at that critical juncture in the country'.[12] The 'very exclusiveness and lack of balance in the Court's use of Kelsen's book suggest that it resorted to a ready-made and welcome formula for something the Court had in mind'.[13] The unavoidable outcome of the Supreme Court's judgment has been its open invitation to the never-ending trail of dictators on the readily available grounds accorded to them by the notorious doctrine of the law of necessity.

Mirza's Exit

Both Iskandar Mirza and Ayub Khan made constitutional democracy and the supreme law of the land casualities of their personal whims and vendetta. Mirza particularly never visualized the stark implications of his collusion with Ayub in his reckless action of abrogating the Constitution. Once the vicious and unpalatable process of destroying national institutions was set in motion, events began to take a dramatic turn. On 24 October 1958, President Mirza announced his new Cabinet with General Ayub Khan as its Prime Minister. Describing the new government as a Cabinet 'in the accepted sense of the term', Mirza pronounced his act as a 'joint responsibility', though it had no parliamentary basis.[14] Consisting of non-political personalities, the new Cabinet was sworn in at a ceremony held on 27 October.

28 October 1958 turned out to be the night of long knives for Mirza, when he was forced at gunpoint 'to step aside and hand over all powers' to General Ayub Khan. With Mirza gone, Ayub Khan issued a proclamation worded as follows:

> Major General Iskandar Mirza, lately President of Pakistan, has relinquished his office of President and has handed over all powers to me, General Muhammad Ayub Khan, Chief Martial Law Administrator and Supreme Commander of the Armed Forces of Pakistan. Therefore, I have this night assumed the office of President and have taken upon myself the exercise of the said powers and all other powers pertaining thereto.[15]

Mirza might have had his motives in colluding with Ayub Khan in staging the *coup*, yet he was 'used as a figurehead because the military probably hoped thereby to hasten foreign recognition of the regime'.[16] By the proclamation of martial law, Mirza 'made his own position untenable. It should have been evident to him that the division of power and responsibility between two different persons was an obvious paradox and that he could not enjoy the monopoly of power while the responsibility for the administration lay with the army.'[17] Following the Supreme Court's verdict in Dosso's case on 27 October 1958, legitimizing 'successful revolution', Ayub lost no time in seizing upon the opportune moment to get rid of 'the semblance of dual-control' by unceremoniously deposing Mirza.[18]

Ayub Khan and his military coterie would often term their seizure of power as a 'revolution' and 'benign Martial Law—to assist the civil power to clear up the mess', yet it was neither a convulsive revolution nor a benign administrative action.[19] Instead, it was a classical case of a 'reform *coup*' as borne out later by the reforms introduced in various national institutions.[20]

Public Offices (Disqualification) Order

Having achieved his long-cherished ambition of becoming the sole arbitrator of national affairs, Ayub Khan made the government servants and the politicians his prime target of attack. During the years 1947-54, PRODA (Public and Representative Offices Disqualification Act) was employed, though on a limited scale, against politicians holding public office. Being cognizant of PRODA, the martial law regime promulgated in March 1959 the Public Offices (Disqualification)Order(PODO). An enquiry under PODO was to be conducted according to the provisions of the Criminal Procedure Code for trials before a High Court. PODO provided that the President or the Governor, on their own or on an application by a citizen, could institute an enquiry in a tribunal against anyone who had held any public office since Independence.

Contrary to the regime's motives and expectations of shooting the politicians and Government servants 'with deadly accuracy', PODO proved ineffective. First, it was confined only to the politicians who had held public office; second, the procedure for investigating the authenticity of the charges was tedious and cumbersome; third, there was no mention of a time limit within which the enquiries were to be completed. PODO's failure led to the promulgation of an other stringent order, i.e., EBDO.

Elective Bodies (Disqualification) Order

From the public acquiescence to the imposition of Martial Law, Ayub Khan gained the faulty impression that 'he was the man of destiny for Pakistan, and that, in accepting him, Pakistanis had rejected politicians, parties and parliamentary government for all times to come'.[21] The image that he portrayed of politicians was that of 'disruptionists, political opportunists, black marketeers and other social vermin, sharks and leeches.'[22] On the other hand, projecting himself as a national reformer and a 'colossus of justice, bestriding the corrupt world of Pakistan', Ayub tried to scavenge national politics from the politicians.[23]

By calling the politicians 'devils' who exploited the masses for ulterior motives, Ayub portrayed federal parliamentary government with political parties as 'divisive of and injurious to the national unity'.[24] He opined that, if federal parliamentary government was adopted again, 'a bloody revolution would overtake the country within six months.'[25] For all such ills and curses, the panacea he held out to the masses was the exclusion of all political parties and their leadership from the federalist polity of the country. He wished to be the sole interpreter of the popular will and the single operator in the national political milieu. For exercising his avowed absolute dictatorship in an independent and unfettered manner, Ayub Khan enacted the draconian law, EBDO. The parochial politics of EBDO covered Ayub's whole political career and was aimed at subverting all political forces and emasculating them for perpetuaing his personal rule in the country.

While superseding PODO, EBDO was applied 'to chasten' any person who held any public office or position, including membership of any elective body in the country, under charges of bribery, corruption, jobbery, favouritism, nepotism, and wilful maladministration, misappropriation and any 'abuse of whatever kind of official power or position, and any abetment of misconduct'. The term 'misconduct' was to include subversive activities and actions detrimental to political stability. For the implementation of EBDO, three tribunals were constituted, one for the Centre and one each for the provinces. Besides the non-application of the Criminal Procedure Code to such cases, the accused were arbitrarily deprived of the assistance of counsel. The provisions of EBDO were to apply retrospectively from 14 August 1947.

In accordance with the provisions of EBDO, several politicians were served notice to appear before the tribunals enquiring about their misconduct. The *modus operandi* of the proceedings was that any person found guilty was to stand disqualified in active politics till 31 December 1966, and that he would have to make restitution of ill-gotten gains to the public exchequer. In case the accused was to voluntarily retire from public life, the enquiry against him would stop forthwith.

Consequent upon such repressive measures, many prominent politicians were either disqualified or made to retire from public life 'voluntarily'. Amidst political inactivity, Ayub's autocratic rule was unchallenged. The possible hurdles to the prolongation of his authoritarian rule could have been the politicians of past regimes whom he wanted to hold responsible for bringing the country to the brink of disaster. Conceived with extreme slyness, the coercive weapon of EBDO was at his disposal, and 'it was relatively easy for the President to pick the targets one by one and with the complete power that he had, he could shoot them with deadly accuracy'.[26]

ADVENT OF CONTROLLED DEMOCRACY

Having barred the politicians through EBDO, Ayub Khan became exclusively dependent on the muscle of the civil and military bureaucracy to run the country's affairs. While the eventual return of political parties and politicians presented him with the worst of nightmares, the civil and military bureaucratic set-up perhaps could not provide the requisite legitimacy to sustain his autocracy. For confronting the politicians whom he considered anathema and for legitimizing his rule by establishing a new cadre of rural politicians who would enlist popular support for the regime, Ayub devised a system of controlled democracy, the Basic Democracies, which he said suited the genius of the 'unsophisticated and illiterate' people of his country. Such a 'system was intended to perform multiple functions: it would secure a clientele for the regime, undertake developmental work and provide units of local government'.

On the first anniversary of his seizure of complete power, Ayub Khan, on recommendation of the sycophantic clique around him, conferred upon himself the title of Field Marshal and simultaneously presented the system of Basic Democracies to the nation. It was a four-tier system, comprising 80,000 Basic Democrat Wards, each consisting of 1000 to 1200 people. The four tiers of the system were:

- Union Councils in rural areas and Union Committees/ Town Committees in urban areas.

- *thana* Council for each *thana* (sub-district) in East Pakistan and a *tehsil* Council for each *tehsil* in West Pakistan.

- District Councils (for each district).
- Divisional Councils (for each administrative division).

In the pyramidal system, the first rung was to consist wholly of elected members, while the upper three tiers were a curious blend of elected and selected government officials as members.

Between 26 December 1959 and 9 January 1960, elections to the Basic Democrat units were held in both wings of the country. The elected members formed an Electoral College to elect the President and members of the provincial and national Assemblies, in a referendum through secret ballot. The referendum to elect the President was held on 14 February 1960, and Ayub Khan, being the only candidate, received 95.6 per cent of the votes cast.

The BD system, supplemented by an extensive public works programme, helped in enlisting the active and constructive participation of the masses and thus diverted 'the energy of vast numbers of rural leaders from traditional political activities, e.g., petitioning, civil disobedience, and strikes, to modern leadership roles such as organizing programmes, mobilizing rural masses, and working out local problems'. The system directly involved the people and the new cadre of relatively younger and more literate leaders in the affairs of their local areas. The induction of governmental officials in the system was meant to bring the elected members under government patronage and constant bureaucratic surveillance.

GALLING CENTRALIZATION

If the problem of provincial autonomy remained unsolved during the era of Pakistan's experience in the parliamentary system (1947-58), the military regime (1958-62) wilfully sacrificed it for the sake of galling centralization and a colonial style of executive authority. When the states and provinces in the western wing were merged into One Unit for the purpose of achieving parity between the eastern and western wings of the country, Ayub (besides being the C-in-C) was a powerful federal minister in the 'Cabinet of talents' in 1954-55. He was privy to and a staunch protagonist of such schemes, achieved through outright coercive tactics against the units in West Pakistan. By thwarting the February 1959 general elections (through his pre-emptive coup) whose results would definitely have done away with One Unit, Ayub Khan, very much in keeping with his cherished ambitions, inherited only two provinces in the country.

Under the umbrella of martial law (1958-62), Ayub Khan evolved a highly centralized and autocratic presidential system in the country. Far from assuaging the demands of the autonomists, Ayub Khan, by his executive actions and official pronouncements, completely did away with the federal parliamentary structure in Pakistan.

Throughout the period of his personal rule (1958-69), Ayub Khan introduced the system of 'governors conference', a periodic high level meeting, participated in by the President, the two governors, cabinet ministers, and senior bureaucrats. Being totally dependent for their individual survival in the government on one man, the President, every participant in the 'governors conference' was supposed to ex- ecute Ayub's whims and policies, both at the Centre and at the provincial levels. Ayub Khan and his coterie discouraged anything approaching provincial autonomy or a parliamentary system of government. Such centralization negated the concept and practice of the federal principle in Pakistan.

With the extreme centralization and the executive supremacy of the military regime, Ayub Khan had visualized his future role as an authoritarian President heading a strong Centre, in 1954-55:

> The President should be made the final custodian of power on the country's behalf and should be able to put things right both in the Provinces and the Centre should they go wrong. Laws should be operative only if certified by the President . . . . No change in the Constitution should be made unless agreed to by the President.[27]

Constitution Commission

On 17 February 1960, when Ayub Khan was sworn in as the 'elected' President via the Electoral College, he announced the setting up of a Constitution Commission to be chaired by Justice Muhammad Shahabuddin, with a mandate to examine the progressive failure of parliamentary government in Pakistan and determine the causes and nature of the failure, and to recommend how a recurrence of similar causes could be prevented; to submit proposals for a Constitution which would embody recommendations on how best to achieve a democracy adaptable to changed circumstances and based on the Islamic principles of justice, equality, and tolerance; and to formulate proposals for consolidation of national unity and a firm and stable system of government.

The Commission prepared a questionnaire containing forty questions and distributed it to certain organizations and prominent citizens of the country. Moreover, the Commission interviewed several hundred leading public personalities hailing from both wings of the country. On the basis of public opinion sought in this way, an analysis of the working of the parliamentary system in Pakistan, the causes of its failure, along with recommendations as to the future Constitution of Pakistan, the Commission presented its report to President Ayub Khan on 6 May 1961. The Commission pinpointed the following as the causes of the failure of the parliamentary form of government in Pakistan:

- lack of proper elections and defects in the Constitution;

- undue interference by the Head of State in the ministries and political parties, and by the Central Government in the functioning of governments in the provinces; and

- lack of leadership, resulting in the lack of well organized and disciplined parties, the general lack of character in politicians, and their undue interference in the administration.

The Constitution Commission presented the following recommendations for inclusion in the future Constitution of the country:

- A Presidential system with adequate checks and balances.

- An independent bicameral legislature at the centre and unicameral legislature at the province level.

- The Constitution was to be federal with powers distributed between three lists of subjects: central, provincial, and concurrent.

- The direct election of the President, the Vice President, and the members of the National and Provincial Assemblies on a restricted franchise.

- A system of separate electorate.

- Fundamental rights and the directive principles of state policy as enunciated in the 1956 Constitution were to be adopted.

- Political parties were considered vital to the smooth functioning of the constitutional structure thus framed.

The Constitution Commission's report with all its commas, semi-colons, and full-stops was wholly unpalatable to Ayub Khan. From its very inception, the Commission, consisting of lawyers and businessmen of 'mediocre standing', was under constant pressure to accommodate Ayub's personal views on the Constitution.[28]

With his discourses on the unworkability of the parliamentary form of government and the imperatives of a strong centre, Ayub had been talking about the possible contours of a constitutional report which he wished to extract from the proposed Constitution Commission. Two months prior to the framing of the said Commission, he had observed that 'if the Constitution Commission made impractical proposals, they would not be accepted'.[29] The farcical nature of the Commission, expecting special pleadings from it, was evident from the following statement made by Ayub:

> The Commission... was not being appointed to tell us what we should do. We know what we should do. We are clear in our mind that we cannot adopt the parliamentary system.[30]

II

THE 1962 CONSTITUTION — FACADE OF AUTOCRACY

In utter disregard of the Constitution Commission's recommendations, Ayub Khan ladled out the 1962 Constitution on 1 March 1962, embodying all his preconceived notions. The 1962 Constitution, the 'brainchild' of Ayub Khan, contained a Preamble, 250 Articles divided into 12 parts and 3 Schedules. Ayub Khan described the Constitution as a 'blending of democracy with discipline: the two prerequisites to running a free society with stable government and sound administration'.

The Constitution provided for a Presidential system of government, the philosophy of which was as under:

> We have adopted the Presidential system as it is simpler to work, more akin to our genius and history, and less liable to lead to instability—a luxury that a developing country like ours cannot afford.[31]

The salient features of the 1962 Constitution were as follows:

- The country would be called the Republic of Pakistan.

- The Constitution was federal in name only and provided for a strong government at the Centre and also in each of the two provinces.

- All executive authority would vest in the President.

- Dhaka would be the principal seat of the Central Legislature, while Islamabad would be the principal seat of the Central Government.

- There would be parity in the Central Legislature, which would have 150 members. In addition, six seats would be reserved for women, three from each province.

- Each province would have maximum autonomy; thus, the residuary powers would be vested in the Provincial Legislatures.

- Urdu and Bengali would be the two national languages of Pakistan.

- A convention was stipulated that if the President was from West Pakistan, the Speaker would be from East Pakistan, and vice versa.

- Only three candidates were allowed to contest for Presidentship and a panel of three was to be nominated by the Central Assembly, in case there were more than three.

- During the absence of the President, the Speaker of the National Assembly would officiate in his place.

- The President would have power to appoint ministers from amongst persons qualified to be elected to the National Assembly.

- A two-thirds majority could amend the Constitution with the concurrence of the President. If the President did not concur, three-quarters of the member of the National Assembly could override his veto. In that event, the President would have the option of referring the matter to a nation-wide referendum or of dissolving the National Assembly.

- An 'Advisory Council of Islamic Ideology', recommending moral and spiritual values, would be set up.

- The Constitution provided for setting up of a Supreme Judicial Council, comprising the Chief Justice of the Supreme Court, the two next seniormost Judges of the Supreme Court, and the Chief Justice of each High Court. The Council could issue a code of conduct to be observed by the Judges of the Supreme Court and High Courts.

- The original Constitution did not provide any list of fundamental rights. Later on, through the first Amendment(1963) a list of fundamental rights(with a rider clause excluding some subjects from the operation of the Act of Fundamental Rights) was provided.

- A list of rhetorics containing the Islamic provisions and the directive principles of state policy, somewhat similar to that of the 1956 Constitution, was also provided.

The Constitution was formulated without the aid or consent of any Constituent Assembly. Made behind closed doors by a Cabinet Committee, the Constitution was intended to protect an individual who was to reign supreme in national affairs. In the words of the late Prime Minister Chaudhry Muhammad Ali (the author of the 1956 Constitution), the 1962 Constitution had given birth to a government in Pakistan which was 'a government of the President, by the President and for the President'.[32] From the original recommendations of the Constitution Commission to the final outcome of the 1962 Constitution, 'the emphasis clearly shifted from what the people want to what is best for the people'.[33]

Two features of the 1962 Constitution, Presidential powers and the quantum of provincial autonomy, were particularly prominent. At the expense of the Central and Provincial Legislatures, the following powers were conferred on the office of the President:

- All executive authority of the Republic was vested in the President.

- He had direct powers of legislation to make ordinances when the National Assembly was not in session and, in a grave emergency, to issue a Proclamation of Emergency.

- He could summon, prorogue, and dissolve the National Assembly.

- In the event of a conflict between the President and the National Assembly on any matter, the President might refer it to referendum, seeking a 'yes' or 'no' answer from the Electoral College.

- The national annual budget, once sanctioned, could not be altered by the Assembly without his permission. Prior approval of the President was needed to move money bills, namely, proposals for taxation, appropriation of public revenues, borrowing of money, etc.

- He enjoyed unfettered authority to appoint federal ministers, governors of the provinces, the Advocate General, the Auditor General, judges of the Supreme Court and the two High Courts, the chairmen and members of the Election Commission, the National Finance Commission, the Advisory Council on Islamic Ideology, and the National Economic Council.

- Being the Supreme Commander of the Defence Forces, he was empowered to *inter alia* appoint the chief commanders of the three defence services without reference to any other body.

- A Council of Ministers was to assist him in executive matters of national affairs but he was not duty-bound to accept its advice. He could induct and dismiss ministers without assigning any reason.

- The President could be impeached but the method was cumbersome, bordering on impossibility.

The veto and the other huge discretionary powers had made the President the cornerstone of the new system provided in the 1962 Constitution. It was almost impossible to impeach the President. Not answerable to the unicameral federal legislature, the President could legislate by ordinances (Article 29), and the National Assembly could not exercise the power of veto over such legislation. The interpretation of such an anomaly in the form of a strong centre was explained by Ayub Khan himself in 1964:

> I may tell you my interpretation of a strong Centre is a central organisation, an organisation which should be able to resolve the quarrels between the various parts of the country and different groups of people. As long as there is no friction, these various regions and different groups should be free to work as they like. But whenever there is difference of opinion, then it is imperative that a central organisation should have the complete authority and complete responsibility of resolving such differences.[34]

Such a self-professed inclination for a strong centre not only betrayed Ayub's faulty understanding of federalism but also demonstrated his personal penchant to be the arbiter of centre-province relations. It should have been evident to him that centre-province disputes could not be settled by executive writs; rather, they had to be referred to higher courts for adjudication.

The unlimited and arbitrary powers of the President under the 1962 Constitution are indicative of the strong central government. There was no statutory division of powers between the Centre and the provinces. Unlike the other late Constitutions of Pakistan, the 1962 Constitution provided only one list of subjects for legislation. Besides 49 items reserved in the Centre's legislative list, Article 131 granted the Centre overriding powers to legislate 'for the whole or any part of Pakistan', whenever the national interest in relation to security, economic and financial stability, planning, or co-ordination of the achievement of uniformity in any matter in different parts of the country so required. In case of conflict between the Centre and the provincial laws, priority was to be accorded to the former's legislative powers over the latter. The National Assembly was to act as arbitrator in case of a conflict between the Governor and the Provincial Assembly in provincial matters.

The Governor was to be appointed by and subjected to the 'direction' of the President (Article 80). Such a constitutional provision relegated the provincial Chief Executive to a mere agent of the Centre. Above all, the members of the provincial Councils of Ministers were to be appointed and dismissed with the prior approval of the President.

Having promulgated the 1962 Constitution on 1 March 1962, the Ayub Government held elections to the National Assembly on 28 April 1962, on the basis of Basic Democracies. The indirectly elected National Assembly held its first session on 8 June 1962, and on the same day martial law was lifted. With the martial law lifted and the normal law of the land restored, elections held, and Assemblies summoned, the Ayub regime began to assume a civilian facade. The new Assemblies comprised an entirely different breed of politicians. The relentless use of PODO and EBDO had weeded out the actual political rivals of the regime.

For weathering the gathering storm of political convulsions in the changed circumstances and providing for the perpetuation and smooth sailing of the quasi-civilian rule, Ayub Khan desperately needed some sort of political organization to back him. For this purpose, on 14 July 1962, the President got the National Assembly to pass the Political Parties Act, legalizing the formation of political parties and their participation in the elections. In a press conference on 20 July, Ayub Khan called on 'right-minded' Pakistanis to form a broad-based nationalistic political party with a progressive outlook, indicating that he himself might join such a party.[35]

The passage of the Political Parties Act created ripples in the stagnant national political life and enlivened the activities of some of the lately banned political parties. Several political leaders, who had been EBDOed, preferred to sit back. They faced the dilemma of whether to revive their parties or to continue their political hibernation and wait for an opportune moment for the working of a democratic system. Such indecisiveness among politicians gave birth to factionalism among their ranks, some favouring the revival and others opposing it. Taking stock of the political split, Ayub Khan decided to monopolize the Muslim League and jumped on the bandwagon of the party's 'Conventionist' faction, who favoured its revival on a broad base.

The Conventionists, hijacked by Ayub Khan and grouped into the Convention Muslim League, were often dubbed 'the Palace Party' by the other two factions, the Council Muslim League led by Khawaja Nazimuddin and a non-revivalist faction led by Nurul Amin. The parties opposed to Ayub's brand of democracy announced on 4 October 1962 the formation of a National Democratic Front, with the Council Muslim League, the Awami League, the National Awami Party, the Krishak Sramik Party, the Nizam-i-Islam Party, as well as sections of the Republican Party and the Jamaat-i-Islami under its umbrella.

The newly formed Front pressed *inter alia* for the introduction of adult franchise, the restoration of fundamental rights, the parliamentary system of government, and the reverting of Karachi to the capital of the country. To introduce fundamental amendments in the 1962 Constitution, the Front insisted on the convening of a Round Table Conference between the government and the weeded out (EBDOed) political stalwarts. To their utter dismay, Ayub Khan outrightly rejected their demand, labelling it as an extra-constitutional measure.

To avert any possibility of agitation in favour of the Front's demands, the Ayub Government promulgated, on 7 January 1963, the Political Parties(Amendment) Ordinance, which provided that the EBDOed politicians would become liable to two years imprisonment if they indulged in any political activity. In pursuit of his carrot and stick policy towards the politicians, Ayub Khan simultaneously issued another Ordinance, empowering himself to remit or reduce the period of disqualification of any disqualified person on application to him, personally.

In 1964, the National Assembly approved some government sponsored constitutional measures for holding presidential, national assembly, and provincial assemblies elections. This provided for the election, by adult suffrage, of 80,000 electors (BD members) who in turn would elect the President of the Republic, the National Assembly, and the two Provincial Assemblies early in 1965. The Presidential Election Bill, approved on 16 August 1964, was a novel piece of legislation in the crisis-ridden constitutional history of Pakistan. This Bill laid down *inter alia* that the sitting President would remain in office until his successor was elected. The election of a new President would precede the election of a new Assembly. The selection of the Presidential candidate would be carried out by the existing National Assembly and not by the newly elected Assembly.

Such constitutional engineering, to benefit Ayub's personal rule, was vehemently denounced by the opposition within and without the Assembly. They made the method of indirect election of the President the prime target of their attack and they urged his election by direct vote on the basis of adult franchise. The constitutional wisdom of many made them question why the President was so obsessed with obtaining a mandate for his office from the outgoing Assembly instead of from its successor. Perhaps Ayub feared that the untested 'genius' of the members of the new Assembly might not repose confidence in him as their next President.

In accordance with the provisions of the 1962 Constitution, the first term of President Ayub('elected' via the 1960 referendum) was to expire on 8 August 1965. But Ayub Khan, for reasons best known to himself, amended Clause(2) of Article 226 of the Constitution and reduced his term by a period of about four and half months, ending on 2 March 1965. 2 January 1965 was fixed for the Presidential election. In the fall of 1964, Ayub Khan's Presidential system faced a major test, when five major opposition parties banded together to form the Combined Opposition Party(COP): the Council Muslim League, the Awami League, the left wing Awami Party, the Nizam-i-Islam Party, and the ultra orthodox Jamaat-i-Islami. They persuaded Miss Fatima Jinnah *(Madar-i-Millat* or Mother of the Nation) to contest the Presidential election as their joint candidate.

From the first rung to the last of the bureaucratic structure, i.e., patwaris, tehsildars, deputy commissioners, and so on each applied all the coercive tactics in their bag to force BD members to cast their votes in favour of Ayub Khan. Consequently, Ayub Khan was re-elected President of the country for a five-year term on 2 January 1965, defeating his main opponent, Miss Jinnah, by a majority of almost 2:1. Besides country-wide criticism of the regime's election rigging strategy, Miss Jinnah charged:

> There is no doubt that these elections have been rigged . . . the entire conduct of these elections has been marred by flagrant official interference, police high-handedness, intimidation, corruption and bribery . . .[36]

III

DEMANDS FOR REGIONAL AUTONOMY

The curse of neglecting provincial autonomy and constitutionalism had plagued the federalist polity of Pakistan since Independence. Ayub's authoritarian unitary system(though with a quasi-democratic facade), and his unscrupulous attempts to destroy an all Pakistan leadership, readily translated the grouse of autonomists into resuscitated demands for a confederation. Ayub's imposition of a fully centralized administration and the abolition of provincial autonomy (in whatever form it existed) forced the EBDOed national leadership in East Pakistan to promptly limit its sphere of political operation to mere parochial demands and regional aspirations.

Dissatisfied with the centralized, though nominally federal system evolved under the 1962 Constitution, the demands for provincial autonomy particularly in East Pakistan assumed extreme tendencies, approaching secessionism. Undeniably, 'in EBDOing for personal and political reasons the national leaders with whom he could have easily worked out a viable national framework for the future Pakistani polity, Ayub had, perhaps unwittingly, caused irreparable damage to politics at the national level, national political organisations, the prevailing political culture and the concept of Pakistan'.[37] His unimaginative politics had polarized national political forces, disbanded democratic politics and allowed the regional ethos to grow at the cost of national unity.

While the ruling Muslim League in the 1950s had failed to cultivate either the old or the emerging elite in the eastern wing, Ayub Khan perfected the legacies he inherited from his predecessors. In the turbulent political permutations and combinations of Bengali politics, the League, for its reorganization, owed much to the dynamic contributions of A. K. Fazlul Haq and Huseyn Shaheed Suhrawardy. Both these legendary political personalities were maltreated at the hands of the whimsical ruling elite at the centre.

A. K. Fazlul Haq was one of the founding fathers of the Muslim League and headed the United Bengal Ministry from 1937-41. Endowed with charismatic traits, oratorical skills, and sincerity of purpose, A. K. Fazlul Haq was the one who seconded the 23 March 1940 Lahore Resolution. Suhrawardy was credited with securing an overwhelming electoral victory for the League in the 1945 elections in Bengal. Being head of the Bengal Ministry, he moved an amendment to the 1940 Resolution in the 1946 Delhi Convention of Muslim Legislators for the purpose of removing some ambiguities in the said document. Throughout the 1940s, both politicians continued to rally the Bengali Muslim masses behind Jinnah's strategy of achieving Pakistan. Despite the distinction of this immense historical and national credit in their patriotic record in the Pakistan movement, both were shabbily treated by the League stalwarts in the 1950s.

The reality of East Pakistan's grievances is evident from the preceding chapter. However, the Bengali politicians like Suhrawardy had still not lost hope of being able to redress their grievances through political means. For that end, they had pinned great hopes on the proposed first general elections in the country, to be held in February 1959. By then, Suhrawardy, with political roots in both wings of the country, seemed 'poised for victory'.[38] Such a scenario was acceptable neither to President Iskandar Mirza nor to General Ayub Khan—the latter particularly disliked Suhrawardy, was afraid of him, and considered him an enemy of the army.[39] That is why, opines an analyst, Ayub

> outfoxed Suhrawardy by pulling a coup in October 1958, imposed martial law, abrogated the Constitution, abolished the Assemblies, banned the political parties, arrested politicians and set himself up as the philosopher-king. As if the 44-month martial law rule was not harsh enough for East Pakistan, Ayub incarcerated Suhrawardy, Mujibur Rahman and scores of Awami Leaguers under the Security of Pakistan Act just when martial law was about to be lifted and political activity permitted. The restriction on the political activities of Suhrawardy and on his party were not lifted until almost his death in 1963.[40]

Suhrawardy was arrested in early 1962. With his impeccable credentials of supporting the League and the Pakistan movement, the distinguished leader was charged with acting 'in a manner prejudicial to the security and defence of Pakistan and indulging in activities of a highly prejudicial nature ever since the inception of Pakistan'.[41] A victim of Ayub Khan's personal venom and vendetta, the former Prime Minister, whom the unscrupulous regime labelled as having indulged in anti-state activities, was even denied the right of writ petition in the High Court because Ayub Khan had promulgated an Ordinance, precluding the High Court from issuance of *habeas corpus* in case of detainees arrested under the Security Act.[42]

Far from submitting to the ulterior wishes of Ayub Khan, Suhrawardy decided to contest the charges levelled against him. However, as expected, he was pronounced guilty by those who had worked for the British when Suhrawardy and his contemporaries were in the forefront of the struggle for Pakistan. Ignoring his major contribution to the creation of Pakistan, Ayub Khan, with a virulent media campaign, subjected the patriot to all sorts of serious and non-serious charges, including disloyalty to the country. While Ayub Khan's action of disqualifying politicians proved to be a great tragedy for the federation, the consequent political vacuum could not be filled by the band of sycophants gathered around him.

The incarceration of popular Bengali politicians, the conspicuous absence of Bengalis in the top echelon of the civil and military bureaucracies, and above all, Ayub's steps towards over-centralization had completely alienated East Pakistan. For undoing the gross economic disparities between the two wings of the country, Ayub accelerated the pace of development projects and inducted Bengalis into the civil and military cadres. Yet his deliberate hesitation in involving the popular Bengali leadership in the Centre's decision-making process caused him to lose the support of the eastern wing. While equating Ayub's rule with West Pakistan, bound to the Centre via the tightened grip of the bureaucracy, the overwhelming majority of the Bengali masses strongly denounced the economic exploitation and political suppression of their province. The hardening Bengali perceptions began to controvert all the national institutions at the centre, thus hanging the justification for maximum regional autonomy on the peg of continuous politico-economic neglect of their province.

EFFECTS OF THE 1965 WAR

The 1965 India-Pakistan war, which was exclusively fought in the western wing, exposed the physical vulnerability of the eastern wing. Some analysts opine that the war proved to be 'a watershed' in east-west relations.[43] During the 17-day war, the fact that East Pakistan was left on its own(with some vague Chinese guarantees for its defence), obliged Bengali public opinion to draw the following unpleasant conclusions, with immense implications for the federation:

- India's deliberately refraining from attacking East Pakistan demonstrated that New Delhi entertained no aggressive designs against the eastern wing.

- The defence forces of Pakistan were apparently meant for the security of West Pakistan only, while the eastern wing, 1500 kilometres away, was left completely at the mercy of Indian military muscle.

- The diversion of the development funds of both wings in the wake of the 1965 war, to meet the swelling security budget, was perceived by the eastern wing as 'undergoing sufferings in the interests of West Pakistan'[44], because the country's defence machine was concentrated in West Pakistan and was practically utilized to defend it. Thus 'their [Bengalis'] relationship with West Pakistan and the survival of Pakistani nationhood were both subordinate to the ultimate interests of West Pakistan'.[45]

- For reasons of national integration and boosting of the morale of the masses in the eastern wing, the presence of the Bengali personnel fighting in the western wing was given huge publicity in the officially-controlled media. Far from achieving its avowed objectives, such propaganda emboldened the disillusioned masses 'to take a more radical stand on autonomy'.[46]

- The complete disruption of the communications network during the war, besides contributing to the sufferings of the eastern wing, awakened the Bengalis to the need to develop self-sufficiency in isolation.

The 1965 war weakened the already fraying national ties between the two wings. The neglect of the eastern wing's defence was utilized by the confederalists to ignite public opinion by drawing wild conclusions and preaching hatred against the western wing. For instance, Sheikh Mujibur Rahman articulated his views thus: 'the 17-day war has proved that the President or his Chiefs of the Armed Forces cannot stand by us in times of such a danger . . . .'[47]

In the wake of the 1965 India-Pakistan war, the following political trends, with far-reaching constitutional implications had crystallized in the country's politics: the overwhelming majority of politicians in East Pakistan clamoured for greater provincial autonomy. The over-centralization, the exclusion of the Bengali elite from the national decision-making process, the deliberate and unfortunate playing down of the Bengali parliamentary majority via the notorious parity formula, discriminatory allocation of development funds to the disadvantage of East Pakistan, and the ever-swelling military and civil institutions to the exclusion of, and at the expense of East Pakistan, substantially contributed to the emerging Bengali nationalism and to the regionalization of their aspirations. Such realities were ultimately translated into Mujib's six-points for the salvation of the Bengali masses.

The dominant political outlook in West Pakistan favoured the induction of a full-fledged parliamentary democratic dispensation in the country. Having gone through the mill of the repressive martial law and the quasi-civilian rule, the opposition parties had grasped the fact that they could not dislodge the Ayub regime through constitutional devices. With their backs to the wall, the opposition leaders resorted to agitational politics to uproot a system vital to the sustenance of Ayub's regime.

The jolt of the 1965 War and the subsequent alleged 'sell-out' of the Kashmir cause at Tashkent had placed the Ayub regime on the defensive. Ayub's illness further loosened his grip on the intractable horse of civil and military bureaucracy.

While the Awami League was gaining ground by exploiting Bengali grievances against the centre, the launching of the Pakistan Peoples Party (with leftist overtones and an attractive manifesto of *roti, kapra aur makan*) by Ayub's dynamic former minister, Zulfikar Ali Bhutto, had radically changed the political climate of West Pakistan.

Amidst such kaleidoscopic political trends, Ayub Khan made a rod for his own back by embarking upon an ill-conceived, ill-planned, and ill-timed programme to celebrate his 'Decade of Reforms'. While officially sponsored jubilations marking the climax of a decade of reforms and development were meant to hoodwink the masses, Ayub had acquired, or for that matter was conferred upon(by the sycophants around him), several cliched titles: the Saviour of the Nation, the de Gaulle of Pakistan, the beloved President, the dynamic leader, the soldier-statesman, the Saladin Ayubi of Pakistan. Ayub and his coterie's obfuscating strategy for befooling the people notwithstanding, the swelling opposition termed the whole show as the celebration of a decade of authoritarianism and ruthless suppression of the vital democratic principles of constitutionalism and federalism

Ignoring the unpleasant realities of One Unit, Ayub Khan had continued to discourage debate on and opposition to the clumsy integration of West Pakistan into a single province. Choosing to ignore the political, economic, and ethno-cultural hardships emanating from such a single province, Ayub Khan, in his 'megalomaniac unwillingness to consider facts and an apparant inability to listen to opinion which did not coincide with his own', branded the demands for dissolving it as anti-Pakistan.[48] After widespread political unrest had erupted in both wings of the country against Ayub's rule, the eastern wing and the former smaller units in West Pakistan (i.e., Sindh, Balochistan, and the NWFP) were unanimous in demanding the dissolution of one unit. If the political parties in the eastern wing had made regional autonomy their main demand, the voices representing the smaller units in the western wing took up the anti-One Unit call, putting the regime on the defensive. In the whole scenario:

> As far as the One Unit was concerned, Ayub's habit of riding roughshod was missing, and the Government showed itself more and more to be on the defensive. It became both the price and the test of loyalty to the administration that leaders in West Pakistan should declare their support for the One Unit and expound its virtues. There were threatening hints directed towards those who persisted in the seditious notion of wanting to break it . . . the topic was still sacrosanct and any adverse mention of it might carry a charge of sedition, for sedition had come to signify any opinion which did not correspond with that held by Ayub Khan . . .[49]

The post-Tashkent constitutional politics in the country meant the beginning of the end of Ayub's authoritarianism. The overwhelming thrust of the rising demands in West Pakistan was for the dissolution of One Unit, undiluted constitutionalism, and a federal parliamentary system based on adult franchise. All the political forces in the eastern wing in general and the rising crescendo of the Awami League in particular, 'did not ask the Centre to do more for the Bengalis'. Rather their demand was 'to let the Bengalis act for themselves'.[50] To put it briefly, while the western wing was asking for federalism and constitutionalism, the eastern wing was poised for confederalism. The common elements in the otherwise divergent demands of both wings were dissolution of One Unit, and the setting up of a parliamentary system based on adult franchise.

Ever since the mid-1950s, the popular political parties in the eastern wing had demanded a full democratic Constitution, providing *inter alia* the sole supremacy of the parliament to which the people's representatives would be elected directly on the basis of adult franchise. Against the omnipresent centralization, they had asked for full regional autonomy. The 1956 Constitution did not satisfy Bengali aspirations. The repressive constitutional order under Ayub Khan frustrated the Bengali masses and alienated them from the mainstream of national politics.

Exploiting the pent-up aspirations of the Bengali masses, Sheikh Mujibur Rahman presented his Six Points—the charter of survival(as it was propagated)—in February 1966. These were:

- A federal parliamentary structure providing for direct elections on the basis of adult franchise.

- The powers of the federal government to be limited to national defence and foreign affairs and, to a limited extent, to the issuance of currency.

- Either two currencies which were freely convertible or one currency with adequate constitutional provisions provided to ensure no flight of capital from the East or West.

- All powers of taxation to be left in the hands of the federating units, while the Centre would receive some fixed share for the expenses it incurred.

- All foreign trade and foreign exchange matters were to come within the sphere of provincial powers. The Centre was to rely on the federating units for a fixed ratio of the foreign exchange earnings to meet its requirements.

- The federating units would have their own militia or paramilitary forces as found necessary for preservation of national security.

The death of Suhrawardy in 1963 had made Mujib, by all accounts a mediocre demagogue and second-rate politician, the undisputed leader of the East Pakistan Awami League. By supporting Miss Fatima Jinnah in the 1964 Presidential elections, Mujib endeavoured to thrust himself to the forefront of the political permutation of volatile Bengali politics. After the 1965 war, the accumulated Bengali grievances and the boiling cauldron of the autonomy cause found a leader in him. Ignoring these realities, the Ayub regime, far from fulfilling the exigencies of politics and holding a pragmatic dialogue with the autonomists including Mujib, preferred to jail the latter.

When Mujib announced his Six Points, he hinted that his programme was 'negotiable' and that it 'was not the Bible'.[51] For making Mujib and his party uncompromising and for rallying agitating public opinion in their favour, 'Ayub chose what he called the language of weapons, and not the weapons of the language'.[52] The ill-conceived tactic of incarcerating Mujib ultimately transformed him into the symbol of Bengali aspirations.

While in the first half of the 1960s, various combinations of political parties had failed in their attempts to dislodge the Ayub regime, the second half was marked by the presentation of the manifestos of individual parties demanding radical restructuring of the Constitution. Mujib's Six Points had already been announced when a conference of opposition parties held in Dhaka in April 1967 resulted in the immediate formation of the Pakistan Democratic Movement, a motley collection of leaders of the National Democratic Front, the Council Muslim League, the Nizam-i-Islam Party, Jamaat-i-Islami, and the West Pakistan Awami League of Nawabzada Nasrullah Khan.[53] Following is the summary of the 'Eight Point Programme' endorsed by the PDM:

- A parliamentary federal form of government with direct elections by adult franchise, and guarantees of fundamental rights, free Press, and independent judiciary on the basis of the 1956 Constitution.

- Federal powers limited to defence, foreign affairs, currency and federal finance, and inter-provincial communications and trade.

- Full regional autonomy with residuary powers vested in the provincial governments as established by the Constitution in both wings of the country. Removal of economic disparity within ten years, with foreign exchange at the disposal of the provinces earning it.

- Currency, banking, foreign exchange, foreign trade, and inter-wing trade and communications to be managed by a board elected on the basis of parity by the members of the National Assembly from both wings of the country.

- Parity in all central services, including autonomous bodies and the Supreme Court, within ten years.

- Parity in defence, fighting and fire power in the two wings, transfer of Naval Headquarters to East Pakistan, and constitution of a defence council on the basis of parity.

- Points 2 to 7 to be incorporated in the 1956 Constitution by the National Assembly as the first order of business after its election.[54]

Without touching the sensitive issues, i.e., One Unit, foreign policy, and demands for nationalization of industry, the PDM's Eight-Point Charter did sound sensible. Yet it was outrightly rejected by the East Pakistan Awami League on the plea that it negated its Six Point manifesto. The NAP, led by Bhashani, condemned it for sidetracking the real issues and 'for defending the semi-feudal, semi-colonial socio-economic order now existing in Pakistan'.[55] The absence of political cohesiveness, splits in the alliance, and dubbing of its demands by the left-wing parties as reactionary, meant that the PDM could not transform itself into an effective platform. The perpetual student unrest in both wings of the country, the eruption of political violence, the endless series of demonstrations and processions, and the emergence of the PPP as a dynamic political force in the otherwise stale politics of West Pakistan rendered the PDM ineffective.

His trial in the 'Agartala conspiracy case' made a martyr of Mujib. The case, with tainted evidence, and the regime's blunder in constituting a special tribunal and then according it widespread publicity, ushered in far-reaching implications for the entire political spectrum of Pakistan. Whatever the nature of the charges against Mujib and his 34 'accomplices', their trial, at the height of political agitation against dictatorship, cast doubts on the prosecution case.

Meanwhile, Ayub Khan fell ill, and the constitutional imperatives provided for the Speaker of the National Assembly(then a Bengali) to immediately assume duties as acting President. With Ayub convalescing in London, the country was run without a Chief Executive for two months. The gross constitutional violation provided the stimulus to the autonomists in the eastern wing to express doubts about the possibility of any Bengali(citing the example of the Speaker) ruling the Centre.

Amidst the continuing state of emergency(imposed since the 1965 war), the celebrations of the decade of development, 'intended merely for the idle nourishing of Ayub Khan's personal egotism', invited the wrath of deprived and alienated masses.[56] His celebration of the so-called 'decade of development' proved to be a source of great annoyance and provocation to the public at large. The masses viewed the excessive publicity of 'celebration' as spitting in the already ugly face of poverty.

Characterizing the agitating politicians as 'the morbid minds of irresponsible persons', the Ayub regime loudly talked about its golden era of development, made possible because of 'stability' in the country. Besides so many other cliches, the word 'stability' invited adverse criticism. For instance, while debunking the 'stability' of the Ayub regime as a myth, Bhutto opined:

> Stability certainly does not mean that a regime should remain in power for a decade. It means that a government's policies should be given time to show results and not keep changing. It means that there must be institutions to provide for an orderly transfer of power from one government to another. Neither of these conditions exists in Pakistan.[57]

The much-trumpeted era of 'progress', 'stability', and 'revolutionary reforms' has euphemistically been compared to the Fifth French Republic under President General de Gaulle. Ironically, installed through a military coup, later confirmed in power by a rigged referendum and controlled elections, Ayub Khan was pleased to be called 'the de Gaulle of Pakistan' by the sycophantic coterie around him. Ignoring what he had done to the Federation, the coterie would label him as the 'saviour of nation', making ceaseless efforts to better the lot of the masses. Ruling the country in viceregal fashion for about eleven years, Ayub retired in isolation. Far from repenting over his fundamental role in causing the country to disintegrate, he would exhibit bitterness to private visitors who came in contact with him before his death in 1974, the quintessence of what he felt 'were injustices committed against him by an ungrateful people'.[58]

IV

THE TWO-ECONOMY THESIS

The concentration of all levers of political power in the capricious hands of the President, the vicious circle of indirect elections(that too, under the direct surveillance and coercive apparatus of civil servants), and the constitutional docility of a unicameral parliament, had completely eroded the concept of federalism. Such a highly centralized system aroused the intense antagonism of the Bengalis, expecting socio-economic and political dividends in the federal parliamentary system. The ever-ascending civil-military bureaucracy under Ghulam Muhammad, Mirza, and Ayub had made repeated attempts 'to strengthen the Centre and resist the East Pakistan demands for what were termed extreme forms of autonomy bordering on secession'.[59]

Completely excluding the popular Bengali leaders from the national system's decision-making and power-sharing process, the Ayub regime committed itself to some economic and development policies to remove inbuilt structural imbalances and gross economic disparities, particularly between the two wings. By responding to the Bengali economic and development imperatives, the regime wished to blunt the sharp edges of the eastern wing's wholesale opposition to Ayub's 'constitutional autocracy' and repressive political system.

Ever since the 1950s, the Bengali political elite had been demanding guarantees for a just and equal share of foreign exchange earnings, central grants, and aids for industrial, commercial, educational, and agricultural development. They called for 'parity' in the sharing of economic dividends in the national budget, to remove the growing disparity and disequilibrium in economic development and the standard of living in the two wings of the country. The 1949 manifesto of the Awami League, the 21-point programme of the Jugto Front, the 9-point programme of the COP, the 6 points of the Awami League, the 8 points of the PDM, the 11 points of the Students Action Committee, and finally, the 8 points of the DAC, had demanded the immediate attention of the omnipresent Centre for removing structrual disparities, particularly in the eastern wing.[60]

The Bengali desire to ensure 'fullest autonomy' to the eastern wing was augmented by the propounding of 'the theory of two economies' by East Pakistan economists at Chittagong in 1956.[61] Disagreeing with the thesis of integrated economic development for both wings of the country, they argued for treating each region's economy as a distinct entity, which should have its own fiscal and monetary control and priorities.[62] While providing 'theoretical justifications' for autonomy to the eastern wing, the East Pakistan economists suggested that 'though for preservation of national unity and solidarity an overall planning authority is essential...yet for maximum economic development greater emphasis should be laid on regional planning with respective autonomous planning units than an overall planning for the whole country. . . these are not sentiments but hard facts of national economy'.[63]

The major arguments advanced in favour of the two-economy thesis can be summed up in the following:

- The peculiar geographic milieu and the distance between the two wings did not favour the pursuance of one economic policy for the country.

- The level of development, price differentials, trade imbalances, and structural differences between the two wings of the country dictated distinct treatment for the economy of East Pakistan.

- The foreign exchange earned by the raw material as well as the money in the eastern wing was utilized in West Pakistan.

- All bodies connected with planning and its execution were heavily centralized and they were all based in West Pakistan.

Amidst widespread publicity and popularity of 'the theory of two economies', Ayub Khan's *coup* and his ambitious bids for centralization of everything provided additional impetus to the *sui generis* nature of East Pakistan's development imperatives. Branding it a prelude to disintegration of the country, the Ayub regime rejected the two economies thesis and, instead, began to make efforts to reduce the existing disparities between the two wings. While hastening the pace of development in East Pakistan, the Ayub regime continued to eulogize the centralized strategy of co-ordinated economic development.

After the lifting of martial law, the Ayub Government (via the 1962 Constitution) made the fast erosion of economic disparities its constitutional obligation. Article 144 provided for the establishment of a National Finance Commission and Article 145 for a National Economic Council(NEC). The basic aim of the NEC was to ensure that interregional and intraregional disparities, in terms of per capita income, were removed. The national resources of the country, including foreign exchange, were to be allocated to the federating units in a

manner conducive to the removal of disparities. The rationale for
instituting the National Finance Commission was to recommend the
distribution of taxes between the Centre and the provinces and to
make a report on the progress of the targeted objectives in Article
145 of the Constitution. The latter Article also provided that the
objective of removing disparities was to be achieved 'in the shortest
possible time'.

However, as in most other matters, the 1962 constitutional structure
provided the Centre with overriding powers in the domain of national
economic planning and co-ordination. While the crucial subjects concerning economic planning and co-ordination were reserved for the
exclusive operation of the Centre, Article 131(2) read:

where the national interest of Pakistan in relation to:

a) the security of Pakistan, including the economic and finan-
    cial stability of Pakistan;

b) planning or co-ordination; or

c) the achievement of uniformity in respect of any matter in
    different parts of Pakistan so requires, the Central Legisla-
    ture shall have power to make laws ... with respect to any
    matter not enumerated in the Third Schedule.

The central legislative supremacy over economic planning and
co-ordination notwithstanding, Article 30 of the 1962 Constitution
provided that 'if the President is satisfied that a grave emergency
exists(a) in which Pakistan or any part of Pakistan is(or is in imminent
danger of being) threatened by war or external aggression or(b) in
which the security or economic life of Pakistan is threatened by
internal disturbances beyond the power of a Provincial Government
to control', he could issue a proclamation of emergency. On the basis
of Articles 131 and 30, Feldman opines, that 'with respect to economic
planning and development, as with practically everything else, the
powers of the Provincial Governments could be nullified or
abrogated by an appeal to this supervening power at the Centre'.[64]
Justice Munir(one-time Law Minister in the Ayub Government)
could not fail to observe such an absurdity of the so-called distribution
of powers between the Centre and the provinces. He remarked that:
'This distribution is qualified in favour of the Centre in so many

respects that, as a matter of constitutional law and political science it is impossible to describe the Constitution as federal'.[65]

Besides complaining about the continuing underdevelopment of their province, the Bengali politicians had often referred to big projects like the Indus Basin Treaty and the construction of the new capital at Islamabad. They demanded investment of equal capital in the eastern wing as well. Their autonomy aspirations brushed aside, their numerical strength converted into 'parity', their popular leadership EBDOed and alienated in the system's decision-making and power-sharing process, the Bengalis seemed determined to get rid of the clumsy manipulators in the western wing.

Suppression of provincial rights by force and centralization had meant the patronizing of provincialism of the worst kind. It would be an abject and extreme travesty of truth to hold the eastern wing responsible for provincialism. The absence of democratic dispensations and Ayub Khan's visible hesitation to devolve power on the federating units were singularly responsible for the secession of the eastern wing. The one-man dictatorship, the totally unjustified continuation of the state of emergency and the ever-increasing imposition of arbitrary laws took away the rights and civil liberties of the people. Such a ghastly process aggravated the people's frustrations with the system itself, ultimately manifesting themselves in the form of disintegration of the Federation.

Signposts

- Barring the Martial Law period (i.e., 1958-62), there was a Constitution (i.e., the 1962 Constitution), yet there was absolutely no constitutionalism and federalism in Pakistan.

- From 1962 to 1969, there was an 'elected' President of the country, but the two provincial chief lords were selected by the former. The Governors were not answerable to the provincial legislatures but to the President alone. The Governors were to appoint and dismiss their Council of Ministers with the prior approval of the President.

- An oft-quoted joke equated the 1962 Constitution to the *Ghanta Ghar* of Faisalabad from where all roads originated and where they converged. Similarly, from whichever direction one looks at the 1962 Constitution, one would always see Ayub Khan in it.

- Although the 1962 Constitution was announced after much careful constitutional engineering to protect, enhance, and sustain an individual in power, Ayub Khan had to issue several ordinances to make it operational.

- Like various regimes in the 1950s, the Ayub government looked upon the Bengali demands for greater provincial autonomy as ostensibly backed by subversive anti-Pakistan elements, i.e., the communists, the Hindus, and by Indian agents across the border, etc.

- Unlike the 1956 Constitution, the 1962 Constitution had made the provincial executive directly responsible to the President and it turned centre-province relations into subordination rather than co-ordination in the Federation.

- Unlike the 1956 Constitution, the 1962 Constitution created a 'Republic of Pakistan', excluding the word, 'Islamic'. Though such connotations demonstrated trends towards secular orientations of the polity, yet, under mounting pressure of the religious lobby, Ayub Khan had to introduce an amendment to the Constitution to dispel such a notion.

CONSTITUTIONAL CRISES TAKE THEIR TOLL: YAHYA KHAN'S CATASTROPHIC INTERLUDE 1969-1971

'Tweedle Khan Takes Over'

This was the pejorative headline of an article in the London-based *The Economist* (29 March 1969), depicting Yahya Khan's take-over from Ayub Khan. Giving a parting kick to his own Constitution, Ayub Khan, contrary to popular demands for constitutionalism and federalism, invited Yahya Khan to 'save the country from utter chaos and total destruction'. Ironically, Ayub Khan, in his own military take-over in October 1958, had used more or less the same rhetoric.

'A document of despair'—such was the harsh and unjust pronouncement of Ayub Khan on the late 1956 Constitution.[1] When he seized power in the dark of night, Ayub Khan had pledged to bestow a befitting Constitution upon his nation. But to the utter dismay of everybody, the masterpiece of Ayub's careful constitutional engineering (i.e., the 1962 Constitution), over which he 'sweated blood' for making it an ideal expression of his people's genius, was ultimately undone by its own creator. Mutilating his own brainchild, Ayub Khan, in a letter to the Commander-in-Chief General Yahya Khan, handed over his people to the latter, authorizing him 'to fulfil his legal and constitutional responsibility' to defend the country from within. One wonders what the legitimate constitutional reference and sound authority was on the basis of which Ayub Khan 'authorized' Yahya Khan 'to fulfil his legal and constitutional responsibility', i.e., abrogating the 1962 Constitution and plunging the whole nation into political chaos via a military *coup d'etat*.

Like his 1958 military *coup*, Ayub Khan euphemistically hung the justification of 'handing over power' to Yahya Khan on the erroneous peg of nation-wide political turmoil, 'deliberately created by well-tutored and well-backed elements'.[2] In his letter to the Commander-in-Chief, General Yahya Khan, and in his radio speech on 25 March 1969, Ayub gave an intriguing statement that 'he found no option but to step aside'. Was the imposition of martial law the only option to avert what he wrongly asserted was the 'liquidation of Pakistan'? Certainly not. If one reads the late 1962 Constitution, apart from its abrogation via martial law, the document provided for the following five constitutional and legal means for the peaceful change of President in the country. These were:

1. The President may resign his office by writing under his hand addressed to the Speaker of the National Assembly. (Article 12(3).)

2. If guilty of misconduct and violation of the Constitution, the President could be impeached by the members of the National Assembly. (Article 13.)

3. The President could be removed 'on the grounds of his physical and mental incapacity'. (Article 14.)

4. The President could vacate the high office by his refusal to take oath when elected by the 80,000 Basic Democrats.

5. He could dissolve the National Assembly and voluntarily vacate the office of President and in that event the Speaker of the National Assembly would step into his shoes.

None of the aforementioned constitutional and legal options imply that the President could only 'step aside' by inviting his coadjutor 'to fulfil his legal and constitutional responsibilities' via martial law. Ayub Khan had not handed over power to Yahya Khan for the sake of 'maintaining' or 'restoring' democratic and constitutional norms. The underlying ignominious idea behind the whole exercise was to perpetuate the monopoly over the coercive levers of the state of the top echelons of the military and civil bureaucracy. Had he been so caring about democratic order and constitutionalism in the country, Ayub Khan would have invited the Speaker of the National Assembly to assume power by becoming President of Pakistan.

Thus the spring of 1969 witnessed the overnight transformation of one extreme form of authoritarianism into another one. When Yahya Khan rose to the high office of President and CMLA, the advocates, instigators, and organizers of the movement for ousting Ayub Khan had posed the following demands:

- Greater provincial autonomy.

- The dissolution of One Unit.

- Direct elections on the basis of adult franchise.

- Democratization.

- Restoring economic and financial rights of the federating units in general and the eastern wing in particular.

- Abrogation of black laws aimed at victimization.

- Nationalization of big business and industry and ending of the concentration of wealth in a few hands in the country.

The unfolding political milieu with the aforementioned demands differentiated the ushering in of Yahya Khan's military rule from that of Ayub Khan in October 1958. Amidst the wrangling of politicians, the horse-trading in the sordid era of Mirza, and the deteriorating socio-economic order, the appearance of the armed forces was welcomed as a 'promising act'. However, when Ayub Khan relinquished his office, the 'administration was gravely discredited along with the man himself. His Basic Democratic system had proved to be a mockery of democracy; corruption had further increased; the privileged few were more securely entrenched than ever; and his much-vaunted Constitution had proved to be putty in his hands, to be moulded as he wished.'[3] In view of his performance of more than a decade, Ayub Khan's entry and exit were greeted with equal enthusiasm and relief by the public at large.

Having watched carefully the mass movement against Ayub Khan, the civil-military ruling elite under Yahya Khan's martial law adopted, perhaps for tactical reasons, a defensive posture towards politicians and their political parties. The advent of Yahya Khan's martial law 'was described in certain quarters as Ayub's political order without Ayub'.[4] That might have been the original hope of the military junta, yet 'the four-month political movement had raised too many expectations and encouraged too much political activity not permitted during the Ayub era, and thus a reversion to Ayub's system was simply not possible'.[5]

For placating the pressing demands of political parties in both wings of the country, the CMLA Yahya Khan exhibited *ab initio* a very conciliatory tone. Far from arresting the politicians, banning the political parties, or filibustering (like Ayub Khan in October 1958), Yahya Khan pledged to 'put the administration on the rails'. While arrogating to himself and his military junta the decisive roles of arbitrators and power-brokers, Yahya Khan in a broadcast to the nation on 26 March 1969, declared:

> I wish to make it absolutely clear to you that I have no ambition other than the creation of conditions conducive to the establishment of constitutional government... [He promised] the smooth transfer of power to the representatives of the people elected freely and impartially on the basis of adult franchise. It will be the task of these elected representatives to give the country a workable Constitution.[6]

On 31 March 1969, Yahya Khan assumed the office of President, under the plea that it was 'necessary to assume the office of Head of State until a new Constitution was framed'.[7] The Chief Martial Law Administrator/President issued on 4 April 1969 the Provisional Constitutional Order, stating that:

- Notwithstanding its abrogation, Pakistan would be governed as nearly as possible in accordance with the provisions of the 1962 Constitution;

- The Sections of the 1962 Constitution relating to fundamental rights were suspended; and

- The Courts could not question any order issued or any sentence passed by a military court under Martial Law Regulations.

THE LEGAL FRAMEWORK ORDER 1970

For the realization of his 'intentions' to smoothly transfer power to the elected representatives, Yahya Khan spelled out the then available constitutional options and their *modus operandi* in his address to the nation on 28 November 1969. He dilated upon the following options:[8]

1. To have an elected Constitution Convention whose task should be to formulate a new Constitution, after which it could be dissolved. In Yahya Khan's opinion, such a method of constitution-making had two distinct disadvantages: it would require two elections, one to the

Constitution Convention and the other to the National Assembly based on the Constitution made by such a Convention. Secondly, such a method of constitution-formulation might cause unnecessary delay in the transfer of power to the elected representatives.

2.   The second available alternative was to revert to the 1956 Constitution and revive it. But the widespread political opposition to 'parity representation' and 'One Unit' schemes, the two salient features of the 1956 Constitution, outrightly discouraged the revival of this document.

3.   The third option, said Yahya Khan, was to formulate a Constitution which could then be presented to the people of Pakistan for a referendum. While discarding this alternative too, Yahya Khan opined that such an option was loaded with certain practical difficulties, as a simple 'yes' or 'no' by way of an answer could not possibly be given by the voters to such a comprehensive national document.

4.   To evolve a legal framework for general elections on the basis of consultations with various groups and political leaders, as well as the study of the 'late' Constitutions of Pakistan and the general consensus in the country.

Notwithstanding Yahya's arbitrary rejection of the proposal of an elected Constitution Convention, this could have served as the state's future legislative organ after it had framed the Constitution. However, in his search for a 'steelframe' to limit the National Assembly's freedom of legislation and at the same time legalize his authoritarian rule, Yahya Khan opted for the misnamed 'provisional' yet exhaustive Legal Framework Order (LFO). The LFO, published on 29 March 1970, comprised 27 Articles and contained rules relating to the holding of general elections and framing of the future Constitution of Pakistan. Its salient features, which were to be incorporated in the new Constitution, are as under:

1.   The National Assembly would consist of 313 members of whom 300 would occupy general seats and 13 seats would be reserved for women. Of these, 162 general seats and 7 women's seats would be held by East Pakistan while the remaining 138 general seats and 6 women's seats were to

be allocated to West Pakistan's four provinces and the centrally-administered Tribal Areas.

2. There would be a Provincial Assembly for each province of the Federation.

3. Polling for elections to the National Assembly would commence on 5 October 1970, and for the Provincial Assemblies not later than 20 October 1970.

4. According to Sections 20, 21, and 22 of the LFO, the Constitution would be so framed as to embody the following fundamental principles:

   i) Pakistan shall be a Federal Republic to be known as the Islamic Republic of Pakistan.

   ii) Islamic ideology, which is the basis for the creation of Pakistan, shall be preserved. The Head of State shall be a Muslim.

   iii) Adherence to the fundamental principles of democracy shall be ensured by providing direct and free periodical elections to the Federal and Provincial Legislatures on the basis of population and adult franchise.

   iv) The fundamental rights of the citizens shall be laid down and guaranteed.

   v) The independence of the judiciary shall be ensured.

   vi) All powers, including the legislative, administrative, and financial, shall be so distributed between the Federal and the Provincial Governments that the provinces shall have maximum autonomy, that is to say, maximum legislative, administrative, and financial powers; but the Federal Government shall also have adequate powers, including legislative, administrative, and financial powers, to discharge its responsibilities in relation to internal and external affairs and to preserve the independence and territorial integrity of the country.

vii) It shall be ensured that: a) the people of all areas in Pakistan shall be enabled to participate fully in all forms of national activities; and b) within a specific period, economic and all other disparities between the provinces and between different areas in a province are removed by the adoption of statutory and other measures.

5. The Constitution shall contain in its preamble an affirmation that:

   i) The Muslims of Pakistan shall be enabled, individually and collectively, to order their lives in accordance with the teachings of Islam as laid down in the Holy Quran and the *Sunnah*; and

   ii) The minorities shall be free to profess and practise their religion freely and to enjoy all rights, privileges, and protection due to them as citizens of Pakistan.

6. The Constitution shall provide that the National Assembly constituted under this Order shall be the first legislature of the Federation for the full term and the same would be the case for the Provincial Assemblies.

7. Section 24 stated that the National Assembly shall frame the Constitution in the form of a Bill to be called the Constitutional Bill within a period of 120 days from the date of its first meeting, and on 'its failure to do so shall stand dissolved'.

8. Section 25 stated that the Constitutional Bill as passed by the National Assembly shall be presented to the President for his assent and authentication. The National Assembly shall stand dissolved in the event that the President's authentication is refused.

9. Section 27 provided that the interpretation of the provisions of the LFO would rest with the President and that he, not the National Assembly, would have power to amend it.

10. The Constitution shall set out the directive principles of state policy by which the state shall be guided in the matter

of promoting an Islamic way of life, observance of Islamic moral standards, providing facilities for the teaching of the Holy Quran and Islamiat to the Muslims of Pakistan; and that no law repugnant to the teachings and requirements of Islam as set out in the Holy Quran and the *Sunnah* is made.

The specification of limits and the tight parameters of the future Constitution indicated that the military regime of Yahya Khan had strong perspectives on the fundamental nature and direction of the national document. Making the validity of the future Constitution dependent on the personal authentication of the CMLA, the military regime adopted a two-pronged political strategy to act arbitrarily and play the role of an active power-broker in the multi-party representative system in the parliament. Besides arrogating to the President the power of withholding his assent to the Constitutional Bill, the other potential weapon in the regime's hand was a deliberate omission in the Third Schedule of the LFO regarding the clear voting procedure for the passage of the Constitutional Bill in the National Assembly. While calling it a 'patent void', Mr Bhutto interpreted it 'as a favour left to the National Assembly'[9] (about voting procedure only); others believed that 'it was left to the Assembly out of sheer mischief in the belief that most of the 120 days allowed would be consumed in arguing over this very topic....'[10] However, Mr Bhutto attacked the LFO for the following lacunae:

> While the Order provided for a federal and parliamentary system of government, it left unsettled the important question of whether the federal legislature was to be unicameral or bicameral... it [LFO] left vague and open the central issue of provincial autonomy, and, by allowing an over-long period for election campaigning, it permitted this issue to become explosive. Perhaps these omissions occured on the basis of the miscalculations that the complexion of the National Assembly would be one of small conflicting parties and that no major parties would emerge to dominate the Assembly and dictate their will.[11]

Highly mandatory as it was, the LFO 'purported to set out a number of constitutional matters on which the Assembly was instructed what it must do', while subjecting its decisions and manoeuvrability to the final approval of the CMLA.[12] These implications meant, firstly, that Yahya Khan, the usurper in the high office, snatched away the sovereign status of the National Assembly which was to write the fundamental law of the land. Secondly, it was an open expression of the junta's 'distrust' in the constitution-making ability of the elected representatives of the people. Thirdly, the junta bound the elected representatives in the steel frame of the LFO to legislate only within its preconceived parameters of constitutionalism and federalism in the country. Fourthly, by defining limitations and mandatory injunctions, Yahya in effect promulgated a Constitution in the form of the LFO itself. Fifthly, no higher court in the country had judicial power to interpret or review the LFO, and the CMLA reserved unto himself the sole prerogative of changing the Order. Lastly, though unspecified in the LFO, the CMLA/President, while rejecting the Constitutional Bill, was not bound to assign any reason for his arbitrary action.[13] Thus, the overall legal and constitutional position of the LFO was nothing other than Yahya Khan himself in his military uniform.

Whether one can call it a serious legal lacuna or deliberate mischief, but Sections 24 and 25 of the LFO seemingly favoured Yahya. If the National Assembly were to fail in preparing the Constitutional Bill within 120 days (a mandatory requirement of the LFO) or if it succeeded, but in that event authentication was denied by the CMLA/President, it stood dissolved![14] What would happen then? In that event, two courses were open: either the military regime would hold fresh elections or itself could formulate a constitutional draft (following in the footprints of Ayub Khan). However, the CMLA in his broadcast on 28 November 1969, had expressed his version of the 120 days:

> I would be happy if they [i.e., the elected representatives in the National Assembly] can finalise it before the expiry of this period. If, however, they are unable to complete the task by the end of the stipulated period, the Assembly would stand dissolved and the nation will have to go to polls again.[15]

The most intriguing aspect of the LFO scheme was the simultaneous elections to the National Assembly and the five Provincial

Assemblies. While the National Assembly was supposed to act firstly as a constituent body, and then as the higher legislative organ of the land, what purpose were the Provincial Assemblies to serve? Under what Constitution were they to be formed to carry out the functions of the provincial legislatures? There was again complete silence in the LFO regarding the fate of the five Provincial Assemblies, if the National Assembly were dissolved. If one links this intriguing aspect of Yahya Khan's election exercise to his radio address on 3 December 1970, saying 'if no Constitution were evolved, Martial Law would continue',[16] the intent of the military junta can easily be ascertained. In the event of refusing authentication to the Constitutional Bill and the National Assembly being dissolved, the Provincial Assemblies could be used to legitimize the indefinite continuation of the junta's authoritarianism in the country.

FEDERALISM AND THE DISSOLUTION OF ONE UNIT

The question of One Unit had gravely impaired the integration of the national polity. Thanks to Ayub Khan's martial law, the abominable scheme of One Unit had continued in the 1960s. The political parties in both wings of the country were unanimous in demanding its dissolution and the restoration of the original provinces. The One Unit scheme had done more damage than good to the national integration process. In his 28 November 1969 speech, Yahya Khan had recognized such a harsh reality. He promulgated the Province of West Pakistan (Dissolution) Order on 30 March 1970, and on 30 June/1 July 1970, One Unit ceased to exist. It gave way to four provinces, i.e., Punjab, Balochistan, the NWFP, and Sindh. Under the CMLA's Order, Bahawalpur went to the Punjab, Karachi to Sindh, and Lasbela to Balochistan.

With the dissolution of One Unit, Lieutenant-General Atiqur Rahman, who had been sworn in as Governor of West Pakistan, was appointed Chairman of the Council of Administration, which consisted of the governors of the four provinces. The basic purpose of constituting such a council was to deal with joint issues concerning the restoration and administration of the four provinces. The main provisions of the dissolution of the One Unit structure are summarized in the following:[17]

1. Islamabad would be Federal Capital territory, and the President of Pakistan would have exclusive powers in relation to its administration. It would be within the jurisdiction of the High Court at Lahore.

2. The President would have powers with regards to West Pakistan Railways, WAPDA, the West Pakistan Agricultural Development Corporation, and the West Pakistan Small Industries Corporation. The President would appoint advisory boards with representatives of the new provinces for these bodies.

3. Each of the new provinces would have a High Court whose Chief Justice and other judges would be appointed by the President. The Provincial Governments of two or more provinces might agree to establish a common High Court.

4. All civil, criminal, and revenue courts and all tribunals would continue to exercise their respective jurisdiction and functions, and persons holding offices in such courts and tribunals would continue to hold their respective offices.

5. The West Pakistan Public Service Commission would cease to exist, and each province would have its own Public Service Commission. Two or more Provincial Governments might agree to establish a single Public Service Commission.

6. Persons serving the West Pakistan Government, other than those in the Central Civil Service, would be deemed to be serving the province in which they were for the time being serving.

7. All existing laws would continue in force until altered or amended by a competent authority.

8, Any question of doubt pertaining to the provisions of the Order, or any Order thereunder, would be resolved by the decision of the President, which would be final.

The constitutional issue of dissolving One Unit was linked to the overall relationship between the Centre and the provinces. Besides undermining the majority voice of the eastern wing in national affairs, the question of One Unit had acquired sinister undertones in Sindh, Balochistan, and the NWFP. Recognizing the impelling public pressure and its distasteful implications (i.e., the issue degenerating into the Punjabi v. non-Punjabi confrontation) in the forthcoming general elections, Yahya Khan hastened to get rid of the lingering legacy of the abhorrent 'parity formula'. But dissolution of One Unit without hammering out the complicated issue of provincial autonomy meant inevitable disaster. For such a 'blunder', Yahya Khan was censured particularly by the PPP leadership in West Pakistan. In Mr Bhutto's perspective, it was a huge mistake to dissolve One Unit without settling the issue of the quantum of provincial autonomy, and to allow the election in East Pakistan to be contested on this 'divisive issue'.[18] While considering provincial autonomy as the central issue in the whole gargantuan constitutional malaise in the country, he opined:

> The [Yahya] regime failed to appreciate the full significance of the demand for provincial autonomy in its scheme for the restoration of democracy. It could have followed several other courses to satisfy this demand. One course would have been for President Yahya Khan to have called a conference of leaders soon after the imposition of Martial Law to settle the quantum of autonomy for the provinces, the main problem. The regime should have put the leaders on notice by telling them that it was prepared to abolish One Unit and Parity and hold general elections provided there was an agreement, but not otherwise.[19]

Notwithstanding Bhutto's wise counselling on the provincial autonomy, it was the cherished desire of Mujibur Rahman to leave the vital issue of centre-province relationships to be decided by the National Assembly,[20] because in that august forum the clear Bengali majority plus the support of autonomists in the western wing could constitutionally reduce the powerful Centre to an impotent entity. Though Yahya Khan had pledged maximum provincial autonomy to the federating units, that stand was devoid of any legal character.

In his 28 November 1969 address, Yahya Khan had identified three fundamental issues: 'First, the question of One Unit; secondly, the issue of "one man, one vote" versus parity; and thirdly, the relationship between the Centre and the federating provinces.'[21] While he conceded the first two demands (i.e., one man, one vote, and the abolition of the amalgamation of West Pakistan into a single province) on the plea that they were inevitably connected with the holding of general elections and must be solved prior to committing the politicians to the hustings, he deliberately left the issue of federalism to be decided by the restive majority of autonomists in both wings of the country. His recognition of the gargantuan question of Centre-province relations is evident in the following:

> As regards the relations between the Centre and provin-
> ces ... the people of East Pakistan did not have their full
> share in the decision-making process on vital issues ...
> they were fully justified in being dissatisfied with this state
> of affairs. We shall, therefore, have to put an end to this
> position. The requirements would appear to be maximum
> provincial autonomy to the two wings of Pakistan as long
> as this does not impair national integrity and solidarity of
> the country.
> One of the main aspects of the whole relationship be-
> tween the Centre and provinces in Pakistan today lies in
> the financial and economic spheres. Federation implies
> not only a division of legislative powers but also that of
> financial powers. This matter will have to be dealt with in
> such a manner as would satisfy the legitimate require-
> ments and demands of the provinces as well as vital
> requirements of the nation as a whole. People of the two
> regions of Pakistan should have control over their
> economic resources and development as long as it does
> not adversely affect the working of the national govern-
> ment at the Centre.[22]

Despite the chorus of sycophantic praise that followed Yahya Khan's prompt recognition of maximum provincial autonomy, the undecided question of autonomy was the cause of an intense row in the ensuing general elections. If he could promulgate the LFO (a Constitution in itself) and dissolve One Unit, Yahya could easily hammer out a satisfactory solution to the problem of provincial autonomy as well. By following such a course of action, he would not have provided the autonomists an election plank to whip up public passions. Yahya Khan's blunder of leaving the sensitive question of autonomy open obliged the Awami League to present to the Bengalis its Six Points as the *Magna Carta* of their regional aspirations. What Mujib and his party needed was to enrol the majority in the eastern wing and pamper the smaller provinces (consistently complaining against the Punjabi domination of their resources and aspirations) to transform the country into a confederal structure. Was Yahya Khan trapped or did he simply acquiesce in Mujib's strategy? The question remains unanswered.

If Yahya Khan sincerely believed in what he considered the imperatives of 'maximum provincial autonomy' for both wings of the country, why was he hesitant to concede it in his LFO? By the time he stepped in to fulfil his legal and constitutional responsibilities to save the country from 'within', the following undeniable facts must have been clear to Yahya Khan:

- The issue of provincial autonomy was one of the major causes in delaying the constitution-making process in the years 1947-56.

- The detrimental system of One Unit was not established to serve the cause of provincial autonomy but to suppress the regional autonomy aspirations of the people of the eastern wing in particular. Such an oppressive structure was not liked by the smaller units in the western wing either.

- Besides imposing strident centralism on the country's otherwise federal polity, Ayub Khan's deliberate attempts to eliminate popular politics and incarcerate the politicians had alienated the Bengalis who viewed regional autonomy as the only viable alternative for their dignified 'national' survival.

- While Mujibur Rahman and his Awami League had presented the Six Points (a confederal scheme) as a panacea to all the ills and curses of the Bengalis, the politicians in the smaller units in the western wing were all for maximum provincial autonomy. Hyder Buksh Jatoi in Sindh, Mir Ghous Buksh Bizenjo and Ataullah Khan Mengal in Balochistan, and Wali Khan in the NWFP had emerged as ardent champions of provincial autonomy. The dissolution of One Unit had not fulfilled the aspirations of autonomists in the western wing; rather, it had stimulated their urge for genuine federalism.

- The demand for provincial autonomy remained the salient feature of every combination and alliance of various political parties (i.e., PDM, DAC, COP, etc.), formed in the late 1960s to oust Ayub Khan.

In view of the aforementioned political milieu, it was incumbent upon Yahya Khan to take a definite decision on the extent and form of provincial autonomy rather than merely recognizing the need for it. It was the strong apprehension of the non-Awami Leaguers in the eastern wing in general and the leadership in the western wing in particular that 'unless provincial autonomy were defined, Mujib would have a strong edge on them by preaching the gospel of Bengali nationalism and his Six Points which had become popular in East Pakistan'.[23] It was also feared that the promise of maximum regional autonomy, contained in the Six Points, could expedite the unchecked crescendo of Bengali nationalism, ultimately leading to the disintegration of the country itself.

Ironically, if Yahya Khan had accepted genuine and maximum provincial autonomy for the federating units, 'so why did he not put an end to this potentially dangerous issue by giving real autonomy and then firmly declaring: this far and no further?'[24] Such an act of setting limits to the extent of provincial autonomy by building up a consensus among the politicians and political parties would definitely have discouraged the use of this potent plank in the 1970 general elections. Bhutto opines that 'the regime should have put the leaders on notice by telling them that it was prepared to abolish One Unit and parity and hold general elections, provided there was an agreement on autonomy, but not otherwise. The necessity of fulfilling this condition precedent would have forced the leaders to work out a satisfactory solution on autonomy. Otherwise they would have incurred public anger and stood condemned for thwarting the restoration of democracy'.[25]

Yahya Khan did not take such precautionary and pre-emptive steps for averting the aforementioned dangers, the consequences of which seemed so dreadful to contemplate. He did nothing to hold back the rising tide of Bengali nationalism. What seems more intriguing is that the junta had the unmistakable intention of prolonging its rule. What it had concluded was a divided mandate in the forthcoming general elections, in which no party would be in a position to command a clear majority in the National Assembly. In that event, while the politicians were fighting among themselves over reconciling their divergent perspectives on provincial autonomy and the form of federalism in the country, Yahya Khan and his coterie would continue to rule at the Centre. Either by withholding presidential authentication of the Constitutional Bill or on the pretext of the National Assembly's inability to formulate the Constitution within the stipulated period of 120 days, the latter would stand dissolved.

However, the LFO specified the dissolution of the federal legislature and not the Provincial Assemblies. If one links Yahya Khan's deliberate omission of the delicate issue of provincial autonomy to that of the continuation of the Provincial Assemblies even after the dissolution of the National Assembly, the junta's ignominious plans for prolonging its rule indefinitely is proved beyond any shadow of doubt.

THE 1970 ELECTIONS

Although Yahya Khan continued to characterize his regime as 'temporary', this was apparently not agreed to by the rest of his 'comrades' at GHQ.[26] Far from creating conditions conducive to the establishment of a constitutional government, the military junta seemed heading towards adopting a two-pronged strategy: firstly, in order to appease the agitated minds of the politicians and thereby bring law and order under control, Yahya Khan acquiesced in some of their demands. Secondly, the military regime embarked upon an ambitious plan of introducing wide-ranging reforms in the state structure. Such a strategy did not fit in with the 'temporary' aspects of the military junta's solemn pledges 'to create conducive conditions' for the transfer of power to the future elected representatives of the people.

Despite the foregoing substantial doubts, Yahya Khan fixed 5 October 1970 for elections to the National Assembly and 22 October for elections to the five Provincial Assemblies. However, a massive natural calamity in the form of floods in the eastern wing of the country obliged Yahya Khan to move the election dates to 7 December 1970. The procedural details for the general elections had already been spelled out in the LFO. For the first time in the history of Pakistan, free and direct elections based on adult franchise seemed a step towards evolving a political order based on constitutional parliamentary democracy. By the time the election campaign was to unfold itself in the beginning of 1970 (amidst a plethora of political groups and parties), the PPP led by Mr Bhutto and the Awami League led by Mujibur Rahman had emerged as the two parties of real political significance in the country. Given the continuing antipathy and distrust between the two wings of the country, both the PPP and the Awami League had their actual political strength in the west and east wing of the country respectively.

Amidst the already polarized politics of the country, the lingering issue of provincial autonomy and the glaring economic disparities, particularly in the context of East Pakistan, dominated the first electioneering process in Pakistan. Totally at variance with the intelligence reports of the Yahya regime and the euphemistic expectations of many within and without the country, the election results were surprising. Having passed off quite peacefully and without major irregularities, the 7 December 1970 general elections accorded an overwhelming majority in the eastern wing to the Awami League and to the PPP in the western wing. While the unexpected election results led to an immediate East-West confrontation, it also deprived the ruling elite of its mediatory role. Besides such painful aspects of the 1970 general elections, the following were the other striking features of the election results:[27]

- The total defeat of the Convention Muslim League and the victory of the PPP and the Awami League demonstrated the complete rejection of Ayub Khan's political and constitutional system.

- The right wing religious parties, contesting elections on the much discredited slogan of 'Islam is in danger', were outrightly rejected by the electorate. This also shows that the influence of the *ulema* was much less than was generally believed or propagated in the country.

- The candidates belonging to the armed forces and parties advocating strident centralism in the country were generally defeated.

The Awami League's electoral victory was mainly attributed to its Six Points programme for autonomy for the eastern wing. The PPP had won elections on the planks of economic radicalism, federalism, and an anti-India posture, and, above all, the dynamic political profile of its leader, Zulfikar Ali Bhutto. Overall, the net outcome of the 1970 general elections had left the destiny of the whole country in the hands of Mujib, Bhutto, and General Yahya Khan. Mujibur Rahman had hinted prior to the elections that his Six Points were not the 'Bible', and they could be suitably amended. Yet soon after the stunning election results, his tone hardened and he asserted that the Constitution of Pakistan would be based on his Six Points only. Mujib began to hurl threats at his political opponents, saying that if anyone opposed the framing of the Constitution on the basis of Six Points, the Awami League would launch a massive movement.[28]

Contrary to Mujib's perspectives on the future Constitution, Bhutto, who represented the western wing, insisted on not only power-sharing in the federal government but also in playing an active role in constitution-formulation. Opining that 'majority alone does not count in national politics', Bhutto unveiled his perspectives on the future Constitution of Pakistan in a press conference on 27 December 1970, in the following:

> In a federation a consensus of all the federating units was essential for ensuring the durability of any future Constitution. Thus the integration of West Pakistan into One Unit, to which Bengal and the Punjab had consented, had failed because the minority provinces were unhappy about it. There was a difference between forming a Government and making a Constitution; for one party or region to impose its majority in forming a Government did not matter much, but it certainly would in the process of Constitution-making. If the majority party insisted on making a Constitution to its own liking he would step aside, but in such an event the People's Party would not be responsible for the consequences that would ensue.[29]

The hundred days that followed the December 1970 elections were very crucial for the destiny of the Federation. The confederal promise contained in Mujib's Six Points presented a dilemma not only to the major actors, i.e., Yahya, Bhutto, and Mujib, but to the whole nation as well. The meetings between Bhutto and Mujib to hammer out major constitutional differences had yielded hardly any positive results. While Mujibur Rahman, flanked by extremist elements in the Awami League, continued to adhere to his Six Points, envisaging complete independence of the eastern wing from the Centre (except in defence and foreign affairs), Yahya Khan announced on 13 February

1971 that the first National Assembly session would be held in Dhaka on 3 March 1971.

So far, no consensus on constitutional issues had been arrived at and the political future of the entire Federation looked very bleak. Having won a landslide electoral victory in the eastern wing, Mujib projected himself as completely inflexible. Adopting an uncompromising attitude towards Mujib and his Six Points, Bhutto declared that 'under the present circumstances' it was pointless for the PPP 'to make the journey to Dacca merely to endorse a Constitution in the framing of which they would have no say'.[30]

The Pakistan Muslim League (Qayyum Group) also announced, on 24 February 1971, at the Party's convention in Peshawar, its inability to attend the National Assembly's opening session in Dhaka, regretting Mujib's 'unbending attitude'.[31] Khan Qayyum opined that his party, while advocating maximum provincial autonomy consistent with a viable Centre, did not accept any constitutional arrangement which jeopardized the very basis of the Federation.[32]

While terming the stiff opposition to his Six Points as 'dark conspiratoral forces', Mujib attacked the western wing leadership, saying that 'It is they who are about to inflict a mortal blow on the integrity of Pakistan by frustrating the last opportunity that the people of Pakistan have of evolving for themselves, through a democratic and constitutional process, a basis for living together. . .'[33]

Besides the hardened perspectives of Mujib and his Awami League on the Constitution formulations to their own liking, the actual rationale of their complete rejection of the stand and contentions of other parties on the Constitution were different. Throughout the 1970 election campaign, Mujib and his Awami League had created political hysteria among the people of the eastern wing. The opportunity for electioneering was utilized to ride on the rising crest of Bengali frustrations, alienation, and exclusion from the decision-making process at the Centre. After the election, the Awami League, so as to deter the military regime from taking any action against it and to formulate a Constitution to the liking of its supporters in the eastern wing, whipped up the tempo of hatred against the Centre, which was projected and identified completely with the western wing only.

However, the West Pakistan leadership had expected that, after the elections, Mujib and his Awami League would soften their hard stance on the future federal structure, that Mujib might amend his

Six Points. But they found the Awami Leaguers labelling them as 'exploiters and dacoits'. The Generals at GHQ and the bureaucratic clique in the Civil Secretariat were equally baffled by their faulty assessment of the election results. The ruling Generals 'had never accepted the Six Points formula but they allowed the Awami League to contest elections on that basis in the hope that the Awami League would not secure an absolute majority and it would then be willing to make a compromise. Now these calculations were upset'.[34]

TOWARDS A HOLOCAUST

Bhutto seriously considered the Awami League's Six Points as a confederal scheme for outright secession from the Federation. Besides, the PPP leadership started growing restive as it increasingly apprehended that it might be rendered irrelevant in the future constitution-formulation in the 313 member Assembly. Having failed to reach a compromise with Mujib over constitutional and political issues, Bhutto adopted a tough line towards the Six Points of the Awami League. On 15 February 1971, Bhutto announced in Peshawar that unless his party received a positive and clear assurance from Mujibur Rahman about the accommodation of the PPP's reasonable demands in the future Constitution, he and his party would not attend the National Assembly session to be held on 3 March 1971 in Dhaka.[35]

The Awami League's politico-constitutional assertions in the wake of its stunning electoral victory had upset Yahya Khan and his coterie at GHQ and they were anxious to wield power and prolong their 'legal' authority by playing one politician against another. Amidst the crisis of constitutional consensus and political legitimacy, mounting in intensity, the ruling military elite faced the dilemma of regaining the political initiative which it had lost to the Awami League via the 1970 elections. However, in their search for pressure tactics to bend the uncompromising Mujib and his Awami League, the Generals at GHQ found Bhutto and his PPP's stance on the Six Points to be a great relief. That is why Mujibur Rahman and his Awami League increasingly perceived an abject collusion between Bhutto and the Generals. The latter were getting restless in their desire to thwart constitution-formulations and to frustrate the democratic transfer of power to the elected representatives of the people.

On 1 March 1971, Yahya Khan, finding an excuse in the fact that the PPP, the largest party from West Pakistan, was not attending the session, postponed the convening of the first session of the National Assembly. While it exposed the blatant discrimination of the ruling elite at the Centre, Yahya Khan's postponement of the first National Assembly session gave Mujib a pretext to unleash a ferocious massive political reaction in the eastern wing. Mujib and his Awami League openly asked the Bengalis not to pay taxes until the transfer of power and returning of the military to barracks. The ensuing serious political storm crippled the provincial administration and embarrassed the Centre, as the political milieu in the eastern wing pointed to the strong possibility of an independent Bangladesh.

Contrary to the outright demands for an independent Bangladesh by the Bengali militants, Mujibur Rahman merely insisted on a Constitution based on his Six Points. However, while rejecting Yahya Khan's call for a meeting of all parliamentary groups at Dhaka on 10 March 1971, Mujib demanded at a public meeting (7 March) the fulfilment of seven preconditions for attending the National Assembly session. They were:[36]

- Withdrawal of martial law.

- Return of troops to their barracks.

- Immediate transfer of power to the elected representatives.

- Ceasing of the transfer of troops from West Pakistan to East Pakistan.

- Prompt termination of firing on civilians.

- Non-interference by military authorities in the functioning of the government in the eastern wing.

- The maintenance of law and order to be left to the Bengal Rifles and the Awami League Volunteers.

In such a delicately-poised situation, with the hardened perspectives at the Centre and of the Awami League, the appointment of Lieutenant General Tikka Khan as the new Governor of East Pakistan added fuel to the fire. By then, Mujib and his Awami League had set up a parallel government in Dhaka. When Tikka arrived in Dhaka, he was greeted with a garland of shoes and the then Chief Justice of the Dhaka High Court blatantly refused to offer him oath of office.[37] Notorious as he was for his 'firmness' and obeying of 'orders', Tikka's appointment as a Governor signalled the subsequent military crackdown on the Awami Leaguers. Tikka's arrival in Dhaka coincided with the fast inflow of military troops into East Pakistan from the western wing. This left the Awami League and its leadership intensely suspicious and resentful in the unfolding scenario of using military means for political ends.

Bhutto's refusal to attend the National Assembly session and his meetings with Yahya Khan provided his political opponents the opportunity to heap acrimonious criticism on him. His growing association with the army was interpreted as 'enigmatic'. Knowing full well the political stunts of the defeated leaders in West Pakistan and their ignominious intent of heaping responsibility for the whole political mess in the eastern wing on Bhutto's shoulders, the latter should have avoided such insinuations by direct political dealings with Mujib and his Awami League. Had he maintained political links with Mujib and attended the Assembly session on 3 March, he would definitely have placed the entire burden of the subsequent tragedy on the shoulders of Yahya Khan and his advisers. By accommodating the political demands of Mujib, and not those of Yahya Khan who wielded power without the concurrence of the people of Pakistan, Bhutto would certainly have been on a much higher moral and political ground. That too, when the military dictator was arrogating unto himself the decisive prerogative of accepting or rejecting the Constitution, and dissolving the National Assembly (a sovereign body) at his whim.

FROM BALLOT TO BULLET

When the province-wide strike and the massive movement of civil disobedience launched by Mujib and his Awami League was giving nightmares to Yahya Khan and other generals at GHQ, the military regime adopted a two-pronged strategy: to appease Mujib through negotiations and to deter him by reinforcing military means in the eastern wing. Yahya and Mujib began their constitutional dialogue on 16 March 1971 and, under the facade of political negotiations, the junta completed its preparations for a heavy crackdown on the Bengalis. With the sands of time running out, Bhutto joined in the beleaguered negotiations as well. Now, instead of insisting on framing the Constitution based on the Six Points, Mujib opined that the members of the National Assembly should meet separately for their respective wings of the country, meaning thereby to evolve two Constitutions for the future confederal structure of Pakistan. Such intransigence on the part of Mujibur Rahman led to the final breaking off of the negotiations, forcing the coercive levers of state to assert their writ at the wrong time.

The murderous campaign of the military against its own people wiped out all hopes of an integrated Federation. While the military junta looked at everything in the eastern wing in conspiratorial terms, the Awami League, in view of the military's atrocities against the people, declared the independence of Bangladesh on 26 March 1971. What happened later is beyond the scope of this study. Suffice it to say that 16 December 1971 witnessed the final falling apart of the uneasy Federation. Besides all other unpalatable conclusions, it was established beyond any shadow of doubt that whenever soldiers, sailors, and airmen interfered in the complex permutations of politics, the results were disastrous. The generals at GHQ and their comrades in the Civil Secretariat were the real culprits, while Mujib and Bhutto remained mere pawns in the whole politico-military drama leading to the secession of East Pakistan.

CONCLUSION

Continuous authoritarian assaults on the vital principles of federalism and constitutionalism by the military-bureaucratic regimes had scuttled the representative system and led to the demise of the spirit of federalism, eventually leading to the tragic secession of the eastern wing, the largest province of the Federation. The dictatorial spells at the Centre had eroded all pretensions to the existence of even a modicum of provincial autonomy in the country. The constitutionally uncontrolled, politically unaccountable, and (by personal inclination) unbridled regimes of Ayub Khan and Yahya Khan, the two military dictators believing in a 'strong Pakistan' had blatantly mauled the pluralistic nature of the country, attempting to weld it into a single entity. They had highlighted their 'golden periods' by prompt promulgation of black laws and ordinances to incarcerate the protagonists of provincial autonomy. Ironically, those who visualized that the strident centralism and anti-constitutionalism of the dictators might lead to doom and destruction were readily detained and ruthlessly crushed as 'anti-state elements'. That is why an odious milieu of arbitrariness and outright political suppression plunged the whole nation into a long nightmare in December 1971.

8

MAKING OF THE 1973 CONSTITUTION: CONSTITUTIONALISM AND FEDERALISM UNDER BHUTTO

PICKING UP THE PIECES

After Yahya Khan's treacherous act of presiding over the destruction of the Federation, Zulfikar Ali Bhutto stepped in on 20 December 1971. Beginning inauspiciously with a civilian martial law, Bhutto faced the most difficult task of picking up the pieces of Pakistan, lest the example of Bangladesh infect the remaining federating units in the western wing.

Bhutto had assumed power amidst confusion, apprehensions as to the possible further breakup of the country, pent-up public emotions, and anguish against the licentious military junta. Indeed, this was the worst crisis of the state. However, the reputation of the military being at the lowest ebb, Bhutto's ascent to the highest office had the major political advantage of receiving popular acclaim and the support of the masses. But power to Bhutto was not transferred under any constitutional scheme nor, for that matter, was it voluntarily relinquished by the military junta. Bhutto owed his ascent to the office of President and the civilian CMLA to a mini-coup and to the complete loss of the military's credibility among the people of Pakistan.

Bhutto's reasons for donning the seemingly potent cap of CMLA were: a) to establish civilian supremacy over the Bonapartism of the generals at GHQ; b) to effect his party's socio-economic reforms through the coercive levers of military authority against the scheming bureaucrats, rapacious feudal lords, and defiant industrialists; and c) the extreme difficulty of summoning the National Assembly to get any constitutional scheme ratified at the shortest notice.

From the time that Bhutto assumed power, he pledged to start with 'a clean slate'. He withdrew the ban on political parties and annulled the results of inconclusive by-elections conducted by the military regime after 25 March 1971. Besides effecting a number of reforms in the socio-economic structure of the state, Bhutto seemed determined to give the nation a Constitution, a prerequisite of viable national survival and democratic order.

TRIPARTITE ACCORD

With the avowed objective of constitution-making, the Bhutto Government held consultations with the major political parties, i.e., the National Awami Party (NAP) and the Jamiat-i-Ulema-i-Islam (JUI). After protracted negotiations, the PPP on the one hand and the JUI-NAP on the other hand agreed upon the following, relating to the formulation of the Constitution:[1]

- Martial Law would be lifted on 14 August 1972.

- The National Assembly would be convened on 14 April 1972 for a period not exceeding three days. It would be reconvened on 14 August 1972.

- An Interim Constitution would be prepared on the basis of the Government of India Act, 1935, read with the Indian Independence Act of 1947, with consequential amendments.

- A committee of the National Assembly would draft a Constitution and finalize its report by 1 August 1972.

- Until the permanent Constitution was framed by the National Assembly, the Central Government would have the power to appoint Governors in the provinces but, by way of compromise, the Central Government would, during the interim period, also appoint Governors in consultations with the majority in the provinces of Balochistan and the NWFP, where the JUI-NAP had a majority.

- The JUI and the NAP, being majority parties, had the right to form Provincial Governments in the NWFP and Balochistan.

- After 14 August 1972, the National Assembly would act both as the constitution-making and the legislative organ of the state, until a permanent Constitution was passed and adopted.

The presentation of the draft of the Interim Constitution to the opposition parties on 11 April 1972, to solicit their views and gain their political backing, deepened the already wide gulf between the PPP and its political rivals. The opposition parties demanded a parliamentary form of government but the draft of the Interim Constitution presented to them had provided for a presidential system. The National Awami Party, led by Khan Abdul Wali Khan, characterized the draft of the Interim Constitution as according Bhutto the status and powers of 'the Governor-General of India, the Viceroy of India, the American President and everything else'.[2]

Besides the powers and status of the President, the opposition parties specifically objected to the distribution of powers between the Centre and the federating units, the presidential prerogative to dissolve the National Assembly, etc. Mir Ghous Buksh Bizenjo, President of the Balochistan NAP, criticized the anti-federal character of the Interim Constitution as it did not equitably distribute resources between the Centre and the provinces.[3] His other significant demand was that the ministers should be made responsible to the legislature and not to the President alone.

In the background of the aforementioned and other similar objections, when the draft of the Interim Constitution was presented before the National Assembly for its approval and adoption till the formulation of the permanent Constitution, Bhutto stated that 'over 100 members of the Assembly had promised to vote for the continuation of Martial Law until 14 August but he had decided that if the Assembly adopted the Interim Constitution, Martial Law should be lifted on 21 April'.[4] Such a dramatic announcement took the opposition members by surprise; they had no alternative except to endorse the Interim Constitution. During the same session, Bhutto was elected President of the National Assembly with 104 votes, his rival candidate, Sardar Sherbaz Khan Mazari, getting 38 votes. The Assembly unanimously adopted a resolution reposing confidence in Bhutto as President.

By virtue of the tripartite accord between the PPP and the JUI-NAP, martial law was to continue in the country till 14 August 1972, yet Bhutto, in a characteristic move, lifted it on 21 April. Why did Bhutto hasten to lift martial law from the country? The appropriate answer, besides Bhutto's personal desire to take the credit for this, lies in the announcement of the historic judgment by the Supreme Court of Pakistan in *Miss Asma Jilani v. The Government of Punjab and others* on 20 April 1972. The Supreme Court declared Yahya

Khan's martial law to be illegal and confirmed the principle of civilian supremacy in the national political system. The steps taken by the National Assembly in approving Bhutto's presidency, and the adoption of the Interim Constitution for the country were held valid in the same case.

THE 1972 INTERIM CONSTITUTION

The Interim Constitution introduced on 21 April 1972 was unilaterally prepared by the Federal Government. It was never discussed, debated, or deliberated upon, or decided by voting in the National Assembly. It was simply presented as 'One Man's Legislation' in the Assembly and got approval without an amendment or alteration.

The Interim Constitution named the country as an Islamic Republic. It was divided into twelve parts (288 Articles) and seven Schedules. The preamble of the Constitution incorporated the Objectives Resolution of March 1949. Pakistan was recognized as a Federation. Besides the huge discretionary powers of the President relating to the Executive, Judiciary, and Legislature, the Governors in the provinces also possessed substantial powers. The Governor had the power to dismiss the Chief Minister if the Provincial Assembly passed a no-confidence motion, naming his successor. The Governor might appoint a Chief Minister who was not a member of the Assembly, on the condition that he was to be elected to the Assembly within twelve months.

The Courts were barred from challenging the Interim Constitution. The President and the National Assembly were to continue for a five-year term. The President was empowered to approve the annual budget for the year 1972. The President and the provincial Governors were required to submit reports to the Legislatures on the observance and implementation of the principles of state policy enumerated in the Constitution. The President was to exercise executive authority with the assistance and advice of the Council of Ministers. He was the Supreme Commander of the Armed Forces. The President had the power to suspend fundamental rights during a national emergency. He was to be advised on Islamic ideology by the Islamic Council appointed by the President himself.

MISS ASMA JILANI V. THE GOVERNMENT OF PUNJAB: THE EMASCULATION OF THE DOCTRINE OF NECESSITY

An Overview

The principal dilemma of Pakistan's constitutional history has been the emergence of despots who dared not only to wreck the constitutional foundations of the state, but provided for notorious brakes on the democratic process using the dubious notions of 'controlled democracy', 'basic democracy' and 'Islamic democracy'. The overriding concern and passion of the ruling elite were to perpetuate themselves by hook or by crook. At various historic points in the over four-decade long history of Pakistan, the higher Courts of the land were required to pass their verdicts on extra-constitutional issues, emerging out of the abrogation or the putting in abeyance of the various Constitutions. By virtue of these verdicts on various occasions, the doctrine of necessity emerged as a cliche in the context of the constitutional history of Pakistan. The upshot of the whole dilemma could be explained in the words of Dieter Conrad, who opines:

> One distinguishing feature of Pakistan's unhappy constitutional history is the persistence of legalistic effort accompanying the most abrupt political changes and break-offs. This effort clearly has been directed towards ensuring a measure of continuity and legal coherence in the teeth, as it were, of recurring irregularity and constitutional upheaval. Repeatedly, the Courts have been involved in the paradoxical task of delineating, from first principle, some constitutional contours of extra-constitutional action. They have thus produced a whole series of judicial pronouncements dealing at explicit length with the validity of extra-constitutional emergency measures and revolutionary changes.[5]

Until the promulgation of the 1972 Interim Constitution, the doctrine of state necessity seemed an effective weapon and rationale to capture power and dispense with the existing constitutional arrangements. Ever since 1955, the fragmented constitutional history of the country had been dominated by sanctimonious doctrine. However, in the Miss Asma Jilani case, the Supreme Court of Pakistan pronounced its historic judgment, which in the words of a British constitutionalist, Leslie Wolf-Phillips, could be briefly characterized as 'Usurpers, Beware!'[6]

Facts

The petitioner's (Miss Asma Jilani's) father, Malik Ghulam Jilani, was arrested on 22 December 1971, under the Defence of Pakistan Rules (DPR). Subsequently, the said detention order was modified and substituted by another order, purported to have been issued by Malik Ghulam Mustafa Khar, the civilian Martial Law Administrator, Punjab, under MLR 78. The Lahore High Court dismissed the petition on the preliminary objection that it was debarred from entertaining *habeas corpus* petitions under the Martial Law Orders 'Jurisdiction of Courts (Removal of Doubts) Order 3 of 1969'. However, the Lahore High Court gave the petitioner a certificate to appeal in the Supreme Court of Pakistan.

The editor of the daily *Dawn*, Mr Altaf Gauhar, was also arrested in February 1972 under the same Martial Law Regulation, and the Sindh High Court granted the petitioner, Mrs Zarina Gauhar, a certificate to appeal in the Supreme Court. Thus, the hearings of Criminal Appeal No. 19 of 1972 (Miss Asma Jilani vs. The Government of the Punjab) and Criminal Appeal No. K-2 of 1972 (Mrs Zarina Gauhar vs. The Province of Sindh), decided by the Supreme Court of Pakistan on 20 April 1972 (PLD 1972 SC 139), are known as the Miss Asma Jilani case.

The precise question of law for determination before the Supreme Court was whether the High Courts had jurisdiction under Article 98 of the 1962 Constitution to enquire into the validity of the orders of detention issued under MLR 78 in the face of provisions contained in the Jurisdiction of Courts (Removal of Doubts) Order 3 of 1969, which barred the Courts from questioning such validity. Besides, a further question arose, whether the principle of law laid down in the State vs. Dosso (PLD 1958 SC 533) was a correct exposition of law.

Chief Justice Hamoodur Rahman observed that it was the duty of the judge to see that the law which he is called upon to administer is made by a person or authority legally competent to make the law, and that the law is capable of being enforced by the legal machinery: the two tests of legitimacy and efficacy. Considering the validity of Yahya Khan's takeover in March 1969, the Chief Justice wrote:

> It is clear that under the Constitution of 1962, Field Marshal Muhammad Ayub Khan has no power to hand over power to anybody. . . he could resign his office . . . could also proclaim an emergency. . . and may be for the present purpose that he also proclaim Martial Law if the situation was not controlled by the civil administration. It is difficult, however, to appreciate under what authority a military Commander could proclaim Martial Law . . . the military Commander had no power also to abrogate the Constitution . . . The assumption of power by Agha Muhammad Yahya Khan as Chief Martial Law Administrator and later as President of Pakistan was an act of usurpation, and was illegal and unconstitutional. All the legislative and administrative measures taken by this unauthorised and unconstitutional regime cannot be upheld on the basis of legitimacy, but such laws and measures which are protected by the doctrine of necessity, that is to say which were made for the welfare of the nation and for ordinary orderly administration of the country, can deemed to be valid . . . Martial Law Regulation No. 78 of 1971 under which the two detenus were held is an illegal regulation which cannot enjoy the protection of the law of necessity.

Having declared Yahya Khan's Martial Law illegal and unconstitutional, the Chief Justice dilated on the legal recognition that had been given to 'successive manoeuvring for usurpation of power under the pseudonym of Martial Law' by the Supreme Court in the Dosso case. The theory that a successful *coup* is a revolution if it annuls the Constitution and the annulment is effective was in particular reviewed by the Chief Justice.

The Court held that in laying down such a novel juristic principle of such far-reaching importance, the Chief Justice in the case of the State vs. Dosso proceeded on the basis of certain assumptions, namely: (i) 'That the basic doctrines of legal positivism', which he was accepting, were such firmly and universally accepted doctrines that 'the whole science of modern jurisprudence' rested upon them; (ii) that any 'abrupt political change not within the contemplation of the

Constitution' constitutes a revolution, no matter how temporary or transitory the change, if no one has taken any step to oppose it; and (iii) that the rule of international law with regard to the recognition of states can determine the validity also of the state's internal sovereignty. These assumptions were not justified. Kelsen's theory was by no means a universally accepted theory, nor was it a theory which could claim to have become a basic doctrine of the science of modern jurisprudence, nor did Kelsen ever attempt to formulate any theory which 'favours totalitarianism'. The Court, after its detailed reasoning, came to the conclusion:

> With the utmost respect, therefore, I would agree with the criticism that the learned Chief Justice [Muhammad Munir CJ] not only misapplied the doctrine of Hans Kelsen, but also fell into error that it was a generally accepted doctrine of modern jurisprudence. Even the disciples of Kelsen have hesitated to go far as Kelsen had gone . . . I am unable to resist the conclusion that [Muhammad Munir] erred both in interpreting Kelsen's theory and applying the same to the facts and circumstances of the case before him. The principle enunciated by him is wholly unsustainable, and I am duty-bound to say that it cannot be treated as good law either on the principle of *stare decisis* or even otherwise.

Having repudiated the judgment in the State vs. Dosso case, the Chief Justice upheld the following universally recognized democratic and constitutional norms:

> No single man can give a Constitution to the society which, in one sense, is an agreement between the people to live together under an Order which will fulfil their expectations, reflect their aspirations and hold promise for the realisation of their selves. It must, therefore, embody the will of the people which is usually expressed through the medium of chosen representatives. It must be this type of Constitution from which the norms of the new legal order will derive their validity . . . A person who destroys the national legal order in an illegitimate manner cannot be regarded as a valid source of law-making. Maybe, that on account of his holding the

coercive apparatus of the state, the people and the Courts
are silenced temporarily, but let it be laid down firmly that
the order which the usurper imposes will remain illegal
and Courts will not recognise its rules and act upon them
as *de jure*. As soon as the first opportunity arises, when
the coercive apparatus falls from the hands of the
usurper, he should be tried for high treason and suitably
punished. This alone will serve a deterrent to would-be
adventurers.

Besides overturning the Dosso case, the judgment in the Asma
Jilani case emasculated the doctrine of necessity—a readily available
excuse for usurpers to validate their extra-constitutional adventures.
In the opinion of a jurisconsult, Kamal Azfar, Asma Jilani's case 'has
ever since been the bright star in Pakistan's constitutional firmament.
Bold though the decision in Asma Jilani's case was, it cannot be
forgotten that the Court declared Yahya Khan a usurper only after
he had ceased to hold office. The Court has yet to perform the painful
duty of questioning the legitimacy of a *de facto* sovereign while he is
in office.'[7]

MAKING OF THE 1973 CONSTITUTION

During the three-day session of the National Assembly in April
1972, a special committee of 25 members of the Assembly, representing both the ruling and the opposition parties, was formed to
draft the Constitution. The Committee, headed by Mahmud Ali
Kasuri, was faced with discord and violent controversies over the
major constitutional issues. The differences chiefly centred on the
following points:

- the presidential or parliamentary form of government.

- federalism, i.e., the division of powers between the Centre
  and the provinces.

- the powers of the head of government.

- the Islamic provisions in the Constitution.

Notwithstanding the aforementioned disagreements, the Constitutional Committee, as orginally proposed, was to submit its draft of

the Constitution on 14 August 1972. However, the Committee was unable to meet the deadline and the delay was ascribed to serious differences between the ruling PPP and the NAP over the form and extent of federalism in the country; and to the debating of the 1972 Simla Agreement in the National Assembly. When the Assembly met on 14 August 1972, it unanimously extended the time for submitting the Draft Constitution till 31 December 1972.

Meanwhile, Mahmud Ali Kasuri, the Chairman of the Constitutional Committee, resigned in the first week of October, and Abdul Hafeez Pirzada was elected its Chairman. To accelerate the pace of constitution-making, on the invitation of President Bhutto, a conference of various parliamentary groups in the Assembly was convened in Rawalpindi on 17-20 October 1972. The intense and co-operative deliberations of the participants led to an agreement on a formula, providing for a federal and parliamentary form of government in the country. The constitutional accord signed on 20 October provided for the following imperatives to be incorporated in the draft Constitution:[8]

1. The Head of State would be the President, to be elected by an absolute majority of the total membership of the Federal Legislature. The President had to be over 45 years of age, and Muslim by religion.

2. Islam would be the state religion.

3. The Prime Minister would be the Chief Executive, and his advice would be binding on the President.

4. The Prime Minister would be elected by the National Assembly and he and his Cabinet would be responsible to the Federal Legislature.

5. Besides being a Muslim, the Prime Minister would have to be a member of the National Assembly.

6. The National Assembly would consist of 200 members directly elected by universal adult franchise. For a period of ten years, ten seats would be reserved for women, to be elected by the members of the Assembly.

7. The upper house of the Federal Legislature would be known as the Senate, and would consist of sixty members.

Each provincial legislature would elect fourteen Senators by a single transferable vote. The members of the National Assembly from the Tribal Areas would elect two Senators, and two would be elected by the National Assembly or selected by the President from the Federal Capital Territory.

8. The minimum age for members of the National Assembly would be twenty-five years and for Senators, thirty years.

9. Any vote of no confidence in the Prime Minister would have to name his successor, and for a period of fifteen years or three electoral terms, whichever was greater, any such motion would have to be adopted by a majority of two-thirds of the total membership of the National Assembly. If the no-confidence motion were defeated, such a motion might not be introduced for the next six months. A no-confidence motion might not be introduced during the budget session of the National Assembly.

10. The Prime Minister might ask the President to dissolve the National Assembly at any time.

11. The Constitution would include a list of subjects reserved for the Federal Government and a concurrent list of subjects on which both the Federal and Provincial Governments might legislate. All other subjects would be reserved for the Provincial Governments.

12. Amendments to the Constitution would require approval by a two-third majority in the National Assembly and a simple majority in the Senate.

13. A Council of Common Interests (CCI), consisting of the Provincial Chief Ministers and four Central Ministers, would decide upon specified matters of common interest.

14. The federating units would be represented in the Planning Commission of Pakistan.

15. The constitutional provisions ensuring a parliamentary system at the centre would apply *mutatis mutandis* to the provincial legislatures.

The Constitutional Committee of the National Assembly resumed its deliberations in the light of the 20 October Accord on 2 December 1972. Despite lingering disagreements and differences, the Committee was able to place the draft Constitution before the National Assembly on 31 December 1972, together with the objections and dissenting notes of five out of the twenty-five members. Prior to the introduction of the Draft Constitution as a Bill on 2 February 1973, the opposition parties in the Assembly resolved that they would 'resist all efforts to pass an unIslamic, undemocratic, non-parliamentary, and non-federal Constitution, and that if their legitimate amendments were not accepted, they would have no choice except to go to the nation'.[9] However, when the National Assembly opened debate on the Constitutional Bill on 7 February, the ruling PPP seemed willing to seek the co-operation of the opposition parliamentary groups 'in rectifying whatever mistakes might have crept into the draft'.[10]

Meanwhile, the opposition continued its boycott of the National Assembly. Despite boycotts and walk-outs by the opposition, pressing for a Constitution of its choice and inclinations, the ruling party continued efforts to hammer out a compromise even outside the Assembly. For effecting amendments in the Draft Constitution, the opposition (both left and right groups) formed a 'United Democratic Front', which increasingly characterized the Bill as immoral, undemocratic, and unIslamic. Finally, the Government of the day had to give in to seven out of the eleven constitutional demands of the UDF. Thus, the Constitutional Bill was finally adopted without a dissenting vote on 10 April 1973. It was signed during a session of the National Assembly by the 137 members as the Constitution of the Islamic Republic of Pakistan. The ruling PPP felt miraculously lucky to have got unanimous authentication of the Constitution. After a thirty-one gun salute, President Bhutto remarked:

> The Consititution of the Islamic Republic of Pakistan is the Constitution of the people of Pakistan and they are best suited to speak for it. The document is their property and they are best suited to protect it. It is our hope and belief that under the inspiring guidance of God Almighty, the people of Pakistan will speak for their Constitution and will protect it for all times to come.[11]

The 26th anniversary of Independence Day coincided with the promulgation of the 1973 Constitution in the country. Having been elected as the Prime Minister of Pakistan under the new constitutional arrangements, Bhutto addressed his nation and said:

> The Constitution ensures that our people will not again be subjected to the arbitrariness, the exploitation and the suppression which had turned the cherished Muslim dream of an independent homeland into a long nightmare. The Federal provisions of this Constitution and the existence of a bicameral Federal Legislature are meant to allow the various regions of Pakistan to play their full part in the nation's social, political, and economic life. The Constitution embodies the principle of Islamic Socialism in order that we can eradicate poverty and want from our land.
> No Constitution in the world is ever perfect. All Constitutions undergo transformation through amendments in the light of a nation's experience. But no Constitution is ever workable without the patience, the tolerance, the search for accommodation that are necessary to the preservation of democracy.[12]

SALIENT FEATURES OF THE 1973 CONSTITUTION

Having been adopted on 10 April and formally promulgated on 14 August 1973, the Constitution created a truly federal parliamentary system of government and reflected contemporary democratic principles. This Constitution was the third in the history of the country, the first having been adopted in 1956 and abrogated two years later, and the second introduced by General Ayub Khan in 1962 and abrogated by General Yahya Khan in 1969. The first ever framed by directly elected representatives of the people, the 1973 Constitution put the country back on the rails of democracy after fifteen years of political frustration. The salient features of the 1973 Constitution can be summarized as follows:

- Consisting of 280 Articles and six Schedules, the 1973 Constitution provided for a parliamentary form of government with a federal structure, an independent judiciary to protect the fundamental rights of the people, and a statement of the principles of policy which should guide the formulation of laws. Embodying the spirit of the March 1949 Objectives Resolution, the Preamble of the Constitution envisaged the exercise of state power and authority through the chosen representatives of the people of Pakistan. While seeking to create an egalitarian society, the Preamble assured fundamental rights, including equality of status, of opportunity, and equality before law, social, economic, and political justice, and freedom of thought, expression, belief, faith, and association.

- The high treason clause (Article 6) was incorporated for the preservation of democratic order and protection of the Constitution from power-hungry adventurers.

- Islam was the state religion. A Council of Islamic Ideology would bring the existing laws in conformity with the tenets of Islam, and recommend ways and means of enabling Muslims to order their lives in accordance with Islamic principles.

- Religious minorities were guaranteed equal protection of law, and freedom to practise and propagate their religions and to develop their cultures. Seats would be reserved for the minorities in the Legislature.

- The President, symbolizing the unity of the Republic, would be elected by a simple majority at a joint sitting of the Parliament. No order of the President would be valid unless it was countersigned by the Prime Minister. The Prime Minister was required to keep the President informed on policy matters, international relations of Pakistan, and all legislative proposals.

- The Prime Minister and his Ministers would form the Federal Government, and they would be collectively responsible to the Parliament. The Prime Minister would be elected by a simple majority of the members of the National Assembly. The Prime Minister could not be removed from his office except through a no-confidence motion or new elections to the Assembly.

- The National Assembly would consist of 200 members directly elected by adult, free, and secret suffrage, and 10 women members elected by the Assembly. The total strength of the Senate would be 63.

- All money bills would originate in the National Assembly and would not go to the Senate.

- The Constitution contained a list of subjects reserved for the Federal Government and a concurrent list of subjects on which both the Federal and Provincial Governments could legislate. The residuary subjects belonged to the federating units. The Council of Common Interests (CCI) and the National Finance Commission (NFC) were the striking features of federalism in the Constitution.

- The Supreme Court of Pakistan was empowered to interpret the Constitution and to issue orders enforceable throughout the country. The Constitution provided for separation of the judiciary from the executive.

FEDERALISM AND CONSTITUTIONALISM UNDER BHUTTO

Having assumed the office of President/CMLA of the residual state on 20 December 1971, Bhutto addressed his nation:

> I have come in at a decisive moment in the history of Pakistan. We are facing the worst crisis in our country's life, a deadly crisis. We have to pick up pieces, very small pieces; but we will make a new Pakistan . . .

Having taken over the reins of government, Bhutto pledged to move fast in managing the crisis of state. The systemic crisis of 1971 had ruptured the political system of the country and Bhutto took some bold steps to rejuvenate and consolidate it. The stupendous task involved the quick evolution of political consensus and legitimacy for the remaining federating units of the truncated country to live together. There was no valid constitutional framework and the National Assembly could not be convened or the Constitution framed in those extraordinary circumstances. Somehow or other, Bhutto was able to tackle the complex political situation and his positive response to the pressure of political parties and the public helped in improving his credibility with the people. His preference for constitutional and political means, the lifting of the ban on the functioning of political parties, and allowing the JUI-NAP to run the provincial administrations in the NWFP and Balochistan earned him public acclaim.

However, prior to drawing any hasty conclusion on the functioning of constitutionalism and federalism under Bhutto, it seems imperative to revert to PPP's earlier perspectives, particularly on federalism. For instance, J. A. Rahim, an influential member of the PPP's Central Committee drafted *Outlines of a Federal Constitution for Pakistan* in 1969 and he eulogized federalism in the following:

> The essential conditions for a unitary system of Constitution are not fulfilled by Pakistan, where diversity rather than uniformity reigns in all the major aspects of national life: multiplicity of languages, inequality of economic and social standards, differences between privileged and under-privileged regions. If a unitary system were imposed under such circumstances, it would work only as an open or veiled dictatorship, abandoning or falsifying democratic procedures. This is what happened under the 1962 Constitution.

J. A. Rahim went on to maintain in the same document:

> It is a special merit of the federal system that it harmonises differences, dissimilarities and divergences, enabling disparate groups, to live side by side in a symbiosis of mutual benefit. Given the same conditions, the unitary system tends to make cleavages and gulfs wider. A unitary system is excellent provided the conditions for it are present—uniformity, homogeniety, limited variety, sameness of language, few divergences of customs and habits. The unitary Constitution is an expression of already existing unity in the major aspects of national life; it cannot produce unity where it is absent.[13]

The aforementioned views of J. A. Rahim were upheld by no less a person than Bhutto himself, who elaborated on them in his speeches, statements, and more cogently in his booklet entitled *The Great Tragedy*. Bhutto was well aware of the fact that the absence of federalism and constitutionalism had taken its toll in the form of the secession of the eastern wing, and that it was utterly essential to define the limits and powers of the Centre and the federating units in the new circumstances. Bhutto admitted the difficulty of the task on the floor of the National Assembly on 10 April 1973, when he described the federating units of Pakistan as 'the most difficult provinces in the subcontinent. Always historically they have been a free people . . . [they] have fought always for individuality, personality, freedom . . . they have that tradition; they have that history.'[14]

From the very beginning, relations between Bhutto's central government and the NAP-JUI governments in the provinces of the NWFP and Balochistan remained tense. Besides the central government's accusations that the two provincial governments were violating their authority in the Interim Constitution, the official media charged Sardar Ataullah Khan Mengal (the Chief Minister of Balochistan) and Khan Abdul Wali Khan, the NAP Chief, on 10 September 1972, for conspiring with Sheikh Mujibur Rahman of Bangladesh (the aforementioned three figures were in London at that time). The so-called conspiracy, readily termed by the media as the 'London Plan', was later contradicted by the NAP leadership and President Bhutto, when asked to comment on such an anti-state act, refused to own the allegations.[15] Meanwhile, Sardar Akbar Khan Bugti, aspiring to the gubernatorial post in the province of Balochistan, joined the central government in accusing the Balochistan government of conspiring with Afghanistan and of importing arms and money to destabilize the Federation. However, on his return from London, Mengal counter-charged the central government with creating a law and order situation and held the central Home Minister Khan Abdul Qayyum Khan responsible for instigating the disturbances in the Lasbela district of Balochistan.[16]

Amidst charges and counter-charges about the civil disturbances in Balochistan, the Bhutto government, on the pretext of the discovery of a cache of arms in the Iraqi Embassy in Islamabad (allegedly for supporting a secessionist movement in Balochistan) dismissed the governorship of Bizenjo in Balochistan and Arbab Khalil in the NWFP. Akbar Bugti and Aslam Khattak were appointed the new Governors in Balochistan and the NWFP respectively. After these appointments, Bhutto got the Mengal government dismissed through the Provincial Governor, alleging that it had failed to maintain law and order in the province. The central government then clamped President's rule in Balochistan. In view of such developments, Maulana Mufti Mahmud, the Chief Minister of the NWFP, offered his government's resignation in protest against the dismissal of the NAP government in Balochistan and the removal of the two Governors. Mufti's resignation was accepted on 21 February 1973.

These unpleasant political developments had taken place when the National Assembly was busy in its constitution- making process. The NAP-JUI leadership accused Bhutto of liquidating the opposition and imposing one-party rule in the country.[17] However, despite such allegations, the NAP and the JUI cast votes in favour of the 1973 Constitution in the National Assembly. Why did the NAP and JUI, despite such utter humiliation perpetrated on their governments in the two provinces, help in the unanimous adoption of the 1973 Constitution? An analyst, Shahid Javed Burki, opines:

> The sixteen months of the Bhutto regime operating within the 'viceregal' framework of the Interim Constitution were enough to convince the NAP leadership that some curtailment in the powers of the central authority would be better than a stalemate on the Constitution issue. This view was strengthened by the departure of the urban democrats from the PPP—an event that was interpreted as an important step towards the development of countervailing forces for checking Bhutto's drive towards centralisation and authoritarianism. It was the NAP's belief that, with the help of the PPP dissidents, it could effectively check Bhutto provided the opposition was allowed to function effectively ... The NAP acquiesced to the PPP's constitutional proposal in order to provide a legal framework for interaction between the government and the opposition ...[18]

The ruling PPP's visible initial political accommodation and the consequent spirit of national consensus which facilitated the formulation of the 1973 Constitution began to fade due to Premier Bhutto's impatience towards political dissent. The Centre's interference in the provincial domain exposed the Bhutto government's inability to settle centre-province disputes through political means, which consequently entangled it in a political mess. Premier Bhutto cherished the notion of building the whole edifice of the political system around his personality for which he opted for personalization of power and its base. And the means adopted by Bhutto to achieve this goal were grossly unfair. His dictatorial inclinations accentuated the intense sense of dissatisfaction within and without the ruling PPP against his person.

On 27 April 1973, Jam Ghulam Qadir, a member of the Muslim League (Qayyum group), was sworn in as the Chief Minister of Balochistan. Giving the lie to the claims of the new Chief Minister that his Government commanded a majority in the Provincial Assembly, the NAP held a mammoth demonstration in Quetta on the day when Jam was administered oath and presented to the audience 11 out of the 21 members of the Assembly.[19] Undeterred by the complete exposure of its false claims, the central government installed Inayatullah Khan Gandapur as the Chief Minister of the NWFP on 29 April 1973. Such abhorrent political developments in the two provinces where the NAP, the largest opposition political party in the country, commanded majorities, confirmed the obsession and overriding passion of Premier Bhutto to instal governments of his own liking in the federating units and that too in utter disregard of the imperatives of federalism and constitutionalism.

The uprooting of majority governments and the suspension of fundamental rights undermined provincial autonomy. The ardent champions of federalism 'had signed the Constitution in the legitimate expectation that, with time, better working arrangements between the centre and the provinces would emerge. The power of the Federation would be diluted. The process of politics would evolve mechanisms which would augment the role of the provinces in the affairs of the state. This dream was not realized.'[20]

Despite the singular credit of formulating the unanimously adopted Constitution, Bhutto has often been accused by his critics of being simply interested in establishing the validity of the basis of his authority.[21] Once he achieved that 'objective validity' in the form of the 1973 Constitution, he was quick to bend powerful institutions, parties, and personalities 'to suit his style and purpose'.[22] Bhutto's excessive interference in provincial affairs not only eroded the concept of federalism in the Constitution but also pitted his central Government against dissidents who were demanding provincial autonomy.

Bhutto's desire to institute governments of the PPP in the two provinces after his dismissal of NAP-JUI coalitions could not be fulfilled. The suspension of the constitutional machinery in Balochistan had obliged the Centre to extend President's rule in Quetta. Amidst a welter of accusations and counter-accusations, a tribal uprising emerged in the province, which assumed the proportions of an ugly crisis. While the opposition political parties maintained that the Balochistan crisis was contrived by the central government for denying power to the NAP, the ruling PPP blamed the NAP-trained guerillas who had stepped up their secessionist activities, thus making the intervention of the federal government necessary. The anti-insurgency military operations at the behest of the federal government kept the regular troops engaged in Balochistan for the next four years.

With the resignation of Mufti Mahmud's provincial government in the NWFP, the Pakhtunistan issue was given wide publicity by the officially-inspired media in the country. To tarnish the image and erode the political base of the NAP, the strongest rival of PPP rule, the central government had used every trick in its bag to malign its leadership and establish that it had links with neighbouring Afghanistan. For some time, relations between Pakistan and Afghanistan had deteriorated, mainly because of hundreds of refugees from Balochistan had fled across the Durand Line. Moreover, the Afghan government through its statements had indicated a revived interest in the Pakhtunistan issue. The establishment in July 1973 of the Daud regime had led to an exodus of Afghan refugees to the areas inhabited by Pakhtuns in Pakistan. Pakistan's central government time and again held the Daud regime responsible for abetting the insurgency in Balochistan and accused the NAP of active connivance with Kabul.

Meanwhile, Hayat Muhammad Khan Sherpao, the Chief Minister of the NWFP, fell victim to a bomb explosion while he was presiding over a ceremony at Peshawar University on 8 February 1975. Bhutto, who was on an official visit to the United States, cut short his tour, returned home and ordered the arrest of leading NAP members under the Defence of Pakistan Rules. Having arrested the top echelon of the NAP, the central government moved fast to take restrictive measures. The NAP was banned under an executive order of the President, its funds and property confiscated on the pretext that the party was 'operating in a manner prejudicial to the sovereignty and integrity of Pakistan'.[23]

An emeregncy session of the Parliament was convened in the second week of February 1975, and on the strength of its majority, the PPP government passed two bills empowering the Centre to detain members of the National Assembly and Provincial Assemblies while these were in session. Besides amending the Political Parties Act, the government introduced the Third Amendment Bill, abolishing *inter alia* the constitutional requirement that a state of emergency might not be extended beyond six months without legislative approval; it also empowered the government to detain a person for three months (instead of a month) without reference to a judicial authority.[24] Having got parliamentary sanction for such legislation, the central government dissolved the NWFP Cabinet on 17 February 1975, and placed the province under governor's rule on the pretext that 'a neighbouring foreign power is actively involved in disturbing normal life in the province, and there can hardly be any doubt that this is a situation which is beyond the power of the Provincial Government to control'.[25] In the tense political atmosphere, governor's rule continued in the province till 4 May 1975, when Nasrullah Khan Khattak was sworn in as the new Chief Minister of the NWFP.

Having banned the NAP via an executive order on 10 February 1975, the federal government had filed a reference in the Supreme Court of Pakistan to the same effect. A full bench of the Supreme Court unanimously upheld the federal government's order declaring the NAP illegal on 30 October 1975. The Supreme Court's judgment held that the NAP 'had never reconciled itself to the existence and ideology of Pakistan, and had attempted to bring about the secession of the North-West Frontier Province and Balochistan through insurrection, terrorism, and sabotage. To destroy the idea of a single Muslim nation it had promoted the concept that Punjabis, Pathans, Balochis and Sindhis comprised separate nations, each of which had the right of self-determination, and had attempted to propagate hatred of Punjab in the other provinces.'[26]

After banning the NAP, the Centre used the politics of 'guns and gold' to induce defections from amongst independent politicians and the banned NAP ranks. The coalition consisting of the PPP and the Qayyum Muslim League began to swell, and the Provincial Governments' position emerged distinctly favourable by September 1975.[27] Then the JUI-NAP members were sitting on the opposition benches, the PPP and its supporters had a strength of twenty-one members in a house of forty-two members, and that too without any fresh elections. Thus, based on the humiliation of the NAP-JUI members, the Centre had fulfilled its political ambition of installing its own government in the NWFP.

In pursuit of his political strategy of complete control over the federal and provincial governments, Bhutto antagonized both his friends and political rivals. The federation had been experiencing the pulls and pressures of regionalism since the fall of East Pakistan, yet Bhutto's excessively personalized form of government and his efforts to instal governments of his own choosing in the federating units provided vehemence and momentum to regionalism in the country.

Until the unceremonious dissolution of One Unit in 1970, Balochistan had never been recognized as a province in the federation of Pakistan. The first ever elected government, that of Sardar Ataullah Mengal, was installed in the province in 1972 under the Interim Constitution. Unfortunately, that was allowed to function only for a few months, and stood dismissed in February 1973. Sidetracking the constitutional imperatives, the Bhutto regime applied coercive tactics to deal with regional aspirations, and banned the party (i.e., the NAP) demanding democracy and provincial autonomy.

Far from yielding any positive political dividends, Bhutto's calculated strategy of suppressing autonomists proved to be a veritable millstone around the neck of the PPP government. Without paying adequate attention to the real cause of unrest in Balochistan, Bhutto moved to change provincial administrations in quick succession. Thus, on 31 December 1975, the federal government suspended the government of Jam Ghulam Qadir Khan and dissolved the Provincial Assembly. Having imposed Governor's rule, headed by the Khan of Kalat, the Centre advanced the grotesque explanation that 'the provincial government has failed to make good use of the sizeable allocations made by the Federal Government for the development of Balochistan ... the Federal Government has received a report from the provincial Governor to the effect that certain measures are urgently needed to rejuvenate the provincial administration, and that the suspension of normal constitutional provisions was necessary in order to create conditions in which the representative institutions of the province will function according to the highest standards of democracy and the interests of the people of the province'.[28]

Ironically, Bhutto was misled by the Army's assessment of the situation in Balochistan and the NWFP. The prolongation of the military operation in Balochistan and the treatment meted out to the Baloch leadership negated the PPP government's democratic pretensions. Opting for military solutions at the expense of political realities, and depicting political opponents in the NWFP and Balochistan as 'traitors' meant in fact following the model of Yahya Khan's military crackdown in the erstwhile eastern wing. From the time that he took the ill-advised step of ordering the military operation in Balochistan, Bhutto remained under constant pressure from the military generals to crush the NAP leadership. While Bhutto had tarnished the spirit of democracy and federalism by subjecting the two federating units to coercive state strategy, the Army was restoring its tainted image by flood-relief operations and fighting against those whom the PPP Government was portraying as 'traitors' in the media.

When Bhutto realized the consequences of his blunder in ordering military action in Balochistan, constituting of the Hyderabad tribunal to try the NAP leadership, and foregoing of the political option, it was too late. The PNA (Pakistan National Alliance), formed in opposition to Bhutto, had included the release of the NAP leadership, dissolution of the Hyderabad tribunal, and withdrawal of the military from Balochistan in its 32-point Charter of Demands. Kausar Niazi, a former federal minister in the Bhutto cabinet opines that, on the basis of the PNA demands, the Army generals based their whole strategy of dispensing with the PPP Government.[29] The Chief of Army Staff, General Ziaul Haq and the Corps Commanders *prima facie* were totally against the withdrawal of the Army from Balochistan and 'wished' Bhutto to decline these demands of the PNA.[30] On the other hand, the same military coterie had connived with the PNA leadership, particularly Air Marshal (retired) Asghar Khan, to avert any possible political compromise with Bhutto. Unaware of Zia's strategy, Bhutto continued to send signals to Begum Nasim Wali Khan and Sherbaz Mazari of conceding their demands, but Asghar Khan, at the behest of Bhutto's 'loyal' generals, subverted such channels of communications and kept both leaders away from the Prime Minister.[31]

The fact that Bhutto's hand-picked COAS, General Zia, used every trick in his bag to create a stalemate in the PPP-PNA negotiations for his meticulously devised scheme of clamping martial law on the country is corroborated by Asghar Khan as well. Despite being used as a tool to sabotage the negotiations, Asghar Khan opines that 'Bhutto probably used to diffuse the situation and gain time, little realizing that somebody else, who wanted a breakdown in the talks and consequently a stalemate, was waiting around the corner'.[32]

More than anything else, the notorious Federal Security Force (FSF), a special task force created in October 1972, earned odium for the Bhutto government. The actual rationale in raising such a force was to lessen the civilian government's reliance on the military in times of crises, civil disturbances, and numerous other situations pertaining to law and order in the country. After its creation, the FSF assumed the form of 'storm troopers' and a private force at the disposal of Bhutto's federal government. With such a potent instrument, the Centre silenced its critics, intimidated the dissidents within the ruling party, and harassed political opponents, lest they challenge the party leader. Equipped with modern semi-automatic weapons, effective communication systems, and modern transport facilities, the FSF could step into situations where the provincial police feared to tread. Whatever the theoretical rationale of its creation, the FSF was, in practice, employed to complete Bhutto's control over the entire civil administration and to terrorize the political dissidents.

Notwithstanding his professions to the contrary, Bhutto rehabilitated the discredited and notoriously coercive levers of the state just to satisfy his personal whims. Unfortunately, the same were employed to expedite his physical extermination. The most outstanding trait in his otherwise flamboyant personality was that he suffered fools gladly—as long as they were loyal to him. During his tenure, sycophants and political adventurers were embraced, and friends in need and those having links with the masses were rejected, jailed, coerced, humiliated, and often subjected to untold miseries. In fact, Bhutto sought to deceive himself.

Besides pulling the country out of the morass of 1971 trauma, Bhutto's foremost contribution was the formulation of the unanimously accepted 1973 Constitution, the sole legitimate basis of future constitutional developments in Pakistan. He successfully curbed the role of the armed forces in the political permutations of the country and subordinated it to the civilian leadership. He also demolished the supremacy of the bureaucracy in political affairs by effecting reforms in the civil services. He succeeded in evolving political and economic institutions, yet he miserably failed to embrace democratic norms, thus shaking the foundations of parliamentary democracy and federalism in Pakistan. He routed the majority governments in the federating units and brought the judiciary under control of the executive by effecting constitutional amendments. Consequently:

> The political culture which Bhutto symbolised was characterised by complete intolerance of democratic opposition, irrespective of the means which may have to be adopted for the purpose. Physical violence, which had always played an important role in the politics of Pakistan, got further stimulus under Bhutto's rule. The disruption of opposition rallies, the kidnapping of opposition

leaders, attacks on their houses or families, assassination attempts on them and acts of arson and looting against them were a frequent occurrence throughout Bhutto's rule. What lent a touch of tragic irony to the situation was that even stalwarts of the People's Party, who dared express an independent or non-conformist opinion within the party, were also not exempted from this kind of treatment.[33]

Despite his inability to either establish democratic traditions of constitutionalism and federalism or to meet the rising crescendo of the people's expectations, Bhutto awakened the political consciousness of the masses. He was successful in generating resentment among the people against the centuries-old socio-economic exploitative system, and gave the common man a sense of his rights. While pulling the whole nation out of the 1971 East Pakistan tragedy, Bhutto instilled hope, courage, and pride in the armed forces of his country. Unlike the political pygmies around him and in the opposition, he had tremendous faith in the people's power. Bhutto's act of stimulating the appetite of the masses for democracy has proved to be a *bete noire* for the present-day rulers and their allies elsewhere, whose base intent is to rule the country without seeking a mandate at the hustings. That is why Zia, with all the coercive levers of state at his disposal, could not tame the people and completely erase the legacy of Bhutto.

Finally, to borrow an observation from Dr Henry Kissinger, 'his (Bhutto's) courage and vision in 1971 should have earned him a better fate than the tragic end his passionate countrymen meted out to him that belied their reputation for mercy'.

9

ZIA MUTILATES THE 1973 CONSTITUTION

Pakistan's continuous wrangling over a suitable constitutional framework had seemingly ended with the formulation of the 1973 Constitution. Validly enacted and unanimously adopted, the 1973 Constitution was an expression of the mutual contract and general will of the people of Pakistan to live together. However, after 5 July 1977, it became what Professor Leslie Wolf-Philips calls, 'merely the expression of the will of the military Generals'.[1] With Zia's military *coup*, promulgation of martial law, and striking down of Bhutto's constitutional government, the ugly phenomenon of 'constitutional mortality' was reintroduced.[2]

In absolute breach of Article 6 of the 1973 Constitution, open violation of the Supreme Court of Pakistan's judgment in the *Miss Asma Jilani Case* (PLD 1972 SC 139), and lacking any legal sanction whatsoever, Zia and his 'accessories and associates' indulged in their breach of duty to the state, allegiance to the society, and its Constitution. Was it the irresponsible act of an individual? Certainly not. An analyst opines that Zia had the blessings and support of several individuals and institutions who helped him in the execution of his *coup* plan and then helped him to stay in power. Zia was backed by the Corps Commanders, who had already decided to topple Bhutto, the then President who acquiesced in the *coup* by accepting the unconstitutional arrangement, the Chief Justices of the four High Courts who acknowledged the military regime by having themselves installed as the acting Governors of the provinces, and finally the politicians who welcomed the advent of the military government and joined its Cabinet.[3] Thus, innumerable opportunists, job-seekers, and tricksters, while turning their backs on all democratic norms and constitutionalism, jumped on the bandwagon of martial law and trumpeted its necessity.

Zia's military *coup d'etat* on 5 July 1977 was the culmination of the agitation launched by nine opposition political parties (the Pakistan National Alliance, PNA) in the wake of general elections for the National Assembly held on 7 March 1977. At that sordid juncture in the constitutional history of the country, nobody could foresee that the *coup* leader had the base intent of staying in power as long as possible and that the military take-over would usher in the night of long knives.

Bhutto's decision to hold mid-term polls was welcomed by his admirers as well as the opposition. Although Bhutto could extend the tenure of the existing Assembly with the consent of the Assembly members, for the sake of political legitimacy he thought it necessary to seek a fresh mandate. Having some solid national achievements to his credit, Bhutto intended to set the tradition of periodic elections in a country where despots had forced the people of Pakistan to fight for their democratic rights. Divided amongst themselves, the disunity of the opposition parties and their working at cross-purposes seemed another reason for the ruling PPP to win the people's mandate. However, the sudden formation of the PNA came as a surprise to Bhutto and his ruling PPP.

Being a motley collection of the right, centre, and left-of-the-centre parties, the PNA pledged to usher in an all-pervasive Islamic social order, replace income tax by *zakat* and *ushr*, introduce an interest-free economy, impose a total ban on gambling and the consumption of alcohol, enact laws providing for Islamic penalties for crimes, and abolish family planning centres. The PNA leadership indulged in character assassination of their political rivals. Having little hope of winning the elections, the PNA leadership had devised a strategy of propagating the theory, even prior to the hustings, that the elections would be rigged. This is what precisely happened on the eve of the general elections, and the Bhutto government was charged with massive rigging. Boycotting the provincial elections on 10 March 1977, the PNA, while demanding fresh polls and the immediate resignation of Prime Minister Bhutto, the Chief Election Commissioner, and the members of the Election Commission, adopted a course of confrontational politics.

In the determined conspiracy to oust Bhutto's government by all means and to thwart the democratic process in the country, the COAS Ziaul Haq encouraged both the government and the opposition to harden their attitudes against each other. Asghar Khan of the PNA ensured that political negotiations between the PPP and the PNA did not lead to a meaningful agreement.[4] Zia adopted a double-faced stance: he assured the Bhutto government of the military's all-out support in restoring law and order and, on the other hand, he conspired with the PNA leadership, particularly Asghar Khan, encouraging it to shun agreement with the government and continue to create conditions suitable for the imposition of martial law in the country. Zia had assured the PNA leadership that he would hold general elections in the country within ninety days of his take-over.

The Press and political scientists agree that it was Asghar Khan who played the most intriguing role in the PNA agitation of 1977. Bhutto having been toppled, Asghar was tipped as the next Prime Minister of Pakistan. However, since Zia had *mala fide* intentions in the whole dubious game of the PNA agitation, he deemed it fit to crush Asghar Khan's flights of fancy as to the latter's political role after the installation of the military regime. After his military take-over, Zia, in his first meeting with the PNA leadership, told Asghar Khan that his manner of addressing letters to the Corps Commanders was not to his liking. On Asghar Khan's defence that there was nothing wrong in it, Zia warned him bluntly that 'it was sedition, and he would like to try him for that'.[5] Such a distasteful first encounter with Zia not only caused Asghar Khan's notions of being prime minister to evaporate but also left him high and dry in his future political career. However, it would have been appropriate for Asghar Khan to tell Zia that he too had violated Article 6 of the Constitution, for which he could be sentenced to death.

In an interview in May 1985, Sardar Abdul Qayyum Khan, the then President of Azad Kashmir, gave his views on the ouster of Bhutto through Zia's military *coup d'etat*. In his perspective, the Army had planned in advance to impose martial law and Zia was not in favour of an agreement between the PNA and the ruling PPP. Zia tried his best to sabotage negotiations between the rival political forces, and Sardar Qayyum maintains that 'they [military generals] did not take-over because of a break-down in negotiations, rather the break-down in negotiations took place due to their planning'.[6]

LAW OF NECESSITY SPREADS ITS TENTACLES

Amidst continuation of riots in the major urban centres of the country and the PNA's agitation to oust Bhutto, the federal government on 21 April 1977 imposed martial law in Karachi, Hyderabad, and Lahore, empowering the armed forces to set up courts for the speedy trial and punishment of offenders in those cities. However, the legality of imposing martial law and effecting the Seventh

258 The Myth of Constitutionalism

Amendment to the 1973 Constitution were challenged in separate petitions in the Lahore and Sindh High Courts respectively. It was contended by the petitioners that the Constitution did not permit the imposition of martial law and that the Parliament could not change the framework of the Constitution by depriving citizens of their fundamental rights enshrined in the Constitution, or prevent them from seeking redress of their grievances through the Courts.

While the Sindh High Court upheld the validity of the Amendment and suspended the hearing of the petition, the Lahore High Court, on the other hand, ruled on 2 June 1977 that there was no provision in the 1973 Constitution empowering the federal government to impose martial law and the said Amendment, therefore, was declared null and void. While refusing to validate the imposition of martial law, the Lahore High Court contradicted the arguments of the Attorney General that the federal government's action was necessitated by the grim law and order situation in the city of Lahore. On the assumption that the Constitution was in force and democratic institutions functioning throughout the country, the Court could be guided by no other legal consideration except 'the rule of law'. It was argued that the Constitution contained no provision as to martial law, hence the federal government's act was illegal, unconstitutional, and, therefore, null and void. The Federal Government preferred an appeal in the Supreme Court; this was not accepted, and the government then filed a review petition.

Meanwhile, General Zia ousted Zulfikar Ali Bhutto through his military *coup* on 5 July 1977, placed the 1973 Constitution in abeyance, proclaimed martial law, dissolved the Parliament, and promulgated the Laws (Continuance in Force) Order, 1977. This Order debarred the higher Courts from entertaining any writs against the Chief Martial Law Administrator (CMLA) and those carrying out their duties under him. The Order also stated that the country was to be governed as nearly as possible in accordance with the provisions of the 1973 Constitution.

Subsequent to the imposition of martial law, Mr Zulfikar Ali Bhutto and ten other leaders of the Pakistan People's Party were arrested under Martial Law Order 12 of 1977. Begum Nusrat Bhutto, wife of the deposed and detained Prime Minister, filed a petition under Article 184(3) of the 1973 Constitution in the Supreme Court of Pakistan, challenging the detention of her husband and ten others under Martial Law Order 12 of 1977. The first legal issue before the

Court was whether, after martial law had been imposed and a law promulgated debarring the Courts from entertaining writs against martial law, the writ filed by Begum Nusrat Bhutto could be heard by the Supreme Court. The second and by far the most important question was whether the imposition of martial law was legal or not. If martial law itself was illegal, then all laws taking away the jurisdiction of the courts were null and void.

Relying on the Asma Jilani case, the counsel for the petitioner, Mr Yahya Bakhtiar, contended that Zia's imposition of martial law amounted to high treason under Article 6 of the 1973 Constitution, and his Order 12 of 1977 was without any lawful authority; that the arrests and detention of the PPP leadership were highly discriminatory and tainted with *mala fide* intentions to prevent the PPP's electoral victory in the forthcoming elections; and that the detention orders were flagrant violations of the fundamental rights provided in the Constitution.

Mr Sharifuddin Pirzada and Mr A. K. Brohi representing the CMLA and the Federation of Pakistan argued that, up to 5 July 1977, the country was governed under the 1973 Constitution and the promulgation of the Laws (Continuance in Force) Order on that day gave birth to a new legal order, altering the jurisdiction of the Court itself. The counsels for the Federation further submitted that the actions taken on 5 July 1977 were not 'the usurpation of power' but were intended 'to oust the usurper who had illegally assumed power' after Bhutto's 'massive rigging' of the 7 March 1977 general elections in the country (PLD 1977 SC 673-4); and that the stated purpose of the CMLA was to remain in power for a limited period so as to prepare the ground for holding of free and fair elections and the establishment of a democratic order in the country. Both the counsel for the petitioner and the counsels representing the Chief of Army Staff reviewed at length the cases already decided on the subject of law of the necessity.

Validating the imposition of Zia's martial law, the Supreme Court held that the new regime was only for a limited purpose and it represented 'a phase of constitutional deviation dictated by necessity'. Besides, the Court empowered the CMLA to perform all such acts and promulgate all legislative measures including the power to amend the 1973 Constitution, and do other similar acts which tended to advance or promote the good of the people and for the orderly running of the state. In the end, the Supreme Court 'expected' the

CMLA to create conditions conducive to the holding of free and fair elections, leading to the restoration of democracy as pledged by the COAS and that the Court expected him 'to redeem his pledge'. What happened can best be summed up in the words of a jurist:

> This was constitutional rewriting of the worst kind. The Court had no power or authority or any convincing reason to authorise any single person to change the Basic Law of the country in a manner which violated not only the spirit but also the letter of the Constitution. The Court no doubt retained with itself the power to review the legality of all the actions of the military regime on the touchstone of necessity. It was naive to expect that once the Court handed over a loaded gun to a military dictator, he would seek the leave of the Judges every time he wanted to use it.[7]

ZIA'S REDEMPTION OF A PLEDGE

A sinister smile on the face and a religious garb may hide the leopard's spots yet it cannot change his nature and intentions. Having toppled the constitutional government of his benefactor, Zia, in order to deceive and outmanoeuvre the political forces, held out solemn pledges to restore democracy and the Constitution. He lied to the whole nation, to the judiciary, and to everyone who came in contact with him. By propagating the pretence of being the head of an interim regime, Zia not only got condonation of his usurpation of power from the Supreme Court but also a free hand to amend the Constitution. There appeared a wide gulf between the spirit of the Court's judgment and Zia's intention of restoring 'the civil order' in the country. The fact that the Court was 'misled' by Zia's wrapping of his actual intentions in the palatable guise of 'operation fairplay' is evident from its judgment:

> The new Legal Order is only for a temporary period, and for a specific purpose . . . the Court would like to state in clear terms that it has found it possible to validate the extra-constitutional action of the Chief Martial Law Administrator not only for the reason that he stepped in to save the country. . . but also *because of the solemn pledge*

given by him that the period of constitutional deviation
shall be as of short duration as possible, and that during
this period all his energies shall be directed towards
creating conditions conducive to the holding of free and
fair elections . . . the Court, therefore, expects the Chief
Martial Law Administrator to redeem this pledge [emphasis added].

Far from redeeming his pledge, Zia began to create conditions to
do quite the opposite. Going beyond his solemn pledges, he created
a wide gulf between his words and his deeds, so that CMLA came to
mean 'Cancel My Last Announcement'. He ruled over the country by
issuing personal decrees and commands in the form of Martial Law
Regulations and Martial Law Orders. This was the climax to
Pakistan's history of constitution-breaking and disfiguring. Having
the unbridled authority of martial law at his disposal, he made every
institution of the country his handmaiden. Zia placed himself above
law and indeed became a 'lawgiver' to his captive nation.

Besides making structural changes in the actual format of the 1973
Constitution, Zia deliberately introduced controversies so as to blunt
the sharp edges of public criticism that he had virtually killed the
unanimously agreed upon Constitution. For instance, he found faults
with the 1973 Constitution for not containing enough Islamic
provisions and he 'emphasized' the urgent need for its 'Islamization'.
By declaring the 1973 Constitution 'unIslamic', Zia had, in fact, joined
the ranks of those who intended to dispense with it altogether.

Having cancelled the October 1977 elections, despite a solemn
assurance given to the people of Pakistan, to the Supreme Court, and
to the General Assembly of the United Nations (by Agha Shahi, the
Chief Delegate of the country) just three days before the cancellation,
the imperatives of the Islamization of politics, the Constitution, and
society as a whole began to figure prominently in the sermons of Zia
and his coterie. The dubious process of Islamization and accountability of the ousted regime were said to have priority over the holding
of the elections. In early 1978, Zia and his junta found faults with the
political parties and expressed their serious intentions of limiting the
number of parties and switching over to the presidential form of
government as it, in their opinion, was closer to Islam.

By 1979, the military regime had made itself the chief custodian of
the 'ideological frontiers' of the country and the vanguard for a

theocratic state. From the very beginning, the Zia regime had 'devised a strategy whereby the political leaders were to be held responsible for the postponement of elections. They were portrayed as unfit to hold high office, while the army was depicted as willing, even anxious, to uphold democracy. This public subterfuge camouflaged more sinister concerns. The military was acutely aware that 'the most significant threat to its retention of power came from Bhutto.'[8] Accordingly, the junta arranged what Ramsey-Clark, the former Attorney-General of the United States of America, called 'not a trial but an assassination'.[9] Through pressures, abject machinations, and manoeuvring in appointing and promoting judges, the Zia regime was able to perpetrate what commonly came to be known as 'judicial murder' and 'corruption of justice'.[10]

Having hanged Bhutto, the military junta felt triumphant in its ignominious deed and felt no hesitation in cancelling elections indefinitely. Political parties were banned, censorship imposed, and those journals and magazines which 'had been engaged in anti-national activities' were forced to close down. There was much talk of amending the Constitution in order to give the Armed Forces a constitutional role. Then one would hear that ninety per cent of the people in the country did not care who ruled them as long as their basic needs were fulfilled.[11] There was wholesale propaganda against the 1973 Constitution, which Zia and his cronies often depicted as 'a failure'. When there was mention of the general elections, the General would remind the nation that the elections would be held when he was sure of their 'positive' outcome and that the future elections would be held on a non-party basis, without campaigning and 'all candidates would have to be strictly vetted'.[12]

PROVISIONAL CONSTITUTIONAL ORDER

By 1981, it seemed that Zia had moved far ahead from the austere wording of the Supreme Court's validation of his military *coup d'etat* of 5 July 1977. The prospects of representative government were not visible on the political horizon of the country. It seemed that the notorious law of necessity was still in force, and whenever someone criticized Zia's regime and exposed his blatant lies, the tyrant's plain answer was: 'I am empowered by the Supreme Court of the country. . . .' And there seemed no end to the dark tunnel.

Zia, like a 'barbarian military tyrant', viewed the judiciary 'as an instrument of the state which should facilitate the exercise of government's authority rather than restrict it'.[13] Unsatiated with the control and use of all the coercive levers of the state, Zia directed his Machiavellian intrigues towards cowing down the judiciary lest it question his illegitimate authority. The military regime had made the conscious use of state-sponsored terrorism a potent instrument to contain civilian agitation against its rule. For demobilizing and excluding the political workers of the PPP from the political process, the regime had effected arrests on a large scale. However, the judiciary had begun to reassert itself because an increasing number of political detenus began to seek justice from the higher Courts. Moreover, the higher Courts began questioning the military courts and their jurisdiction. The judiciary's initiatives of scrutinizing and judging the politically decisive executive actions of the regime for containing its rivals merely served to strengthen Zia's base resolve to stay in power longer.

On 24 March 1981, the CMLA promulgated a Provisional Constitutional Order, seeking to put a formal end to the 'necessity' regime as sanctioned by the Supreme Court in the Begum Nusrat Bhutto case. The PCO was to remain in force as long as Pakistan was under martial law. It did away with the provisions for elections to the Parliament and with fundamental rights. The PCO purported to validate everything done by the Zia regime since its *coup* and such validation was not to be called into question in any court on any ground whatsoever. It required the judges of the High Court, the Federal Shariat Court, and the Supreme Court to take new oath of office to uphold the PCO. The Courts were deprived of jurisdiction over members of the armed forces and any judicial order concerning them was null and void. A higher court might not release on bail a person detained under the preventive law, a person against whom a complaint had been made before any court or tribunal, a person convicted under a military law, order, or regulation, or a person against whom a case had been registered in a police station. The PCO effectively extinguished the jurisdiction of the higher courts in cases involving issues of political substance. Blatant interference in the composition, jurisdiction, and independence of the judiciary on such a massive scale was unprecedented in the history of the country.

The abject obedience of the judges was sought by imposing another oath of office on them by specifically referring to the PCO. Confronted with such an offending scenario, a substantial number of judges, including the Chief Justice of the Supreme Court and the Chief Justice of the Balochistan High Court, two Supreme Court judges, Mr Justice Dorab Patel and Mr Justice Fakhrudin Ebrahim, and at least five provincial High Court judges refused to take the new oath and accordingly lost their offices. Besides, seven other judges were retired without being asked to take oath, including an acting Supreme Court judge, Mr Justice Maulvi Mushtaq Hussain, and Mr Justice Khuda Bakhsh Marri of the Balochistan High Court. It may be mentioned here that for the purpose of Zia's vendetta and prolongation of his tyrannical rule, Justice Maulvi Mushtaq Hussain, being the Chief Justice of the Lahore High Court, played a pivotal role in seeking what later was termed as 'the judicial murder' of Bhutto. Yet 'the Machiavellian Prince' did not deem it proper even to retain the worthy judge on the panel of the Supreme Court judges.

The way Zia exerted pressure on the judiciary to make it an instrument of his misdeeds is evident from the remarks of Justice Anwarul Haq. Justice Haq remained the Chief Justice of the Supreme Court during almost half of Zia's martial law; he presided over the appeal of Bhutto and provided Zia with judicial sanction to amend the 1973 Constitution. Justice Anwarul Haq dilates on the military regime's treatment of the judiciary as follows:

> The oath which Judges were required to take under PCO was extremely humiliating. The relevant article of the PCO was something like this: the Judge who will take oath, he will not allow in any case the challenge to any Martial Law order. The judgement which I gave as Chief Justice in the Nusrat Bhutto case was nullified by the imposition of the PCO. Therefore, it was inconceivable for me to take oath under it. Besides, Martial Law authorities prepared a list of a dozen Judges who were not asked to take oath. This included Chief Justices of Punjab, Sindh and Balochistan High Courts. These Judges and the nation have never been told why they were not administered the oath. Were they dishonest and incompetent? This has never been explained. Besides these twelve Judges, there were several judges who refused to take oath because they did not want to go against the dictates of their conscience by taking oath under the PCO which insulted the judiciary.[14]

It is a cardinal principle of constitutional law that the judiciary of any country is not a legislator but an interpreter and custodian of the Constitution and laws enacted by the legislature. It was indeed a serious mistake, if not judicial misconduct, of the full bench of the Supreme Court judges to empower the CMLA/COAS (on the basis of the 'good intentions' which the judges had attributed to Zia) to legislate and amend the 1973 Constitution.[15] The Court had no power to enable an individual to tamper with the fundamental law of the land. Such an act of jurisdiction was without precedent; neither the Constitution's text nor its spirit allowed the judiciary to assume the power of conferring upon a person the sovereign right to legislate. Some of the judges who had legitimized Zia's new order, and even empowered him to amend the Constitution and legislate, after their retirement or quitting of the judiciary, attempted a volte face on the Begum Nusrat Bhutto case. For instance, Justice Dorab Patel floated the myth (more than four years after the judgment in the Begum Nusrat Bhutto case) that the sentence to amend the Constitution was added at the last minute.[16] That may be the case, yet not a single dissent was expressed even at that last minute.

TOWARDS A THEOCRATIC STATE

Having banned political parties, ousted those judges whom he suspected of not doing his bidding, curtailed the freedom of speech and of the Press, and after arranging the judicial murder of Bhutto, Zia headed for legitimizing his oppression of the whole nation vide discriminatory and barbaric laws in the name of religion. Now the military dictator was the self-appointed President of Pakistan, and was amending, revoking, or making laws as and when his whims required. He had created a climate of terror by the *Hudood* Laws relating to offences against property, *qazf*, adultery etc. The intriguing mix of religion and politics manifested itself in institutions like the Council of Islamic Ideology, Federal Shariat Court, *Majlis-i-Shura*, Islamic Research Institute, Islamic University, Ansari Commission, Acceleration of Islamization Committee, Ijtehad Committee, etc. In his bid to establish theocratic institutions for perpetuating himself in power, Zia was actively supported by the Muslim League and the Jamaat-i-Islami.

The black laws in the garb of 'Islamization' stabilized the position of the clergy, particularly the Jamaat-i-Islami and the traditional *ulema* who controlled the mosques and *madrasahs*. To demolish political consciousness and social liberalism, Zia completely identified himself with the Jamaat-i-Islami and involved the latter in governmental institutions. Political coercion, Jamaat-style, was combined with an Islamization policy which brought immense benefits not only to the regime but to the adherents of theocracy as well.

The discrepancy in the ideals and practice of Zia's 'Islamization' was witnessed on 18 December 1979. Professor Abdus Salam (a renowned scientist) was awarded the Nobel Prize for physics. He was invited by Zia to visit Pakistan for celebrating his achievement. Besides, the Quaid-i-Azam University intended to confer an honorary doctorate on the scientist. The ceremony took place in the auditorium of the defunct Parliament House and Zia, being the Chancellor of the Quaid-i-Azam University, conferred the degree on Dr Abdus Salam. Though the worthy scientist belonged to the Ahmediya community, which the National Assembly under Z. A. Bhutto had declared non-Muslim, Zia, being the self-styled 'commander of the faithful', called the physicist 'the true soldier of Islam'. However, to appease the agitating *ulema* who proved to be the backbone of the dictator's rule, Zia began persecuting the Ahmedi sect to which Dr Abdus Salam, the 'true soldier of Islam' belonged.

Besides making the superior Courts (via the PCO) subservient to his capricious will, Zia introduced a new hierarchy in the form of the Shariat Courts. The Federal Shariat Court was to decide whether or not any existing law or its provision was repugnant to the injunctions of the Holy Quran and the *Sunnah*. For this purpose, the military General, who had assumed unto himself the exalted status of 'lawgiver', added Articles 203-A, 203-B, 203-C, 203-D, and 203-F to Article 203 of the 1973 Constitution. The judges of the Federal Shariat Court were to hold their offices during the 'pleasure' of the President, and the terms and conditions of their service could be modified at any time by the President. If the President wished, they could be transferred to perform any other function which the President might deem fit for them.

Tailoring of such special provisions, relating to the appointment and terms of service of the Federal Shariat Court judges, was motivated by ulterior objectives. A pointer to such an assertion is the manner in which the first Chief Justice of the Shariat Court was removed in 1981. He was dismissed on the day when he pronounced his judgment on the question whether *rijm* was an Islamic punishment. The Court had declared it an unIslamic punishment, and such a judgment obviously contradicted Zia's promulgation of an ordinance on the said issue. The Chief Justice was summarily dismissed overnight. Another Chief Justice was appointed, and the General made an amendment in the powers of the Federal Shariat Court to review its own judgments. Thus, a review petition was filed by the government, and the Court reversed its previous judgment to fulfil the imperatives of the President's 'pleasure'.

DYARCHY UNDER THE KHAKI-COLOURED CONSTITUTION

Zia's proclivity for making alterations in the basic law of the land had given rise to an apprehension that his regime would end up by giving the country a 'khaki-coloured' Constitution. Zia's assertion that he was given powers to amend the Constitution by the Supreme Court remained controversial. How could the Supreme Court, a creature of the Constitution, which itself was unable to exercise amending power, grant that privilege to the dictator, the product of a military *coup d'etat*? The very concept of martial law is the violation of human rights and repudiation of democratic norms and constitutional principles. The legislation enacted during martial law cannot be consistent with the rule of the law. Had the judiciary not ruled that forcible capture of power was acceptable (as it became a precedent and a law unto itself), the judiciary and the people of Pakistan would not have been humiliated and forced to suffer at the hands of military dictators as they did during the martial laws of Ayub Khan, Yahya Khan, and Zia.

Notwithstanding the contents of the judgment in the Begum Nusrat Bhutto case and Zia's promise to hold elections within ninety days, after a lapse of almost five years the CMLA/President Zia was talking of sanitizing the 1973 Constitution by Islamizing it. He had installed the *Majlis-i-Shura* (a hand-picked motley collection of self-seekers and opportunists), which was presented as a substitute for an elected parliament. The nominations to that *Majlis-e-Shura* were to be made by the President, by his colleagues, and 'certain other persons', meaning thereby perhaps the intelligence agencies. To weaken the political parties and to make them irrelevant in the political landscape of the country, the military regime had held local bodies elections (in 1979, 1983, and 1987) on a non-party basis.

Such a political process of participation at the grass-root level was intended to break the organizational structure and strength of the political parties, and to coerce and contain them. In the early 1980s, it seemed that there were no prospects of early elections or lifting of the ban upon political activities. The PCO had virtually ended the independence of the judiciary and Zia was openly asserting that the judiciary's job was to interpret the law and not to challenge the administration. While harping on the theme of formal military participation in the future constitutional arrangements of Pakistan, Zia remained evasive on the question of holding general elections in the country. In his view, elections could be held when the country had achieved political, economic, and social stability, and national trade and industry were progressing. When the MRD (Movement for the Restoration of Democracy) demanded elections and restoration of the 1973 Constitution, Zia banned reporting of all political news in the country in July 1982. Though it did not succeed in ousting the military dictator, the MRD shook the very foundations of the regime in 1983.

For his ambitious scheme of prolonging personal rule, Zia would deliberately generate ambiguities to gain time and to keep his opponents in the MRD guessing. However, in August 1984, Zia unfolded his plan for staying in power by 'sharing power' rather than 'transferring' it to the people's representatives in the upcoming elections. For legitimizing his dictatorial spell, the regime arranged a presidential referendum in December 1984, and a positive vote was manipulated through the dubious exercise on paper, mandating Zia as President for the next five years. Having secured his political future via the rigged referendum, Zia felt secure enough to hold national elections in February 1985 on a non-party basis. With the exclusion of the political parties and a proliferation of independent candidates, the election campaign was closely regulated by the military regime. Indeed, 'the military elite had carefully orchestrated the 1985 elections and were skilful in selecting who should participate in these elections. It had little difficulty in establishing a patron-client relationship with the civilian leadership which had social origins in the land-owning elites and commercial-industrial groups.'[17]

The first joint session of the partyless Parliament was held on 23 March 1985, in which Zia took oath of office under the 1973 Constitution and Muhammad Khan Junejo was appointed as the civilian Prime Minister. Martial law was not lifted and Zia remained

CMLA/COAS. Guileless and completely devoid of the art of double-talk common in the political permutations of Pakistan, Junejo was catapulted to the office of premiership unexpectedly. In the rather blunt political estimation of a veteran journalist, Mir Jamilur Rehman:

> If left to himself, Junejo had as remote a chance of becoming Prime Minister as for the sun to rise from the west. He had neither the mental aptitude nor political acumen nor the ambition to embroil himself in political horse-trading, an essential element for the acquisition of power. He would have remained a silent spectator throughout the life of the House, had he not been nominated the Prime Minister.[18]

MUTILATION OF THE CONSTITUTION

Soon after the induction of Junejo as the Prime Minister, an intriguing game of give and take resulted in the Eighth Amendment to the 1973 Constitution. The Amendment received the assent of its architect, Zia, on 9 November 1985, and was enacted as Act XXXVIII of 1985. Containing 20 Articles and one Schedule, the said Act apparently provided for the amendment of only 17 Articles, yet in effect it amended and validated a very large number of amendments made earlier by Zia in various Articles of the Constitution. Prior to analysing the consequences of the adoption and validation of all those illegal instruments by the stamp put on them by the National Assembly and the Senate under duress, it seems essential to revert back to earlier Amendments to the 1973 Constitution.

Between 15 August 1973 and 5 July 1977, the Bhutto Government effected seven amendments to the Constitution, through the Parliament.

The First Amendment came into force on 8 May 1974, and it related to the recognition of Bangladesh. Through this Amendment, the territories mentioned in the Constitution were redefined and the eastern wing was excluded.

The Second Amendment was effected on 21 September 1974 declaring all those persons who did not believe in the absolute and unqualified finality of the Prophethood of Muhammad (pbuh) to be non-Muslims.

The Third Amendment was passed on 18 February 1975. This Amendment empowered the government to extend the period for which a person could be detained without trial from one month to three months. The scope of the grounds on which such order could be passed by the Government was enlarged by the addition of anti-national activities and acts prejudicial to the integrity, security, and defence of Pakistan.

The Fourth Amendment was enacted on 25 November 1975, enlarging the scope of protected laws and adding to the restrictions on the freedom of association. Through this Amendment, two seats in the National Assembly were added for the province of Punjab. Moreover, the duration of an interim order passed by the High Court in writ jurisdiction which affected realization of public dues was reduced to two months.

The Fifth Amendment came into force on 15 September 1976, and dealt with the functioning of the higher Courts in the country, the appointment of governors, and distribution of taxes between the Federation and its units. This Amendment increased the period for the separation of the judiciary from the executive from three to five years. It fixed a tenure of five years for the Chief Justice of the Supreme Court and four years for the Chief Justice of a High Court. Clause 3-A of Article 199 in the Constitution was deleted and substituted by Clauses A to C, which prohibited High Courts from making or suspending the operation of an order for the detention of any person, an order for the release of a person on bail detained under preventive laws, grant of bail before arrest, or passing an order prohibiting the registering of a case at a police station. Through the same Amendment, Article 206 was amended to provide that if a judge of a High Court did not accept appointment as a judge of the Supreme Court, he would be deemed to have retired.

The Sixth Amendment was enacted on 4 January 1977. Articles 179 and 195 were amended to provide that the Chief Justice of the Supreme Court of Pakistan and the High Court, on attaining the age of 65 years and 62 years respectively, could continue to hold that office for a term of 5 years and 4 years respectively.

The Seventh Amendment was adopted on 16 May 1977, and it provided that the Prime Minister might seek a vote of confidence from the people through a referendum, and that if he failed to receive more than half of the votes cast, he must resign. This provision was to remain in force till 30 September 1977. The Seventh Amendment further provided that a High Court could not exercise any jurisdiction under Article 199 of the Constitution in relation to an area in which the armed forces of Pakistan were for the time being acting in aid of the civil administration. It must be mentioned here that the Lahore High Court on 2 June 1977 ruled that there was no provision in the Constitution for the imposition of martial law and the said Amendment was therefore null and void. When the Federation appealed to the Supreme Court to set aside the ruling of the High Court, a bench of three judges refused the appeal. However, the Federal Government's review peition was accepted, and a seven-judge full bench was constituted to hear the appeal on 6 June 1977.

EIGHTH AMENDMENT

Zia had conferred the title of Prime Minister on Muhammad Khan Junejo, yet the former was not ready to relinquish power and accept his position in the new hierarchy as merely the constitutional Head of State. Zia insisted on remaining the supreme source of law and the highest authority in the country. For such ambitions, he forced two major legislations as a precondition for the lifting of martial law: first, the Eighth Amendment to the 1973 Constitution; and second, the Political Parties (Amendment) Act, which revised the Political Parties Act, 1962, primarily to limit their role in the body politic.

The way Zia mutilated the 1973 Constitution had never been contemplated by the Supreme Court while validating his extra-constitutional act in the Begum Nusrat Bhutto case. The Court had empowered Zia to amend the Constitution to the extent necessary for the restoration of the democratic order in the country. The Court never empowered him to perform major surgery to prolong a dictatorial spell in Pakistan. The way the military dictator got the document of treachery (the Eighth Amendment) authenticated, can be ascertained from the following editorial comment of a newspaper, *The Muslim* :

> When the dictator realized that the time had come for
> him to lift the curse of martial law, he used his Assembly,
> composed mostly of individuals without any conscience,
> to destroy the 1973 Constitution. He employed some of
> the most diabolical legal tricksters to draft what was

called the Eighth Amendment. It was this document
which the military dictator used as a bargaining lever to
perpetuate his personal rule under the screen of a constitutional arrangement. Threats, blackmail, bribery and
every evil stratagem, was used to convert the members of
the Assembly to the General's point of view. It was this
perfidious alliance between a military dictator and a
supine Assembly which drove the country into the quagmire of the Eighth Amendment.[19]

The Eighth Amendment was never passed by the captive Parliament in the way contemplated in the 1973 Constitution. Article 239,
which was the amendment Article of the 1973 Constitution, was itself
amended by Zia through the Revival of Constitution Order of 1985.
However, by virtue of Zia's amendment to Article 239, no Constitutional Amendment Bill could be passed unless it was approved by a
majority vote rendered in all the provincial legislatures of the Federation. The Eighth Amendment was never placed before a single provincial legislature. The validation of laws, as approved under duress, was
restricted to Martial Law Orders, and the Presidential Orders and the
Eighth Amendment was never protected even under Article 270-A of
the Constitution.

Zia's unscrupulous tampering with and addition of his
'commandments' to the 1973 Constitution, changed the entire complexion of the supreme law of the land. While retaining elements of
both the parliamentary and presidential forms of government, the
Eighth Amendment tilted the balance of power in the latter's favour.
While making the office of the President the fulcrum of power, the
Eighth Amendment reduced the status of the Prime Minister, making
him subservient to the 'desires' of the former. Removing the
'excessive' powers of the Prime Minister in the original 1973 Constitution, the Eighth Amendment grafted presidential 'discretion',
without the protection of a system of checks and balances.

The 'balance' Zia struck between powers of the Prime Minister and
the President began to tell immediately on the new political system
of Pakistan. The popular will had been flouted and the entire
spectrum of national politics changed from parliamentary democracy
to dictatorship. Zia's main obsession was to keep himself in power at
any cost—constitutional democracy, national integrity, national institutions, etc. Thus, he deliberately contrived constitutional devices

in which he, as life-long President of the country, was above the parameters of law, Constitution, and accountability to the people.

The Eighth Amendment left the President in an effective position of command over the Chief Executive of the country. In its new shape, the Constitution was not workable as it demolished the executive authority of the federal government. While in a federal parliamentary system, the dissolution of the legislature was the prerogative of the Prime Minister, the Eighth Amendment kept the Prime Minister's power to this effect intact and also authorized the President to exercise similar powers. Article 52(2) (b) of the Constitution, spelling out this queer prerogative of the President, is relevant:

> Notwithstanding anything contained in clause (2) of Article 48, the President may also dissolve the National Assembly in his discretion, where in his opinion, (b) a situation has arisen in which the government of the Federation cannot be carried on in accordance with the provisions of the Constitution and an appeal to the electorate is necessary.

The foregoing deadly constitutional weapon in the hands of the President unquestionably placed him in a very powerful and unique position. *Via* the Eighth Amendment, the President became the sole spokesman of the civil-military establishment in the country, because the Prime Minister, who represents the majority in the Assembly, has no effective say in the military, civil, and even election affairs of the nation. Such a dispensation gives the President a surrogate Parliament and a puppet Chief Executive.

Having been appointed, allowed to form the government, and then dismissed unceremoniously by General Zia on 29 May 1988, Junejo and his cronies ironically claimed 'restoration' of constitutional democracy in the country! Their other so-called democratic 'deeds' apart, passing of the Eighth Amendment to the unanimously adopted Constitution of 1973 gave the lie to their whole democratic track record. Some might argue that Zia's military dictatorship remained only for eight years (i.e., 1977-85), and the rest was civilian rule under Prime Minister Muhammad Khan Junejo. One wonders how an army-appointed politician could claim his political independence — nay, of the whole nation — from his 'puppeteer'. Even though Prime Minister Junejo and his Cabinet colleagues were elected under Zia's own novel formula of partyless elections in 1985, he found the Prime Minister and the Assemblies completely unacceptable to his version of constitutional democracy, and thus sent them packing.

RULE OF THE PROCONSULS

Terming the 1973 Constitution a mere document which could be torn up by him at any time, Zia reached the nadir in the country's history of 'constitution-breaking'. Having arranged not only the criminal trial but also the assassination of the architect of the 1973 Constitution, the military junta under Zia headed fast for the total suppression of the two vital pillars of stability—constitutionalism and federalism—in the country. In suppressing the federal principle particularly, Zia surpassed all the previous regimes in Pakistan. He appointed military proconsuls in the federating units, wholly negating all norms of federalism. Remaining an absolute master over the entire federation, Zia personally equated the centre-province relations with the CMLA dictating to the DMLAs.

Zia's suppression of provincial autonomy and the people's rights converted the demands for greater autonomy into regionalist fires. The excessive use of military force to suppress the demands for provincial autonomy and the restoration of democracy alienated the smaller units of the federation. Barrister Makhdoom Ali Khan opines that during the Zia era:

> Far more people and sections of society started asking for more powers for the provinces. Even the moderates began to insist that the powers of law and policy-making institutions at the Centre be drastically curtailed. There were those who were not willing to allow the Federal Government to retain anything more than four subjects i.e. defence, foreign affairs, communications and currency. The more radical in Sindh and Balochistan started talking about solutions outside the federal framework.[20]

Provincial autonomy was essentially a political and constitutional demand, which was viewed as alien by the country's administrative set-up presided over by the COAS/President. A military leader, wishing to see his personal orders executed down to the lowest rung, could hardly comprehend the psyche of a people demanding constitutional democracy and provincial rights. Zia and his military governors ruled the country for over a decade, yet:

> The barren decade made a shambles of the whole concept of provincial autonomy, as the units were ruled by pro-consuls, which almost erased the political/administrative demarcations within the country. It was an indirect reinstitution of the One Unit, which was now divided into four zones, with little to differentiate one from another, except the facade of cartographic provincial boundaries. It would have been bizarre to expect any of the military governors to come fuming and fretting to Islamabad, demanding provincial rights for his unit.[21]

Effecting the Eighth Amendment to the 1973 Constitution and installing Mr Junejo as the Prime Minister in 1985 was not seen as the establishment of a democratic and federal order in the country. It was regarded as a facade to shield military rule from excessive criticism of the masses. Junejo was constitutionally not a powerful Chief Executive and, working under the shadow of the COAS Zia, he was unable to strike a balance between the Federation and its units. The Junejo Government, in its three-year tenure, could not go beyond verbally upholding the rights of the provinces. Except putting up an elaborate 'show' of an 'elected' government, the Junejo interlude could not restore the kind of provincial autonomy that was promised in the original 1973 Constitution.

What the Zia era lacked conspicuously was the presence of national integration and pro-federation politics. He deliberately introduced cleavages of regionalism, provincialism, ethnic groups, linguistic loyalties, local, and *mohajir* sentiments, and above all, the division of the national polity on religious lines. The whole nation was fragmented into tribes, castes, *biradaris*, etc. The vertical and horizontal cracks were employed to suppress the possible common struggle of the 'have-nots' in the socio-economic parlance of federal politics.

Minorities

Since the 1950s, the *de facto* custodians of 'the ideological frontiers' of the country had been subjecting the minorities to abject discrimination. Yet the ghastly process of humiliating and ignoring the minorities was perfected in the Zia era. The system of separate

electorate, death penalty for blasphemy, induction of the *ulema* in
the Senate, making the Constitution subservient to the Objectives
Resolution, the institution of the Federal Shariat Court and empowering it 'to judge' the laws of the land on purely religious lines,
subjected the minorities to the potential onslaught of the majority
and the repressive state apparatus.

During the Zia era, various religious groups were encouraged to
demand that their rival groups be declared non-Muslims. Thus, a
disgusting trail of *fatwas* and demands—like the *Anjuman-i-Sipahe-
Sahaba*, a self-styled representative of the *Sunni* sect demanding
declaration of the *Shia* sect as non-Muslim, and the *Deobandi* sect
clamouring for *Zikris, Ismailis, Barailvis,* etc. to be declared *kafirs*—
surfaced in the already strife-ridden political permutations of Pakistan. Hiding his guile and brutality under the mask of humility and
ostentatious religiosity, Zia relied on two powerful pillars of
authoritarianism, the military and obscurantism. These were reck-
lessly employed to suppress every legitimate demand of human rights,
constitutionalism, and federalism in the country.

The 1973 Constitution in its original form allowed the minorities
a right to vote in and contest from all the general seats, giving them
the additional advantage of reserved seats for the sole purpose of
ensuring their adequate representation in the Parliament. This was
in line with Jinnah's thinking and perspectives on the rights of the
minorities. By resorting to the system of separate electorate through
the Eighth Amendment, Zia's constitutional engineering violated the
rights of the minorities and alienated them from the mainstream of
national politics. The 1949 Objectives Resolution, which had the
potential to reduce the minorities to the status of second-rate citizens,
was inserted by Zia in the 1973 Constitution.

Zia exploited the deeply-held religious sentiments of various factions and set them against the minorities for the perpetuation of his
hold on them. There is a consensus among political scientists that Zia
employed the civil and military intelligence agencies to create and arm
ethno-cultural and communal groups and entangled them in a confrontation with other sections of society which were reluctant to yield to
his ignominious rule. While deliberately generating the kalashnikov and
heroin culture, Zia completely neglected socio-economic development
and thoroughly corrupted all aspects of national politics.

10

GHULAM ISHAQ KHAN SUBVERTS THE CONSTITUTION

Ghulam Ishaq Khan (GIK), by scrupulously following the time-honoured bureaucratic technique of never upsetting persons in high positions, had got quick promotions in the 1950s. He had held key bureaucratic positions under a succession of authoritarian figures from Ayub Khan to Zia. Through an assurance of complete loyalty to every dictator, Ghulam Ishaq Khan rose to the Chairmanship of the Senate in the mid-1980s. By his wheeling and dealing in the corridors of power, Ishaq Khan had made himself indispensable to the military regime of Zia. Being the Chairman of the Senate, he was sworn in as Acting President of Pakistan after the sudden death of his mentor, General Ziaul Haq in the C-130 plane crash on 17 August 1988.

After his death, Zia's execrable political heritage, with all its commas, semicolons, and full-stops, devolved upon Ghulam Ishaq Khan. The day he assumed the office of President, Ghulam Ishaq Khan began to run the affairs of the federation according to his own bureaucratic lights, as he attempted to subvert, misinterpret, and misapply the Constitution. He began to exercise powers in a manner that undermined the faith of the people in the sovereignty of the Parliament. Zia's mutilation of the 1973 Constitution (via the Eighth Amendment) had proved helpful in Ishaq's assumption of the country's Presidency. The sycophants' praise showered on Ishaq Khan for his treading the 'constitutional path' notwithstanding, it may be mentioned here that he never followed it at all.

Ishaq Khan started with a declaration of a state of emergency in the country, though the internal and external affairs of Pakistan did not warrant such an extreme measure at all. For the ulterior motive of being the sole arbiter of national affairs, he stuck to his predecessor's political order. The country was being run without a prime minister since 29 May 1988, and Ishaq Khan continued the unconstitutional legacy of the military dictator. He flatly refused to accede to popular demands and constitutional imperatives to appoint a caretaker prime minister. Devoid as Pakistan is of exemplary political traditions, constitutional conventions, and democratic norms, Ishaq Khan tended to treat the Constitution as a political football.[1]

Inheriting the unconstitutional and anti-democratic heritage of the Zia era, Ishaq Khan used the National Identity Card as the criterion for the right of franchise in the country. This, in the opinion of many, amounted to victimization. Such an intriguing condition placed some political parties in an extremely disadvantageous position. Having made foolproof arrangements for eliminating the much-trumpeted massive mandate of the PPP, Ishaq Khan was able to fortify his position via the bureaucratic levers of the state. He had prepared the ground well for his future moves to seize and control all levers of power by behind-the-scene machinations.[2]

Ghulam Ishaq Khan, in active collusion with the openly politicized COAS, Mirza Aslam Beg, had asked the then Inter-Services Intelligence (ISI) Chief, General Hamid Gul, to organize an effective alliance of right wing parties to counter Ms Benazir Bhutto's seemingly bright prospects of winning the 1988 general elections.[3] However, when Ms Bhutto emerged as leader of the largest parliamentary party in the November 1988 elections, Ghulam Ishaq Khan kept her nomination as the Prime Minister pending. For Machiavellian ends, he enabled the political opponents of the PPP to form governments in two provinces and particularly in the Punjab during that decisive interregnum.[4] Besides, he made Ms Bhutto commit herself to his election as the President. Moreover, Ishaq Khan pressurized Ms Bhutto to leave, though unofficially, certain key cabinet portfolios to be managed by the President himself.[5]

Even after having appointed Ms Bhutto as the Prime Minister, Ishaq Khan never reconciled himself to being a neutral umpire in the country's unfolding political scenario. Ignoring the expected role of a father figure, he began to indulge in shady political deals with the opposition parties, for the purpose of undermining the authority of the federal government. He exercised his powers under the Constitution in a subjective manner and reduced the Parliament and its sovereignty to a nonentity.

Ishaq Khan, as Zia's successor, continued the same policy of contempt for the popular mandate. Seemingly power-drunk, he ignored the constitutional imperative that the 'President shall act on the advice of the Prime Minister'. Closely associated with Zia's military junta, Ishaq Khan appeared to be set upon completing the 'divine mission' of his predecessor.

THE FIRST BENAZIR GOVERNMENT

While openly impeding the policies and programmes of the PPP government, Ishaq Khan adopted the colonial policy of 'divide and rule'. He thus played a princely part in aggravating Centre-province relations in the country. Indulging in 'constitutional impropriety' and 'conduct unbecoming', he missed no chance to malign the Benazir government. He prevented its political rivals from effecting compromise or harmony with the Centre.

The government of Ms Benazir Bhutto became the target of confrontationist and conflictual crises, especially those created by the government of Nawaz Sharif in the Punjab. Treating the people's representatives as wares on sale, and by spreading vile and vicious rumours against the federal government, Ghulam Ishaq Khan outrightly encouraged the Chief Minister of the Punjab to challenge the authority of the federal government, as a prelude to the dissolution of the National Assembly.[6] The Centre-Punjab tussle, a unique event in the history of the federation, far from revolving around the federal principle, remained a personal rivalry between Benazir Bhutto and Nawaz Sharif and their respective parties.

The Chief Minister of Balochistan, Akbar Khan Bugti, having his own grievances against the PPP and boosted by Ghulam Ishaq Khan, joined hands with the over-ambitious Nawaz Sharif in destabilizing the Centre. Aimed at rocking the Centre, the demands for maximum provincial autonomy raised by the Punjab and Balochistan governments did not serve the cause of federalism at all. The Punjab, which had always admonished the smaller provinces for their repeated demands of provincial autonomy in the past, was now at the forefront in championing the rights of the federating units. Ghulam Ishaq Khan, with an overwhelming ambition for life-long Presidency, lent full support to Nawaz Sharif in creating hardships for the federal government.

In principle, it was essential to strike a balance between the powers of the Centre and the provinces. But the Centre-Punjab confrontation in the late 1980s reduced the actual issue of federalism to political and personal polemics. Interestingly, those (the Muslim League, Jamaat-i-Islami, etc.) who used to dub the autonomists as 'traitors' and 'anti-Islamic', emerged as the advocates of federalism, especially in the Punjab. They had always exploited the religious sentiments of the people in order to contain the adherents of democracy and federalism in the country. Failing to generate any positive moves towards the cause of federalism and constitutional democracy in the country, the Centre-province confrontation fostered political corruption of the worst kind in Pakistan.[7]

The Benazir government had publicly opposed the Eighth Amendment. However, lacking sufficient parliamentary strength, the PPP was unable to repeal the Eighth Amendment because its political rivals perceived the law as part of their power politics. Ghulam Ishaq Khan, a strong believer in non-parliamentary and non-electoral politics, saw great advantage in retaining the conspiratorial document called the Eighth Amendment. This abiding scar on the unanimously adopted 1973 Constitution engendered a plethora of legal and political problems for the federal government. Assuming himself to be all-powerful in the lingering dyarchy created by the subverted Constitution, Ishaq Khan struck at the government of Ms Benazir Bhutto on 6 August 1990, and dissolved the National Assembly as well. Ignoring the letter and spirit of the Constitution, the President made the lifespan of the Assembly and the elected government contingent on his capricious will.

The long list of Ishaq's charges of corruption and official misconduct against the PPP Government can be summarized in the following allegations:[8]

- Rampant corruption through the misuse of authority, and indulgence in 'horse-trading' of the Assembly members.

- Confrontation with the provinces in general and the Punjab in particular, thus impeding the constitutional framework of the Federation.

- Failure of the National Assembly to legislate.

- Massive civil disturbances in the province of Sindh.

- Misuse of the President's constitutional prerogative to grant pardon to prisoners in December 1988. (Ishaq arrogated this power to himself via Article 45 of the Constitution).

- Issuing derogatory statements against the Senate and belittling its constitutional role in the Parliament.

- Deliberate failure to convene meetings of the Council of Common Interests and National Finance Commission.

- Launching of the People's Works Programme, an encroachment on provincial rights, etc.

Ishaq's allegations against the ousted PPP and his controversial indictment were nothing new for the people of Pakistan. More or less the same stance was assumed by Ghulam Muhammad in 1954 to dismiss the Constituent Assembly, as was taken in October 1958 by Iskandar Mirza and Ayub Khan to abrogate the Constitution and dismiss the federal government. Likewise, in July 1977, the COAS General Zia had used similar pretexts to oust Zulfikar Ali Bhutto's government. Again, in May 1988, Zia employed such a strategy to summarily dismiss his own hand-picked prime minister, Muhammad Khan Junejo. Thus, the dismissal of Ms Benazir Bhutto's government became part of the unsavoury political traditions of the country, while the future remained uncertain and confrontational, because of power-hungry rulers like Ishaq Khan, who cared little for constitutional and democratic norms.

Ms Benazir Bhutto's dismissal as the prime minister, and the dissolution of the National Assembly were followed by a plethora of charges, the worst kind of insinuations, cajolements, and veiled threats. Ghulam Ishaq Khan filed a number of references against Ms Bhutto and her husband, Asif Zardari. The latter was arrested on criminal charges. While ousting the PPP government, Ishaq Khan had installed in its place the bitter political rivals of Ms Bhutto, with unbridled powers and financial leverage to rig the next election.[9] The President patronized the stalwarts of the *Islami Jamhoori Ittehad* (IJI, Islamic Democratic Alliance) in every conceivable fashion. He directed his 'accountability process' against the PPP leadership with excessive venom. Its orientations earned the disparaging epithet of 'Kangaroo courts'.

Ghulam Ishaq Khan displayed manifest antipathy for pro-people politics. For counteracting the genie of popular politics, he had already cobbled together a motley collection of groups and parties into the IJI, headed by Nawaz Sharif. The Inter Services Intelligence Directorate (ISI) had carried out an extensive constituency-wise exercise to gauge the position of the various parties and the voters' inclinations in the 1990 elections.[10] Enjoying the extraordinary support of the President and the COAS Mirza Aslam Beg, Nawaz Sharif's prospects of winning the elections were bright. The President and the COAS had asked him to concentrate only on the Punjab, while the tyrant Jam Sadiq Ali worked in Sindh, in close co-operation with the military intelligence and the Mohajir Qaumi Movement (MQM).[11] The intriguing political set-up in the 1990 elections seemed formidable to the extent that the chances of the opposition's comeback to power were more or less foreclosed in the foreseeable future.

THE NAWAZ SHARIF GOVERNMENT

Consequent upon Ishaq Khan's rigging plan, the spectacular election victory scored by the IJI in the 1990 elections looked dubious to the extent that many winners found the unexpected results a stark embarrassment to them. The voters felt cheated and lost their confidence in the sanctity of the ballotbox. Ghulam Ishaq Khan, the godfather of the IJI, felt jubilant over the complete exclusion of the PPP from the corridors of power. He installed Nawaz Sharif, his faithful disciple, as Prime Minister.

Having done so, the triumphant President expected the new incumbent to be a docile protege who could be bent to make Ghulam Ishaq Khan the ultimate authority of the Federation. By ousting the PPP and offloading General Beg, Ishaq Khan amended the Rules of Business of the Federation to bring all levers of power, 'discretions' and 'pleasures' under the umbrella of his Presidency. Thus, the new Prime Minister 'found the field barbed and spiked with demands of Presidential discretion and pleasure. The Prime Minister was expected to play, happily and voluntarily, a subordinate if not servile role allowing President Ishaq to administer the affairs of the Federation without advice or assistance from the Federal Cabinet and any control by the Parliament.'[12]

Initially perceived as a pliant product of the establishment, Nawaz Sharif surprised his political rivals and stunned Ghualm Ishaq Khan, who had politically underestimated the Prime Minister. Although the Nawaz-Ishaq dyarchy was able to survive for two years, the political threats of the opposition led by Ms Bhutto, the Eighth Amendment and the heterogeneous elements constituting the 'troika' created huge cracks in it. The Nawaz-Ishaq dyarchy worked well till early 1993. Both had allegedly protected each other in their corrupt practices, bungling of public money, and, above all, keeping Ms Bhutto and her PPP at bay.[13] With his strong desire to be an effective Chief Executive, Nawaz Sharif began to take an aggressive position and a confrontationist course with the architect of his government. However, because of his avowed ultimate designs, Nawaz Sharif had to face the wrath of an antagonized President.

While Ghulam Ishaq Khan seemed anxious to avail of a second five-year term of office, Nawaz Sharif was out to remove the discretionary powers of the President in the Constitution. With his vigorous training in intolerance of democracy and popular politics, Ghulam Ishaq Khan became allergic to Nawaz Sharif, who questioned his supra-constitutional powers. The moment the hand-picked protege displayed symptoms of operating independently, Ishaq Khan decided to guillotine the Nawaz Cabinet along with the National Assembly.

Ishaq's ambitions for lifelong Presidency had degenerated into a phobia. For seeking another five-year term, he laid the foundations of political crisis by dismissing governments and dissolving Assemblies. Ghulam Ishaq Khan lost all patience when Nawaz Sharif addressed the Senate in March 1993, seeking the repeal of the Eighth Amendment. Ironically, having experienced the President's unfettered powers under the Eighth Amendment in demolishing her democratically elected government, Ms Benazir Bhutto was imploring Ghulam Ishaq Khan to strike down the Nawaz government as well. The consummate manipulator of Assemblies, Nawabzada Nasrullah Khan, was once again in the forefront, demanding the dissolution of all the Assemblies. The Nawabzada's agenda was: dissolution of Assemblies and declaration of emergency.

'Nawaz Sharif must go' was the one-point agenda of Ghulam Ishaq Khan. For his drastic action of ousting the Prime Minister, the President prepared the ground in the following way:

> The pliable members were encouraged to resign from the Assembly and Ishaq's emissaries were in touch with his first victim, Ms Benazir Bhutto, whom he had kept on the run ever since the dismissal of her government. Ishaq Khan offered her partnership in the new arrangement and once again the lady stooped to conquer, lured by the 'art of the possible'. Her husband would be released and might even find a place in the federal government. That would be nemesis indeed and a thundering vindication of her family. Ishaq had calculated that with the People's Party on his side, he would easily crush any popular demonstration that Nawaz Sharif might be able to drum up in his support.[14]

The PPP and its leadership played a Machiavellian role in real-politik for the dismissal of the Nawaz government. Ms Bhutto's government, which was brushed out as 'corrupt' by Ghulam Ishaq Khan on 6 August 1990, was washed spotlessly clean. All the 'sins' of Ms Bhutto and her husband, stringed together in a long list of complaints and pending court cases, were suddenly forgotten for making the 'oust-Nawaz-campaign' successful. Consequently, the PPP leadership became controversial for seemingly indulging in the worst kind of opportunism and naked lust for power. For a while, Ghulam Ishaq Khan appeared to be successful in restoring the inhibitive bureaucratic supremacy over the increasingly restive parliamentary leadership, and above all, bringing together strange bedfellows in the caretaker cabinet of Balakh Sher Mazari on 18 April 1993.

On 17 April 1993, Prime Minister Nawaz Sharif had addressed the nation on radio and television, pledging that he would never submit to dictation from the President. While asserting that he would neither resign nor dissolve the National Assembly on the desire of Ghulam Ishaq Khan, Nawaz Sharif charged the President with intrigues and conspiracies against the federation in general, and his government in particular.[15] Never before in the whole history of Pakistan had any Prime Minister challenged the mighty Head of State.[16] Ghulam Ishaq Khan was stunned; he dissolved the National Assembly and dismissed the Nawaz government on charges of corruption, misuse of power, etc. on 18 April 1993.

The drastic action of dismissing the Nawaz government and dissolving the National Assembly was not taken to avert any public uprising, agitation, or insurgency, but to create one. The deliberately created and artificially sustained political crisis, far from pacifying the tension-ridden people, contributed to their persistent antagonism to the Byzantine palace intrigues of Ishaq Khan. Ms Bhutto, who was fully involved in the dismissal of the Nawaz government by the President, artfully manipulated the differences between Nawaz and Ishaq. However, Nawaz Sharif, aggrieved by the dissolution of the National Assembly and the dismissal of his government, decided to seek the aid of law. He went straight to the Supreme Court and challenged the President's order dismissing his government and dissolving the National Assembly.

MUHAMMAD NAWAZ SHARIF V. PRESIDENT OF PAKISTAN AND OTHERS (PLD 1993 SC 473)

Muhammad Nawaz Sharif, the petitioner, as Prime Minister, had developed a row with Mr Ghulam Ishaq Khan, the President of Pakistan, over constitutional and political issues relating to the running of the affairs of the Federation. On 17 April 1993, Nawaz Sharif had addressed the nation on radio and television, charging Ghulam Ishaq Khan of persistent patronization of disgruntled political elements and of working against his government. The Prime Minister alleged that the President was hatching conspiracies against the Federation of Pakistan.

Ghulam Ishaq Khan, who was already in search of some excuse to dismiss the government, declared on 18 April 1993 that the speech of Premier Nawaz Sharif, and other acts of his government, had convinced him of its inability to work in accordance with the provisions of the Constitution. Consequent upon these and other charges of corruption, nepotism, etc., Ghualm Ishaq Khan, in exercise of his powers under Article 58(2) (b) of the Constitution, ordered the dissolution of the National Assembly, dismissed the Prime Minister and his Cabinet, and called for general elections on 14 July 1993.

Aggrieved by the drastic action of the President, Nawaz Sharif filed a petition under Article 184(3) of the Constitution in the Supreme Court under its Original Constitutional Jurisdiction, on 25 April 1993. The dismissed Prime Minister prayed that the order of dissolution of the National Assembly and dismissal of his government be declared *mala fide,* without lawful authority, null and void, and of no legal effect, and all steps taken in implementation of or as a result of the aforesaid order of dissolution, including the appointment of a 62-member cabinet under the caretaker Prime Minister Balakh Sher Mazari, be also declared null and void.

When the said petition came up for preliminary hearing before a full bench of eleven judges of the Supreme Court on 26 April 1993, the Attorney-General objected to its filing under Article 184 of the Constitution directly in the highest Court, and thus liable to be dismissed on this ground alone. However, after hearing the Counsel of the petitioner, the Court proceeded to join the question of the maintainability of the petition, along with the other main questions arising on merit, to hear and decide them together. The two main questions were:

- Is this petition under Article 184(3) of the Constitution, maintainable? and

- If so, has the President exceeded the powers conferred on him under clause (b) of Article 58(2) of the Constitution, in ordering the dissolution of the National Assembly?

The basic objection of the learned Attorney-General, Mr Aziz A. Munshi, was that the petition for seeking the enforcement of fundamental rights under Article 184(3), merely guaranteed the right to form a political party and the right to be a member of a political party, and no more.[17] Contrary to this argument, the Counsel for the petitioner maintained that his grievance was that though the tenure of his office had not expired, yet he was being deprived of the right to continue as Prime Minister on account of the unlawful order of the President.

In view of the submissions of the Attorney-General and Mr S. M. Zafar, that the rights guaranteed under Article 17(2) of the Constitution extend only to the right to form a political party and the right to become a member of a political party, or merely extended to all the political processes culminating in the election of its members to the National Assembly, and no more, the Court observed[18]:

> Article 184(3) pertains to original jurisdiction of the Supreme Court and its object is to ensure the enforcement of fundamental rights referred to therein. This provision is an edifice of democratic way of life and manifestation of responsibility cast on this Court as a protector and guardian of the Constitution. The jurisdiction conferred by it is fairly wide and the Court can make an order of the nature envisaged by Article 199, in a case where a question of public importance, with reference to enforcement of any fundamental right conferred by Chapter I of Part II of the Constitution is involved. Article 184(3) is remedial in character and is conditioned by three prerequisites, namely:
>
> i)   There is a question of public importance.
>
> ii) Such a question involves enforcement of fundamental right; and
>
> iii) The fundamental right sought to be enforced is conferred by Chapter 1, Part II of the Constitution.

The Court dealt at length with the concept of 'political justice' and 'political rights'. The Court held that the illegal and unconstitutional denial of the right to run the government as long as one enjoyed the support of the majority of the House amounted to denial of political justice, guaranteed under Article 17 of the Constitution; that in every democratic society, political parties compete for the right to form the government. The party winning a majority of the seats should have complete control of the government. Thus, the Court held that there was no valid basis to sustain the objection to the maintainability of the petition under Article 184(3) of the Constitution which, on account of infringement of fundamental right, lay before the Supreme Court.

After rejecting the preliminary objection, the Court came to the second question requiring adjudication, namely, whether the President, in ordering the dissolution of the National Assembly, exceeded the powers conferred on him under Article 58(2) (b) of the Constitution. The Court held that Article 58(2)(b) contemplates one and only one situation for dissolution of the National Assembly, and that is where, in the opinion of the President, the government of the Federation cannot be carried on in accordance with the provisions of the Constitution and an appeal to the electorate is necessary.[19]

The Court held that the grounds mentioned by the President in his dissolution order on 18 April 1993 had no nexus with his constitutional powers. The President punished the National Assembly for not withdrawing its support to an 'insolent' Prime Minister and his Cabinet. The dissolution order was passed in a fit of anger and vengeance and under a totally mistaken view that the Constitution had conferred any such power on the President. The Court held:[20]

> The President unfortunately assumed to himself the position of a Judge sitting on the performance of the Government and thought that he had the power to punish the Cabinet for acts of omission and commission as ascertained by him. He, therefore, taking himself as the Authority and the Cabinet as civil servants, inflicted on them the major penalty, as under the Efficiency and Discipline Rules. He was, however, totally mistaken that the Constitution conferred any such power on him. The exclusive power in respect of all the charges levelled by him vested in the National Assembly, to whom the Prime Minister and the Cabinet were accountable.

Upon evaluation of the lengthy arguments of the parties, the Court felt that the contentions of the respondents did not outweigh the arguments advanced on behalf of the petitioner. On 26 May 1993, a full bench of the Supreme Court of Pakistan gave an almost unanimous (10:1) verdict, holding that President Ghulam Ishaq Khan had acted unlawfully in dissolving the National Assembly and dismissing the Nawaz government on 18 April 1993. The Supreme Court announced:

> On merits by majority (of 10 to 1) we hold that the order of the 18th April, 1993, passed by the President of Pakistan is not within the ambit of the powers conferred on the President under Article 58(2)(b) of the Constitution and other enabling powers available to him in that behalf and has, therefore, been passed without lawful authority and is of no legal effect.

The people of Pakistan had watched with disgust the unfolding drama of the dissolution of Assemblies and subversion of the Constitution by Ghulam Ishaq Khan. The verdict of the Supreme Court was, indeed, an indictment of the President by the highest judicial forum of Pakistan. The main judgments written and released later dealt mainly with the President's conduct and his powers in the Constitution. The salient features pertaining to the Supreme Court's verdict can be summarized as follows:

- The President, being a symbol of the unity of the country, is entitled to respect. It is contingent upon the President to conduct himself with the utmost impartiality and neutrality. Their Lordships concluded that President Ghulam Ishaq Khan had ceased to be neutral and had aligned himself with the elements which were trying to destabilize the Nawaz Government.

- The Prime Minister was neither answerable to the President nor subordinate to him.

- The only way open to the President under the Constitution for deciding whether the Prime Minister does, or does not command the confidence of the majority of the member of the National Assembly is by summoning the National Assembly and requiring the Prime Minister to obtain a vote of confidence from the Assembly. Any other method adopted for achieving the object, for forming an opinion, and for giving effect to it is impermissible.

- The allegations of corruption, maladministration, and incorrect policies being pursued in matters of financial, administrative, and international affairs, are independently neither decisive nor within the domain of the President for action under Article 58(2)(b) of the Constitution. These are wholly extraneous and cannot sustain the impugned order.

- The advice of the Prime Minister is binding on the President.

- In the matter of appointing the services chiefs, the President is empowered to appoint in his 'discretion' only the Chairman, Joint Chiefs of Staff Committee.

- The President cannot preclude the authority of the Federal Government from the FATA.

- In formulating the policies of his government, the Prime Minister is answerable to the National Assembly alone.

The Supreme Court judgment in Muhammad Nawaz Sharif's case completely demolished the myth of the President's overlordship of the National Assembly and the Prime Minister. It was erroneously assumed, on the basis of the dissolution of the National Assembly three times in the past, that Article 58(2)(b) was a potent weapon with which the President could repeat such an act at will. General Zia had made first use of Article 58(2)(b) on 29 May 1988, when he dissolved the National Assembly and dismissed Prime Minister Junejo. The order of the said dissolution was challenged in the Lahore High Court, where it was held that the impugned order bore no nexus with constitutional power and was, therefore, unconstitutional. An appeal was made to the Supreme Court by the Federation, and it was rejected after thorough scrutiny. The Supreme Court, in the *Federation of Pakistan v. Haji Muhammad Saifullah Khan* (PLD 1989 SC 166), had held that Article 58(2)(b) was introduced in the Constitution for preventing a wrong, rather than securing a right for the President to dissolve the Assembly at his whim.

On 6 August 1990, Ghulam Ishaq Khan, under the same provision of the Constitution, had dissolved the National Assembly and the government of Ms Benazir Bhutto. The said dissolution order was challenged in various High Courts. Five of the petitions came up before the Lahore High Court for adjudication. However, the Court, following the case of Haji Saifullah Khan, unanimously held that the grounds which weighed with the President for dissolving the National Assembly had direct nexus with the preconditions prescribed by Article 58(2)(b) of the Constitution. Thus, according to the High Court's judgment, the government of the Federation could not be carried on in accordance with the provisions of the Constitution and an appeal to the electorate was necessary.[21]

In appeal, the Supreme Court, by majority, in a case reported as *Ahmed Tariq Rahim v. Federation of Pakistan* (PLD 1992 SC 646), upheld the decision of the Lahore High Court pertaining to the dissolution of the National Assembly on 6 August 1990. In the two cases of Haji Saifullah Khan and Ahmed Tariq Rahim, Article 58(2)(b) was looked at from a different perspective. In these two cases, the acts of omission and commission of the Prime Minister and the Cabinet were made the basis of the dissolution of the National Assembly. However, in the case of Muhammad Nawaz Sharif, the Supreme Court observed that the President had neither the power to dismiss the Cabinet nor was he supervisor of the National Assembly. The President is compelled to accept and give his assent to whatever is done by the Cabinet, on the one hand, and the National Assembly along with the Senate, on the other.[22]

The Supreme Court judgment in Muhammad Nawaz Sharif's case was distinct from another perspective, if compared with Haji Saifullah Khan's case. The government of the petitioner, Muhamamad Nawaz Sharif, alongwith the National Assembly, as a consequence of the declaration of President's dissolution order as illegal and unconstitutional, was restored forthwith. However, in Haji Saifullah Khan's case, such relief was denied. The proceedings in Haji Saifullah Khan's case were taken up after about three months of the passing of the impugned order on 29 May 1988, by General Zia, when the November 1988 elections process had reached its crucial stages. The Supreme Court refused consequential relief, after holding the impugned order unconstitutional, on the ground that:[23]

> [The] whole nation is geared up for elections and we do
> not propose to do anything which makes confusion worse
> confounded and creates a greater state of choas which
> would be the result if the vital process of elections is
> interrupted at this juncture.

The 1985 partyless elections had been boycotted by some of the major political parties, rendering their representative character doubtful. The Court refrained from giving relief because, in its opinion, greater harm was likely to be caused than that sought to be remedied. That the individual interests must be subordinated to the collective good of the nation was the main consideration of the Supreme Court at that critical juncture.

The circumstances prevailing at the time of the restoration of the Nawaz Government and the Federal Cabinet were entirely different from those of the Junejo dismissal and dissolution of the National Assembly on 29 May 1988. Although the Court had held the impugned order of dissolution of the National Assembly and the Junejo Cabinet to be unconstitutional, it had refused relief because at that time an appeal to the electorate was necessary. However, in the Muhammad Nawaz Sharif case, a situation had not arisen in which the government of the Federation could not be carried out and, therefore, an appeal to the electorate was not necessary. Moreover, in the background of the reckless dissolution of two Assemblies by Ghulam Ishaq Khan, financial and political considerations did weigh heavily with the Supreme Court in the restoration of the National Assembly and the Nawaz Cabinet. The Supreme Court held:[24]

> [The] premature dissolution of an Assembly is a very severe punishment to members and more so to the people and the national exchequer. The members lose their remaining term of office, provided by the Constitution, and they have to spend millions on fresh elections, with no guarantee of success. The nation is deprived of the continuance of policies and projects, is exposed to instability and uncertainty, loses the confidence of the governments and investors at home and abroad, faces economic and administrative chaos and is required to spend crores of rupees on the new election . . .

POLITICAL CRISIS

The judgment of the Supreme Court restoring the National Assembly and the Nawaz government on 26 May 1993 was hailed by the people of Pakistan as a unique piece of justice. Many thought that the rule of law was firmly established and the notorious assumptions of the doctrine of necessity would not rescue the wreckers of the constitutional system in future. Such aspirations were optimistic.

Ghulam Ishaq Khan and his political allies did not extend due deference to the verdict of the highest Court of the land. While Ms Bhutto had openly criticized the judgment as, in her 'wisdom', it would generate political problems, Ghulam Ishaq Khan maintained hypocritically that he 'respected' the judgment of the Court.[25] Prior to the announcement of the historic verdict against his action, the President's 'visitors', 'emissaries', and the sixty-two member cabinet had, through some journalists, spread all kinds of degrading jokes, rumours, and wild insinuations against the judges of the Supreme Court.[26] They had held out threats that if the Supreme Court gave a verdict against the dissolution of the National Assembly, the President would undo it by the proclamation of an emergency in the country.

The judgment had held the President to be partial, biased, political, partisan, and acting unlawfully against the government of Nawaz Sharif; and that Ishaq Khan had been guilty of exceeding his powers and of acting illegally in matters of the Federation. Thus, constitutional propriety and respect for the highest office demanded that Ishaq tender his resignation immediately.

However, to prove that the judgment of the Supreme Court had given birth to intricate political problems, and that his 'wisdom' in dissolving the National Assembly was indubitable, Ishaq Khan got the provincial assemblies of the Punjab and the NWFP dissolved, in active collusion with his cronies. This was done to create problems for the smooth functioning of the federal government and to deny it a base in the two provinces. Ghulam Ishaq Khan's mischief and his subversion of the Constitution became more apparent when the Punjab Assembly was dissolved within seven minutes of its restoration by the Lahore High Court. The Governor (a close friend of Ishaq Khan) had wrecked the Court-restored Provincial Assembly on the advice of the Chief Minister. Without the slightest compunction about committing an unlawful act, Ishaq Khan was determined to strangulate the fragile democracy and political order of Pakistan for the sake of defeating the imperatives of the Supreme Court's verdict.

After the restoration of the Nawaz Government, Nawabzada Nasrullah Khan and Ms Bhutto were instigating Ghulam Ishaq Khan to re-stage the dissolution act, already declared 'unlawful' by the Supreme Court. They had formed, at the behest of Ghulam Ishaq Khan, the All-Parties Conference (APC), a collection of heterogeneous political elements, to oust the Nawaz government and to hold mid-term polls. By playing one against the other, Ms Bhutto's highly manipulative political strategem had created a stalemate in the Ishaq-Nawaz dyarchy at the Centre. Amidst wide cleavages, uncertainty, and confusion in the dyarchical system, the APC issued a call for a 'Long March' on 16 July 1993, on the Capital from various cities of the Punjab and the NWFP. By conniving and backing the APC's call for agitational and confrontationist politics, Ghulam Ishaq Khan, along with his entire establishment, was bent upon obstructing the federal government's writ.

CRISIS BRINGS NAWAZ GOVERNMENT TO A HALT

In the wake of the restoration of the National Assembly and his government by the Supreme Court, Mian Nawaz Sharif was expected to be magnanimous on account of his legal victory, while Ms Benazir Bhutto was expected to be gracious in accepting the Supreme Court's verdict. Likewise, Nawaz Sharif was expected to himself ask for the dissolution of the National Assembly to seek a fresh mandate from the people. Instead, Nawaz Sharif decided to assert his suzeranity all over the country. He did not wait for the final outcome of the writ petitions filed against the dissolution of the Punjab and the NWFP Assemblies. He lured the majority of the Punjab MPAs and lodged them in the luxurious Marriott Hotel, Islamabad. These turncoat legislators from the Punjab did not earn any respect. Rather their own image was tarnished and such legislators were characterized with the pejorative epithet of 'lotas' by the assertive national media and Nawaz Sharif was widely accused of 'horse-trading' by his political opponents.

Nawaz Sharif was acclaimed by the masses for his courage in standing up against the arbitrary dissolution of the National Assembly and the dismissal of his government by Ghulam Ishaq Khan. With the wide support of the people, Premier Nawaz Sharif had the rare opportunity of getting rid of Zia's abominable legacies. Failing to avail of such opportunities for shedding his undemocratic image, he went straight to the grave of Zia on 26 May 1993, and exhorted his supporters and cronies to fulfil 'the mission' of the deceased dictator. Such an affirmation of adherence to the latter's legacies hurt Nawaz Sharif's image.

In his ambitious bids to sieze control of the federating units, the major blunder committed by Nawaz Sharif was to call a joint session of the Parliament for the passage of a law to take over the administration of the Punjab in a surreptitious manner. The Speaker of the National Assembly, working in active collusion with the Nawaz government, did not disclose the actual purpose of the joint session of the Parliament. The federal government did not deem it proper to take the opposition into confidence nor did it ever spell out its real intent about the joint parliamentary session which commenced on 29 June 1993. Given the complete breakdown of communication between the President and the Prime Minister, the federal government was demonstrating indecent haste to grab Punjab. Amidst pandemonium, heightened by the opposition's walkout from the Parliament, the Treasury Benches passed a Resolution under Article 234 of the Constitution, enabling the federal government to take over the provincial administration.

The Nawaz Government's political hysteria did not end with the passage of the said Resolution. The Law Minister, seemingly bereft of even a modicum of political sense, asked the Federal Cabinet Secretary to issue a proclamation in the name of President Ghulam Ishaq Khan, without his approval, authorizing the federal government to assume the functions of the Punjab govenment under Article 234 of the Constitution. On 30 June 1993, President Ishaq Khan told the Press that he had not received, approved, or signed any such proclamation.[27] For further complicating the tense political situation, the federal government maintained that a resolution adopted in a joint session of the Parliament was mandatory and did not require the authentication of the President. Ms Benazir Bhutto and her political allies depicted the government's move as 'cheating' and 'foul play', tantamount to 'high treason'.[28] All steps taken in quick succession by the federal government in this respect backfired and placed the beleaguered Prime Minister on the defensive.

Although a resolution passed in the joint session of the Parliament was mandatory and the President could neither amend it nor refer it for reconsideration, it would have been appropriate for the Nawaz government to obtain the signature of the President (who believed in technicalities) on the summary. For its part, the Punjab government flatly refused to obey the proclamation, as it had not been signed by the President. Subsequently, the federal government asked the Rangers to arrange to take over the provincial administration. In a counter-move, the Punjab government ordered the local police to resist such moves of the federal government. GHQ stepped in to call off the Rangers from taking over the Punjab government, as it did not deem it proper to involve the para-military forces in the Centre-province confrontation.[29] By then, Punjab had two governments, two chief secretaries, and two police chiefs. Failing in its desperate moves, the Nawaz government denied having ordered the Rangers into action against the Punjab government and, as a face-saving measure, decided to consult the Supreme Court on whether the proclamation under Article 234 of the Constitution required the President's signature. However, this did not happen.

Against the backdrop of these developments, the governments of the Punjab and the NWFP resorted to extra-constitutional strategies to obstruct the policies and programmes of the federal government under Nawaz Sharif. Disregarding due deference to the Centre, these two governments, in close collaboration with Ghulam Ishaq Khan, had sidetracked all avenues of legality in favour of generating civil unrest and political confusion in the country. While the government of the Punjab behaved like an autonomous state, Ghulam Ishaq Khan pretended to be supremely unaware of such activities.

The writ of the Nawaz government had been virtually reduced to Islamabad and its outskirts and, due to Ishaq Khan's instigation, not a single Governor or Chief Minister was extending the due protocol of receiving the Prime Minister. Nawaz Sharif might have then recalled his own acts of confrontation with Prime Minister Benazir Bhutto on Ghulam Ishaq Khan's behest, while he served as the defiant Chief Minister of the Punjab. Then the politicking COAS, Mirza Aslam Beg, the politicized ISI, and the almighty Ghulam Ishaq Khan were on his side and, unfortunately, the political agenda was similar: to create trouble in every conceivable manner for the government at the Centre.

Moved by the compelling desire to die in the saddle, President Ghulam Ishaq Khan unleashed his seasoned bureaucratic skills and political surrogates to guillotine the political process. The Leader of the House and the Leader of the Opposition remained irretrievably locked in confrontation because of such manipulations. Ghulam Ishaq Khan was, allegedly, the moving spirit behind all the 'long and short marches', the extra-constitutional stratagems, and back-door machinations to flout the writ of the federal government. Even the Supreme Court was belittled for pronouncing a pro-democracy judgment on 26 May 1993.

In spite of his well-known conspiracies against the federation, Ghulam Ishaq Khan often talked about his half century of service to the nation. While questioning the track-record of his service, the Islamabad-based daily, *The Muslim,* wrote:

> [S]ervice to whom? Essentially to himself. That alone explains his rise, if rise it really be. He has served every dictator, every autocrat. He has been an obedient servant not of the people, but all anti-people usurpers. He was a particularly loyal and dedicated servant of the darkest and the longest of all dictatorships.[30]

In July 1993, all the major political parties and their leaders seemed to be outmanoeuvring one another, little realizing the actual implications of their infighting. Prime Minister Nawaz Sharif was repeating his old mistakes, which had exposed his regime to charges of incompetency and corruption. Ms Benazir Bhutto was bent upon ousting the Nawaz government and was being labelled by her critics as an accomplice of Ghulam Ishaq Khan. However, it was an insult to the track-record of all the politicians that the COAS was dictating to them how to behave. The much touted myth of civilian supremacy in national affairs was laid to rest and the Army exhibited all visible signs of being the leading player in the political permutations of the country. It was on account of this reality that Ms Benazir Bhutto had to obey the 'advice' of the COAS General Abdul Waheed, by calling off the long march. The Nawaz-Ishaq uncompromising dyarchy had to abandon the highest offices to make room for a novel caretaker set-up at the behest of the Army. In their bids for maximizing power or uprooting their rivals, all the politicians, including Ghulam Ishaq Khan, had caused incalculable damage to the democratic process and, indeed, to the federation.

THE NEW SET-UP

The Ishaq-Nawaz confrontation, with all its ugly potential, degenerated into a crisis of state. Besides making a laughing stock of both the personalities, the unabated rivalry negated constitutional and democratic trends in the country. The two dignitaries, who had been enjoying power in collusion with one another, had unhesitatingly thrown political restraint and national interests to the winds. The frenzied quest for ascendancy and the desire to outsmart each other had led to their reciprocal abdications. The politically thrilling drama of the Ishaq-Nawaz dyarchy stepping down set the scene for general elections in October 1993.

The circumstances in which the caretaker government of Moeen Qureshi was installed reflected the Pakistani politicians' distrust of one another's motives. Moeen Qureshi, an unknown entity on the political landscape of Pakistan, was 'imported' as the caretaker Prime Minister. The day the Ishaq-Nawaz dyarchy fell, the political legitimacy accorded to the rigged 1990 elections went by the board. The people seemed grateful to the country's Armed Forces who had facilitated the continuity of the fragile democratic process.

The October 1993 general elections under the supervision of the Army were definitely the fairest and the freest on record. Consequent upon these elections, Ms Benazir Bhutto became the Prime Minister for the second time. Notwithstanding the rare distinction of having five Prime Ministers (i.e., Mian Nawaz Sharif, Mir Balakh Sher Mazari, Mian Nawaz Sharif again, Mr Moeen Qureshi, and then Ms Benazir Bhutto) in 1993, and plagued with extraordinary political pulls and stresses, Pakistan's constitutional order apparently remained intact.

Farooq Ahmed Khan Leghari's election as President of Pakistan has been widely hailed, equating it to a breath of fresh air in the suffocating tangle of the country's internal differences. President Leghari seems to be maintaining neutrality in the potentially combative political permutations of Pakistan. For that avowed end, he has gone through the traditional ritual of resigning his membership of the PPP. With a record of fighting against the ruthless dictatorship of Zia, President Leghari is expected to uphold the norms of constitutionalism, encouraging the federal government and its legitimate pro-people policies, and avoiding parochial political perspectives.

After the October 1993 elections, though the federal government seems stable, all the provincial governments have, as usual, been at the mercy of opportunists who keep changing their loyalties for the sake of money and ministerial posts. The opposition led by Mian Nawaz Sharif has charted a confrontational course of agitational politics. He seems determined to create all sorts of hurdles in the smooth functioning of the federal government at all levels. The insinuations of corruption, financial irregularities, and misuse of state resources for partisan considerations have become a common phenomenon. The 'long march,' the 'train march', and strike calls have entered the recognized parameters of Pakistani politics. While the opposition prefers to continue to destabilize the entire government structure through negative political means, the party in power is obsessed with the expansion of its power base. If it continues in the foreseeable future, such a phenomenon of combative politics and politicians will create a sort of suicidal political environment in the country.

After the prolonged dictatorial spell in which Zia and his destructive legacies reigned supreme, the chequered career of statehood and the crisis-ridden politics of Pakistan have been given a breathing space to tread the path of constitutional democracy. Under the prevailing circumstances, the politicians are expected to exhibit qualities of statesmanship instead of opting for incessant strife for power. To that end, the constitutional imperatives crying out for the urgent attention of all the saner political elements can be listed as follows:

- Restoration and legitimization of, and respect for the supremacy of Parliament.

- Cleansing of the 1973 Constitution of the abhorrent vestiges of the Zia era.

- Subordination of the Establishment to legitimate political authority.

- Reorganization of the federating units and devolution of power to them.

- Utilization of state authority purely for the benefit of the masses.

- Restoration of confidence in and dispensation of justice by the judiciary.

- Reverence for popular sovereignty and sanctity of the ballot box.

- Enforcing the principle of accountability.

11

FOUNDATIONS OF A SUCCESSFUL FEDERATION: PLURALISM AND DEVOLUTION OF POWER

Consequent upon strident centralization, outright denial of autonomy to the federating units, and the Centre's authoritarianism, regional aspirations amounting almost to secessionism have acquired ascendancy in the political milieu of Pakistan. Short-sighted acts of suffocating the spirit of federalism have prevented the process of national integration from taking root. While tarnishing the image of the nation, the extent of centralization has obliged the autonomists to cast doubts on the very genesis of Pakistan. The unpalatable developments pertaining to federalism in the country have acquired such dangerous dimensions that it is freely asked: Is Pakistan one nation or a multi-nation state?

The notion of 'nationalities' is catching on fast among the smaller provinces in the country. In the mid-1970s, the Supreme Court of Pakistan in its judgment on a reference by the federal government had banned Wali Khan's National Awami Party in the NWFP because, besides other reasons, the NAP maintained that Pakistan was composed of more than one nationality. Notwithstanding such constitutional and legal measures, at present the concept, existence, and rights of the provincial 'nationalities' have become the creed and manifesto of several political groups operating in Pakistan. Those who deny such a harsh reality seem to be labouring under a delusion. Yet, taken to its logical conclusion, the notion of 'nationalities' lends itself to further fragmentation beyond contemporary provincial boundaries. Decentralization means neither parochialism nor provincialism but grass-roots, doorstep, local democracy, catering to the urgent day-to-day problems of basic needs and human rights, be they sociocultural, ethnolinguistic, or politico-economic.

The presence and diversity of ethnic, linguistic, cultural, and geographic traits are not anathema to nation-building in the contemporary nation-state system. Many states in the world have such diverse traits, yet they have become, with the passage of time, very stable, integrated, and viable entities. That seems to be the result of a fair, fraternal, and free political process in which various linguistic, ethnic, and cultural entities were allowed and, indeed, encouraged to cut across the 'discontinuities'. Where the political process was blocked, aspirations for group identity curbed, and the local and regional elite alienated from the national/federal framework, it gave birth to polarization and fragmentation of the national polity itself. If linguistic, cultural, and ethnic entities are neglected, coerced, and kept away from the national power structure for the purpose of creating a monolithic and all-embracing abstract nation-state, they present the frightening scenario of viewing one another as staunch adversaries. In the words of a renowned theorist on integration, Karl W. Deutsch, the concept of nation-building is both mechanistic and voluntaristic, and, for the achievement of such an extraordinary process, he suggests:

> [A]n architectural or mechanical model. As a house can be built from timber, bricks, and mortar in different patterns, quickly or slowly, through different sequences of assembly, in partial independence from its setting, and according to the choice, will and power of its builders, so a nation can be built according to different plans, from various materials, rapidly or gradually, by different sequences or steps, and in partial independence from its environment.[1]

PERSISTENT PROBLEMS

From the discussion in the preceding chapters, it seems that the following factors have had an adverse effect on the federal issue in the constitutional and political milieu of Pakistan:

1. centralization of power;

2. centralization of economic and development planning; and

3. the denial of provincial rights, absence of political process, and the emergence of ethno-cultural and linguistic entities.

For all such ills and curses affecting the cohesion of the federation, (thanks to over-centralization), the following alternative scenarios are suggested to avert any unpleasant variation of the tragic model of East Pakistan:

1. multiplication of provinces;

2. separation and devolution of power to the federating units;

3. decentralization of economic and development planning and implementation;

4. uninterrupted continuation of the political process; and

5. independence of the judiciary.

Multiplication of Provinces

The successive ruling elites in Pakistan have faithfully stuck to the federal structure that the country inherited from the colonial power. The present provincial boundaries are neither sacrosanct nor unalterable. They were arbitrarily drawn by the colonialists to serve and sustain their administrative system. Neglecting geographical, cultural, linguistic, and ethnic imperatives, the British stamped the present provincial boundaries to subdue the political aspirations of the local people. Thus, in the changed circumstances, when sociocultural, educational, and politico-economic modernization has become essential, it is imperative to redraw provinical boundaries on realistic contours so that the federation should have culturally homogeneous, economically viable, and administratively manageable units.

Various schemes have been suggested for redrawing and multiplying the provinces in the country. Such schemes were presented for administrative convenience, ending strident centralization, satisfying the legitimate rights of regional groups, and facilitating the process of national integration—through participative, local, doorstep democracy. However, far from responding to the vital issue of restructuring the federation in a pragmatic manner, the varied vested interests have chosen to depict such demands as provincialism, regionalism, and the curse of the nationalities, amounting to an anti-Islamic act. Even the genuine demands for provincial autonomy have been labelled as highly treasonous acts. To exclude the masses and various regional groups from sharing power, both at the central and provincial levels, the successive ruling elite have harassed, persecuted, and repressed the adherents of provincial rights.

Contrary to military-bureaucratic thinking, with its emphasis on centralization and One Unit schemes, neither the multiplication nor the redrawing of the present provinces seems inimical to the viable existence of the federation of Pakistan. Having tasted the bitter fruit of East Pakistan's traumatic separation, it is high time to avoid the vicious process from being repeated in the 'new' Pakistan. For fulfilling the regional ethos and group aspirations, and allowing the masses to manage their own affairs, the issue of increasing the number of provinces is both structural and objective.

In Pakistan's immediate vicinity, Afghanistan has twenty-eight provinces; Iran over thirty provinces, that too, with a population less than half of Pakistan. Turkey consists of sixty-five provinces, Iraq has eighteen provinces, and India has twenty-five states (provinces) with some additional Union-administered territories, Sri Lanka, with a much smaller territory and population, comprises of twenty-two provinces. It may be mentioned here that on the eve of independence, India consisted of fourteen units evolved under the British Raj. However, to satisfy regional aspirations and to establish the firm basis of its Union, the Indian leadership did not hesitate to redraw and demarcate the boundaries of its states on linguistic and ethnic lines and for administrative convenience. With this objective, the first linguistic state, Andhra Pradesh, was established in 1953. This act did not erode the strength of the Indian Union; rather, it has eliminated administrative encumbrances and allowed the linguistic and ethnic groups to rule themselves in their respective states.

Failing to learn from its neighbour's wisdom in satisfying regional aspirations by a multiplication of units on the basis of rational and natural affinities, the ruling elite in Pakistan created clumsy structures like One Unit. Moreover, the Byzantine bureaucracy, with its complex and corrupt mechanism based at Lahore (the capital of One Unit), began to aggravate the problems of the people, particularly those in far-flung areas. Hardly contributing any thing positive to the federation of only two provinces (i.e., East and West Pakistan), the One Unit system hastened centrifugalism and added to the political and socio-economic frustration of the small regional groups in the country.

Yahya Khan's decision to scrap the artificially-created province of West Pakistan, held together by coercion and political expediency, was welcomed by the exponents of autonomy. Consequent upon such a decision:

> not a tear was shed over its demise, nor an accusing
> finger pointed towards the General who had given it

an unceremonious burial. The enthusiastic welcome to
his decision in the smaller Provinces proved that unification by force was a Himalayan blunder for which the
nation had to pay a high price. There was no parallel or
precedent in any other Federation . . .[2]

The demand for more provinces or divisional democracies or
administrative units carries weight because the present four federating units have not fulfilled the aspirations of the population of various
regions in the country. The tendency of neglected areas, aggrieved
groups, and smaller provinces to be offended by the dominating
attitude of the Punjab has been the root cause of the federation's
problems. Thus, treating demands for provincial autonomy, more
provinces, and regional rights as treasonable and unpatriotic seems
intended to perpetuate socio-economic exploitation and denial of
democratic rights to these groups.

For the multiplication of provinces, various suggestions have been
put forward in the chequered constitutional history of Pakistan.
When it was evident that Yahya Khan was going to do away with One
Unit, some suggested the setting up of provinces on linguistic and
ethnic lines. Without visualizing any pragmatic scheme to serve the
cause of the federation, Yahya Khan decided to restore the old
provinces. When the 'new' Pakistan chartered the 1973 Constitution,
Bhutto also did not attempt to recognize the imperative of establishing administrative units on a realistic basis. When Zia clamped
his martial law on the country, besides other controversies, the issue
of more provinces also raised its head. General Zia, both in his public
speeches and private conversations, talked about dividing the country
into almost twenty-five provinces.[3] He did not give his scheme
practical shape, and this, like so many other promises, remained
unfulfilled.

Those who argue in favour of the multiplication of units suggest
the following rationale for their schemes:

Administrative Convenience: Smaller units are more easily manageable and convenient for solving the local problems of people. Shorter
distances and better communication facilities allow the people to
reap the benefits of budgetary allocations. For instance, the Punjab
is too large in territory and population, and it is difficult to reach
out to the southern and western areas of the province from Lahore.
Moreover, the members of the provinical Assembly live in the

provincial capital, and the bureaucracy rules the widespread and scattered areas. But the situation becomes more manageable if there are smaller administrative units. The case of the Punjab applies to Balochistan as well. It is difficult to reach out to the other regions of the province from Quetta, the provincial capital.

Preventing Parochialism: Smaller units based on realistic lines would definitely curb the rising crescendo of provincialism in the country. There are regions, (i.e., the Seraiki, the Hazara, the Potohar, etc.,) which are entities in themselves. They have socio-economic grievances against the ruling elite of their provinces. They would feel satisfied if they were to acquire local self-government. The main condition for the success of a federation is that its constituent units must have a sense of fulfilment and of belonging to the national polity; that the people of one region should not feel that they are being dominated politically and economically or being ruled by another region. The vital question of national integration is linked with the satisfaction of the federating units. The present federal system does not unite the nation but divides it instead.

Minority Relations: The majority-minority syndrome, reminiscent of pre-partition days, has centred on the abhorrent pattern of the remaining units versus the Punjab. Moreover, because of administrative difficulties and lack of budgetary allocations, the Seraiki belt and the whole of the Potohar region feel neglected. Thus, the sense of deprivation of the existing federating units, and the large linguistic and cultural entities is quite understandable. Indeed, no federal structure can work smoothly where one federating unit is larger than the rest combined. 'Unless the structural problem of the country is resolved', maintains Senator Amir Abdullah Khan Rokari from Mianwali, 'it is virtually impossible to find a lasting cure for this disease of provincialism eating away at the integrity of the country like a deadly gangrene.'[4]

Decentralization: Whether the number of federating units is twenty or more or less, it is not too large for a country like Pakistan. Besides ending the colonial maladjustment of local provincial boundaries and groupings, the multiplication of federating units would also allow decentralization of power.

Secessionism: Provincial fragmentation will reduce the tendencies for secessionism on the basis of size and strength. For elaboration of this point, Nigeria's experience of multiplication of federating units can be cited here. In the past, Nigeria was plagued with secessionist activities of its three large regions, i.e., the northern, eastern, and western regions. The African giant divided its federation into nineteen provinces and was successful in subduing the separatist elements in the large country. Having almost the same population and territory, Pakistan can follow suit and emerge as a stable federation.

Decisive Factors

While the multiplication of federating units on some rational and pragmatic lines seems to be essential, the following factors should be kept in mind to effect this:

1. administrative convenience;

2. the satisfaction of the regional, cultural, linguistic, and ethnic ethos;

3. the socio-economic imperatives of regional entities and major groups;

4. the distances and communication systems in the proposed new administrative seats of management;

5. while redrawing the administrative boundaries of the present provinces, it should be assumed that such an act would contribute to, and not adversely affect, national integration. Every administrative unit so created must realize that its viable existence, socio-economic welfare, and overall future lies within the Federation and not outside its orbit; and

6. before finalizing any scheme for the multiplication of provinces, national and political consensus would need to be ensured. Otherwise, such an exercise might provide the much sought for opportunity to parochial political elements to fish in troubled waters. Unfortunately, the most common element in various schemes for multiplying the federating units is that all its adherents look towards military dictators to do the job. This is a negative approach.

Keeping all the apprehensions and implications of linguistic, regional, and ethnic interests in mind, many political scientists suggest that the

306 The Myth of Constitutionalism

present number of divisions, with adequate adjustments, might be successfully converted into full-fledged basic administrative units. Such a scheme, in the perspective of its advocates, would bring double benefits to the federation. Firstly, by geopolitically fragmenting the present provinces into the proposed twenty-two people's Divisional Democracies, it would be possible to reduce provincialism. Secondly, it would avert the possibility of centrifugalism on the basis of ethnicity and language.

Whether the new administrative structures (consisting of divisions) would be twelve, twenty two, or more, the rationale of such a scheme is provided by Jamil Nishtar in the following terms:

> these Provinces would not, by any means, be small administrative entities. In fact, in accordance with world standards, they will still be substantial. For instance, the largest Province, Lahore Province, would be the 32nd largest country in the world, if it were an independent State. In other words, it will be larger than about 100 independent sovereign countries. Even the smallest Province, Mekran Province, would be at 126 in the league of countries. In other words, larger than about 40 independent sovereign states around the world.[5]

Such a scheme favours geopolitical fragmentation of the existing provinces in the form of the present divisions as administrative units. If economics and ethnicity justify the present provinces, then by the same logic, they provide the rationale for further geopolitical fragmentation at the regional and local levels. This scheme scrupulously avoids the colonial gubernatorial term, 'provinces'.

Devolution of Power to the Federating Units

The devolution of power to the federating units is a prerequisite for the viability of any federation in the world. If there is too much concentration of power at the Centre, it becomes a unitary system. The penchant of the ruling elite in Pakistan for centralization has left the question of provincial autonomy unresolved. The ignominious attempts of successive regimes to sweep this burning issue under the rug resulted in the alienation of the people of East Pakistan.

Despite experiencing the gruesome tragedy of East Pakistan, the extent and degree of centralization in the present constitutional and political set-up of Pakistan is spectacular. A brief analysis of the distribution of Centre-province powers will reveal that the federation is still at the starting point of August 1947. For instance, in the Government of India Act, 1935 (as the Provisional Constitution of Pakistan 1947-56), the Federal List consisted of 61 subjects, the Provincial List was of 55 subjects, and the Concurrent List of 37. In the 1956 Constitution of the country, the Federal and Concurrent Lists consisted of 30 and 19 subjects respectively. The Provincial List of subjects was increased to 94. The 1973 Constitution contains only the Federal and Concurrent Lists and all the residual powers rest with the provinces. Yet, the increasing of the Federal List to 67 and the Concurrent List to 47 subjects, has reduced the units almost to nonentities, whereas the Centre enjoys powers to legislate over a total of 114 subjects.

In view of such over-centralization, it has been suggested that the Centre must have the minimum number of subjects, namely, defence, currency, foreign affairs, and communications only.[6] The rest of the subjects must be vested in the federating units. This, in the opinion of political analysts, is justified in the light of the country's past experience of over-centralization.

Mr M. P. Bhandara, a prominent minority leader, opines that the salient trend in the over four decade long history of Pakistan, 'in terms of the division of power, has been a one-way street, with the federal government in *de jure* and *de facto* manner usurping the powers of the provinces. The same axiom is true in respect of provincial capitals usurping the powers of the districts and the divisions . . . Everyone knows that the pettiest and the meanest of decisions have to be referred to Lahore, Quetta, Karachi or Peshawar by the divisional authorities . . . The worst hit case, because of its size and number is that of Punjab, where outlying districts and divisions queue up for the power dispensation of Lahore.'[7]

While Mr Bhandara suggests a system of smaller units as a panacea for the aforementioned malaise of centralization, Dr Mubashir Hasan, a founding member of the Pakistan People's Party, on the other hand, proposes changing the constitutional rules and management grids to ensure the sharing of power on an equitable basis by the people of Pakistan. In his perspective, the Constitution of the country should be amended in such a manner that the devolution of power from Islamabad right down to the village level is ensured. Moreover, sweeping changes must be effected in the administrative system of the country allowing for transfer of power from the 'officer class' to elected bodies and persons.[8]

In the contemporary constitutional scenario in Pakistan, the people's representatives are unable to voice the wishes of those who elect them. Throughout the country, power is exercised by a hierarchy of officers. While the jurisdiction of the elected representatives is restricted at all levels through legal impediments and technicalities, the people's destiny is perpetually mortgaged in the unscrupulous hands of officials who exercise absolute powers. The entire structure of administration needs to be changed in favour of the elected representatives. The existing laws, rules, and regulations of administration should be so restructured as to confer full powers and responsibilities to elected bodies at the grass-root level.

Decentralisation of Economic and Development Planning

Besides the absence of devolution of substantial powers to the federating units, the centralized development, planning, and revenue system have adversely affected federalism in Pakistan. The heavily centralized system of planning, for the sake of so-called uniformity, has eroded provincial autonomy. Besides gaining effective control over subjects falling exclusively within the provincial sphere, the Centre has been able, through the potent instrument of financial grants, to dominate the provincial administration.[9]

All the five-year plans have been formulated by the Centre and handed down as 'orders' to the provinces as 'subservient units'.[10] Failing to create any sense of 'partnership', the federating units were asked, at the most, to prepare their own limited plans on the basis of development priorities and financial targets set out by the Planning Commission of Pakistan. Euphemistically assuming that all sectors of the national economy are interlinked, a highly centralized economic structure has been established in the country. Shahid Kardar, an economist, opines that:

> The Planning Commission attempts to bring all the Provinces within the ambit of what it regards as the national plan, leaving the Provinces with little autonomy in determining their own development plans. It prepares a national plan on a sector-wise basis, which is then broken-up into Annual Development Plan allocations for the Centre and the Provinces, even if the plans are not

appropriate to each Province's resource endowments and stage of development'.[11]

Dr Mahbubul Haq, a former Finance Minister of Pakistan, holds the biased system of distribution of development powers between the centre and the provinces responsible for the ill-will between the two. Dr Haq opines:

> The present situation is extremely unsatisfactory. Provincial governments face a deficit . . . in their current accounts. They have to turn to the Centre for every teacher they hire, every doctor they employ, every policeman they need to strengthen their internal security. This leads to constant battles and ill-feeling between the Centre and the Provinces about the genuineness of provincial expenditures and the correct level of their deficits . . . If there is provincial surplus on the current account, it is taken away by the Centre and placed in the common financial pool for federal and provincial expenditures. If there is a provincial deficit, it is financed by the Centre, irrespective of its size . . . such a formula encourages competition among the provinces to become deficit.[12]

Continuation of the Political Process

In the over four decade long history of Pakistan, the military-bureaucratic elite, for their own vested interests, have inflicted decisive blows on the political and democratic process in the country. The illegal and unconstitutional dissolution of Assemblies and abrogation of Constitutions have had a powerful negative impact on Centre-province relations. From Ghulam Muhammad (1951) to Ghulam Ishaq Khan (1993), with several generals in between, the central leadership has dismissed provincial governments without fulfilling constitutional requirements. Federalism and democracy are the two essential pillars of political stability in a country like Pakistan. However, from the very inception of this country, neither democracy nor federalism has been allowed to take root.

The unilateral forcible acts of assuming power, dismissal of provincial governments, suspension of constitutional machinery, imposition of Governor's rule, declaring of the federalists demanding provincial autonomy as traitors by the powers that be, and other such acts amounting to defederalization had driven the autonomists to the point of no return during Zia's military dictatorship. The intensity of deprivation was quite visible when a vetern Baloch politician known for his integrity and patriotism, Mir Ghous Bukhsh Bizenjo, angrily demanded in 1978 the insertion of a constitutional provision in 'the future constitution' of Pakistan that if the democratic and provincial rights were snatched away again, the minority provinces shall have the right to opt out of the Federation.[13]

Perennial Bonapartism has eroded the political process, thereby affecting the foundations of the federation. Confrontationist and agitational politics have allowed parochial entities to create a situation of fragmentation in the federal polity of Pakistan. While the ruling elite has turned the provinces into mere extensions of the Centre, those who demand maximum provincial autonomy seem determined to transform the federation into a nonentity. The best solution to avert any unpleasant confrontation between the autonomists and centralists would be to allow democratic and constitutional processes to take their due course, peacefully and unimpededly. Any attempt to curb the political process further would be suicidal for the federation.

In a country like Pakistan, based as it is on plural entities, it is essential to preserve the Constitution and to discourage the strong-arm tactics of those who, under cover of darkness, snatch power and ridicule the verdict of the people. Despite attempts to deny it, the people of Pakistan have demonstrated on various occasions that they want constitutional democracy. Democratic ideals and idealism, democratic aptitude and ambitions, democratic norms and nomenclature, democratic vision and visualization, democratic precepts and concepts, fit in very well with the national polity and political culture of Pakistan.

Independence of Judiciary

A Constitution is a fundamental framework of immense importance for political interaction, co-operation, crisis management, and conflict resolution between the federation and its units. Besides being the state's general framework of political existence, a Constitution contains those primary rules of law and binding conventions which regulate the structure of the main governmental organs and their relationship with one another and with the federating units. If there is some ambiguity and conflict in the operation of those constitutional principles, it is the supreme responsibility of the superior courts in the country to interpret the Constitution. Interpretations independently arrived at are respected by the federation and its units. However, such a judicial process has remained mythical in Pakistan and sometimes over-protected under the outdated colonial concept of contempt of court.

The judiciary in Pakistan has often been criticized for its failure to uphold the rights of the citizens and the federating units. The judiciary legitimized every regime which tended to promote centralism. More often than not, the higher courts in the country made themselves available to those who wanted to legitimize their unconstitutional and extra-constitutional acts. The Supreme Court of Pakistan's acquiescing in abrogation of Constitutions, via the so-called law of necessity, has become a joke in local politics. The judiciary extended respect to successful coup-makers as if they were an elected parliament. This impotence of the higher courts has left an adverse impact on the federating units which wish to get their due share from the Centre through the judicial process. Thus, it is in the interest of the democratic process and federalism in Pakistan that the higher Courts should recognize their supreme role as custodians of the Constitution.

Recurring political turmoil and the worst kind of constitutional engineering for promoting centralism by the military regimes have curtailed judicial powers as well. What is even more surprising is that the judges have never prepared themselves for an activist role. In most of the cases, they dutifully obliged the federal government. Consequent upon such a practice and tradition, a constitutional expert opines that:

> In disputes between the Federal and Provincial Governments, or between two Provincial Governments, under the Constitution, the Supreme Court has no power to deliver a binding judgment (Article 184). It can only make declaratory pronouncements which cannot be executed and can be ignored. In many federations the units can rely on the judicial power for protection against ambitious federal policies. The courts provide a convenient and relatively independent forum for the adjudication of outstanding centre-state issues. This power is denied to our

courts. In the entire federal structure not a single
safeguard has been built to protect the provinces from the
abuse of power by the Centre. If their rights are infringed
by the Centre, all that they can do is complain. The
Constitution does not provide any forum from which they
can seek a redress of their grievances. They have to learn
to live with Federal excesses.[14]

NEW SOCIAL CONTRACT

Social contract connotes a phenomenon whereby an understanding
of a fundamental nature signifies a consensus on the need to live
together and regulate the collective sociopolitical life of a group.
This multi-dimensional philosophical and political concept has
unfolded over a period of time. Hobbes, Locke, and Rousseau
elaborated the concept of social contract. However, without entering
into the perilous journey of explaining it further, suffice it to mention
that the idea is neither a new one nor is it confined to any particular
geographical area or political group.

In Pakistan, Prime Minister Benazir Bhutto has emerged as the
champion of introducing the concept in the sociopolitical milieu of
the country. She unveiled her perspectives and understanding of the
social contract a few years back on the occasion of the twenty-fifth
anniversary of the founding of the PPP. Ms Bhutto advocated radical
reforms in the local self-government structure, with devolution of
substantial authority from the Centre to the federating units and
down to the district level. Ms Bhutto characterized it as the 'New
Social Contract', aimed at establishing a balance of power between
the federation, the provinces, and the local bodies.

In the wake of becoming the Prime Minister for the second time in
October 1993, Ms Bhutto's government appears to have pledged itself
to effecting pragmatic changes in the local bodies system. According
top priority to her programme of setting up district governments, the
federal government appointed a task force, headed by a veteran
politician, Kamal Azfar. The task force came up with a comprehensive
report on the programme for the New Social Contract. The 67-page
report has proposed the setting up of district governments and has
attracted much publicity, critical evaluation, and even harsh comments.

Despite its publication with great fanfare, the government of Ms Benazir Bhutto has failed to implement its social contract so far. It is stated that each district will have a district government, headed by the district mayor. The chairman of the union council will be a member of the district assembly which will pass the annual budget, make by-laws, exercise the powers of the district council, and frame rules of business for the district government. The deputy commissioner will be appointed in consultation with the district mayor. He will be the head of the district secretariat and will assist the mayor in running the district government. The essential functions of the commissioner and the division would be reallocated at the district level. The district mayor would represent the state at the district level as the governor does at the provincial level.

In principle and as ideal visualization, there is nothing wrong in every district having its elected assembly, its own government overseeing the functions of the local bodies, local resources being spent on local problems, etc. Yet the critics of district government apprehend the introduction of a peculiar phenomenon of power politics at the district level, whereby feudalism would undermine the emerging trends of democratization and industrialization in the country. The new system may tilt the sociopolitical bias further in favour of the repressive ruling elite. Generally aimed at improving the socioeconomic plight of the masses and solving problems at their doorstep, this idealism may degenerate into a permanent monopoly of a few over the levers of local government.

The need to radically reform the local bodies system is a real one. Local government is usually helpful in solving civic problems locally. The apprehensions about the proposed district government are mostly based on the present malpractices in the Pakistani political system. It is widely questioned whether the district government would not open another market for horse-trading. Such pertinent queries notwithstanding, there should not be any hesitation in removing the most unproductive, outdated, and abhorrent system with a new one which vows to concentrate on the grass-roots level and which at least visualizes progressive changes in the society.

CONCLUSION

Suffice it to say that the geopolitical fragmentation of the present provinces or the multiplication of federating units, devolution of power in practical terms to the provinces, allowing constitutional democracy to take root in the country, decentralization of development planning, and the independence of the judiciary are the best devices to save the Federation from the scourge of corrosive parochialism. Any steps taken contrary to the foregoing popular remedies appear fraught with terrible consequences for the whole federation. Mere frequency of elections, whether regular or mid-term, without other essential democratic checks and balances and moderating forces, may only add fuel to the fire of confrontationist agitational politics. Systemic structural fragmentation seems to be inevitable. The *status quo* of traditional vested interests must give way to regional revolutionary forces, creating a democratic and futuristic collective leadership rising to the challenges, opportunities, and responsibilites of the twenty-first century.

The unresolved problem of provincial autonomy has become one of the most important issues in the contemporary political permutations of Pakistan. The absence of federalism and constitutionalism has led to unpalatable consequences for the federation in the past (in the creation of Bangladesh). And if the present state of affairs continues, the remainder of the federation may experience serious strains on its viable survival.

The continuation of semi-military and semi-civilian rule by, or through, an authoritarian civil and military bureaucracy throughout the country's history has already accentuated the sense of provincial alienation, leading to parochialism and even secessionism. There has been a noticeable absence of initiative to accommodate or even to consider the demands of the autonomists. Far from taking positive constitutional steps to fulfil the aspirations of the people, the ruling elite adopted tactics which stalled the democratic process itself. While opting for centralization as their political creed, almost every federal government has dealt severe blows to constitutionalism and federalism. Little has it been realized that the strength of a federation does not stem from the federal government but from the devolution of power in the nation as a whole, and that political co-operation between the federating units and the federal government, and self-restraint in the exercise of power are the hallmark of a successful federation.

The discussion in the preceding chapters amply demonstrates that the vital democratic principles of federalism and constitutionalism became the target of the whims of power-grabbing influential individuals from Ghulam Muhammad to Ghulam Ishaq Khan. No

Governor-General in the 1950s acted as a constitutional figurehead, Khwaja Nazimuddin being the exception. Similarly, with President Fazal Elahi Chaudhry an exception in the Bhutto government (1973-77), no President acted as a constitutional figurehead in the whole history of the federation. Either the prime ministers or, in most cases, the chief ministers of the provinces, were readily available prey to political predators.

Between the period 1947-71, barring Liaquat Ali Khan, none of the prime ministers (about eight) were either elected or ever received a vote of confidence from the National Assembly. Not a single government, either federal or provinical, has so far been changed in the country through a normal, legitimate constitutional process. Provincial governments have often been forced out, not to foster federalism or provincial autonomy, but to provide for pliable provincial heads. Similarly, the military-bureaucratic elite have ousted federal governments, not to restore any particular Constitution or democratic order, but to perpetuate centralization and authoritarianism.

There was a time when the adherents of provincial autonomy were dubbed as traitors by the vested interests. However, the times seem to have changed. The people can no longer be misled by officially-inspired anti-autonomy propaganda. It is high time that the vital issue of federalism is addressed in a cool, dispassionate, and far-sighted manner. The emerging trends of regionalism and secessionism, particularly in the smaller provinces, might provide the long-awaited opportunity to Pakistan's hostile neighbour to dismember the country on the pattern of East Pakistan. Both the opposition and the government must learn to evolve a pragmatic consensus on the issue of provincial autonomy and solve it once and for all through a viable *modus operandi*.

12

PAKISTAN 1947-1995
THE HERITAGE OF CONSTITUTIONAL POLITICS

I

The Pakistan of today appears to be a country where the ruling elite is consistently busy in fashioning all kinds of whips for the masses, where dissent is pathologically abhorrent, where arbitrariness is an accepted norm, where the human spirit struggles to breathe in a stifling environment, where financial pillaging is practised as an art, where fanaticism is made palatable, where obscurantism is preached as a code, where everything is said to be ordained by Almighty Allah, where the deference due to the judiciary is on the decline, and where legislators have a price tag on them. In such a sordid sociopolitical milieu, it seems ridiculous to talk about constitutional propriety, civil rights, moral standards, human values, and the dignity of man. The mighty Roman empire was assaulted, mutilated, and torn to pieces by 'foreign barbarians'; in Pakistan, we have bred our own to do that job.

The country's ruling elite, abiding by its creed of absolutism, has kept the whole nation in a state of turmoil. As the rulers indulge in deceit, huckstering, injustices, and plunder, Pakistan has earned a reputation for financial embezzlement, forsaken beliefs, impossible loyalties, love for arbitrariness, and disdain for federalism and constitutionalism. Meanwhile, the professed guardians of the faith, via their dabblings in constitutional jurisprudence for ulterior ends, have obfuscated the liberal social aspirations and democratic inclinations of the people.

Devout merely in the pursuit of absolutism, the ruling elite has entrenched itself by trading the obsolete model of colonialism for draconian emergency laws, the infamous doctrine of necessity, and the spectre of martial laws. The desire to remain perpetually in power, and that too without facing the masses at the hustings, has become fashionable. The prospects of holding general elections in a fair and democratic manner sound like a death-knell to the politicians. The ruling elite seems interested only in contriving situations to evade taxes, waste the national money, and to amend or distort the Constitution for partisan gains.

The patience of those who have suffered the extortions of the Byzantine bureaucracy, ruling the country unconstitutionally and pillaging the national exchequer, is amazing. The tyrannical whims of despots from Ghulam Muhammad to Ghulam Ishaq Khan and the capacity of the suffering people to endure humiliation, oppression, and abject exploitation, are all remarkable. Yet more peculiar is the popular psyche which, off and on, realizes the unacceptable cost of living under sociopolitical enslavement, risks confrontation with dictators, and effects their downfall in the process.

While enslaving the entire nation, the rulers promise to match and surpass past glories, erase past shames, avenge betrayals, and bring a utopian world to the doorstep of every citizen. The dissolution of Assemblies, abrogation of Constitutions, and the dismissal of governments are justified as a purging of the holy precincts of politics from degraded politicians. Then follow proclamations of reinforcing the majesty of constitutional law and establishing a sanctified political order in the country. Contrary to these pretensions of the rulers, the ugly phenomenon of disrupting constitutional governments gives birth to rampant corruption. Yet it is an irony of Pakistan's politics that those who indulge in the worst form of corruption, abrogation of Constitutions, and usurpation of power in the dark of night, are acclaimed as 'heroes' and eulogized as 'saviours'. What else is this if not abject hypocrisy, to label such unscrupulous dictators as 'soldier-statesmen' and call their nefarious acts 'missions'?

Dictatorships in Pakistan, both military and civil, were frequently wrapped in theological justifications. The leaders who made great claims of making the country safe for democracy played a great role in making it unsafe for such norms. They flooded the liberal social environment with novel, anti-democratic, anti-parliamentary, and anti-people theories. Most of the nation's democratic and constitutional institutions were facile imitations of contemporary institutions elsewhere. They were theoretically adopted and hypocritically maintained, without the slightest consideration for the socio-economic and political environment in which they were to operate. The net outcome was that not a single government could function with even a fair degree of regularity and legality. Every 'late' Constitution was adopted to set high political standards, yet each collapsed along with its promulgator.

318 The Myth of Constitutionalism

The ruling elite has never respected 'late' Constitutions, not considering them even worth the paper on which they were written. It was the height of such insolence towards the 1973 Constitution when a military dictator openly asserted that it was a booklet of a few pages which could be torn up at any time by him. Such gallantry earned him the 'sacred' title of *mard-e-momin, mard-e-haq*, bestowed on him by none less than the pious *ulema* of this country. A constitutional critic might malign such a despot for his treacherous and irresponsible act of scuttling the democratic and constitutional process in the country, yet he symbolized the collective thinking of 'dacoit kings' towards the Constitutions throughout the political history of Pakistan.

Pakistan's political contentions have usually centred on the Constitution: its restoration, abrogation, sustenance, holding in abeyance, amendments to it, its secular or theocratic character, its Islamization, and its inadequacies. Notwithstanding the assertions of the politicians of holding constitutional principles very sacred, they have never confronted the dictators who abrogated, put in abeyance, or violated the highest law of the land. Every prominent politician of the country has indulged at one time or another in the uncivilized practice of scuttling the constitutional process, in active collusion with dictators.

While the military dictators invariably oppose the continuation of constitutional democracy, the overwhelming majority of politicians has acted as a pliable tool for the 'cause' and in the hands of the former. The contention that the self-seeking lot would unhesitatingly accept even a Hitler or Stalin is not devoid of truth.

While attending the Silver Jubilee celebrations of the Punjab Provincial Assembly in February 1988, a Turkish delegate, Mr Enrole Kose, made some perceptive remarks about the working of the constitutional and democratic system in Pakistan. The delegate opined, on the basis of his own country's experience, that each martial law takes the country back several years, introducing huge impediments in the process of re-establishing institutions of legitimate civilian and representative government; and that Pakistan's federal and provincial legislatures were exclusively manned by individuals who did not belong to the strata they were supposed to represent.

Hailing from the well-to-do and privileged sections of the society, the majority of the people's respresentatives seem determined to recover the cost of their electioneering and increase the benefits of plunder by switching from one party to another in their search for official patronage. With legal sanction for looting the national exchequer, they first get loans from financial institutions and then get them written off by political bribery. They seem to be above the law of the land. The laws of insolvency and bankruptcy are applicable to small fry while the dacoits and big sharks are above such routine matters of the Pakistan Penal Code. These unscrupulous power-brokers often don the garb of religion to enhance their public image, yet it is their notorious and shady financial backgrounds that distinguish them.

Opportunism, political immaturity, self-interest, lack of democratic conventions, disgust for the opposition, and lust for power have created a frightening sociopolitical stalemate in the country, leading to virtual collapse of the system. The contemporary political culture of Pakistan is permeated with unprincipled politics with shameful connotations of horse-trading (*lotas*), with rank rottenness and naked lust for power all around. The whole political system is apparently hostage to mafia politics and the power of the drug barons.

II

In Pakistan's contemporary sociopolitical environment, the majority of the politicians claim to speak in the name of religion. They use the sacred name of Allah as an investment and as an argument to condemn others. While asserting their moral and political superiority, they pronounce verdicts on their rivals as *kafirs*. Embodying the evils of dogmatism, fanaticism, and abject hypocrisy, such politicians wish to perpetuate dogma, ritualism, and social stagnation. Using religion as a device to gain power and then hang on to it, the fundamentalists in Pakistan have the base intent of depriving the people of their fundamental rights. Failing to persuade the masses, they wish to attain their ends by manipulating lesiglatures. Amidst recurring crises of change in the modern era, the adherents of theocracy intend to drag the whole nation back into the medieval ages.

The period beginning with the end of the fifth century, and continuing for about the next five centuries, is called the Dark Ages in Western political history. The major trait of the political philosophy of the Dark Ages was the supremacy of Christian scriptures and theology over the state, society, and law. Papal authority was supreme throughout the European continent, interfering with and controlling the sociopolitical lives of the masses. In the shadow of the Holy Roman Empire, the political and institutional orientations had centred on the dictum that 'Prayers superseded thought and Faith prescribed knowledge'. Marked by papal political ascendancy, theological generalizations, and religious influence, the Dark Ages retarded the process of change and political evolution.

Ignoring these historical considerations and socio-economic realities, and shunning the political philosphy of the modern state and constitutionalism, the orthodox *ulema*, *muftis*, and *grand muftis* in Pakistan are pressing the government and persuading the people to return to orthodoxy. However, the overwhelming majority of the people in Pakistan seems to have rejected the *ulema's* quest for theocracy. Such an assertion is borne out by the rout of religious groups in the 1993 elections in Pakistan.

III

Lack of vision, sense of direction, and adequate leadership qualities among politicians in the 1950s facilitated the hijacking of the country's top positions by the bureaucracy. The whimsical and authoritarian bureaucratic structures disrupted the political life of the country. The bureaucratic and military ascent to power, led by Governor-General Ghulam Muhammad and Iskandar Mirza, meant that all levers of state power were used to erode the basis of all-Pakistan leadership in country. In preference to national leaders, insignificant personalities with parochial, regional, racial, religious, and provincial allegiances were encouraged and eulogized by the oppressive state apparatus.

After Ayub Khan clamped his martial law in October 1958, the Establishment began recruiting politicians as 'informers', 'agents', and even 'pimps' to sustain the authoritarian structure. They began to be rewarded for their 'valuable services' to 'the State'. Those who refused to succumb to such lucrative temptations or who tried to be 'clean and principled' were promptly victimized and often sent to special torture cells for 'correction', to ween them away from treading the 'unpatriotic' path of opposing the government. General Yahya Khan introduced the most humiliating punishment of whipping political workers for the same end.

Prime Minister Zulfikar Ali Bhutto had the rare opportunity to institutionalize the supremacy of political rule over the Establishment. By then, the conventional power-brokers, i.e., the military generals, the civil bureaucrats, and the traditional ruling elite, had been completely discredited in the eyes of the public. The falling apart of the Federation in 1971 was a traumatic experience for the Establishmet and it had reluctantly handed over power to Premier Bhutto. Far from keeping the civil and military bureaucracy under the control of political authority, Bhutto sought ways and means to strengthen it. His resorting to army action in Balochistan, the establishment of the Federal Security Force to crush his political opponents, and to rule the country single-handedly, through the coercive state apparatus, vitiated the imperatives of political rule over the Establishment.

Zulfikar Ali Bhutto's politics never appealed to the Establishment. The military regime of Zia dispensed with Bhutto, aiming to make a horrible example for such would-be politicians. With rare exceptions, the process of 'enrolment' attained its height during the Zia regime. Zia created not only a 'new' brand of politicians but showered upon them huge bank loans to be written off later. The objective behind such corruption was to keep these politicians on his side and blackmail them subsequently, if and when they tried to be clean and principled. The tradition so established began to pay immense dividends to the Establishment. The majority of the politicians were imploring the Zia regime for conferrment of political roles in the 1980s.

Zia unhesitatingly employed the services of the Establishment for exterminaton of his political opponents. The tactics used for such avowed ends led to the division of the society on ethnic, sectarian, regional, linguistic, and caste lines. Zia, like Ayub Khan and Yahya Khan, wanted to rule Pakistan for the rest of his life and would definitely have tried to do so if he had not been eliminated in the air crash of 17 August 1988.

Ghulam Ishaq Khan arrogated to himself the singular distinction of perpetuating the rule of the bureaucratic clique in Pakistan. Following in the footsteps of Ayub Khan and Ziaul Haq, Ishaq Khan remained the arch enemy of those politicians who enjoyed public acclaim and confidence. He never acknowledged the people as the real source of power. Enjoying the arbitrary powers of dismissing governments and dissolving Assemblies through the Eighth Amendment to the 1973 Constitution, he packed Ms Benazir Bhutto home, though her government had defeated a no-confidence resolution in the National Assembly. His hand-picked protege, Nawaz Sharif, had a comfortable majority in the National Assembly, yet Ghulam Ishaq Khan dismissed him in a similar manner.

If the higher Courts (which took oath to protect the Constitution) joined hands with the constitution-breakers in the past, a trail of 'eminent' jurists helped in changing and chopping Pakistan's 'late' Constitutions as well. Amidst constitutional crises, in the guise of guiding the Courts, they misguided the whole nation. Far from pleading in the interests of public, they entrusted the latter to the whims of dictators. For subverting constitutional structures and flouting the popular mandate, they sided with the usurpers of people's rights. Popularly known as 'the legal eagles' in drafting dissolution orders of the Assemblies for the dictators, they have led dictators to suspend democratic rights and the constitutional machinery of the country since the 1950s. Claiming to be committed professionals, they served their clients from Ghulam Muhammad to Ghulam Ishaq Khan, no matter what they did to the Federation.

IV

The amendment-ridden 1973 Constitution in its present form is full of inconsistencies. The rulers, compelled by their dictatorial propensities have introduced diabolical constitutional provisions, ending up with the latest Twelfth Amendment to the Constitution. The process of mutilating the Constitution had begun during the era of Zulfikar Ali Bhutto, but it was perfected in 1985 when the captive Assembly under duress signed away its attributes of sovereignty. Thenceforth, the National Assembly and the government it elected were incapable of protecting their existence against being summarily snuffed out by Presidential decree through the Eighth Amendment.

The misguided dissolution of the Assemblies by Zia and Ishaq, and the guillotining of the governments which they themselves had appointed, has expedited the pace of recurring political uncertainties in the country. It has created an atmosphere where rumours and disinformation thrive. The people's confidence in the prevalent political order and sanctity of the ballot box has been eroded. The mindless pursuit by the Governor-Generals and Presidents for 'discretion' in the 'late' Constitutions has subverted the smooth functioning of parliamentary democracy in the country.

The legacy of a decade of Zia's military rule still hovers like a juggernaut over democratic institutions. The rule of one man mutilated national institutions and completely blurred democratic values. The 1973 Constitution, a valid basis for the existence of the Federation, has been deliberately beaten out of shape. The Eighth Amendment did not merely add certain Articles to the 1973 Constitution, it completely destroyed its character. This carbuncle in the Constitution has turned into a vicious amalgamation of parliamentary practices and authoritarian decrees. The following political environment in which the Eighth Amendment was conceived and adopted negates its retention in a civilized society:

- Preceding the addition of the Eighth Amendment, the country was run by Zia's PCO—a negation of the 1973 Constitution. Zia held a fraudulent referendum which was supra-constitutional, with gross malpractices on the ground, and declared himself President of the country for the next five years.

- The representative character of the National Assembly that assented to the notorious law was dubious.

- An Assembly which was not the creation of the 1973 Constitution could not pass an Amendment to the Constitution, which had been put in abeyance by the military dictator on 5 July 1977.

- The so-called National Assembly, elected on a non-party basis, was not a sovereign legislature, as martial law was still in force and the COAS was the President who eclipsed the power of every national institution.

- After the Eighth Amendment, the 1973 Constitution became the first of its kind throughout the civilized world wherein the serving COAS is mentioned by name.

- Working under the shadow of the COAS gave the lie to the democratic credentials of the Assembly passing the law.

- By passing the Eighth Amendment, Zia was mainly interested in providing a facade of legitimacy to his dictatorship.

The only viable and dignified solution to the contemporary constitutional malaise lies in the restoration of the original 1973 Constitution, with consequential amendments to make it operative in the present political permutations of Pakistan. The Eighth Amendment must be consigned to the dustbin of Pakistan's chequered constitutional history. The Constitution, in its present form, requires changes to make it an undiluted expression of the will of the people and their representatives, who had adopted it unanimously in 1973. The 1973 Constitution is the only legitimate basis for the Federation, and must be restored. Besides restoring the sovereignty of the Parliament, the restoration of the 1973 Constitution would demolish the scenario of an unscrupulous President confronting a beleaguered Prime Minister.

NOTES

1

1. Keith B. Callard, *Political Forces in Pakistan* (New York: Institute of Pacific Relations, 1959) 8.
2. Ibid.
3. Pakistan has been governed under the following Constitutions: Provisional Constitution:1947–56 (modified and amended version of the Government of India Act, 1935); the 1956 Constitution:1956-8; Interim Constitution under Ayub Khan's martial law:1958-62; the 1962 Constitution:1962-9;The Legal Framework Order/Provisional Constitution under Yahya Khan's Martial Law:1969-71; Bhutto's Interim Constitution (i.e., based on the Government of India Act, 1935, and the Independence Act, 1947):1972-3;the 1973 Constitution:1973-7; Zia's martial law, suspension of the 1973 Constitution, promulgation of the Provisional Constitution Order(PCO):1981-5; the 1985 Constitution(the disfigured form of the 1973 Constitution):1985.
4. Rafi Raza (a former federal minister in Z. A. Bhutto's cabinet, and later in Ghulam Mustafa Jatoi's caretaker cabinet), 'The Continuous Process of Rewriting the Constitution', in Wolfgang Peter Zingel and Stephanie Zingel Ave Lallemant (ed.) *Pakistan in the 1980s:Law and Constitution* (Lahore:Vanguard Books, 1985) 33.
5. Professor Carl J. Newman taught political science and international relations, first at the University of Dhaka and later at the Quaid-i-Azam University, Islamabad. He was a very close observer of the constitution-making process in the 1950s in Pakistan. See his *Essays on the Constitution of Pakistan* (Dhaka: Co-operative Book Society Ltd., 1956) 118.
6. For substantiation of such a perspective, see Ahsan Ali Khan, 'Provincial Autonomy: Roots of the Problem', *The Muslim* (Islamabad) 29 May 1986.
7. Ibid.
8. From a speech delivered by Mr S. M. Zafar on 15 December 1966, in Dhaka, quoted in Lawrence Ziring, *The Ayub Khan Era:Politics in Pakistan,1958-1969* (New York: Syracuse University Press, 1971) 184.
9. Zulfikar Ali Bhutto, *The Great Tragedy* (Karachi: Pakistan People's Party Publication, 1971) 9. Bhutto attributed the ever-worsening economic situation in the country, the continuation of martial law, and the abrogation of two Constitutions (i.e., the 1956 and the 1962 Constitutions) in Pakistan's two-decade history, to wrong political decisions. For his comment that 'by the time President Yahya Khan came to power, Pakistan seemed like a patient in the last stages of tuberculosis', Bhutto relied on Machiavelli's observation. Machiavelli had equated wrong political decisions to tuberculosis which were 'difficult to detect in the beginning

but easy to cure, and, with the passage of time, easy to detect but difficult to cure'.

10. Satish Kumar, 'Problems of Federal Politics in Pakistan', in Pandav Nayak(ed.), *Pakistan: Society and Politics* (New Delhi: South Asian Publishers, 1984) 29.

11. D. Shah Khan, 'Two Pillars of Stability—Democracy and Federalism', *The Muslim* (Islamabad) 11 August 1989.

12. Ibid.

13. Muhammad Ayub Khan, *Friends Not Masters* (Karachi: Oxford University Press, 1967) 217.

14. Dr Mubashir Hasan's interview, *The Frontier Post* (Lahore) 27 August 1990.

15. Ibid.

16. See Makhdoom Ali Khan, '1973 Constitution — The Founding of the Federation', an unpublished paper read at a seminar: 'The Heritage Of Prime Minister Bhutto', in Karachi, 3-5 April 1989; f.n.22, 10.

17. Ibid.

18. Rao Rashid, *Jo Mein Ney Dekha* (Lahore: Caravan Books, 1985) 60.

19. The expression 'corruption of justice' was used by Mr Ramsey Clark, the former Attorney General of the USA, in his address to a seminar: 'The Heritage of Prime Minister Bhutto', in Karachi, 3-5 April 1989.

20. Dr Faqir Hussain, 'Guilty of high treason—IV', *The Frontier Post* (Peshawar) 30 May 1990.

21. Mushahid Hussain, 'Bhutto's Anniversary:focus on judiciary', *The Times of India* (New Delhi) 24 April 1989.

22. Bernard Lewis, *The Arabs in History* (New York:Harper & Brothers, 1960) 42.

23. Dr Muhammad Yusuf Goraya, 'The Prophet of Islam and Constitution' (Urdu) a paper read at a Seerat Conference held on 30 November 1989 at Lahore.

2

1. For some of these connotations, see, for instance, K. C. Wheare, *Modern Constitutions* (London:Oxford University Press, 1958) 46. The Constitution, a fundamental law of the land, as American President Woodrow Wilson used to assert, could not be 'a mere lawyer's document, but in fact the vehicle of a nation's life'.

2. *Encyclopaedia Britannica,* vol.5, 84.

3. See Leslie Wolf-Phillips (ed.), *Constitutions of Modern States:Selected Texts and Commentary* (New York: Frederick A. Praeger, 1968), ix.

4. James Bryce, quoted in Wolf-Phillips.

5. Bolingbroke, *A Dissertation Upon Parties* (1733) quoted in Wheare, *Modern Constitutions*, 3.

6. Thomas Paine, *Rights of Man*, quoted in E. C. S. Wade and W. Godfrey Phillips, *Constitutional and Administrative Law* (London: 1978) 2.

7. William G. Andrews, *Constitution and Constitutionalism* (New York:1963) 24.

8. Muhammad Munir, *Constitution of the Islamic Republic of Pakistan* (Lahore:All Pakistan Legal Decisions,1967) 6.

9. Ibid.

10. Ibid., 6-7; and Wade &Phillips, *Administrative Law*, 2.

11. See for instance Andrews, *Constitutionalism*, 24-5.

12. Ibid., 25.

13. *Encyclopaedia Britannica*, vol.5, 84.

14. Andrews, *Constitutionalism*, 13.

15. Ibid. In the libertarian sense of constitutionalism, the best example would be those restraints that were imposed on the national government by the ten amendments to the Constitution of the USA.

16. Munir, *Islamic Republic*, 5.

17. See M. J. C. Vile, *Constitutionalism and the Separation of Power*, quoted in Wade & Phillips , *Administrative Law*, 5.

18. For substantiation of such views, see Andrews, *Constitutionalism*, 22.

19. Ibid., 22-3.

20. Thomas Paine, quoted in Charles Howard McIlwain, *Constitutionalism: Ancient and Modern* (Cornell University Press: 1947) 2.

21. For elaboration of Paine's definition of Constitution, the author drew insights from McIlwain, op.cit, 8-9.

22. A. K. Brohi, 'Constitutionalism: its theory and practice', *Dawn*, 23 December 1986.

23. George H. Sabine, *A History of Political Theory* (London:1949) 92-3.

24. A. V. Dicey, *Introduction to the Study of Law of the Constitution* (London: MacMillan, 1952) 9th edition, 183-204.

25. International Commission of Jurists 'Declaration of Delhi' (1959) i.e., 'The Rule of Law in Free Society' in *Report of International Congress of Jurists*, quoted in O. Hood Phillips, *Constitutional and Administrative Law* (London:1973) 17-18.

26. A. K. Brohi, 'Some Reflections on the Ideal of Justice and the Legal Order', *All Pakistan Legal Decisions (PLD), Journal*, 1974, 68. Brohi's whole paper is admittedly based on Dr Robert Briffault's work, *Making of Humanity* (London: George Allen & Unwin Ltd, 1928).

27. Dr Robert Briffault, quoted by Brohi.

28. See Daniel J. Elazar, 'Federalism', *International Encyclopaedia of Social Sciences*, vol.5, 354; and K. C. Wheare, *Federal Government* (London:Oxford University Press [4th edition], 1968) 10-16.

29. Elazar, 'Federalism', 353.

30. A. K. Brohi, *Fundamental Law of Pakistan* (Karachi: Din Muhammad Press, 1958) 56.

31. Sir Robert Garran, *Report of the Royal Commission on the Australian Constitution* (1929) 230.

32. Wheare, *Federal Government*, 10.

33. Ibid., 11.

34. Ibid., 15. To assess whether a constitution or government is federal or not, K. C. Wheare in his *Federal Government*, says: 'The test which I apply for federal government is then this:Does a system of government embody predominantly a division of powers between general and regional authorities, each of which, in its own sphere, is co-ordinate with the others and independent of them ? If so, that government is federal.' 33.

35. Lord Bryce's remarks quoted by Morton Grodzins, 'The Federal System' in Aaron Wildasky (ed.), *American Federalism in Perspective* (Boston: 1967) 261.

36. In 1939, Professor Harold J. Laski in his article 'The Obsolescence of Federalism', observed, 'I infer in a word that the epoch of federalism is over'. Professor Laski's pessimistic view is quoted from R. L. Watts, *New Federations: Experiments In The Commonwealth* (Oxford: Clarendon Press, 1966) 5.

37. Max Beloff, 'The Federal Solution in its Application to Europe, Asia and Africa', *Political Studies*, 1953, 114, quoted by Sharada Rath, *Federalism Today* (New Delhi: Sterling, 1984) 1.

38. Newman, *Essays*, 118.

39. See for instance, Wheare, *Federal Government*, 20.

40. Brohi, *Fundamental Law of Pakistan*, 56.

41. Dicey, *Introduction*, 138-80; Brohi, *Fundamental Law*, 56-61; Elazar, 'Federalism' 357-60.

42. These essentials are mostly drawn from Elazar's discussion on federalism, 361.

43. Sabine, *A History of Political Theory*, 471-2.

44. Montesquieu, quoted in Phillips, *Administrative Law*, 14.

45. Blackstone, *Commentaries on the Laws of England* (1765) vol.I, 146, 269.

46. James I of England, quoted in A. Appadorai, *The Substance of Politics* (London: Oxford University Press, 1956) 33.

47. Sibte Hasan, *The Battle of Ideas in Pakistan* (Lahore: Pakistan Publishing House, 1986) 72. This study also presents innumerable examples of rulers legitimizing their dictatorial rule on the basis of the theory of the divine right of kings.

48. Ibid., 67.

49. Ibid., 72.

50. Ibid., 73.

51. See Fazlur Rahman, 'Islam and the New Constitution of Pakistan', in J. Henry Korson (ed.), *Contemporary Problems of Pakistan* (Leiden: E. J. Brill, 1974) 39.

52. Ibid.

53. *Encyclopaedia Britannica*, vol.17, 609; see also, Ernest Baker, *Principles of Social and Political Theory* (London: Oxford University Press, 1967) 11-13.

3

1. Professor Qamaruddin Khan, 'Islam is a society, not a political system', *Dawn* (Karachi) 13 August 1980.

2. Ibid., and his, *Al-Mawardi's Theory of the State* (Lahore: Islamic Book Foundation, 1983); Brohi, *Fundamental Law,* 754.

3. Brohi, 'Thoughts on the Future Constitution of Pakistan', *Dawn* (Karachi) 24 August 1952.

4. Khan, 'Islam is a society'.

5. Brohi, *Fundamental Law,* 750.

6. Muhammad Asad, 'Islamic Constitution-making', *Arafat*, March 1948; quoted in Brohi, *Fundamental Law*, 747.

7. Lewis, *The Arabs in History*, 29.

8. Duncan B. Macdonald, *Development of Muslim Theology, Jurisprudence and Constitutional Theory* (Lahore: The Premier Book House, 1972) 68.

9. Lewis, *The Arabs in History,* 35.

10. This term is adopted from Lewis, 42.

11. Quranic interpretation quoted in Brohi, *Fundamental Law,* 755.

12. William Muir, *The Caliphate*, 84.

13. Macdonald, *Muslim Theology*, 14.

14. Usman's perspective, quoted in S. M. Yusuf, *The Choice of a Caliph in Islam* (Lahore: Islamic Book Service, 1982) 29- 30.

15. Muir, 208.

16. Professor Gibb opines that the monarchical traditions of the empires were introduced in the Muslim polity to check the growing instability of Arab tribal structure and to foster solid foundations of power. Gibb, *Studies on the Civilisation of Islam,* 41. See also Justice (Retired) Javed Iqbal, 'Islamic State—An Ideal or Reality', *PLD*: 1983, *Journal*, 97-8.

17. Philip K. Hitti, *The Arabs—A Short History* (London: MacMillan & Co, 1956) 71-2.

18. *Tyabji's Muhammadan Law*, 10.

19. Macdonald, *Muslim Theology,* 50.

20. Hitti, *The Arabs,* 83.

21. A remark quoted in ibid., 85.

22. Khan, 'Islam is a society, not a political system'.

23. Khan, *Al-Mawardi's Theory of State*, 53-4.

24. Ibid., 54.

25. Ibid.

26. Ibid., 47.

27. Ann K. S. Lambton, *State and Government in Medieval Islam* (London: Oriental Series) vol. 36, 145.

28. Erwin I. J. Rosenthal, *Political Thought in Medieval Islam* (Cambridge University Press, 1988) 52.

29. Professor Qamaruddin Khan, *Ibn Taymiyah*, 183.

30. The essence of Ibn Taymiyah's political thought was that personalities like Umar would not emerge in history to reinstitute the Caliphate on the model of *Khilafat-e- Rashidah*, 'because if the ideal institution can appear in history, the ideal personalities must appear with it, since the one is, logically, inconceivable without the other'. f.n. 3, Khan, *Ibn Taymiya*, 185.

31. Ibid., 63.

32. Rosenthal, *Political Thought*, 60.

33. P. J. Vatikiotis, *Islam and State* (London: Croom Helm, 1987) 21.

34. Manzooruddin Ahmed, *Islamic Political System in the Modern Age* (Karachi: Allied Books, 1966) 128-9; see also, Rosenthal, *Political Thought*, 87.

35. Albert Hourani, *Arab Thought in the Liberal Age* (London: Oxford University Press, 1970) 24.

36. Rosenthal, quoted in ibid., 97.

37. See Nathaniel Schmidt, *Ibn Khaldun* (Lahore: Universal Books, n.d.) 9-16; Rosenthal, *Political Thought*, 102–193; Lambton, *State and Government*, 165-170; Gibb, *Civilisation*, 170-4.

38. Vatikiotis, *Islam and State*, 22.

39. Ibn Jamaa, quoted in Hourani, *Arab Thought*, 15; Lambton, *State and Government*, 141-2.

40. For the expression, 'Gandhi-Khilafat express', see Stanley Wolpert, *Jinnah of Pakistan* (New York: Oxford University Press, 1984) 72.

41. Afzal Iqbal, *Islamisation of Pakistan* (Lahore: Vanguard Books, 1986) 25.

42. Khalid Bin Sayeed, *Pakistan: The Formative Phase,* (London: Oxford University Press, 1968) 199.

43. S. M. Burke, *Pakistan's Foreign Policy* (Karachi: Oxford University Press, 1973) 67.

44. Aziz Beg, *The Quiet Revolution* (Karachi: Pakistan Patriotic Publications, 1959) 73-4.

45. Jinnah's interview with Reuter's correspondent in New Delhi, 1946, quoted in Muhammad Munir, *From Jinnah to Zia* (Lahore: Vanguard Books, 1980) 29.

46. A dialogue between Mahmoud A. Haroon (ADC to Jinnah in 1946) and Jinnah, quoted in Iqbal, *Islamisation,* 37.

47. Ibid., 25.

48. Jinnah's speech, quoted in G.W. Choudhury, *Constitutional Development in Pakistan* (Longman, 1969) 46.

49. Mian Muhammad Mumtaz Khan Daulatana (a veteran Muslim Leaguer) quoted in Iqbal, *Islamisation*, 40.

50. Sayeed, *Pakistan: The Formative Phase*, 14.

51. For Jinnah's reaction to the Nehru Report and his perspectives on the constitutional rights of minorities, see Muhammad Noman, *Muslim India* (Aligarh: 1941) 281.

52. Extract from Jinnah's speech in the Central Assembly, 7 February 1935, quoted in Ayesha Jalal, *The Sole Spokesman* (London: Cambridge University Press, 1985) 14.

53. Jamil-ud-Din Ahmed(ed.) , *Some Recent Speeches and Writings of Jinnah* (Lahore: 1964) 161.

54. Jinnah's address to Aligarh Muslim University students in 1936. See Noman, *Muslim India*, 339.

55. Editorial, 'No Slogan-Mongering', *Nawa-i-Waqt* (Lahore) 16 July 1948.

56. Iqbal, *Islamisation*, 46.

57. Leonard Binder, *Religion and Politics in Pakistan* (Berkeley: 1961) 149.

58. *Report of the Court of Inquiry, Punjab Disturbances 1953* (Lahore: Government of the Punjab Press, 1954) 210.

59. For detailed discussion of the reaction of the minorities to the Objectives Resolution, see Choudhury, *Constitutional Development*, 39-41; and Afzal, *Political Parties*, 130-1.

60. Maulana Shabbir Ahmed Osmani, *Pakistan Constituent Assembly Debates* (Karachi: 1949), vol.5, no.3, 45.

61. Duran Khalid, 'The Final Replacement of Parliamentary Democracy by the "Islamic System" in Pakistan', in Zingel and Lallemant, *Law and Constitution*, .280.

62. Khan, 'Islam is a society'.

63. Ibid.

64. Editorial, *Nawa-i-Waqt* (Lahore) 6 December 1979.

65. Justice (Retired) Hamoodur Rahman 'Islamic Concept of State', a paper published in a report of an international seminar, *Application of Shariah*, held at Islamabad in October 1979, organized by the Organization of Islamic Countries in collaboration with the Ministry of Law and Parliamentary Affairs, Government of Pakistan, 69-70.

66. Ibid., 78.

67. Ibid.

4

1. Quoted in M. Hafeez Ahmed, *Constitutional History of Pakistan* (Lahore: 1974) 1-2.

2. Sir Bartle Frere, quoted in Sir Reginald Coupland, *The Indian Problem: 1833-1935* (Oxford: The Clarendon Press, 1968) 21.

3. Lord Macaulay, quoted ibid., 20.

4. S. M. Burke, *Mainsprings of Indian and Pakistani Foreign Policies* (Minneapolis: University of Minnesota Press, 1974) 36.

5. L. F. Rushbrook Williams, *The State of Pakistan* (London: Faber and Faber, 1962) 16.

6. Russell Brines, *Indo-Pakistan Conflict* (London: Pall Mall Press, 1968) 22-3.

7.   Williams, *The State of Pakistan*, 17.
8.   Ibid.
9.   Maulana Altaf Hussain Hali's biographical note on Sir Syed Ahmed Khan, quoted in Aziz Beg, *The Quiet Revolution—A Factual Story of Political Betrayal in Pakistan* (Karachi: Pakistan Patriotic Publications, 1959) 27.
10.   Burke, *Mainsprings,* 36.
11.   Beg, *Quiet Revolution,* 28.
12.   Remarks quoted from Richard Symonds, *The Making of Pakistan* (London: 1951), 3rd ed., 31. See also for substantiation of such remarks, Coupland, *The Indian Problem*, 155-6.
13.   Even if the allegations of British encouragement in the formation of the Muslim League are true, it is equally true beyond any doubt that the Indian National Congress was created, patronized, encouraged, and often presided over by the higher British officials in the subcontinent.
14.   Burke, *Mainsprings,* 36. For administrative reasons, the 1905 partition of Bengal, and the creation of East Bengal led to the emergence of a Muslim province–foreshadowing East Pakistan (now Bangladesh). Similarly, the 1909 Minto-Morley separate electoral reforms, the concept of communal politics, and electoral representation consolidated the two-nation thesis propounded by Sir Syed Ahmed Khan foreshadowing the emergence of Pakistan in 1947.
15.   For a summary of the Government of India Act, 1919, see Coupland, *The Indian Problem:* 149-150.
16.   See Syed Sharifuddin Pirzada, *Foundations of Pakistan, All India Muslim League Documents* (Dhaka: 1969), vol.I, 558-9.
17.   Ibid., 578.
18.   Jamil-ud-din Ahmed, *The Middle Phase of the Muslim Political Movement* (Lahore: 1969) 84-5.
19.   Noman, *Muslim India*, 291-2.
20.   Ahmed, *Middle Phase*, 101-2.
21.   See Article 41, Part V of the Government of India Act, 1919.
22.   For details of the Simon Report, see Coupland, *The Indian Problem*, 97-102.
23.   The Parliamentary Committee's Report, Part III, titled: 'The Governor's Provinces', quoted in Dr Waheed Ahmed, *Road to Indian Freedom—The Formation of the Government of India Act, 1935* (Lahore: Caravan Book House, 1972) 271-2. Under the Act of 1919, the provincial governments used to exercise 'a devolved and not an original authority'. The Simon Commission gave the following meaning to provincial autonomy: 'Provincial autonomy—a phrase constantly used not to indicate the throwing off of all central control as the ending of dyarchy and the creation of ministry responsible to the provincial legislature in respect of all provincial subjects'.

24. While some termed the 1935 Constitution 'a steel frame', others, like J. Nehru, opined that it was 'a charter of slavery'. See Nehru, *India's Freedom* (London: 1962) 37.
25. *PLD*, 1955 FC 240.
26. For Iqbal's views and his political reaction to the Bill (later the Government of India Act, 1935), see *The Civil & Military Gazette*, 23 November 1934.
27. Jalal, *The Sole Spokesman,* 15.
28. The Resolution of the All India Muslim League, 24th Session, in Sharifuddin Pirzada (ed), *Foundations of Pakistan,* vol.II, 260-1.
29. Wilhelm Von Pochhammer, *India's Road to Nationhood* (New Delhi: Allied Publishers, 1973) 530.
30. C. H. Philips, *The Evolution of India and Pakistan 1947-1958* (London: 1962) 378-82.
31. Syed Sharifuddin Pirzada, *Evolution of Pakistan* (Lahore: 1963) 148-50.
32. On the eve of the Round Table Conference in London, in his famous pamphlet titled: *Now or Never: Are We to Live or Perish*, Chaudhry Rahmat Ali drew up a scheme for the future Muslim entity in the north-west of the subcontinent. In Ali's proposed state, named 'Pakistan', P stood for the Punjab, A for Afghania or the NWFP, K for Kashmir, S for Sindh, and tan for Balochistan.
33. The views of Dr Syed Abdul Latif are mentioned in K. K. Aziz, 'A 1939 Scheme of Confederation for India', *Scrutiny* (Islamabad), January-June 1974, 89-90.
34. Ibid., 90.
35. Ibid., 89-90.
36. Ahmed, *Historical Documents,* 382.
37. Syed Sharifuddin Pirzada, *The Pakistan Resolution and the Historic Lahore Session* (Karachi: 1968) f.n.63, 20.
38. Saleem M. M. Qureshi, 'Politics of the Parties in the Ayub Khan Era, 1962-69', *Scrutiny* (Islamabad) July-December 1975, 60.
39. M. Rafique Afzal, 'Problems of Federalism in Pakistan—The Pre-Independence Dimensions', *Scrutiny* (Islamabad) January-June 1980, 76.
40. Ahmed, *Historical Documents,* 492-3. This Resolution of 9 April 1946 was moved by H. S. Suhrawardy, then Chief Minister of Bengal.
41. Noman, *Muslim India*, 402-3.
42. Jalal, *Sole Spokesman*, 47.
43. Ibid.
44. Lord Linlithgow, quoted ibid., 49.
45. Ibid., 62.
46. Lord Linlithgow's letter to his provincial governors, quoted ibid., 62.
47. Sisir Gupta, *Kashmir—A Study in India-Pakistan Relations* (New Delhi: Asia Publishing House, 1967) 9.
48. Khalid Bin Sayeed, *The Political System of Pakistan* (Boston: Houghton Mifflin, 1967) 43.

49. Ibid.
50. Jalal, *Sole Spokesman*, 174.
51. Ibid.
52. Sayeed, *Political System*, 47.
53. Jalal, *Sole Spokesman*, 178.
54. Quoted by E.W. Lumby, *The Transfer of Power in India* (London: George Allen & Unwin, 1947) 78.
55. Quoted by Maulana Abdul Kalam Azad, *India Wins Freedom* (New York: Longmans, 1960) 218.
56. Choudhury, *Constitutional Development*, 32.
57. Sir Winston Churchill, quoted ibid., 34.
58. Ibid., 35.
59. See for such remarks, Lawrence Ziring, *Pakistan—The Enigma of Political Development* (London: Dawson-Westview, 1980) 31.
60. See Lord Mountbatten's address to the newly-formed Indian Constituent Assembly in New Delhi, 15 August 1947. For remarks on the unusual and rapid degeneration of Britian's 'divide and rule' policy to that of a 'divide and run' strategy, Ziring, *Enigma*, 31.

5

1. Justice (Retd.) Masud Ahmed, *Pakistan: A Study of its Constitutional History-1857-1975,* (Lahore: Research Society of Pakistan, 1978) 34-5.
2. Y.V. Gankovsky and V. N. Moskalenko, *The Three Constitutions of Pakistan* (Lahore: People's Publishing House, 1978) 14-15.
3. Justice Dr Nasim Hasan Shah, *Constitution, Law and Pakistan Affairs* (Lahore: Wajidalis, 1986) 7.
4. See Gankovsky and Moskalenko, *Three Constitutions*, 15.
5. Ibid. Mainly based in East Bengal, the National Congress of Pakistan stood for the joint electorate system, provincial autonomy for East Bengal, and prompt recognition of Bengali as the official language of the country.
6. Choudhury, *Constitutional Developments,* 20.
7. M. Rafique Afzal, 'Problems of Federalism in Pakistan: The Continuing Debate, 1947-54', *Journal of the Research Society of Pakistan,* vol. XVIII, No.4, (1981) 2.
8. Rounaq Jahan, *Pakistan—Failure in National Integration* (New York: Columbia University Press, 1972) 19-20.
9. Ibid., 20.
10. Ibid.
11. Belonging to the Scheduled Castes, i.e. untouchables, Mr Mandal became Federal Minister in the Cabinet of Liaquat Ali Khan. However, in 1950 he left for India and never returned.

12. Jinnah was the father of the Nation, Governor-General, President of the CAP, and President of the Muslim League.

13. The Objectives Resolution was appended to the 1956 Constitution and General Zia included it (as part of his 8th Amendment) in the 1973 Constitution, in 1985.

14. Richard S. Wheeler, *The Politics of Pakistan—A Constitutional Quest* (New York: Cornell University Press, 1970) 110.

15. Inamur Rahman, *Public Opinion and Political Developments in Pakistan: 1947-58* (Karachi: Oxford University Press, 1982) 41.

16. *Pakistan: From 1947 to the Creation of Bangladesh,Keesings Research Report* (New York: Charles Scribner and Sons, 1971) 18-19.

17. Rahman, *Public Opinion*, 16-17.

18. *The Pakistan Observer* (Dhaka). See its editorials on 3,6, and 8 October 1950.

19. *Nawa-i-Waqt* (Lahore), 1 October 1950.

20. Rahman, *Public Opinion*, 43-5.

21. *Keesings Research Report: Pakistan*, 18-19.

22. Ibid., 19-20.

23. For a critical evaluation of the Bengali reaction to the second report of the BPC, see Rizwan Malik, *The Politics of One Unit 1955-58* (Lahore: University of the Punjab, 1988) 7.

24. Ibid.

25. *The Pakistan Times* (Lahore) 27 December 1952.

26. Ibid., 7 October 1953.

27. Rahman, *Public Opinion*, 53-5.

28. Ibid., 54; Malik, *One Unit*, 8-10.

29. *Dawn* (Karachi) 23 January 1953.

30. In February and March 1953, the ulema headed by Ahrar and the Jamaat-i-Islami demanded that the Ahmadiya sect should be declared non-Muslims because it allegedly did not believe that Muhammad (pbuh) is the last Prophet. For some interesting details, see Justice Munir, *From Jinnah to Zia*, 41-73.

31. Miss Asma Jilani v. the Government of the Punjab and others, PLD 1972 SC 139.

32. *Dawn* (Karachi) 6 October 1953.

33. Rahman, *Public Opinion*, 55.

34. Afzal, 'Problems of Federalism in Pakistan: the Continuing Debate', 12.

35. For the original text of Jinnah's speech, see Jamil-ud-din Ahmed (ed.), *Speeches and Writings of Jinnah* (Lahore: Ashraf Publishers, 1964), vol.II, 490.

36. P. Sharan, *Government of Pakistan—Development and Working of the Political System* (Delhi: 1975) 32-3.

37. Ibid.

38. For the text of the 8 Point Language Formula, see *Keesings Research Report: Pakistan*, 33.

39.   Malik, *One Unit*, 25.
40.   Miss Asma Jilani v. the Government of the Punjab and others, PLD 1972 SC 139.
41.   Justice (Retd.) Ahmed, *Pakistan: A Study of its Constitutional History*, 42.
42.   This account is based on the following cases:i) Federation of Pakistan and others v. Maulvi Tamizuddin Khan, *PLD* 1955 FC 240; Usif Patel v. Crown, *PLD* 1955 FC 387.
43.   For a summary and anatomy of Maulvi Tamizuddin Khan's case, see Choudhury, *Constitutional Developments*, 87.
44.   For this dissenting opinion, see *PLD* 1972 SC 139, 214.
45.   In this case, petitioner Usif Patel was declared a *goonda* under the *Sind Control of Goondas Act* and, in the ensuing litigation that came up to the Federal Court, it was contended on his behalf that the Act under which he had been declared a *goonda*, was invalid. See Usif Patel and two others v. Crown *PLD* 1955 FC 387.
46.   See *Dawn* (Karachi), 14 April 1955.
47.   PLD 1955 FC 435.
48.   G. Marshall, *Parliamentary Sovereignty and the Commonwealth* (London: Oxford University Press, 1957) 135; K. K. Aziz, *Party Politics in Pakistan* (Islamabad: National Commission for Historical and Cultural Research, 1976) 52-3.
49.   *The Economist* (London), 8 October 1955, 138, quoted in Aziz, *Party Politics*.
50.   Wheeler, *Quest*, 110.
51.   For the advantages of the One Unit System and the arguments advanced in favour of this scheme, see Choudhury, *Constitutional Developments*, 71; and Rahman, *Public Opinion*, 71-2; see also Ayub Khan, *Friends Not Masters*, 53-4, 187-8.
52.   For this argument, see a letter to the editor, *The Pakistan Times*, 3 August 1954.
53.   Suhrawardy's speech, quoted in *Dawn* (Karachi) 1 October 1955.
54.   Mian Jaffar Shah's speech, quoted in *Dawn* (Karachi) 25 August 1955.
55.   *Dawn* (Karachi), 28 and 29 July 1954.
56.   Sheikh Mujibur Rahman's speech, quoted in *Dawn* (Karachi), 26 August 1955.
57.   Suhrawardy's speech, quoted ibid., 11 and 13 September 1955.
58.   Satish Kumar, 'Problems of Federal Politics' in Pandav Nayak (ed.), *Pakistan: Society and Politics* (New Delhi: 1984) 24.
59.   *Keesings Research Report:* Pakistan, 66.
60.   For some of these arguments, see Ahmed Hussain, *Politics and People's Representation in Pakistan* (Lahore: Ferozsons) 54-55; and Rahman, *Public Opinion*, 89-111.
61.   Ibid.
62.   Ibid.

63. Beg, *Quiet Revolution*, 71.
64. Justice Shah, *Pakistan Affairs*, and Leslie Wolf-Phillips, 'The 1973 Constitution: A Heritage for the Future', *The Pakistan Times* (Islamabad), 14 April 1989.
65. Justice Shah, *Pakistan Affairs*, 20.
66. Norval Mitchell, *Sir George Cunningham: A Memoir* (Edinburgh: 1968) 126; Rafique Afzal, *Political Parties*, 63.
67. Aziz, *Party Politics*, 1; see *Dawn*, 27 August 1947; Lord Birdwood, *A Continent Decides* (London: 1953) 35.
68. Afzal, *Political Parties*, 63.
69. Qayyum Khan's abject high-handedness and coercive tactics could partially be blamed on Premier Liaquat whose penchant for installing loyal ministries in the provinces (at whatever cost) knew no bounds.
70. Afzal, *Political Parties*, 66.
71. Aziz, *Party Politics*, 2.
72. *Dawn*, 9 November 1954.
73. Aziz, *Party Politics*, 30.
74. Ibid., 4-5.
75. Ibid., 5.
76. Ibid., 4.
77. Ibid., 28.
78. Jahan, *Failure*, 13.
79. Rahman, *Public Opinion*, 212-15.
80. *Dawn*, 26 May 1954; Aziz, *Party Politics*, 20.
81. Aziz, ibid., 30.
82. Z. A. Suleri, quoted in Williams, *The State of Pakistan*, fn .71, 129.
83. Callard, *Pakistan: A Political Study*, 172.
84. Ibid.
85. Ibid., 173.
86. See *CAP Debates*, vol.I, 530. 7 September 1955.
87. Wolf-Phillips, '1973 Constitution—A Heritage for the Future'.
88. Mushtaq Ahmed, *Government and Politics in Pakistan* (Karachi: Pakistan Publishing House, 1970) 48.
89. Ibid., 29.
90. Callard, *Pakistan: A Political Study*, 137.
91. M. S. Venkataramani, *The American Role in Pakistan—1947-58* (New Delhi: Radiant Publishers, 1982) 171.
92. Ahmed, *Government and Politics*, 49.
93. Wolf-Phillips, 'The 1973 Constitution—A Heritage for the Future.'
94. Ahmed, *Government and Politics*, 51.
95. Statement quoted in Venkataramani, *American Role*, 288.
96. Kalim Siddiqui, *Conflict, Crisis & War in Pakistan,* (London: MacMillan, 1972) 96-7.
97. Ibid.

98.   Muhammad Asghar Khan, *Generals in Politics* (London: 1983) 6.

99.   Ayub Khan, *Friends Not Masters*, 54-5.

100. See *The Pakistan Times*, 29 March 1956. Contrary to Mirza's assertion, Dr Khan and his Congress Party had opposed the creation of Pakistan. He and his Ministry had reportedly refused to pay respect to the Pakistani flag and never took an oath of allegiance to the new State.

101. *The Pakistan Times*, 3 April 1956.

102. Rahman, *Public Opinion*, 180.

103. Ibid.; *Dawn*, 10 April 1956; *The Pakistan Times*, 17 April 1956.

104. Karl von Vorys, *Political Development in Pakistan* (Princeton University Press, 1965) 126.

105. See for this information, Jahan, *Failure*, f.n.44, 28.

106. *The Pakistan Times*, 21 July 1955.

107. Jahan, *Failure*, 24.

108. Ibid. See also Henry F. Goodnow, *The Civil Service of Pakistan: Bureaucracy in a New State* (Yale University Press, 1964) 51-103.

109. Hasan Habib, 'Provincial Autonomy and the Colonial Bureaucracy', *The Frontier Post* (Peshawar) 15 January 1988.

110. Jahan, *Failure*, 29.

6

1.   Venkataramani, *American Role*, 297; Khalid Bin Sayeed, *Politics in Pakistan—The Nature and Direction of Change* (Praeger: 1980) 45.

2.   Venkataramani, ibid.

3.   Ibid. Such an effective strategy was aimed at subverting the 1959 general elections by a pre-emptive coup. This would impede the coming in of a popularly-elected and broad-based civilian government in the country—a death-knell to Ayub Khan's cherished ambitions.

4.   *The Pakistan Times,* 8 October 1958.

5.   Ibid.

6.   Ibid., 9 October 1958.

7.   See ibid., and Justice(Retd.) Masud Ahmed, *Pakistan: A Study of its Constitutional History,* 49.

8.   Afzal, *Political Parties,* vol.II, 1.

9.   See Province of East Pakistan vs. Muhammad Mahdi Khan, *PLD* 1959 SC 387 (406).

10. The State vs. Dosso and others, *PLD* 1958 SC (533).

11. *PLD* 1972 SC 139.

12. Dieter Conrad, 'In Defence of the Continuity of Law: Pakistan's Courts in Crises of State' in Zingel and Lallemant (ed.), *Law and Constitution,* 145.

13. Ibid.

14. *Keesings Contemporary Archives*, 1958, 16459.
15. Ibid., 16460.
16. Jahan, *Failure*, f.n.21, 54.
17. Munir, *From Jinnah to Zia*, 52.
18. *Keesings Contemporary Archives*, 1958, 16460.
19. Ibid., 16458.
20. Jahan, *Failure*, 51.
21. Qureshi, 'Politics of Parties in the Ayub era', 45.
22. Sayeed, *Political System*, 93.
23. Ibid., 94.
24. Qureshi, 'Politics of Parties in the Ayub era' 45; *Dawn*, 8 April 1962.
25. *Dawn*, ibid.
26. Sayeed, *Political System*, 93.
27. See 'A Short Appreciation of Present and Future Problems of Pakistan' written by C-in-C and Defence Minister in the 'cabinet of talents', General Muhammad Ayub Khan (4 October 1954), reproduced in Karl von Vorys, *Political Development*, 304.
28. C. J. Newman, 'The Constitutional Evolution of Pakistan', *International Affairs*, July 1962, 360.
29. See Herbert Feldman, *Revolution in Pakistan*, (Karachi: Oxford University Press, 1967) 196.
30. *Dawn*, 18 December 1959.
31. *Keesings Contemporary Archives*, 1962, 18857.
32. *Dawn*, 2 April 1963.
33. Ahmed, *Constitutional History*, 82.
34. President Ayub Khan's address at Liaquat Bagh, Rawalpindi, quoted in *Dawn*, 18 October 1964.
35. *Keesings Research Report*, 81.
36. Ibid., 84.
37. S. Mujahid, 'Pakistan's political culture during the Ayub era', *Scrutiny*, January-June 1974, 33.
38. See W. A. Wilcox, 'India and Pakistan', *Foreign Policy Association* (New York), October 1967, 21. This is an indirect reference quoted from Qureshi, 'Politics of Parties', 64.
39. Qureshi, 'Politics of Parties', 64. See also Ayub Khan, *Friends Not Masters*, 37.
40. Qureshi, 'Politics of Parties', 64-65.
41. *Asian Recorder* (New Delhi), 19-25 March 1962, 4482.
42. Ibid.
43. Jahan, *Failure*, 166.
44. M. Nazrul Islam, *Pakistan and Malaysia — A Comparative Study in National Integration* (New Delhi: 1989) 147.
45. Ibid.

46.   Jahan, *Failure*, 166.
47.   *The Pakistan Observer* (Dhaka), 22 March 1966.
48.   Herbert Feldman, *From Crisis to Crisis* (Karachi: Oxford University Press, 1972), 210-11.
49.   Ibid., 208-9.
50.   Islam, *Pakistan and Malaysia*, 148.
51.   This is what Z. A. Bhutto says in his *Great Tragedy*, 69.
52.   Ibid., 70.
53.   Wheeler, *Quest*, 260.
54.   Ibid., 260-1; and *The Pakistan Times*, 3 May 1967.
55.   *The Pakistan Times*, 23 May 1967.
56.   Feldman, *From Crisis to Crisis*, 226.
57.   Bhutto, quoted in Sharan, *Government of Pakistan*, 213.
58.   Robert La Porte Jr., *Power and Privilege: Influence and Decision-making in Pakistan* (University of California Press, 1975) 74.
59.   Sayeed, *Politics in Pakistan*, 67.
60.   A. Muhammad Quddus, *Pakistan: A Case Study of a Plural Society* (Calcutta: Minerva Publications, 1981) 154-5.
61.   Ibid., 155.
62.   Jahan, *Failure*, 85-6.
63.   Shafiqur Rahman, 'The Third Plan—An Analysis of Objectives', quoted in Quddus, *Plural Society*, 156.
64.   Herbert Feldman, 'The Experiment in a Presidential System', in S. H. Hashmi (ed.), *The Government Process in Pakistan* (Lahore: 1987) 34.
65.   Munir, *Constitution of the Islamic Republic*, 448.

7

1.   Ayub Khan, *Friends Not Masters*, 54.
2.   Ayub Khan's letter of 24 March 1969 to General Yahya Khan, the C-in-C.
3.   Herbert Feldman, *Pakistan: 1969-1971—The End & the Beginning* (Karachi: Oxford University Press, 1976) 10-11.
4.   G.W. Choudhury, *The Last Days of United Pakistan* (London: C. Hurst & Company, 1974) 49.
5.   Ibid.
6.   *The Pakistan Times*, 27 March 1969.
7.   *Keesings Research Report Pakistan*, 99.
8.   See Yahya Khan's speech, *Keesings Contemporary Archives*, 3-10 January 1970, 23745.
9.   Bhutto, *Great Tragedy*, 58.
10.   Feldman, *End & the Beginning*, 67.
11.   Bhutto, *Great Tragedy*, 58. The fact that the Yahya regime had miscalculated the results of the forthcoming nation-wide general elections is

also supported by Rounaq Jahan. It is argued that in a divided electoral mandate, Yahya Khan and his military junta hoped to be arbitrators and power-brokers in the emergent political milieu. See Jahan, *Failure*, 188.

12. Feldman, *End & the Beginning*, 68-9.
13. On this issue, Bhutto opines that 'it would not have been possible for an individual, no matter how great his power, to reject without democratic sanction the decision of the National Assembly. Such an affront to democracy would have provoked the final crisis.' Bhutto, *Great Tragedy*, 57-8. One wonders how a usurper, who had abrogated the 1962 Constitution and promulgated the LFO—a Constitution in itself—could be expected to respect the verdict of the National Assembly?
14. Feldman, *End & the Beginning*, 70.
15. *Dawn*, 29 November 1969.
16. *The Pakistan Times*, 4 December 1970.
17. *Keesings Contemporary Archives*, 20 August-5 September 1970, 24157.
18. Bhutto, *Great Tragedy*, 59.
19. Ibid., 58-9.
20. G.W. Choudhury opines that leaving the issue of provincial autonomy to be decided by the National Assembly alone was a major concession to Mujibur Rehman and his Awami League. This is what the Bengalis had been demanding since the 1950s. Such a concession would allow them to decide the maximum provincial autonomy once and for all. See *Last Days*, 87.
21. *The Pakistan Times*, 29 November 1969.
22. Ibid.
23. Choudhury, *Last Days*, 91.
24. Ibid.
25. Bhutto, *Great Tragedy*, 58-9.
26. Choudhury, *Last Days*, 53-4
27. For substantiation of some of these points, see *Keesings Contemporary Archives*, 30 January 6 February 1971, 24413.
28. *The Pakistan Times*, 4 January 1971.
29. *Keesings Contemporary Archives*, 30 January-6 February 1971, 24414. These are extracts from Mr Bhutto's press conference on 2 October 1970. See also *The Pakistan Times*, 28 October 1970.
30. *Keesings Contemporary Archives*, 1-8 May 1971, 24565.
31. Ibid.
32. Ibid.
33. Ibid.
34. Hasan Askari Rizvi, *The Military and Politics in Pakistan* (Lahore: Progressive Publishers, 1986) 183.
35. *The Pakistan Times*, 16 February 1971.
36. *Dawn*, 8 March 1971.
37. Feldman, *End the Beginning*, 118.

8

1. For the salient features, see the text of the Tripartite Accord between the PPP on the one hand and the JUI and the NAP on the other hand, photocopy reproduced in *Constitution-Making in Pakistan* (National Assembly of Pakistan, 1973) 73-5.
2. *Keesings Contemporary Archives*, 8-15 July 1972, 25359.
3. Ibid., 25360.
4. Ibid.
5. Dieter Conrad, 'In Defence of Continuity of Law: Pakistan's Courts in Crises of State', in Zingel and Lallemant (ed.), *Law and Constitution,* 123.
6. Leslie Wolf-Phillips, 'Constitutional Legitimacy in Pakistan: 1977-82', ibid., 90.
7. Kamal Azfar, *Pakistan: Political and Constitutional Dilemmas* (Karachi: Pakistan Law House, 1987) 84.
8. *Keesings Contemporary Archives*, 16-23 December 1972, 25626. See also *Dawn*, 21 October 1972.
9. *Keesings Contemporary Archives,* 21-27 May 1973, 25893.
10. Ibid., 25894.
11. *The Pakistan Times*, 13 April 1973.
12. *Dawn*, 16 August 1973.
13. J. A. Rahim, *Outlines Of A Federal Constitution For Pakistan*, (Pakistan People's Party, Political Series(4), Lahore:1969) 41.
14. National Assembly of Pakistan(Constitution-Making) Debates, 10 April 1973, 2468.
15. *Keesings Contemporary Archives*, 21-27 May 1973, 25893.
16. Ibid.
17. Ibid.
18. Shahid Javed Burki, *Pakistan Under Bhutto, 1971-77* (MacMillan, 1980) 96-7.
19. *Keesings Contemporary Archives,* 21-27 May 1973, 25894.
20. Makhdoom Ali Khan, '1973 Constitution: The Founding of the Federation', an unpublished paper read at a seminar, 'The Heritage of Prime Minister Bhutto', 3-5 April 1989, held at Karachi.
21. Burki, *Pakistan under Bhutto,* 97.
22. Ibid., 98.
23. *The Pakistan Times*, 11 February 1975.
24. Ibid.
25. Ibid., 18 February 1975.
26. *Keesings Contemporary Archives*, 20 February 1976, 27584.
27. Satish Kumar, *The New Pakistan* (New Delhi: Vikas Publishing House Ltd. 1978) 208.
28. *The Pakistan Times*, 1 January 1976.
29. Kausar Niazi, *Aur Line Cut Gai* (Urdu)(Rawalpindi: Jang Publishers, 1987) 160.

30. Ibid.
31. Ibid., 161.
32. Asghar Khan, *Generals in Politics*, 119. Besides keeping the PPP-PNA negotiations in a state of flux, lest the parties struck a political bargain, Asghar Khan addressed a lengthy letter to the three services chiefs not to obey the orders of the Bhutto government because, in his view, it was no longer a lawful authority.
33. Kumar, *New Pakistan*, 330.

9

1. Wolf-Phillips, 'The 1973 Constitution', 16.
2. The expression 'constitutional mortality' is drawn from Ms Benazir Bhutto's address to the members of Sukkur Bar Association on 2 March 1989, See *The Pakistan Times,* 3 March 1989.
3. Dr Faqir Hussain, 'Guilty of High Treason', *The Frontier Post,* 27 May 1990.
4. Ghafoor Ahmed, *Phir Martial Law Aa Gaya* (Lahore: Jang Publishers, 1988) 241-5.
5. Lt. General (Retired) Faiz Ali Chishti, *Betrayals of Another Kind* (Rawalpindi: PCL Publishing House, 1989) 16.
6. Javed Ahmed Siddiqui, *Operation Fairplay* (Urdu) (Karachi: 1987) 114
7. *The Pakistan Times* 10 April 1989.
8. Omar Noman, *The Political Economy of Pakistan: 1947-85,* (London: KPI, 1988) 119.
9. *The Muslim* (Islamabad), 4 April 1989. Remarks made at a seminar held in Karachi.
10. See ibid.; and Dr Inayatullah, 'Law of Contempt and the late Bhutto case', *The Nation* (Lahore) 13 April 1989, 7.
11. *The Pakistan Times,* 28 March 1978.
12. Zingel and Lallemant (ed.), *Law and Constitution,* 76.
13. Muhammad Waseem, *Politics and State in Pakistan* (Lahore: Progressive Publishers, 1989) 387.
14. Justice (Retired)Anwarul Haq's interview, translated and quoted in Inayatullah, 'Law of Contempt'.
15. The judges of the Supreme Court were seemingly impressed by the moral contents of 'the new order' and Zia's personal pledges to restore the democratic order. They rejected Mr Yahya Bakhtiar's contention that Zia had no intention of relinquishing power and holding general elections as 'highly unfair and uncharitable' remarks.
16. Khan, 'The 1973 Constitution: The Founding of the Federation' (an unpublished paper), f.n. 34, 15.
17. Saeed Shafqat, *Political System of Pakistan* (Lahore: Progressive Publishers, 1989) 57.

18. Mir Jamil-ur-Rahman, 'The Undoing of a Prime Minister', *The Nation* (Lahore) 3 June 1988.
19. 'Eighth Amendment: a document conceived in sin, adopted in shame', Editorial, *The Muslim* (Islamabad) 2 March 1993.
20. Khan, '1973 Constitution: The Founding of the Federation', 18
21. D. Shah Khan, 'Two Pillars of Stability — Democracy and Federalism', *The Muslim* (Islamabad) 11 August 1989.

10

1. K. Subrahmanyam, 'SC verdict a victory for rule of law over the Subcontinent', *The Economic Times* (New Delhi) 27 May 1993.
2. Imtiaz Alam, 'Towards a government by the people', *The Frontier Post* (Peshawar), 23 July 1993.
3. Ibid.
4. Ibid.
5. Altaf Gauhar, 'President Ishaq stands indicted for high treason', *The Muslim* (Islamabad) 25 June 1993.
6. Ibid.
7. Terms with pejorative connotations, such as 'horse-trading', 'lifafa' (envelop full of money), 'lota' etc. gained much currency due to Centre-Punjab confrontational politics in the late 1980s.
8. For details of Ghulam Ishaq Khan's charges against the dismissed government of Ms Benazir Bhutto, see *The Pakistan Times* (Islamabad) 7 August 1990.
9. Alam, 'Towards a government by the people'.
10. Ibid., and Gauhar, 'President Ishaq stands indicted'.
11. Ibid., and Altaf Gauhar, 'Ghulam Ishaq Khan must know the limits of his power', *The Muslim* (Islamabad) 30 March 1993.
12. Gauhar, 'President Ishaq stands indicted'.
13. For substantiation of such allegations, see Professor Manzoor Mirza, 'A few questions to Ghulam Ishaq Khan', *The Nation* (Lahore) 29 October 1993.
14. Editorial, 'The present situation cannot hold. Who is trying to tear the country apart?', *The Muslim* (Islamabad) 6 June 1993.
15. *The Pakistan Times* (Islamabad) 18 April 1993.
16. Ibid.
17. *PLD* 1993 SC 473.
18. Ibid., 735.
19. Ibid., 796.
20. Ibid., 800.
21. *PLD* 1991 Lahore 78.
22. *PLD* 1993 SC 473, 795.

23. *PLD* 1991 Lahore 78.
24. *PLD* 1993 SC 473.
25. *The Muslim* (Islamabad) 27 May 1993.
26. Gauhar, 'President Ishaq stands indicted'.
27. *The Muslim* (Islamabad) 1 July 1993.
28. Salamat Ali, 'Squabbling Nabobs', reproduced in *Nawa-i-Waqt* (Rawal-pindi) 16 July 1993.
29. Ibid.
30. Editorial, 'The present situation cannot hold', *The Muslim (Islamabad)* 6 June 1993.

11

1. Karl W. Deutsch and William J. Foltz (ed.), *Nation-Building* (New York: Atherton Press, 1963), 3; Also Ikram Azam, *Pakistan's Security and National Integration* (Rawalpindi: London Book Co., 1974).
2. Mushtaq Ahmed, 'Provincial Autonomy—Still A Live Issue', *Dawn* (Karachi) 19 September 1989.
3. Ibid.
4. Amir Abdullah Khan Rokari, 'Debate on Provinces: Small Provinces, Stronger Pakistan', *The Nation* (Lahore) 15 September 1989.
5. For the thesis of the late Jamil Nishtar on the multiplication of federating units, see M. P. Bhandara, 'The Provincial Question', *Dawn* (Karachi) 11 August 1986.
6. Air Marshal (Retired) Muhammad Asghar Khan, 'The Relation between the Federation and Units', *Jang* (Rawalpindi) 9 September 1989; and, 'MRD Achieves Consensus on Autonomy Issue', *The Muslim* (Islamabad) 21 June 1986.
7. Bhandara, 'The Provincial Question'.
8. Dr Mubashir Hasan's interview in *The Frontier Post* (Lahore) 27 August 1990.
9. Shahid Kardar, 'Provincial Autonomy: The Issue of Financial Independence', in *Provincial Autonomy: Concept and Framework* (Lahore: Group 83 Series, November 1987) 71.
10. Ibid., 70-3.
11. Ibid., and 'Centralised Planning and Provincial Autonomy' *Dawn* (Karachi) 21 August 1988.
12. Dr Mahbubul Haq, 'Charter of Provincial Rights', *Dawn* (Karachi) 4 May 1989.
13. Ghous Bukhsh Bizenjo, conversation with Mushtaq Ahmed at Quetta airport in February 1978. See Ahmed's article, 'Autonomy in Retrospect', *Dawn*, 10 October 1989.
14. Makhdoom Ali Khan, 'Provincial Autonomy: The constitutional impediments' in *Provincial Autonomy: Concept and Framework* (Lahore: Group 83 Series, November 1989) 29-30.

BIBLIOGRAPHY

Afzal, M. Rafique. *Political Parties in Pakistan, 1947-58*. Islamabad: National Commission on Historical and Cultural Research, 1976.

Ahmed, Azizud Din. *Kia Ham Ekhathey Reh Saktey Hain (Urdu)*. Lahore: Maktaba-i-Fikro Danish, 1988.

Ahmed, Manzooruddin. *Pakistan: The Emerging Islamic State*. Karachi: The Allied Book Corporation, 1966.

Ahmed, Mian Hafeez. *Constitutional History of Pakistan*. Lahore: 1974.

Ahmed, Mushtaq, *Government and Politics in Pakistan*. Karachi: Pakistan Publishing House, 1959.

Ahmed, Waheed. *Road to Indian Freedom—The Formation of the Government of India Act, 1935*. Lahore: The Carvan Book House, 1972.

Ali, Chaudhry Muhammad. *The Emergence of Pakistan*. New York: Columbia University Press, 1967.

Andrews, William G. *Constitution and Constitutionalism*. New York: 1963.

Asghar Khan, Muhammad. *General in Politics: Pakistan 1958–82*. New Delhi: Vikas, 1983.

Ayub Khan, Muhammad. *Friends Not Masters*. Karachi: Oxford University Press, 1967.

Azam, Ikram. *Pakistan's Security and National Integration*. Rawalpindi: The London Book Co. 1974.

——— · *Pakistan's Strategy for Survival*. Rawalpindi: 1982.

——— · *Pakistan's Foreseeable Future*. The PFI & AUL. UK. Islamabad: 1989.

Azfar, Kamal. *Pakistan: Political and Constitutional Dilemmas*. Karachi: Pakistan Law House, 1987.

Aziz, K. K. *Party Politics in Pakistan, 1947-58*. Islamabad: National Commission on Historical and Cultural Research, 1976.

Baker, Ernest. *Principles of Social and Political Theory*. London: 1967.

Bhutto, Zulfikar Ali. *The Great Tragedy*. Karachi: Pakistan People's Party, 1971.

Binder, L. *Religion and Politics in Pakistan*. Berkeley: University of California Press, 1961.

Brines, Russell. *The Indo-Pakistan Conflict*. London: Pall Mall Press, 1968.

Brohi, A. K. *Fundamental Law of Pakistan*. Karachi: 1958.

Burke, S. M. *Pakistan's Foreign Policy*. Karachi: Oxford University Press, 1973.

Callard, Keith. *Pakistan: A Political Study*. London: Allen and Unwin, 1959.

———. *Political Forces in Pakistan*. New York: Institute of Pacific Relations, 1959.

Choudhury, G. W. *The Last Days of United Pakistan*. Bloomington: Indiana University Press, 1974.

———. *Constitutional Development in Pakistan*. London: Longman, 1969.

———. *Documents and Speeches on the Constitution of Pakistan*. Dhaka: 1967.

Coulson, N. J. *A History of Islamic Law*. Edinburgh: 1971.

Dicey, A. V. *Introduction to the Study of Law of Constitution*. London: MacMillan, 1952.

Edgar, A. & Schular K. R: *Public Opinion and Constitution-making in Pakistan 1958-62*. Michigan State University, 1967.

Engineer, Asghar Ali. *Theory and Practice of Islamic State*. Lahore: Vanguard Books, 1985.

Feldman, Herbert. *Revolution in Pakistan*. London: Oxford University Press, 1967.

———. *From Crisis to Crisis: Pakistan 1962-69*. Karachi: Oxford University Press, 1972.

———. *Pakistan, 1969-1971: The End and the Beginning*. Karachi: Oxford University Press, 1974.

Ferdinand, Klaus, and Mozaffari, Mehdi (ed.). *Islam: State and Society*. Scandinavian Institute of Asian Studies, 1988.

Friedrich, Carl J. *Constitutional Government and Democracy: Theory and Practice in Europe and America*. London: Ginn and Co, 1946.

Gardezi, H. & Rashid. J. (ed.). *Pakistan: The Roots of Dictatorship*. London: Zed Press, 1983.

Gauhar, Altaf, *Ayub Khan: Pakistan's First Military Ruler*. Lahore: Sang-e-Meel, 1993.

Gledhill, Alan. *Pakistan: The Development of its Laws and Constitution*. London: Stevens & Sons, 1967.

Goodnow. H. F. *The Civil Services of Pakistan, Bureaucracy in the New Nation*. Karachi: Oxford University Press, 1969.

Hamidullah, Muhammad, *Muslim Conduct of State*. Lahore: 1968.

348 *The Myth of Constitutionalism*

Hasan, Sibte. *The Battle of Ideas in Pakistan*. Lahore: Pakistan Publishing House, 1986.

Hitti, Philip K. *The Arabs*. London: MacMillan, 1956.

Hourani, Albert. *Arab Thought in the Liberal Age, 1878- 1939*. London: Oxford University Press, 1970.

Iqbal, Afzal. *Islamization of Pakistan*. Lahore: Vanguard Books, 1986.

Ishaq, Khalid M. *Constitutional Limitations: An Essay on Limits on Exercise of Political Power*. Karachi: Pakistan Publishing House, 1972.

Jafri, Rais Ahmed (ed.). *Ayub: Soldier and Statesman*. Muhammad Ali Academy, 1966.

Jahan, Rounaq. *Pakistan: A Failure in National Integration*. New York: Columbia University Press, 1972.

Jalal, Ayehsa. *The Sole Spokesman — Jinnah, the Muslim League and the Demand for Pakistan*. London: Cambridge University Press, 1985.

Janowitz, Morris. *Military Institutions and Coercion in the Developing Nations*. University of Chicago Press, 1977.

Kelsen, Hans. *General Theory of Law and State*. Cambridge: Harvard University Press, 1945.

Khan, Qamaruddin. *Al-Mawardi's Theory of State*. Lahore: Islamic Book Foundation, 1983.

Klotter, John C. and Kanovitz, Jacqueline R. *Constitutional Law*, Ohio: 1983.

Kochanek, Stanley. *Interest Groups and Political Development: Business and Politics in Pakistan*. Karachi: Oxford University Press, 1983.

Korson, Henry J. (ed.) *Contemporary Problems of Pakistan*. Leiden: E.J. Brill, 1974.

Kumar, Satish. *The New Pakistan*. New Delhi: 1978.

LaPorte, Robert. *Power and Privilege: Influence and Decision Making in Pakistan*. Berkeley: University of California Press, 1975.

Lewis, Bernard. *The Arabs in History*. New York: Harper & Brothers, 1960.

Macdonald, Duncan B. *Development of Muslim Jurisprudence and Constitutional Theory*. Lahore: The Premier Book House, 1972.

Mahmood, Dr Safdar. *The Deliberate Debacle*. Lahore: Muhammad Ashraf, 1976.

McIlwain, Howard. *Constitutionalism: Ancient and Modern*. New York: Cornell University Press, 1947.

Malik, Hafeez, *Sir Syed Ahmed Khan and Muslim Modernization in India and Pakistan*. New York: Columbia University Press, 1980.

Marshall, Geoffrey, *Constitutional Conventions: The Rules and Forms of Political Accountability*. Oxford: Clarendon Press, 1984.

McWilliams, W. (ed.). *Garrisons and Governments: Politics and Military in New States*. San Francisco: Chandler, 1967.

Munir, Muhammad. *Constitution of the Islamic Republic of Pakistan*. Lahore: 1975.

———— · *From Jinnah to Zia*. Lahore: Vanguard Books, 1979.

Newman, C. J. *Essays on the Constitution of Pakistan*, Dhaka: 1956.

Nice, Richard W. *Treasury of the Rule of Law*. New Jersey: Littlefield, 1965.

Noman, Omar, *The Political Economy of Pakistan: 1947-1982*. London: KPI, 1988.

Perry, Michael J. *The Constitution, the Courts and Human Rights*. New Delhi: 1982.

Pirzada, Sharifuddin. *Evolution of Pakistan*. Lahore: 1963.

———— · *The Pakistan Resolution and the Historic Lahore Resolution*. Karachi: 1968.

Rahim, J.A. *Outlines of A Federal Constitution for Pakistan*. Pakistan People's Party, Political Series No. 4, Lahore, 1969.

Rahman, Inamur. *Public Opinion and Political Development in Pakistan*. Karachi: Oxford University Press, 1982.

Ramadan, Said. *Islamic Law: Its Scope and Equity*. Geneva: 1970.

Rashid, Rao. *Jo Mein Ney Dekha*. Lahore: Jang Publishers, 1985.

Rizvi, Hasan Askari. *The Military and Politics in Pakistan*. Lahore: Progressive Publishers, 1987.

———— · *Pakistan's Peoples Party: The First Phase*. Lahore: 1973.

Sayeed, Khalid Bin. *The Political System of Pakistan*. Boston: Houghton Mifflin, 1967.

———— · *Politics in Pakistan: The Nature and Direction of Change*. New York: Praeger, 1980.

Shafique, Muhammad. *Islamic Concept of a Modern State*. Lahore: Islamic Book Foundation. 1987.

Sherwani, Haroon Khan. *Studies in Muslim Political Thought and Administration*. Lahore: 1965.

Siddiqi, Kalim. *Conflict, Crisis and War in Pakistan*. London: MacMillan, 1972.

Syed, Anwar. *Pakistan: Islam, Politics and National Solidarity*. Lahore: Vanguard Books, 1984.

The Myth of Constitutionalism

Taseer, Salman. *Bhutto: A Political Biography*. New Delhi: Vikas, 1980.

Tinker, Hugh. *Ballot Box and Bayonet*. London: Oxford University Press, 1964.

Vatikiotis, P. J. *Islam and the State*. London: Croom-Helm, 1987.

Venkataramani, M. S. *The American Role in Pakistan 1947-58*. New Delhi: Radiant Publishers, 1982.

Von Vorys, Karl. *Political Development in Pakistan*. Princeton: Princeton University Press, 1965.

Waseem, Muhammad. *Politics and the State in Pakistan*. Lahore: Progressive Publishers, 1989.

Wheare, K. C. *Federal Government*. London: Oxford University Press, 1968.

———— · *Modern Constitutions*. London: Oxford University Press, 1958.

Wheeler, Richard S. *The Politics of Pakistan*. Ithaca: Cornell University, 1970.

Wildasky, Aaron. *American Federalism in Perspective*. Boston: 1967.

Wolf-Phillips, Leslie. *Constitution of Modern States*. New York: 1968.

———— · *Constitutional Legitimacy: A Study of the Doctrine of Necessity*. London: Third World Foundation, 1979.

Wolpert, Stanley. *Zulfi Bhutto of Pakistan*. Karachi: Oxford University Press, 1993.

Yusuf, K. F. *Towards a Tri-Polar World*. Lahore: 1975.

Yusuf, S. M. *The Choice of Caliph in Islam*. Lahore: 1982.

Zafar, S. M. *Through the Crisis*. Lahore: 1970.

Ziring, Lawrence. *Pakistan: The Enigma of Political Development*. Boulder, Colarado: Westview, 1980.

———— · *The Ayub Khan Era: Politics in Pakistan 1958-69*. Syracuse: Syracuse University Press, 1971.

ARTICLES

Afzal, Rafique. 'Problems of Federalism in Pakistan: Consensus by Command', *Pakistan Journal of History and Culture*: Islamabad, Vol. IV, No. 2, July - December 1983.

Ahmed, Eqbal. 'Pakistan: Signposts of a Police State', *Journal of Contemporary Asia*, Vol. 4, No. 4, 1974.

Azam, Ikram. 'Democratic Pakistan: Strategy for survival', *The Muslim*, 25 November 1989.

———. 'The Pothwar Pageant', *Dawn* (Karachi), 18 January 1989.

Baxter, Craig. 'Constitution-Making: The Development of Federalism in Pakistan', *Asian Survey*, Vol XIV, No.12, December 1974.

Brohi, A. K. 'Constitutionalism: its theory and practice', *Dawn* (Karachi), 23 December 1986.

Burki, Shahid Javed. 'Politics of Economic Decision-Making During the Bhutto Period', *Asian Survey*, Vol. XIV, No. 12, December 1974.

Diamond, Larry. 'Beyond Authoritarianism and Totalitarianism: Societies for Democratisation', *The Washington Quarterly*, Winter 1989.

Elazar, Danial J. 'Federalism', *International Encyclopaedia of Social Sciences*, Vol, 5.

Goriya, Muhammad Yusuf. 'The Prophet of Islam and Constitutions' (Urdu). A paper read at a Seerat Conference held on 30 November 1989, at Lahore.

Habib, Hasan. 'Provincial Autonomy and the Colonial Bureaucracy', *The Frontier Post* (Peshawar), 15 January 1988.

Haq, Dr Mahbubul. 'Charter of Provincial Rights' *Dawn* (Karachi), 4 May 1989.

Hussain, Dr Faqir. 'Guilty of High Treason,' *The Frontier Post* (Peshawar), 30 May 1990.

Hussain, Mushahid. 'Bhutto's Anniversary: Focus on Judiciary', *The Times of India* (New Delhi), 24 April 1989.

Inayatullah. 'Law of Contempt of Court and the late Bhutto's case', *The Nation* (Lahore), 13 April 1989.

Kardar, Shahid. 'Provincial Autonomy: The Issue of Financial Independence', *Provincial Autonomy: Concept and Framework.* (Lahore: Group 83 Series, November 1987).

Khan, D. Shah. 'Two Pillars of Stability—Democracy and Federalism' *The Muslim* (Islamabad), 11 August 1989.

Khan, Makhdoom Ali. 'The 1973 Constitution: Founding the Federation.' A paper read at a seminar: *The Heritage of Prime Minister Bhutto,* held at Karachi, 3-5 April 1989.

Khan, Professor Qamaruddin. 'Islam is a society, not a political system', *Dawn* (Karachi), 13 August 1980.

Kumar, Satish. 'Problems of Federal Politics in Pakistan' in Pandav Nayak (ed.) *Pakistan: Society and Politics*, New Delhi: 1984.

352   *The Myth of Constitutionalism*

Meer, Khurshid Hasan. 'Judgements on the 1988 & 1990 dissolutions', *The Frontier Post* (Lahore), 5 April 1993.

——— 'The 1973 Constitution: a bulwark against horse-trading', *The Frontier Post* (Lahore), 13 April 1993.

Naqvi, M.B. 'The Constitutional Crisis', *Dawn* (Karachi), 11 April 1993.

Rahman, Mir Jamilur. 'The Undoing of a Prime Minister', *The Nation* (Lahore), 3 June 1988.

Rokari, Amir Abdullah Khan. 'Debates on Provinces: Small Provinces, Stronger Pakistan', *The Nation* (Lahore), 15 September 1989.

Wolf-Phillips, Leslie. 'The 1973 Constitution: A Heritage for the Future'. A paper read at a seminar: *The Heritage of Prime Minister Bhutto;* held at Karachi, 3-5 April 1989.

PUBLIC DOCUMENTS

Constitutional Documents (of Pakistan), Ministry of Law and Parliamentary Affairs, Government of Pakistan, Volumes I to V.

Basic Democracies: Rules and Ordinance 1959-60. Karachi: Government of Pakistan.

Debates of the National Assembly, 1972-77. Islamabad: Government of Pakistan.

Report of the Constitution Commission 1961. Government of Pakistan Press, Karachi.

A New Beginning: Reforms Introduced by the People's Government of Pakistan. Islamabad: Printing Corporation of Pakistan, 1972.

White Paper on the Conduct of General Elections in March 1977. Islamabad: Printing Corporation of Pakistan, 1978.

INDEX

354 *The Myth of Constitutionalism*

Balochistan, 6, 96, 103, 105, 107, 119, 120, 121, 143, 196; new province, 215; 217, 219, 231-32, 244, 246, 248-52, 274, 279, 304, 321
Balochistan High Court, 264
Banu Aws, 48
Banu Khazarij, 48
Bangladesh, 226, 228, 269, 314
Bay of Bengal, 85
Basic Principles Committee (BPC), 127-30, 131, 134
Basic Democracy, 179-80, 207-8
Beg, Mirza Aslam, 11, 278, 281-82, 295
Begum Nusrat Bhutto case, 10, 11, 257-60, 263-65, 267, 274
Beloff, Max, 30
Bengal, 84, 89; partition of, 91-93; 95-96, 107, 112, 121, 191
Bengal, East, 91, 119, 120, 121, 123, 131, 135, 137, 141, 158-59
Bengal Rifles, 226
Bengali-Punjabi tussle, 126, 131, 137, 153-58
Bengali, official language issue, 134-36, 153-54, 157, 159, 184
Berbers, 58, 64
Bhashani, Maulana Abdul Hamid, 199
Bhandara, M.P; 307
Bhutto, Begum Nusrat, see Begum Nusrat Bhutto case
Bhutto, Ms Benazir, 8, 278; the first Government of, 279-81; 282-83, 284, 289, 292, 294-95; the second Government of, 297; and new social contract, 312-13; 321
Bhutto, Zulfikar Ali, 6, 195, 200, 213, 217, 220, 222-23, 225-28, civilian CMLA, 230-33; constitution-making efforts of, 239-42; as Prime Minister, 242; and practice of federalism, 244-53; ouster of, 255-59; 260-61; assasination of, 262; 264-66, 281, 303, 321-32
Bible, 198, 223
Bizenjo, Mir Ghaus Buksh, 219, 232, 246, 310
Blackstone, 36
Bogra Formula, 133-34

Bolingbroke, 19
Bombay, 97, 102
Bombay Presidency, 121
Bonapartism, 230, 310
Brahvi, 134
Briffault, Robert, 28
British Constitution, 21, 35
British Government, 67, 86, 97, 101, 107
British in India, 66-67, 74-75, 85-117, 121-22, 148, 302
Brohi, A.K; 28-29, 45-46, 259
Bryce, James, 19, 29
Bugti, Nawab Muhammad Akbar Khan, 246, 279
Bundestaat, 30
Buksh, Pir Illahi, 153
Burki, Shahid Javed, 247
Buwahid Amirs, 60
Buwahids, 61
Byzantine, 33, 38, 40, 47, 102, 114, 284, 302, 317
Cabinet Mission Plan, 109-10, 112, 117
Cabinet of talents, 180
Cairo, 58
Calcutta, 156
Callard, Keith B., 1, 157, 160
Cambell, Don, 71
Canada, 116
Centre-Punjab tussle, 279-82, 294-95
Chamber of Princes, 94
Charter of Human Rights, 49
Charter of Medina, 13-15, 43, 48-49, 79-81
Chase, Salman P; 32
China, 193
Chitral, 120
Chittagong, 201
Choudhry, Fazal Elahi, 315
Chundrigar, I.I; 163, 165
Churchill, Winston, 111
Civil Disobedience Movement, 106
Clark, Ramsey, 262
CMLA, 16, 33, 79, 81; Ayub Khan as, 167, 169, 173, 176; Yahya as, 207, 213-15; Bhutto as civilian, 230-33, 244; Zia as, 255-76
Combined Opposition Parties(COP), 190, 201, 220

Communal Award, 73, 102
Confederacy of India, 103
Confederalism, 31, 34, 109, 114, 116, 132, 190, 194, 196, 219, 223, 225, 228
Conrad, Dieter, 234
Constituent Assembly of Pakistan, 15, 21, 69, 74-77, 118-20, 123, 125, 127-29, 132, 134-35; dissolution of, 137-42, 145, 150-1, 156; second CAP, 157-58; 160, 161-64, 169
Constitution Commission, 181-83, 185
Constitutional Committee, 238-41
Constitutional Accord, 239-41
Constitutional Bill, 212-13, 215
Constitution, general reflections, 1-17; definition of, 18-22; in relation to constitutionalism, 23-25; in relation to the rule of law, 25-28; in ralation to federalism, 23-25; the doctrine of separation of powers, 35-39; and Islamic theory and practice, 43-69; and Jinnah's visualization, 70-75; and Objectives Resolution, 76-77; the colonial heritage, 82-117; making of the 1956 Constitution, 118-69; Ayub Khan's martial law and the 1962 Constitution, 170-205; the Yahya interlude, 206-29; making of the 1973 Constitution, 230-54; Zia era and the PCO, 255-76; Ishaq's subversion of, 277-98; the heritage of constitutional politics, 316-24
Constitutionalism, 1, 7, 12-13, 17; definition of, 23-25; 33, 37, 43-46, 49-50, 57, 60, 67, 74, 82; pre-indepencence appraisal of, 113-17; efforts for making a Constitution, 118-47; critique of, 149-69; and Ayub Khan, 170-250; and Bhutto, 231-54; GIK's subversion of, 277-98; heritage of, 316-24
Constitution(of 1956), 5, 21, 31, 118, 145-47, 163, 165, 170; abrogation, 171-73, 183, 185, 197-98, 205-6, 210, 242, 307
Constitution(of 1962), 21, 31, 170; saliant features, 183-190; 202-3, 202-6, 235, 242, 245

Constitution(of 1973), 6, 21, 31; making of, 238-42, features of, 242-44; operation, 245-54; 255, 259, 261-62, 265, 267-81, 271, 273, 274-74, 277, 280, 298, 307, 318, 321-24
Convention Muslim League, 188, 222
Cordova, 58
Council Muslim League, 188, 198
Council of Common Interests(CCI), 240, 244, 280
Council of Islamic Ideology, 185-86, 265
Criminal Procedure Code, 177-78
Coupland, Sir Reginald, 94
Cripps, Sir Stafford, 107, 109
Cripps Mission, 107
Damascus, 54, 56, 58
Dar-ul-harb, 68, 71
Dark Ages, 319-20
Dar-ul-Islam, 59, 71
Daud regime(in Afghanistan), 249
Daultana, Mian Mumtaz Muhammad Khan, 132, 154, 159
David, 45
De Gualle, President General, 200
De Gaulle(of Pakistan), 195, 200
Decade of Development, 195, 199-200
Decade of Reforms, 195
Deccan, 84, 103
Defence of Pakistan Rules(DPR), 235, 249
Delhi, 46, 84-86, 93, 105, 112, 191
Democratic Action Committee(DAC), 201, 220
Deobandi, 276
Desai, Bhulabhai, 108
Desai-Liaquat Formula, 108
Deutsch, Karl W., 300
Dhaka, 92, 129, 135, 156, 184, 198, 224-27
Dhaka High Court, 173, 227
Dhaka University, 135
Dicey, A.V., 26
Dir, 120
Direct Action Day, 109-10
Directive Principles of State Policy, 130, 183, 185, 212
Divide and quit India, 107